REGIONAL CONFLICT
AND
COOPERATION

a framework for understanding
global geography

FIRST EDITION

Brian McCabe

California State University — Fullerton

Bassim Hamadeh, CEO and Publisher

Michael Simpson, Vice President of Acquisitions

Jamie Giganti, Senior Managing Editor

Jess Busch, Senior Graphic Designer

Marissa Applegate, Senior Field Acquisitions Editor

Gem Rabanera, Project Editor

Elizabeth Rowe, Licensing Coordinator

Rachel Singer, Interior Designer

Printed in the United States of America

ISBN: 978-1-63189-966-9 (pbk) / 978-1-63189-967-6(br)

www.cognella.com   800-200-3908

CONTENTS

CHAPTER 1

Introduction to Global Geography

1.1 What is Geography?

Fundamentally, geography is the study of Earth's surface and the influences that shape both physical and human landscapes over time. Global geography, also known as *world regional geography*, might be described as the study of both the human and physical landscapes, of key world regions, and the patterns that can be observed within them.

Because geography often encompasses the study of large areas, it has become cooperatively divided, yet eagerly interdisciplinary. For example, physical geography is a topical subfield of geography that examines the natural world. Physical geographers rely on a broad spectrum of scientific fields in order to spatially understand Earth's dynamic physical landscapes. These fields include climatology, hydrology, geology, geomorphology, biology, and marine studies.

Another topical subfield of geography is human geography. Human geographers embrace related disciplines within the social sciences to examine human landscapes and spatial patterns of human activity. For example, they study the movement and diffusion of culture and ideas; economic spaces and the activities that define them; political spaces and the conflict and cooperation they cause between nations; social landscapes; and population studies.

A third subfield of geography is geographic information systems (GIS). GIS is the computerized data management system used to capture, store, manage, retrieve, analyze, and display spatial information. This technology enables us to visualize patterns over space and even time. Maps have never been as informative as they are today because of these technologies. Geography, then, is the ultimate bridge discipline between science and social science.

Geography traces its origin to ancient Greece and to a man named Eratosthenes (276–194 BCE), who became the chief librarian at the Library of Alexandria. He was the first to use the term γεωγραφία, or *geographia*, which literally translates to "describe/write about earth." Specifically, Eratosthenes was interested in "describing earth" mathematically. At that point, no one had attempted to measure the planet. This inspired him to devise a method that would accurately measure not only Earth's circumference, but also its natural tilt and distance to the sun. Although the field still relies in part on mathematically based principles (*geographic coordinate systems* and *geodetic datums*), today the discipline embraces both quantitative and qualitative methods to understand the world.

Earth's landscapes have never been so complex. As a result, geographers specialize in particular subfields. For example, physical geographers may specialize in coastal erosion or the distribution of water resources in a particular state or country. A human geographer, by contrast, might specialize in cultural space within cities or geopolitical issues like regional tensions over natural resources in the Arctic. Despite specialization, geographers study all subfields as part of their education. Thus, all geographers possess fundamental knowledge of how physical and human landscapes interact and influence each other—this is the crux of geography. This textbook will, at its foundation, approach the study of world regions by embracing each subfield in an interdisciplinary way.

GEOGRAPHIC TOOLS

The broad nature of geography makes it difficult to define. Geographers themselves often grapple over definitions that best fit their particular areas of expertise and, in doing so, may inadvertently confuse students. At the same time, students often arrive to class with preconceived notions that geography is simply the study of the names and locations of countries, states, oceans, capital cities, and so on. Neither scenario offers a good start for studying geography. This textbook, then, will propose alternatives to relying on the formal definitions that attempt to encapsulate the academic discipline. Instead, it will focus on several tools that might illuminate how geographers approach a particular area of interest. One such tool is the four (4) spatial questions. These questions lead to a greater spatial understanding. They illuminate what geographers refer to as "the why of where," or, in other words, why things happen where they do. These questions include:

1. How does the physical environment shape human activity?
2. How do humans manipulate their physical environments?
3. What patterns have emerged from this interaction over time?
4. What data can be collected and used to visualize these patterns?

By asking these questions, geographers can dissect and analyze a particular area from several angles. If successful, this will lead to the discovery of patterns that have evolved, explain human activities (agricultural, economic, conflicts, etc.), and eventually become a doorway to more focused studies within that particular space.

BOX 1A CALIFORNIA: MANIPULATED SPACE

Generally, California is a dry state with infrequent, seasonal episodes of intense precipitation. These averages result from California's climate, a physical geographical consideration. California is influenced by a sub-tropical high-pressure system that, in part, determines the amount (or lack of) precipitation the region receives. Between November and early May, this high-pressure system typically weakens and allows the jet stream to dip to lower latitudes, thus delivering the occasional high-intensity winter storm from the Pacific Ocean. Most of the time, however, much of California is dry. Water, then, is a key physical geographical consideration in understanding California and its settlement patterns.

FIGURE 1.1a(1). Pleasant Valley Reservoir Dam. Copyright in the Public Domain.

With this in mind, human activities can then be examined. The Gold Rush (1849) drew tens of thousands to the state and established California as a destination for millions of future migrants. Over time, the state would grow from fewer than one hundred thousand in 1850 to more than thirty-eight million today. This exponential increase in population over a short period can be seen in many ways. Cities like San Francisco, Los Angeles, and San Diego grew into major metro-politan areas, each with millions of residents.

California also has some of the most productive agricultural regions on Earth. Agriculture uses the most water, by far. All this is possible because, over time, people have manipulated California's natural water budget to sustain this level of human activity. Water,

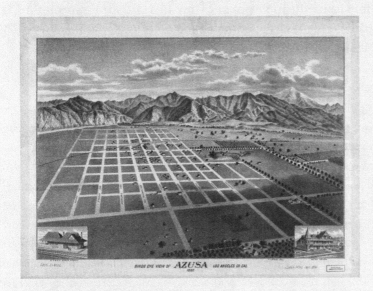

FIGURE 1.1a(2). Bird's eye view of Azusa, Los Angeles Co. Cal., 1887. Copyright in the Public Domain.

as seen in the images, is drawn from distant sources and engineered to travel great distances to areas of need via sophisticated dam and aqueduct systems. At the same time, the devastating effects of California's periodic, powerful storms have been tempered by giant plumbing systems like the paving of the Los Angeles and Santa Ana Rivers, along with the creation of thousands of storm runoff networks. Both of these adjustments to California's natural environment enable large populations to exist with access to water resources and in safety from flooding.

FIGURE 1.1a(3). Caesar Chavez Bridge. Looking Northeast. Copyright in the Public Domain.

To this day, however, California struggles with limited water resources (exacerbated by drought). And because California boasts both the nation's largest population and most robust economy, there is an incentive to effectively manage this resource. This is where a geographer would look for patterns. What patterns have emerged from the relationship between human activity and natural environment? How does California deal with this issue through policy? How has drought altered the state's approach to water management? And what data can be collected and visualized for us to understand this problem better? This is the advantage of employing geographic tools like the Four Geographic Questions.

Another geographic tool is the Core-periphery model. This model is primarily used by human geographers and leads to a better understanding of the diffusion of culture, ideas, technology, conflict, and so on. Diffusion is the movement, over time, of a cultural element or phenomena from a source area outward. This can include agricultural practices, language, religion, urban expansion, disease, and technology. This model is useful because it helps us identify that, although everything has a point of origin, that point seldom remains stationary. It also shows us how things change the further they get from the core. Geographers refer to this as time-distance decay.

European colonization offers a window into how this works. The British, for example, once had the largest empire known, spatially. Through their colonies, and the economic activities they engaged in within those regions, the British spread their culture. This included the diffusion of language, social systems, administrative and governance practices, Christianity, business practices, and even views about race. Over time, however, the purity of this cultural diffusion wanes, dilutes, and alters. If you were to look at countries today that used to be British colonies, you will find aspects and traces of British culture (laws, language, social views), but also differences. Being able to identify these patterns also helps us understand major world regions and the cultures that reside within them.

MAPS, VISUALIZATION, AND GEOSPATIAL TECHNOLOGIES

Maps have long been an important tool for understanding our world on various scales. If you were to visualize your own neighborhood, or your *activity space*, you would likely be able to mentally account for most of the key features and countless small details within that space. Mental maps, or the visualization of an area you know very well, allow us to think about our homes, neighborhoods, and even our towns or cities in a way that reflects our experiences and observations. If you were to transcribe your mental map onto paper, you might illustrate a badge icon where you often see a police officer waiting to catch a speeding car. You might draw an angry dog face over a neighbor's house because of previous run-ins with the owner's pet. You would likely remember to pencil in the new traffic circle your town added or the new coffee shop that opened nearby. Maps allow us to document, organize, and visualize information in useful ways.

Cartography, or the art of map making, leverages computer technology to help us understand the world better than ever. But maps today are only a component of *geospatial technologies*. These include GIS, Global Positioning Satellites (GPS), and satellite and aerial remote sensing. They are, in a sense, the visualization end of an ecosystem of data that comes to us from countless sources. Geospatial technologies transcend maps in many ways because they help us understand what is happening on Earth at any given place, and often in real time.

Smart phones and increased connectivity allow users to view the world in a way that's well beyond their own abilities. Mapping programs use GPS to not only inform you precisely where you are, but also to highlight features, services, and even friends around you. Likewise, your phone's camera geotags the location where the image was taken, and that information can be shared, in an instant, with practically anyone. Naturally, conventional and even thematic maps are still commonly used—as they should be—but, in addition to providing useful services, these geospatial technologies make the user part of the data collection process. Later chapters will provide examples of how these technologies fostered great changes within certain regions.

Although this textbook will not discuss the science behind geospatial technologies, it is important to briefly highlight some functionalities and advantages. Fundamentally, GIS takes a base map and then "layers" on spatial data that can be represented in many ways. For example, the simplest form of a GIS map can be seen in *Figures 1.1b (1), (2), and (3)*.

These simple USGS maps show us a *base map* at various scales, along with recent earthquake data (in this case, the geographic coordinates of the precise location of the earthquake) represented by a colored dot. This information is displayed over the base map as a "layer." As you pan in closer, the scale changes, but the location of the earthquakes does not. The "layer" with the icons is informed by an attribute table that houses each earthquake and the precise location where it occurred. Thus, a user can pan in or out to any specific earthquake event while preserving the precise location. Naturally, GIS gets much more sophisticated than this. Many more layers can be added, and data can be displayed in many ways.

FIGURE 1.1b(1). Earthquake GIS.
Copyright in the Public Domain.

FIGURE 1.1b(2). Earthquake GIS.
Copyright in the Public Domain.

FIGURE 1.1b(3). Earthquake GIS.
Copyright in the Public Domain.

CASE STUDY 1A

Geospatial Technologies: A Practice in GIS and Mapping Datasets

Part 1: Google Earth

Google Earth is a fantastic Geographic Information System that utilizes millions of images, taken at various scales and over time, that show most of the planet. It is free to download and intuitive to use. Perhaps the most interesting aspect of Google Earth is the "layers" that you, as a user, can activate or deactivate, depending on what kind of information you want to see. If you do not have Google Earth, here are some simple directions:

1. Open an internet browser and type "Google Earth" in the search bar.
2. Open the Google Earth website and download the free version.
3. Open on your desktop and explore!

The first thing you will see is Earth. On the top left, you will see a Search bar, and on the bottom left, Layers. Google Earth will likely have predetermined activated layers like Borders, Labels, Places, and Roads. As you can see, there are many more.

Let's do a simple exercise:

1. In the Search bar, type in Manhattan, New York, NY.
2. After it takes you there, double-click on Central Park.
3. Within Central Park, you will see a large pond called the "Jacqueline Kennedy Onassis Reservoir." Pan in closer to this feature.
4. Observe the areas north and south of the pond (a directional compass is provided for you on the upper right). These are softball and baseball diamonds.
5. How many softball and baseball diamonds can you count?

Before you answer, keep in mind that interpreting images is tricky. Sometimes, you must change the scale (pan in and out closer and further from the surface) to find the "best answer." The best answer may not always be the correct answer. As far as we can see, there are about twenty softball and baseball diamonds, combined, at each end of the pond. However, there may be features that look like baseball fields, but are not. There may be trees covering several diamonds. The best you can do is use the tool to observe space beyond your own abilities. It may not always give us the answers we seek, but it can give us perspectives we might lack otherwise.

Part 2: United States Census

Under Title 13 and Title 26 of the US Code, the United States Census Bureau is authorized to be the leading source of quality data about the nation's people and economy. They then take this data and create publically accessible thematic maps. This next simple exercise will enable you to see how data is displayed on digital maps.

Please follow these steps:
1. On your favorite search engine, enter US Census.
2. Enter website and choose Geography tab on top of page.
3. In the left column, choose Maps & Data and then Thematic Maps.
4. Select Agriculture and then Land in Farms as percentage of land area.

This thematic map represents the data they have collected about this particular study. Areas with the least amount of farms per land area are represented by the color yellow, whereas the most are colored brown. These colors are what you see when you travel to these areas. They are simply used to distinguish variability within the dataset, thus being "thematic." Take some time to examine other Census maps.

As you can see, geospatial technologies are not all the same. This textbook has not even covered multispectral band satellite remote sensing or aerial imagery, which are themselves fascinating and complex. What they all have in common is that they allow us to see more than we can. They have become extensions of our own senses and inform us about the world in ways that reveal the good, the bad, and the things we should keep an eye on.

UNDERSTANDING "SCALE"

Scale, in cartography, is simply the ratio of map distance to ground distance, represented by a bar graph. In more practical terms, it is a mathematical way for us to distinguish close from far. This is an important aspect of geography, because quite often studies are done within the context of a certain amount of space. For example, a broad study about the decline of manufacturing in the northeast quadrant of the United States would be represented by a much smaller fraction, because you would need to be further from Earth's surface to see everything from Missouri to Massachusetts. On the other hand, a study about the revitalization of Main Street in Linton, Indiana might require a map that shows just that part of town. This would be a larger scale. Mathematically, the study about manufacturing might be 1:60,000, whereas the study of Linton might be more like 1:1,000. See *Figures 1.1c (1) and (2)*.

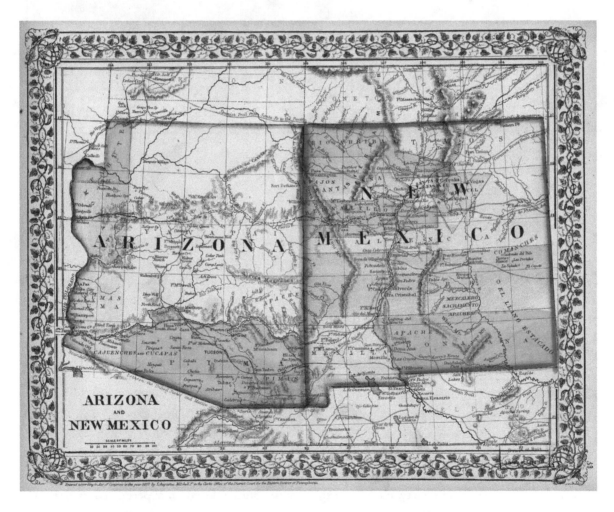

FIGURE 1.1c(1). Arizona and New Mexico.
Copyright in the Public Domain.

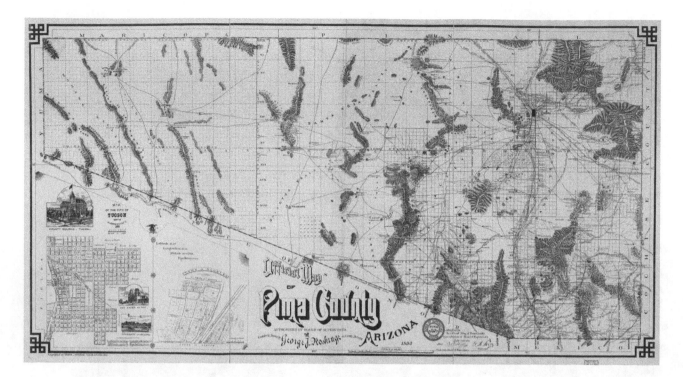

FIGURE 1.1c(2). Official map of Pima County.
Copyright in the Public Domain.

These old maps in *Figures 1.1c (1) and (2)* show the broader region of Arizona and New Mexico as an example of *small scale* and Pima County, Arizona as *large scale.* Geographers, however, do not necessarily consider the fraction in scale, but use scale to provide context to their study. This is how this textbook will use scale, as well. When discussing each region, discussions will be framed in the context of the subject being discussed. This will be done through common terms like *community, local, metropolitan, regional, national,* and so on.

BOX 1B ENVIRONMENTAL DETERMINISM AND POSSIBILISM

Since the Age of Enlightenment, humans have attempted to explain differences between us that can be observed regionally. These observations include differences in physical features, like the color of our skin, or the level or rate of advancement in society. European expansionism during the colonial period led to many assumptions about these differences that still exist.

One such paradigm is environmental determinism. This way of thinking was born in northwestern Europe during a time when countries were expanding their colonial empires around the world. It rooted itself in the belief that a particular culture's environment determines its success. In the case of the British, Dutch, Germans, and other European countries of this region, they believed that their cooler climate and rich resources made them more productive and technologically advanced, thus propelling them forward ahead of subtropical and tropical cultures. They associated tropical climates with laziness and low productivity. This naturally led to a cultural mentality that Europeans were superior,

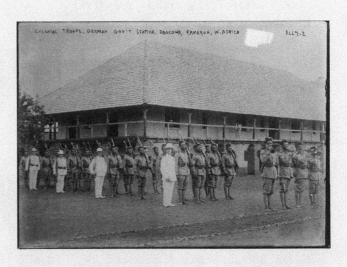

FIGURE 1.1d. Colonial troops, German Government station, Ebolowa, Kamerun [i.e., Cameroon], W. Africa. Copyright in the Public Domain.

and the behaviors associated with this belief system followed. The Europeans, as they expanded into these realms, manipulated, controlled, and even subjugated many cultures and, in doing so, established a racial order that can still be observed to this day.

Environmental determinism, as it turns out, falsely assumes that the environment determines the successes or failures of society. There are many examples of rich, colorful, and productive subtropical and tropical cultures, both historically and today. The ancient Maya and Aztecs, for example, were very sophisticated. The ancient Khmer Empire in modern-day Cambodia, Laos, and Vietnam was very advanced. The field of geography, up until the 1950s, was a supporter of environment determinism. Incidentally, when the theory was disproven, the field of geography suffered and did not recover from the shame of backing such a paradigm until the late 1960s and early 1970s.

Although there have been many new theories, Possibilism can probably be most credited with negating environmental determinism. Possibilism proposes that it is not the environment that determines the success of society, but the choices cultures make within their climates. For example, there are many historical examples of irresponsible deforestation (Romans, Vikings in Iceland, Japanese, Easter Island, etc.), and with each case follows a story of self-inflicted harm and even social collapse. These problems did not stem from the natural climate, but the choices made by those who inhabited these areas. Now this is not to say that environment plays no role. It does. It just does not determine success or failure. This textbook will carefully discuss each region in a way that illuminates the choices cultures made, as opposed to simply connecting their narrative to their respective environments.

1.2 Our Physical World

Understanding Earth's physical geography is an important part of studying world regions. Simply put, Earth's surface is dynamic and characterized by the interaction of various subsystems that shape the physical landscapes we see around us. This symphony of interactions is not evenly applied, but is instead highly variable, depending on where you are. Any given location on Earth is, without external influences, determined by a rather complex combination of natural factors. This could include distance from the equator (or energy received), elevation, wind orientation, proximity to an ocean or large body of water, slope, and

FIGURE 1.2a(1). Earth rotating around the sun, with angle shown.
Copyright in the Public Domain.

precipitation patterns, just to name a few. The goal of this section is to illuminate some key physical geographical concepts that may prove useful as we transition into discussions about specific world regions.

Before we begin a more detailed discussion about our physical world, the stage must be set. Earth is a planet that is part of a solar system. The planets within this solar system revolve around the sun because of the immensity of the sun's gravitational pull. Earth maintains an average ninety-three-million-mile distance from the sun and takes about 365 days (one year) to complete one full rotation. Earth, however, is slightly tilted at a 23.5-degree angle. Therefore, as the planet revolves around the sun, the range of direct solar energy Earth receives shifts from the north to the south, depending on the time of year.

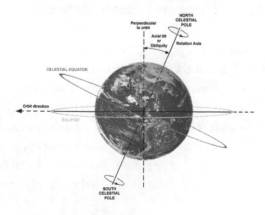

FIGURE 1.2a(2). Earth's angle or "obliquity." is 23.5 degrees.
Copyright © Dennis Nilsson (CC BY 3.0) at https://commons.wikimedia.org/wiki/File%3AAxialTiltObliquity.png .

FIGURE 1.2a(3). Mother Earth.
Copyright in the Public Domain.

This process determines seasons. For example, on June 21, Earth's natural tilt points the Northern Hemisphere at a 23.5-degree angle toward the sun. This results in summer in the north. On December 21, the Northern Hemisphere is tilted 23.5 degrees away from the sun, providing the Southern Hemisphere with more direct radiation (their summer). In between these periods, direct solar energy is directly over the equator, in an event known as an *equinox*. Translated, this means both day and night are of equal length. This happens twice a year, around March 20 and September 22. Therefore, Earth has an established *zone of direct radiation* between 23.5 degrees *N* latitude (*Tropic of Cancer*) and 23.5 degrees *S* latitude (*Tropic of Capricorn*).

Beyond the *zone of direct radiation* are the *middle latitudes* (between about thirty degrees and sixty degrees north and south of the equator) and eventually the subpolar and polar realms (or greater than sixty degrees north and south). These sections of Earth receive oblique, or fractional, energy because of the planet's round shape. This annual allocation of solar radiation influences the interactions and conversations between subsystems on the planet surface. The results, however, are very different landscapes. The coast of Brazil, for example, has very different characteristics than the coast of Maine in the United States. These differences begin with the amount of energy received, but must continue with how the four subsystems interact with each other in those particular locations.

EARTH'S SUBSYSTEMS IN ACTION

Earth's physical processes are fascinating and complex. Generally, a discussion on Earth's dynamic subsystems should begin with a review of some basic terminology. A system can be described as various elements coordinated with each other in an organized way. A subsystem, then, is an independent, yet important, component of a system. Earth's physical landscapes are, essentially, the conversation occurring between the planet's four subsystems at any given time. Earth's four subsystems are:

- Atmosphere: The various layers of gas, from surface to space, that protect Earth.
- Hydrosphere: All the water on Earth (salt, fresh, solid, and gaseous).
- Lithosphere: All rock material on Earth, from surface to core.
- Biosphere: All living organisms on Earth (flora, fauna, bacteria, fungi, spores, etc.)

These subsystems are neither equal partners nor strangers to each other. Depending on location, the interactions between these subsystems can be quite different.

Part of the difference between Earth's regions can be attributed to the amount of solar energy they receive. For example, tropical regions receive the most solar energy and, as a result, have climates and landscapes that are rich with biodiversity. Great expanses of rainforests ring the planet around the equator. This is because of regular direct energy, rising air that creates a thicker atmosphere and fosters abundant rainfall, and soils that are adapted to absorb that amount of water.

The middle latitudes (again, the areas between the tropics and polar realms) are seasonal, in that radiation intensifies during the summer months but then wanes in winter. The interaction between the subsystems, then, is very different than the in the tropics. Climates become more variable in the middle latitudes. Some regions have ample precipitation and rich biomes, whereas others are extraordinarily dry and life struggles to survive.

Finally, the subpolar and polar regions receive the least amount of energy. The atmosphere thins as latitudes increase. There are fewer storms and short growing seasons (if any), and temperatures are often too low to sustain a diversity of life. Understanding the basic relationship between energy and the four subsystems allows us to better understand human landscapes.

THE IMPORTANCE OF LATITUDE

Geographers rely on an *earth coordinate system* in order to identify the absolute location, or a precise place on Earth. It can be described as an invisible grid of *parallels* running east to west and meridians running north to south. Parallels, or *lines of latitude*, begin at the equator (zero degrees latitude) and then are measured by degree point, both north and south, all the way to ninety degrees (poles). Each line of latitude, then, is *equidistant* from each other (about sixty-nine miles apart). Between these lines, each degree of latitude is likewise measured by sixty *minutes*, and between each *minute*, sixty *seconds*. For example, the famous Gateway Arch in St. Louis, Missouri is at 38d 37'28.89" N latitude. This coordinate represents

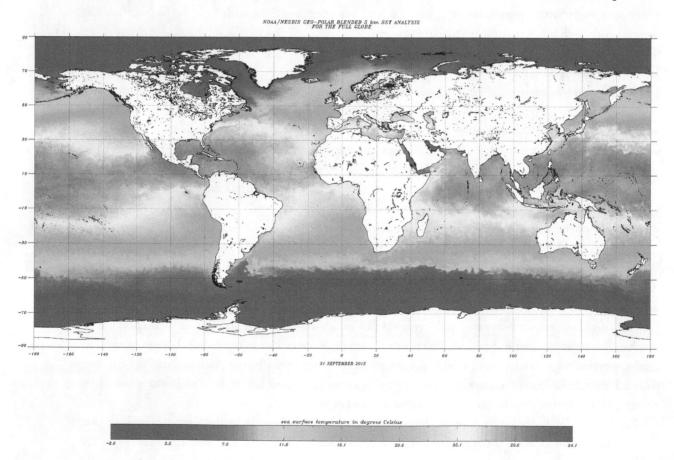

FIGURE 1.2b. A thermo map of the Earth's surface indicates where radiation is received.
Copyright in the Public Domain.

precisely how far from the equator this feature resides. However, this same line of latitude circles the planet and therefore fails to tell us its absolute location. Therefore, a meridian must be used.

Unlike lines of latitude, meridians are not equidistant, because they intersect at the North and South Poles. The Prime Meridian, or zero degrees longitude, runs through the Royal Greenwich Observatory in Greenwich, England, and then east and west until it reaches 180 degrees, or the International Date Line (IDL). Naturally, the IDL does not always fall on 180 degrees longitude, as it must accommodate national interests on occasion. Like lines of latitude, longitude is measured in degrees, minutes, and seconds. Therefore, the Gateway Arch can be located precisely at: 38d 37'28.89" N latitude, 90d 11'05.07" W (or west of the Prime Meridian) longitude. This is the feature's absolute location and will not change.

This textbook will place a greater focus on latitude than longitude. Longitude simply informs us how far we are from a city in England—useful for locating something, but uninformative otherwise. Latitude provides insight into the character of a particular region on Earth because it measures distances north and south. It can be observed that changes in climate occur quicker and more radically as you move north or south of the equator, as opposed to moving in an east–west trajectory. The reason for this can be found in wind patterns and the aforementioned levels of energy received.

As you can see in *Figure 1.2b*, the Earth's *sea surface temperature* is warmer by the equator and then cools to the north or south over a fairly short distance. This is because Earth is essentially a giant energy exchange system. It takes solar energy received in its *zone of direct radiation* and then disburses it via wind and ocean currents to the rest of the planet. Some continents, as will be discussed later, have a north–south axis (South America, Africa) and differences can be easily observed. Understanding the latitudinal position of an area being studied provides us with insight into human activities and culture.

PRESSURE AND WIND PATTERNS

High and low pressure influence wind patterns on Earth. Though this sounds unexceptional, it is actually critical to understanding world regions. At the equator, wind converges and rises. This is known as the Intertropical Convergence Zone (ITCZ), a continuous band of warm, moist air rising and producing copious rainfall. This rising air heads back to the north and to the south, depositing its moisture through precipitation events along the way. This is known as the Hadley Cell (see *Figure 1.2c*). Around thirty degrees north and south latitude (or the northernmost and southernmost ends of the *subtropics*), all this air cools and descends. By this point, the air is dry, and as it swirls clockwise down to Earth's surface (Northern Hemisphere), it creates high pressure. This is known as subtropical high pressure zones. Most of the world's deserts exist under the influence of these high-pressure systems. This natural high-pressure belt acts like a gateway into the middle latitudes.

High-pressure systems not only create dry, seasonally hot conditions; they also influence wind orientation in the middle latitudes. As a general rule of thumb, air flows from high pressure to low pressure. Therefore, clockwise-spinning, descending air flows towards low-pressure systems that often form over land. Although the *Hadley Cell* deposits dried out equatorial winds via high-pressure systems around Earth (at about thirty degrees north and south), they form more intensely over oceans. For example, the North Pacific Ocean is home to the relatively stable and powerful *Hawaiian Subtropical High*. Likewise, the

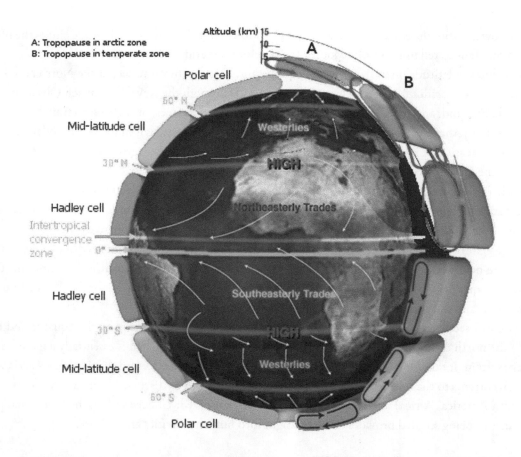

FIGURE 1.2c. This schematic of Earth reveals a lot. Note the Hadley Cell on both sides of the equator. This cell takes rising air from the equator, rings out its moisture, and then it falls down to Earth around 30 degrees North and South latitude.
Copyright in the Public Domain.

Northern Atlantic is home to the *Bermuda Subtropical High* (also known as the *Azores High*). The air descending from these high-pressure systems flows to low-pressure systems over land in North America and Europe, thus influencing a *westerly* wind orientation. These systems also influence the *jet stream*, which can directly influence the trajectory of storm systems. Thus, the allocation of precipitation is influenced by high-pressure zones. These examples provide an important backdrop for understanding the climates and human activities of both North America and Europe.

PHYSIOGRAPHY

Whereas the term *geography* is used to describe Earth, physiography literally means to describe the physical landscape. This is an umbrella term that will be commonly used in this textbook. It is useful because it encompasses various elements and processes that can be observed and recorded in any given region. This might include climate, weather patterns, landforms and features, bodies of water, soils, vegetation, and so on. It can also be considered the product of the interaction between the subsystems. For example, the physiography of the Sahara Desert in North Africa can be described as arid, exceptionally hot, and rocky, with low vegetation and sand dunes. When considering world regions, the physiography provides us with context for human activities.

1.3 Human Landscapes

A central focus of this textbook will be the human landscapes. These can be described as any combination of human activities that shape the character of a particular place or region. Naturally, humans have been extraordinarily influential over time, and there exists virtually countless ways by which the human footprint can be measured. In this section, the textbook will briefly explore a wide range of important human influences on Earth's surface.

FIGURE 1.2d. The oceans receive much of the energy from the sun and therefore store most of the energy from the sun. Copyright © Tiago Fioreze (CC BY-SA 3.0) at https://commons.wikimedia.org/wiki/File%3AClouds_over_the_Atlantic_Ocean.jpg .

EARLY HUMAN LANDSCAPES

The human landscapes we see today would hardly resemble those of early human civilizations. At the same time, by examining early human civilization, we can see the building blocks of the world we now know. By using the *core-periphery model*, geographers can trace many aspects of the human landscapes to areas in which they originated. This allows us to understand the connectivity between various regions over time, and how core activities and human features have diffused and changed.

The First Agricultural Revolution

Perhaps no era better sets the stage for the evolution of human landscapes than the First Agricultural Revolution. This first *nodal point* in human history can be characterized as a great transformative period. Interestingly, there are two connected narratives that may explain this transformation. Through a physical geographical lens, we can see Earth transition from the last Ice Age (the Pleistocene Epoch) into an interglacial period. This lengthy process of deglaciation occurred between about ten to fifteen thousand years ago. During this period, the planet warmed, ice slowly melted, and great watershed zones were formed. These watershed zones carried soils from distant regions and deposited them into fantastic river valleys and deltas in key regions around the planet. Combined with a warmer climate, vegetation within these areas was robust. The result of this physical process was an increased availability of the edible plants preferred by humans.

During the Ice Age, humans were *hunter-gatherers*. *Hunter-gatherers* were a foraging culture characterized by a mixed strategy of survival. Men, for example, would hunt big game for protein. This was a dangerous endeavor, as weapons were primitive and the types of animals hunted were often very dangerous. Women, on the other hand, foraged for berries, nuts, and other sources of food. Because humans lacked advanced technologies, they could not effectively mitigate the dangers imposed by the world around them. As a result, hunter-gatherer societies were typically small in number and tribal in structure.

The beginning of the *Holocene* period, about ten thousand years ago, was the setting for gradual, yet radical, changes in human behavior and human society. This is known as the Neolithic Revolution. Calorie crops (grains, fruit, etc.) were growing more abundantly in the warming climate. Watershed zones, like river valleys and deltas, had ample and easily collectible food sources. Humans, then, began to select the types of calorie crops they liked best, and eventually elected to either grow those varieties closer to their encampments or move closer to those naturally growing sources of food and attempt to grow them in closer proximity to their places of residence. This marked a fundamental change in humanity. Calories had become more accessible, and methods followed that allowed the more efficient cultivation of those foods. And if you have more reliable access to calories, you are more empowered to grow your population. Thus, the *first agricultural revolution* can be paired with increases in human population.

Other impacts of the *first agricultural revolution* and subsequent *Neolithic revolution* were societal in nature. With the shift to cultivation came the need to use land differently. Land planning, then, became an important aspect of human society. As seen in *Figure 1.3a*, human tools become important as well.

Designated areas for agriculture and domesticated animals were planned around living spaces. Structures changed as well. Some structures were for residential use, while others may have been for the storage of surplus grains or housing livestock. Humans' changing how land was used is something that has remained with us to this day.

The Evolution of Society

The *Neolithic Revolution* would induce other major shifts in human society. This could be seen in the following ways:

- Advancements in language and written communication
- Vocational specialization
- Social hierarchies
- Structural religion
- Regional politics/conflicts/alliances
- Technological advances
- Formal education
- New diseases

These changes were predetermined by a shift to agriculture, but evolved out of necessity. As society grew in population and complexity, there was a greater need for more advanced language and written communication. Thus languages advanced and regional patterns of diffusion could be observed. No

FIGURE 1.3a. Early stone tools of the Neolithic Revolution. Copyright © José-Manuel Benito (CC BY-SA 2.5) at https://commons.wikimedia.org/wiki/File%3AMolino_neol%C3%ADtico_de_vaiv%C3%A9n.jpg .

longer was society a simple hunter-gatherer dynamic. In agricultural society, there was a need for specialists. This might include engineers, farmers, administrators, builders, and so forth.

A more complex society meant a more complex social structure. Some people would have power over others. Leadership was needed to coordinate and administrate the people and activities in which they participated. Religion began to reflect the increasing sophistication of society as well. Advanced language and written communication helped structure more advanced belief systems across greater areas. Relationships changed between peoples that shared regions. These relationships could be adversarial or cooperative. If adversarial, there would be a greater need for security (e.g., walls, trained soldiers, defense/offense technologies). New advances in engineering, agriculture, and weaponry redefined regions.

Finally, proximity to livestock put humans in the biological trajectory of new diseases. Many of the diseases we know of today began because early humans shared space with livestock. Animal microbes mutated and became pathogens that inflicted humans with disease. Proximity to cattle, for example, led to diseases like *measles, tuberculosis,* and *smallpox*; the *flu* came from pigs and ducks, and so on. Together or independently, all these changes can be attributed to the first agricultural and *Neolithic* revolutions and would, forever, change humanity.

Diffusion Patterns

A new formula for humanity emerged after transitioning from hunter-gatherers to agriculture. Population grew, technology advanced, and society became more sophisticated. These advances, however, really emerged from specific hearths, or origin areas. For example, the *Fertile Crescent* (seen in *Figure 1.3b*), which includes Mesopotamia and the Nile River Valley and Delta, was one of the early hearths of advanced agricultural civilization. Others included the Indus and Ganges River valleys, West Africa, The Huang He River region, and both the Mesoamerican and Andean cultural regions. Many of the foods we eat today (wheat, rice, corn, fruits, vegetables) come from these early agricultural hearths. Likewise, early advanced *proto languages* came from these regions. Clearly, these ideas did not remain exclusive features of these early hearths. The reason for this is both simple and complex. People, by nature and for whatever reason, move. When they move, they take with them all they have learned. Therefore,

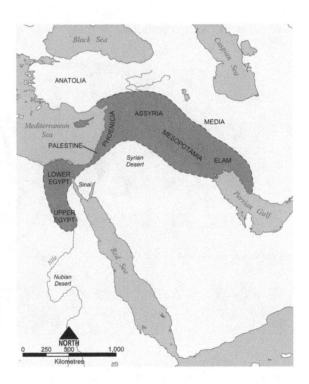

FIGURE 1.3b. Early agricultural hearth known as the Fertile Crescent. Copyright © Norman Einstein (CC BY-SA 3.0) at https://commons.wikimedia.org/wiki/File:Fertile_Crescent_map.png.

understanding movement and diffusion patterns is a key component of regional geography.

This textbook will only focus on two main types of diffusion. One type is contagious diffusion, which might be described as the spreading of an idea from person to person in close proximity and/or from one community or region to an adjacent community or region. This type of diffusion explains how innovations, cultural traits, and technology often have an outward trajectory. The other type of diffusion is relocation diffusion, or the transplanting of ideas, innovations, or culture from one location to another, often through migration. European colonialism would be an excellent example

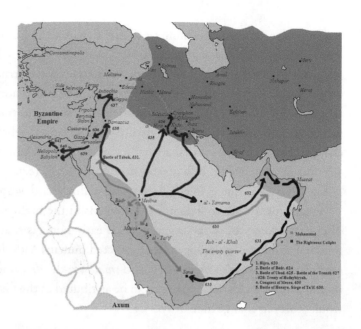

FIGURE 1.3c. The rapid spread of Islam is an excellent example of both contagious and relocation diffusion. Copyright in the Public Domain.

FIGURE 1.3d. The British had a colony on the Cook Islands in the South Pacific and the traditional Polynesians started to dress like British people. As the British pulled out and they became independent, they stopped dressing this way. Too much time passed and they were too far from London to keep up with fashion trends. Copyright in the Public Domain.

of relocation diffusion, whereas the spread of Islam would represent the power of contagious diffusion. Although there are more examples of diffusion, this textbook will focus on these two types.

Resulting from diffusion is what geographers refer to as time-distance decay. This term captures the dilution that commonly occurs as something (language, customs, or some other cultural trait) moves away from a hearth, or the longer it is away. As people move, they carry with them traits from their culture. However, the further they get, the more they interact with other cultures and the more time passes. This process explains why divisions emerge amongst many groups from the same culture. The United States, for example, was originally a British colony. American colonists from England faced very different circumstances than their kin and countrymen at home. Therefore, changes began to occur over time that reflected a new, emerging cultural complex in America. Yet this textbook is written in English, by an American citizen, so some key traits remain, while others are lost entirely.

A final discussion will address why people move. There are three types of movement that will assist

FIGURE 1.3e. American troops deployed during war represents a form of periodic movement.
Copyright in the Public Domain.

with the study of world regions and the conflict and cooperation that have defined them. One is cyclic movement, or one's daily *activity space*. This type of movement examines the patterns of movement locally.

FIGURE 1.3f. Silicon Valley is a highly desired destination for college graduates educated in computer engineering, programming, and design. It has created a "pull factor" for techies around the world. Copyright © Coolcaesar (CC BY-SA 3.0) at https://commons.wikimedia.org/wiki/File%3AEbayheadquarters.jpg .

Where people live, work, and shop can reveal something about their culture, economy, and a number of other things. Periodic movement is moving away for longer periods with the intention of returning. College students, soldiers deployed abroad, or farm hands arriving for harvest are examples of this.

Migration is when someone leaves his or her country of residence or arrives in a new country with the intention of making it permanent. More specifically, an immigrant is someone arriving into a new country. An emigrant, on the other hand, is an individual leaving his or her country of residence. People come and go for many reasons. Geographers break this down into the following terms: *push* and *pull factors*. A **push factor** would be a negative reason or perception influencing a move out of a particular area. A factory closing in a town where it provided the bulk of jobs would influence many to leave to find work elsewhere.

A **pull factor** would be a positive reason or perception about another location, influencing a move there. Recent graduates with technology degrees, for example, might move near Silicon Valley, California, where top computer, Internet, and tech firms headquarter. Finally, there is forced migration, or the involuntary movement of people from their homes (as a result of war, natural catastrophe, slavery, or climate change) to another region or country. The *Atlantic Slave Trade* would be an example of this. See *Figure 1.3g* (1) and (2).

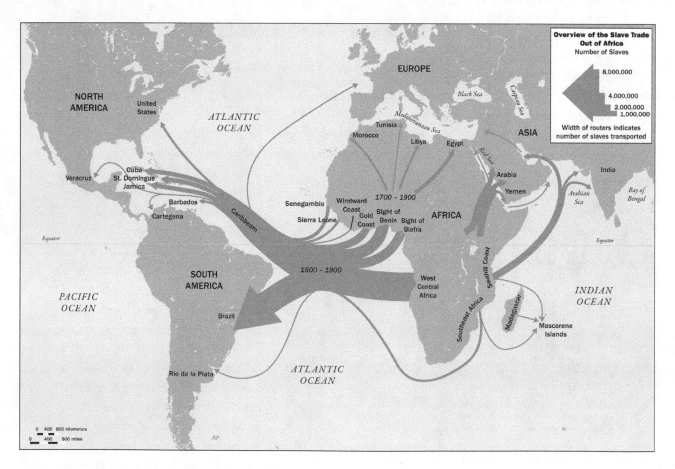

FIGURE 1.3g(1). Overview of the Slave Trade out of Africa, 1500–1900.
David Eltis and David Richardson, "Map 1: Overview of the Slave Trade Out of Africa, 1500-1900," Atlas of the Transatlantic Slave Trade. Copyright © 2010 by Yale University Press. Reprinted with permission.

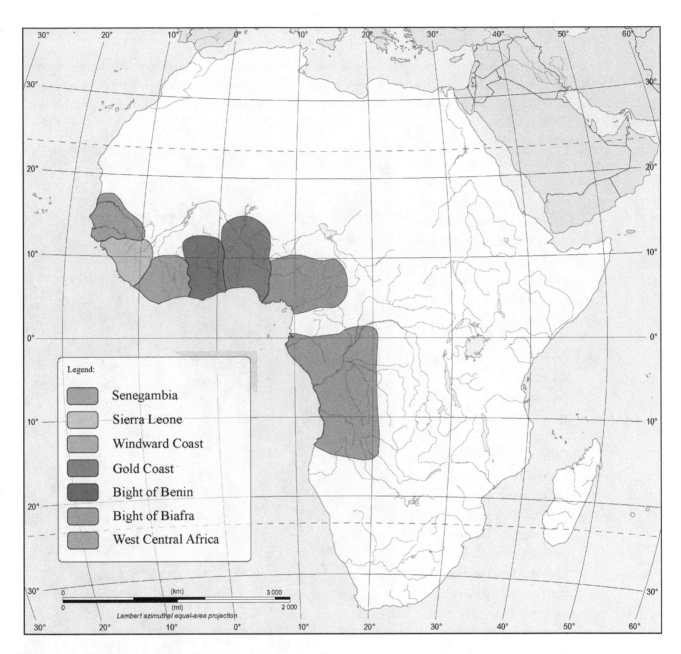

FIGURE 1.3g(2). The Atlantic Slave Trade resulted in several million people forced to migrate to the Americas.
Copyright © Eric Gaba (CC BY-SA 3.0) at https://commons.wikimedia.org/wiki/File:Africa_slave_Regions.svg.

This shameful example of human movement highlights the involuntary migration of approximately twenty million Africans to the New World for the purpose of labor. Other reasons generate refugees or displaced people. Understanding human movement sheds light on how cultural landscapes formed and continue to shape our world today.

CULTURAL LANDSCAPES

The diffusion of ideas from early agricultural hearths outward began to aesthetically change broader regions. Increasingly, human activities like agriculture could be seen along lengthy stretches of river valleys in regions like Mesopotamia. Villages had grown into towns and even cities. All these changes would reflect the values, technologies, practices, and features of a particular culture. A cultural landscape, then, is the imprint of human activity over space—a broad range of human activities, over a natural landscape, that are influenced by the culture that resides within that space. Below are some terms and definitions about culture:

- **Culture:** An umbrella under which various traits, values, rituals, norms, and practices are held together by communication and interaction.
- **Cultural trait:** A single element of culture.
- **Cultural complex:** A particular culture's structure that houses the various elements of culture.
- **Cultural hearth:** The heartland of a particular culture; a place of origin.
- **Cultural landscape:** Imprint of human activity over space. A broad range of human activities, over a natural landscape, that are influenced by the culture that resides within that space.

FIGURE 1.3h. Sri Mariamman Temple, Singapore. Cultures are unique around the world. Copyright © AngMoKio (CC BY-SA 3.0) at https://commons.wikimedia.org/wiki/File%3ASri_Mariamman_Temple_Singapore_3_amk.jpg.

These terms illuminate various aspects of culture. This is often the result of a group having common geographical roots or racial or ethnic similarities. When groups of people share a long history within a particular region, a culture is formed. Naturally, this can take time, and culture can continue to be influenced by others.

Identity, Ethnicity, and Race

Though it is important to understand the evolution and diffusion of cultural landscapes, it is equally as important to discuss differences between people and how those influence human relationships at various scales. A person's identity, where they are from, and what color their skin is (as well as other physical features) influence how they feel about others. Naturally, the study of identity, ethnicity, and race has, and continues to be, deeply explored within the behavioral and social sciences. This textbook will take aspects of these important conversations and use them to examine how they have fostered conflict and cooperation between groups, locally to globally, over time.

Identity refers to how someone sees himself in comparison to others. One's identity is often a reflection of who is around him, his culture, and even his physical features. If a particular culture remains in a geographical area for a very long period, then they begin to identify themselves with both others from this region and the region itself. This refers to ethnicity; a cultural group affiliated with a certain geographical region. A cohesive element of ethnicity is that a particular group or culture often shares the same physical features, like skin color, hair color, or other biological *genotypes* and *phenotypes*. Race, or distinctive biological characteristics that are passed from parents to children, tells us where they are from originally. When exploring world regions and the conflicts and cooperation between cultures and nations over time, discussions related to identity, ethnicity, and race will often provide valuable insights.

POLITICAL SPACE

The world is divided into political space. Maps commonly use color to distinguish the sovereign political space of countries around the world. Encasing the color is a political border, which allows the viewer to see the line where one political space ends and another begins (as seen in *Figure 1.3i*). This division of the world into political units largely defines humanity, and how we interact with each other, to this day.

There are several characteristics of modern political space that might allow a better understanding of the world. First, our current global political structure means that most of humanity can claim citizenship or residency in one of these political spaces. Within these political spaces, people are governed by the laws and have variable access to services, representation, and security. Naturally, some political spaces are in a state of conflict and cannot provide these benefits.

Secondly, the political borders that define these political spaces did not simply appear. Rather, they are human constructs, and there is often a long story behind their inception. Accepting this modern political dynamic leads to some questions: Why would a group of people need its own distinguishable, definable space? What led to the modern system of political space, and how does it define human interaction at various scales? This chapter will briefly explore these questions in a way that fosters a deeper understanding of world regions and the political relationships that define the world.

FIGURE 1.3i. Political space resulting from European need to cooperate with each other.
Copyright in the Public Domain.

Territory, Sovereignty, and the Nation-State

A fundamental human instinct is to protect the space they believe is theirs. This is known as territoriality, or a protective stance over the space which people, communities, or nations occupy. The protection of this space has been, and continues to be, a source of conflict between people. Disputes over territory, invasion of space, and sometimes the unwanted, aggressive expansion of space have been some of the leading causes of human conflict over time. Although conflicts stem from a wide variety of issues, sometimes issues not directly related to territory become territorial issues when different groups engaged in conflict reside in close proximity to each other. This scenario, incidentally, was the inception of the modern political structure we know today.

Sovereignty, or the control over a people or territory by those who reside within that space, arose as the result of great conflicts in Europe. During the early seventeenth century, Europe was engaged in two of the bloodiest concurrent wars the continent has ever known. The Thirty Years' War (1618–1648) and the lengthy Eighty Years' War (1568–1648) were essentially the reaction to the Protestant/Catholic religious divisions following the Protestant Reformation (1516).

So devastating and lengthy were these wars that an attempt to make peace was welcomed by the various actors who were fighting. Until this point, kingdoms, the Holy Roman Empire, and *principalities* (often in conjunction with church power) controlled people and space. But with changing alliances and the division of religious beliefs amongst those who were formally allied, a new system had to be devised. The *Peace of Westphalia* (1648) did precisely that (*see Figure 1.3j*). Essentially, the conference conceived that those cultural groups that had traditionally occupied the same space would form a nation of people. That nation of people, then, would construct, by agreement, borders and sovereign political space in which to conduct their own affairs while being recognized and respected by neighboring sovereignties. Thus was born the modern nation-state. A nation is cultural in origin, while the state is the political structure that defines that space geographically. Within the state are laws, taxes, administrative structures—and eventually citizenship—for those who reside within that space. This new system began to form the political borders we still see today (see *Figure 1.3i*).

The importance of this shift to a nation-state system cannot be underestimated. Not only did the Europeans devise a political system that quelled decades of war, they also created a political template that could be applied to the world through the channels of colonialism. If they were to conduct themselves globally, then imposing or influencing a similar political structure of borders and formalized political space could only play to their advantage. As seen in *Figure 1.3j*, the world has been defined by this system born

FIGURE 1.3j. The Peace of Westphalia in 1648 determined the system of borders we use today.
Copyright in the Public Domain.

in Europe. This textbook will consider the role of the *nation-state* system and how it has fostered both regional alliances and contempt in different regions.

ECONOMIC RELATIONSHIPS

Humans have been engaged in observable and measurable economic activities since the dawn of civilization. Historically, there are many examples of trade and commerce being conducted across great distances and between cultures who share little apart from a common desire to exchange goods and services. The *Silk Road*, for example, stretched from Venice and Constantinople all the way through Persia, India, China, and Korea. This economic artery linked west to east, laying the groundwork for future Western European nations to seek direct trade routes, by sea, to these realms.

The British Empire might also provide a looking glass into how commerce was conducted globally. They were really the first to engage in commerce on a global scale. By 1860, the British controlled one-fifth of the world's economy. This was done by leveraging the natural and human resources of foreign colonies for the benefit of Britain's economy.

Today's economic landscapes are sophisticated and require an interdisciplinary examination. Within this complexity, several key narratives arise:

- *Economic hierarchies*: How the world is divided into core, semi-periphery, and periphery.
- *Social dynamics:* Who trades with each other, and why?
- *Political ties:* What alliances have formed that define global business trends?
- *Cultural limitations*: Who is left out of the globalized world?
- *Geographical observations*: Why are the most powerful economies located in the middle latitudes of the Northern Hemisphere (e.g., North America, Europe, and East Asia)?

Although this textbook cannot address each of these narratives in detail, a discussion about uneven global development may illuminate aspects of the world economy.

FIGURE 1.3k. Super Panamax ship moving goods around the world, because of economic relationships. Copyright © Wmeinhart (CC BY-SA 3.0) at https://commons.wikimedia.org/wiki/File:Colombo.Express.wmt. jpg .

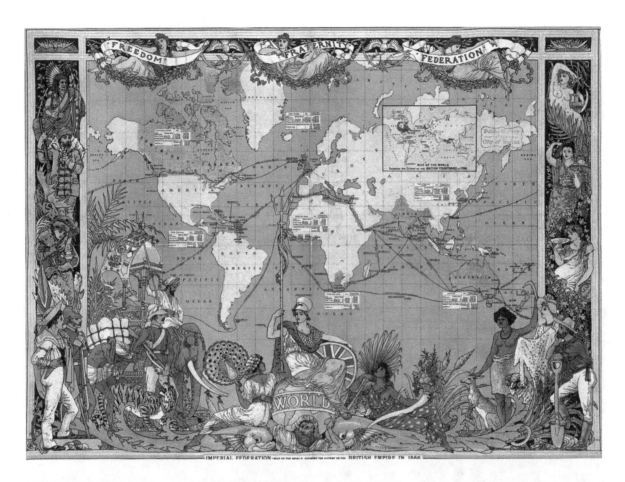

FIGURE 1.3I. Map of the world showing the extent of the British Empire in 1886. Note how people of other races and ethnicities are depicted.
Copyright in the Public Domain.

UNDERSTANDING ECONOMIC GEOGRAPHY

Generalizing the world economy can be difficult, if not irresponsible. There are many mechanisms at play and countless formulas that have together shaped the economic landscapes we can observe today. Economic geography explores various economic activities and the trends and spatial patterns that emerge from those activities. Like other areas of geography, the scale of this discussion can shift from the economy of a particular city to global macroeconomic trends. That is why there are some useful external additions to this textbook (to follow) that will help us understand the successes and challenges of understanding economic geography. Before those sources are examined, it is important to discuss some important concepts and theories.

Observing and Measuring Differences

Broadly, one can view the world economy and identify whether an individual country is mostly characterized by its *formal economy* or *informal economy*. A formal economy can be described as any legal economic activities that are taxed and monitored by government and counted in all measures of the economy (gross domestic product, for example). This would include any licensed business, personal income, corporate profits, sales tax, and so on. An informal economy would be any activity not counted or measured by government as a part of the economy. Countries with a high percentage of poverty are often characterized by informal economic activities.

Another tool used to observe a particular country's economy is its occupational structure. This refers to the dominant sector that a particular nation, region, or locale engages in. Three key structures are:

1. **Primary Sector:** Defined as anything directly extracted from nature, like fishing, silviculture (logging), farming, mining, etc.
2. **Secondary Sector:** Industries that transform a natural resource into a commodity, like manufacturing steel out of coal and iron ore.
3. **Tertiary Sector:** Any person or industry providing a service. This would include retail, teaching, health care, public services, hospitality, etc.

FIGURE 1.3m(1). Tamarack miners, Copper Country. Mining is regarded as one of the "Primary" sector activities. Copyright in the Public Domain.

FIGURE 1.3m(2). A factory worker manufacturing a product works in the "Secondary" sector.
Copyright © KINEX (CC BY-SA 3.0) at https://commons.wikimedia.org/wiki/File%3AWorker_9.JPG .

FIGURE 1.3m(3). Nurses, and others who provide services, work in the "Tertiary" sector.
Copyright © Vlastimil (CC BY-SA 2.0) at https://commons.wikimedia.org/wiki/File%3ANursing_students.jpg .

The reason why these are important to understand is because they can indicate a country's role or place in globalization. A wealthy country like the United States, for example, is characterized by its tertiary sector economy. That is because Americans form one of the largest consumer markets in the world and rely on a robust service sector for economic prosperity.

Walt Rostow's *Modernization Model* (1960) might also provide a glimpse into a particular economy. His five Stages of Growth include:

1. Traditional society
2. Preconditions to Take-off
3. Take-off
4. Drive to Maturity
5. Mass Consumption

This model is useful for studying countries that seek to transform themselves in a way that may allow better economic connectivity with the global economy. India, for example, identified that their stagnant economy, poor infrastructure, and thick bureaucracy of the 1980s limited their ability to be a part of the globalizing economy. This would be their "traditional society" stage. They approached the World Bank and IMF, who are tasked with facilitating development. Once India agreed to the laundry list of requirements, they were loaned a large sum of money to put into action the conditions itemized by the World Bank. This would be the preconditions to take-off stage. India made many of these changes, which attracted more foreign direct investment (FDI), or the investment of capital by foreign sources of revenue, into their country (manufacturing/production, services, etc.). This would be the take-off stage, and so on. Where a specific nation falls within this model often provides insight into its role in a global economy.

A useful tool for examining the economic hierarchies that have formed since World War II is Immanuel Wallerstein's World Systems Theory (see *Fig. 1.3n*). In this theory, Wallerstein divides the world into three basic categories: Core, Semiperiphery, and Periphery. Below is a summarization of each level:

*   **Core:** These nations, like US/Canada, Western Europeans, Japan, and Australia–New Zealand, are characterized by workers with higher-level skills, capital-intensive production, higher levels of education, and robust consumer economies.
*   **Periphery:** These nations, like those found in much of Africa, South Asia, and Central America, are characterized by low-skilled, labor-intensive production, low education levels, and high levels of poverty.
*   **Semi-periphery:** Several nations exhibit characteristics of both the core and periphery. They have low-skilled, cheap labor that fuels robust production operations (often by foreign firms). They have high percentages of poverty and an economy with a high growth rate. These countries include the BRICS (Brazil, Russia, India, China, and South Africa) as well as others like Mexico, Argentina, and Indonesia.

This theory indicates that certain nations have emerged as economic powers who define how goods, services, labor, and production are distributed or allocated at the global scale. Their ability to reach this level,

World Trade

FIGURE I.3n. World Systems Theory map.
Copyright in the Public Domain.

then, might help explain how their societies could reinforce the strength of their economies with institutions of higher learning, specialized labor, and—eventually—a higher *per capita* GDP (gross domestic product) and standard of living. Likewise, it also suggests there are many that remain either external to global economic partnerships or are relied upon only for their resources (cheap labor, raw materials). These economic divisions and interdependencies between nations require a brief discussion prior to moving on to key world regions.

Measuring national economies falls within the field of economics. Economists use a broad range of formulas to measure a nation's economy. Some of those are: GDP (Gross Domestic Product), which measures the total value of a state's services and goods each year. GNP (Gross National Product) is GDP plus profits and incomes earned by citizens and companies abroad. *Per capita* GDP is the total GDP divided by total population. Finally, growth rate, also called *compound annual growth rate (CAGR)*, measures the increase in value of goods and services over the last year. Although this barely skims the surface of what economists use to look at state economies, they will be useful tools for examining world regions, providing context for the uneven development that characterizes the human landscape.

CASE STUDY 1B

CIA World Factbook: One-Stop Shopping for Data

The Central Intelligence Agency (CIA) is a principal American intelligence-gathering agency of the federal government. In addition to the host of duties they perform, they collect and maintain important data about every political state on Earth and publish it in the World Factbook. The World Factbook is available through a website that is accessible to anyone, and it can be a useful tool when seeking information about a particular country's economy, demographic profile, or cultural data.

In this exercise, you will follow the instructions to learn about the economy of Nigeria. Please follow the steps below:

1. Open a web browser and type in "CIA World Factbook," or click the link below: https://www.cia.gov/library/publications/the-world-factbook/.
2. On the right, above the interactive world map, either click on Africa on the map (if you know where it is) or use the pull-down menu on the upper right above the map to find Nigeria (it is in alphabetical order).
3. Once on Nigeria, you will be given several options such as Introduction, Geography, People & Society, Government, etc.
4. Click "Economy: NIGERIA": There you will find a wide variety of current economic data.
5. What is Nigeria's GDP or Gross Domestic Product (2013 est.)?
6. What is Nigeria's per capita GDP?
7. If you were to break down Nigeria's GDP by service, which sector would be the largest of the three?
8. Name three (3) of Nigeria's main industries.
9. What percentage of the people lives below the poverty line?
10. What country is Nigeria's number one exporting partner?

All this and more can easily be found on the CIA World Factbook site. Now, play with the website and choose a country of your own to examine. As this textbook progresses through world regions, use this resource to look deeper into various aspects of countries within those regions.

UNEVEN DEVELOPMENT

The inevitable outcome of examining world regional economies is the discovery that the world has developed unevenly. This is a long and complicated narrative, but there are some key discussions that may effectively illuminate why this has happened.

European Colonialism

A good beginning point to this discussion is European colonialism, which followed the *Age of Exploration*. Colonialism can be defined as the settlement of a foreign nation by a more powerful nation for the purpose of using their human and natural resources for the benefit of the colonizer. The Europeans, specifically the British, French, Spanish, Portuguese, and Dutch, would all leverage the resources of foreign lands they occupied or claimed in order to bolster their respective economies. To secure and maintain these colonies, Europeans established sea routes for products and services to flow between their homeland and their colonies. This was an effective model, at first.

In the case of the British, they managed their American colony in very much this way, and eventually paid the price. *Mercantilism*, or measuring a colonial system by its profitability, defined early British colonies. As long as the colony was profitable, there was indirect supervision of that colony, at most. After the Seven Years' War (a.k.a. the French and Indian War) was over, the British reasserted themselves over the colony and imposed taxes to recover from the cost of the war. American colonists rejected British interloping, went to war, and achieved independence.

The British, having lost their alpha colony, reexamined their colonial paradigm and leaned towards Adam Smith's *Wealth of Nations* (1776) publication for inspiration. Adam Smith talked about the "invisible hand," which proposed that those who felt inclined to be entrepreneurial would benefit society. Smith implied that he who would strive to provide the best product or service to make himself competitive, while giving the consumer better options to choose from, would better society. This "free market" approach would influence a paradigm shift in colonial management. The British, before long, would embrace a *laissez faire*, or "hands-off" economic posture that would deem any nonproductive appendage of society (typically government) unnecessary. Markets, in this view, dictated the success of a state's economy, not government. Thus was born a *classical economics* system of free markets, low regulation, and small government.

The result of this system was the global expansion of the British Empire. They became the largest and most powerful economy on Earth by the mid-nineteenth century. Other European nations (Germany, for example) had similar production abilities and access to raw materials but lacked the trade networks and number of colonies the British established and profited from. This would later become a major source of conflict in Europe.

The Americans, formerly a colony of Britain, adopted many of the same strategies of allowing industry to grow in a largely unregulated environment. As the relationship began to thaw between the Americans and British, a new era of friendship and trade partnership would evolve between the British—and others in its family of nations or with kinship links (North America, Australia, New Zealand)—and profitable colonies like India, Hong Kong, Singapore, and a handful of African nations. This colonial system was likewise put into place by the French in Indochina (Vietnam, Cambodia), and by the Portuguese in

FIGURE 1.3o. US aircraft carrier in the Suez reflects a regular presence of American military power in the region. Copyright in the Public Domain.

Macau and Brazil. These colonial systems, then, would provide the first blueprint of the modern economic landscape.

Global commercial interests are often paired with protectionism and a tendency to control or manipulate affairs abroad. This European interloping had two fronts. One was coercion. In more traditional societies, like India and Africa, the Europeans often imposed strict rules with heavy-handed responses to social unrest. The British, for example, limited access to the cities from which they governed. This helped to quell anti-colonial solidarity in strategic cities with ports, government buildings, and supply chains from the hinterland. This particular dynamic revealed how the Europeans were really the beneficiaries of these colonial economies and used their military prowess to manipulate favorable regional politics when possible.

Industrialization

The other key discussion that helps explain uneven development is industrialization. The Industrial Revolution can be described as an era of technological innovation and mechanization resulting from a deeper understanding (and embracing) of the sciences. This "revolution" began in England around the turn of the century (eighteenth/nineteenth) and quickly spread to other Western European nations and North America. Innovative technologies helped to mechanize labor, increase production outputs, move products and services faster, and to make better, stronger materials that supported growing industries and markets.

The *Second Agricultural Revolution* soon followed, and industrializing nations became epicenters of agricultural production. Better ships, trains, and mobility technologies allowed crops and livestock to move from more peripheral realms to markets in cities. These attributes helped to propel some countries forward, while others that did not industrialize fell behind. As this textbook examines world regions, this division amongst nations and the competition between industrialized nations will be shown as a major source of conflict and cooperation.

BOX 1C COLONIALISM AND NEOCOLONIALISM

Not only are some countries more susceptible to hunger than others, but some are also more limited in their policy options for tackling it. Differences in the power of governments to independently chart their country's hunger and poverty strategies are rooted in their colonial history. European colonialism deeply affected the societies and economies of many of the countries that today experience hunger vulnerability. Colonialism is both a political economic system and an ideology that allows a country to assert control over a people and territory beyond its boundaries. Historically colonial power was exerted for the purported benefit of the subject population, but colonialism benefited the colonizing power to the detriment of the colonized.

European colonies covered 10% of the world's land area in 1750. By 1914 this territory expanded more than three-fold to encompass 35% of the world's land area. See Figure 1.3p(1). Colonial possessions brought prestige to even small countries like Belgium and Portugal, whose African colonies significantly enlarged their land area. King Leopold's personal colony, deceptively named the Congo Free State, was 76 times the size of Belgium (Hochschild 1999). By adding Angola and Mozambique to its colonial possessions, Portugal could proudly proclaim to the world that "Portugal is not a small country." See Figure 1.3p(2).

Colonial authorities sought to control the natural resources and labor of their colonies and to reorient markets to serve the interests of European industries, consumers, and settlers. In Southeast Asia, the Netherlands instituted the "culture system," which required farmers to plant one-fifth of their fields in cash crops like coffee and sugar that were of interest to Dutch companies (Bagchi 1983, 71–73). In Eastern and Southern Africa, the British forced indigenous peoples to move onto reserves so that European settlers could occupy the most productive lands. These reserves, known as Tribal Trust Lands, Communal Lands, and Native Reserves, were notoriously overcrowded and characterized by poor soils and insufficient rainfall. Poverty,

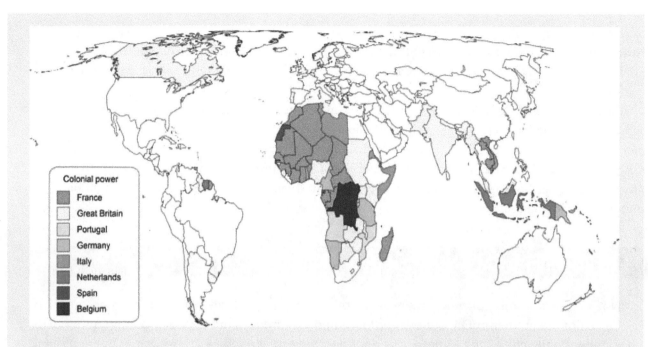

FIGURE 1.3p(1). European colonies, 1914.

hunger, and taxation forced men and women to migrate to settler plantations and mines to work as wage laborers.

In French West Africa, the colonial state coerced rural populations to produce cash crops and work for a pittance in settler logging concessions and coffee and cocoa plantations. French policies in Côte d'Ivoire required savanna farmers to plant a specified area in cotton and then sell it for low prices in markets dominated by French merchants. See Figure 1.3p(3). The little money earned from these transactions was used to pay

FIGURE 1.3p(2). Portuguese government propaganda map showing the size of its colonies in comparison to the land area of Portugal. The title reads: "Portugal is not a small country." Enrique Galvão, *Lithografi a de Portugal* (Lisbon, ca. 1935), private collection.

taxes imposed by the colonial state on adults. This "head tax" had to be paid in French francs. The colonial state also required communities to fill a certain number of sacks with maize, rice, and millet. If a village did not have sufficient quantities of these crops to deliver, it had to buy them in a neighboring village. In this way, colonialism impoverished households and made them vulnerable to poor harvests associated with drought or pest invasions.

Some of the taxes collected in colonies were reinvested in those regions, but colonial investments shaped colonies

FIGURE 1.3p(3). Forced cotton deliveries in Tiébissou, Côte d'Ivoire, circa 1915.
Source: National Archives of France, Overseas Section.

according to European priorities rather than local interests. For example, governments supported research to develop cash crops of interest to European merchants and industries. Food crops important to the diets of local populations received little attention. Similarly, colonial investments in transportation infrastructure were designed to move goods from the interior to the coast, where they could be easily shipped to Europe, not to promote regional economic development.

The regime of forced labor, forced cultivation, dispossession, and taxation intensified during the first and second world wars and the Great Depression of the 1930s. In Africa, famine became common in areas where, prior to colonialism, it had been rare (Watts 1983). Sen (1983) chronicles the devastating famines that occurred in British India, where the entitlements that prevented famine in the past were eroded under colonial rule.

The legacy of authoritarian rule and the orientation of production and markets to serve the colonial powers is apparent in the continuing dependency of many former colonies on the export of primary products and the large numbers of people living in extreme poverty . Former colonies tend to trade with their former colonial rulers, producing and exporting low-value primary goods, which makes them particularly vulnerable to deteriorating terms of trade for their exports. Strong political ties also bind former colonies and colonial powers, as is evident in bilateral aid flows of France and Great Britain (Table 1.1). The top 10 recipients of both British and French aid in 2004–5 were overwhelmingly former colonies.

Having inherited economies that were designed to serve a foreign country rather than local peoples, many former colonies have fragile economic systems that have been vulnerable to instabilities and crises. Often, economic crises have driven these countries to seek the aid of international financial institutions (IFIs) that have provided loans only on the condition that borrowers adopt a set of specific policies aimed at reducing government spending, increasing exports, and "freeing up" markets. In many countries these policies may have deepened poverty and increased hunger vulnerability (Stiglitz 2003). The efforts of IFIs like the World Bank and International Monetary Fund to dictate national social and economic policy resemble the power of European governments during the colonial era. This resemblance has led many critics of the World Bank and IMF to label their interventions as "neocolonial."

TABLE 1.1. Top recipients of French and British official development assistance, 2005

Rank	French aid	British aid
1	Nigeria	Nigeria*
2	Congo Republic*	Iraq*
3	Senegal*	India*
4	Morocco*	Bangladesh*
5	Iraq	Zambia*
6	Madagascar*	Afghanistan
7	Algeria*	Tanzania*
8	Cameroon*	Ghana*
9	Mayotte*	Congo, Democratic Republic
10	Tunisia*	Sudan*

*Former colony
Source: OECD 2007

Poverty & Corruption

The product of uneven development has been a large portion of the world living in poverty. Poverty can be described as a human condition defined by low personal income. In its most extreme form, it can mean poor or limited access to:

- Nutrition
- Fresh drinking water
- Health care professionals and family planning
- Education
- Emergency and other government services
- Land tenure

Currently, about one in five humans on Earth live in abject poverty. Although economic globalization has transformed many societies by moving millions from poverty into the middle class, the lowest quintile of humans living in squalor is still a fixed part of the human landscape.

There are many reasons why poverty at this scale is sustained. Embedded corruption, rigid social systems, gender imbalances, and civil discord account for much of it. Corruption can be described as the fraudulent misconduct of those in positions of power over others, used for personal gain. Corruption can also be seen in government and embedded in all parts of public services, from policing to the state's executive. Although corruption can be found in any state, poor countries tend to have higher corruption rates. Slum dwellers, for example, typically squat on public lands and therefore lack the legal protection afforded to property owners. As a result, they are often forced to pay rent money for services to cartels or slumlords who take control of areas occupied by sometimes tens of thousands of people.

Below is a series of additional resources that help measure and visualize poverty globally.

BOX 1D INCOME INEQUALITY

Differences in political power are often related to income inequality. Income inequality and poverty are related but distinct concepts. In this atlas, "poverty" refers to a condition of absolute deprivation. We have classified people as "in poverty" if they live on less than $2.00 per day (PPP). "Inequality," in contrast, refers to relative rather than absolute conditions. Measurement of income inequality usually tries to gauge the distribution of income, not its level.

One common way to measure inequality in a country is to calculate the share of national income held by the richest and poorest 10% of the population. See Figures 1.3p(4) and (5). If incomes were distributed equally, the poorest 10% would control 10% of the nation's income and the richest 10% would hold the same share. Of course, in the case of complete equality, there would be no richest or poorest 10%, since everyone would have the same income. In general, the larger the share of national income held by the richest 10% or the smaller the share of income held by the poorest 10%, the greater the income inequality in a country.

The implications of income inequality for people's material well-being depend on the amount of income that is available to share. In terms of distribution, the countries of Scandinavia (Sweden, Norway, and Finland) are very similar to those of South Asia (Pakistan, India, Bangladesh). In both regions the poorest 10% claim a large share of national income compared to other countries, while the richest control a smaller share than elsewhere. However, since gross national incomes (GNI) in South Asia are about $2000 (PPP) per capita compared to $30,000 (PPP) per capita in Scandinavia, the poorest 10% in India, Pakistan, and Bangladesh are at vastly greater risk of hunger than are their counterparts in Sweden, Norway, and Finland. Similarly, the poorest 10% in Ethiopia control 4% of the country's income, while the poorest 10% in the United States hold less than 2% of their country's income. Since average income in

Thomas J. Bassett and Alex Winter-Nelson, "Income Inequality," *The Atlas of World Hunger*, pp. 118-121. Copyright © 2010 by University of Chicago Press. Reprinted with permission.

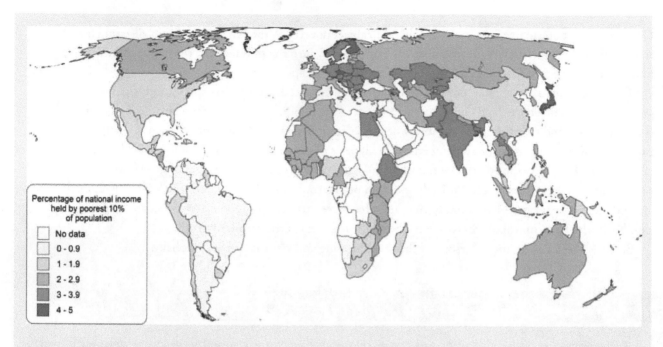

FIGURE 1.3p(4). Income share held by poorest 10%, 1992–2005.

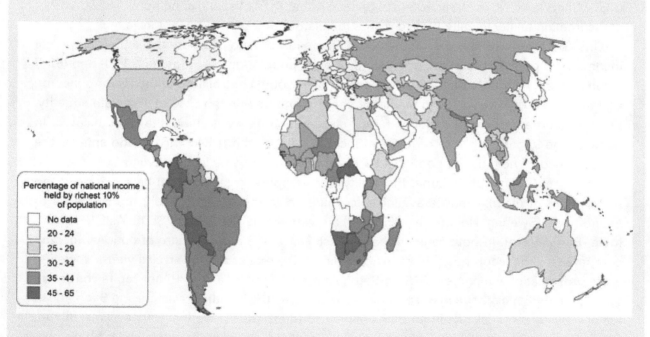

FIGURE 1.3p(5). Income share held by richest 10%, 1992–2005.

the United States is about $40,000 compared to less than $1000 (PPP) in Ethiopia, the poorest Americans have considerably higher incomes than the poorest Ethiopians.

Inequality can influence hunger vulnerability in at least two ways. First, if incomes are not very high, then unequal distribution of income will mean that the poorest people are too poor to get enough to eat. A second and less direct way in which inequality affects hunger is through the political system. If the rich control a large share of national income and the poor control a very small share, as in most of Latin America, it is unlikely that the poor will have much influence in political institutions. Inequalities in income distribution can translate into inequalities in political access. One would not expect governments that are more influenced by the rich than the poor to aggressively address the causes of hunger or to emphasize food and nutrition programs, since undernourishment is not a malady of the wealthy.

At first glance, the maps of income distribution bear little relationship to the mapping of hunger vulnerability. One can find countries like Ethiopia with high hunger vulnerability and low income inequality and countries like Chile with low hunger vulnerability and dramatic

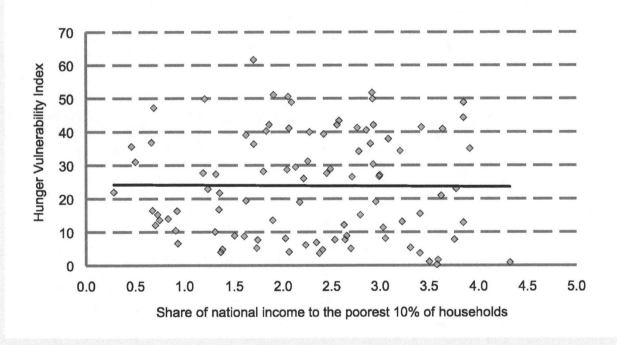

FIGURE 1.3p(6). Hunger vulnerability and income inequality in the world.
Sources: WHO 2008c; FAO 2008b; World Bank, PovcalNet, n.d.; World Bank, *World Development Indicators Online*, n.d.

inequality. This outcome can be explained by the influence of income level in addition to income distribution on hunger outcomes.

Figure 1.3p(6) plots the data on hunger vulnerability and the share of income to the poorest 10% of the population in all countries for which information is available. The distribution in the diagram reveals no clear pattern. This is because in affluent countries high degrees of inequality can exist with low rates of absolute poverty. However, if we look only at those countries in which per capita incomes range between $5000 and $10,000 (PPP) per year, then a more distinct pattern appears. For these countries, the larger the share of national income going to the poorest, the lower the hunger vulnerability tends to be (Figure 1.3p(7)). This relationship does not hold in the poorest countries, as the flat distribution of points in Figure 1.3p(9) shows. The level of income is so low in these countries that marginal increases in the share going to the poor (say from 2% to 3%) cannot influence hunger substantially. In these countries, alleviating poverty requires both increases in total income and more equitable distribution of

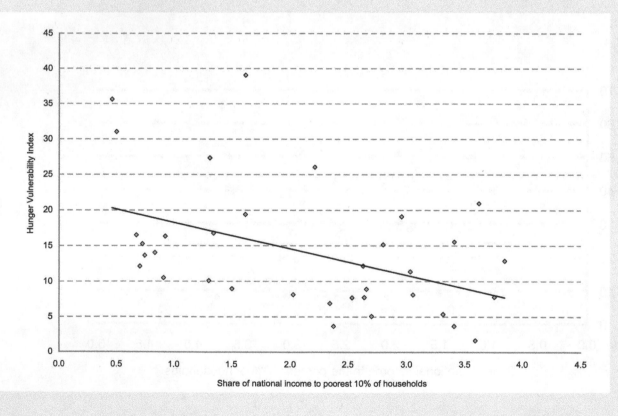

FIGURE 1.3p(7). Hunger vulnerability and income inequality in countries with annual per capita incomes between $750 and $2,500 (PPP).

Sources: WHO 2008c; FAO 2008b; World Bank, PovcalNet, n.d.; World Bank, *World Development Indicators Online*, n.d.

it. Poverty alleviation can take place through government programs that provide jobs, health care, education, and food stamps to the poor. This channeling of public goods and services to assist the poorest requires that institutions and power relations be focused on reducing poverty and food insecurity.

MEASURING INEQUALITY: LORENZ CURVES AND GINI COEFFICIENTS

The maps on inequality reveal the share of national income controlled by the poorest 10% of a country's households and the share held by the richest 10%. A more general presentation of income distribution can be plotted using a Lorenz curve. The Lorenz curve diagram, Figure 1.3p(8), shows the percentage of national income on the vertical axis and the percentage of households or population ordered from lowest to highest income on the horizontal axis. The Lorenz curve maps the cumulative share of income held by progressively larger shares of the population. A Lorenz curve will always end in the upper right corner of the diagram, with 100% of households controlling 100% of national income and will always begin in the lower left corner. The shape of the curve suggests something about distribution.

If a Lorenz curve followed a 45-degree line from the lower left to upper right, the country would have perfectly equal income distribution. The poorest 10% would control 10% of national income; the poorest 40% would control 40% of national income; and so on. The curved solid line in Figure 1.3p(8) shows a more common distribution. Here the poorest 10% have about 5% of national income; the poorest 40% have about 20% of national income; and the richest 20% have 30% of national income. The greater the inequality in distribution, the larger the area between the 45-degree line and the actual Lorenz curve, labeled A in this figure.

The gini coefficient, or gini index, is a measure of inequality based on the Lorenz curve. It is simply the area A in Figure 1.3p(8) divided by the area (A + B). The gini coefficient must fall between zero and 1, with zero representing perfect equality and 1 representing a single individual holding all the national income. Sweden, a country with fairly even income distribution, has a gini index of 0.25. In South Africa, where a history of racial injustice has

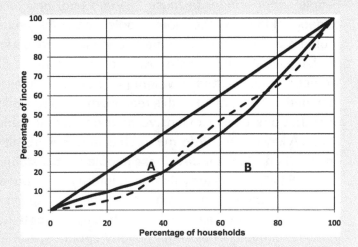

FIGURE 1.3p(8). Lorenz curve diagram.

created highly uneven distribution, the gini coefficient is 0.58. The United States has a gini value of 0.41, while Ethiopia's is 0.30.

The gini coefficient is a useful and widely applied summary measure of inequality. However, it does not indicate the status of people at the extremes of the distribution. Two Lorenz curves could imply the same gini coefficient but different shares of income to the poorest groups. The dotted Lorenz curve in Figure 1.3p(8) has about the same gini coefficient as the solid Lorenz curve, but the poorest households are shown to have

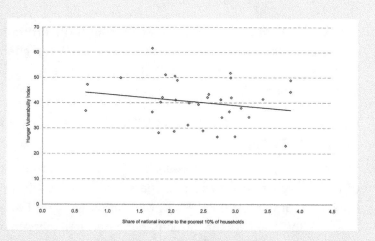

FIGURE 1.3p(9). Hunger vulnerability and income inequality in countries with annual per capita incomes between $750 and $2,500 (PPP).
Sources: WHO 2008c; FAO 2008b; World Bank, PovcalNet, n.d.; World Bank, *World Development Indicators Online*, n.d.

a smaller share of national income with the dotted curve. A focus on hunger implies particular interest in people at the bottom of the income distribution, and concerns about economic and political power suggest emphasis on those at the top. With that in mind, the maps in this atlas show the share of income that goes to the poorest and richest 10% of households.

EXTREME POVERTY

People suffer hunger because they are poor and receive inadequate assistance. Regardless of national income, the more people who suffer poverty in a country, the greater the hunger problem will be. There is some relationship between national income and hunger vulnerability, because countries with lower incomes tend to have more people in poverty. However, we get a better picture of where people suffer poverty by looking at personal income rather than national income. For this reason, the United Nations, World Bank, and other international organizations collect extensive data on incomes and spending among people around the world. A key piece of information that emerges from these data is the number of people living on less than $1.25 per day. These people are considered to be in extreme poverty.

The $1.25/day poverty line is an international poverty line measured in purchasing power parity (PPP) dollars rather than US dollars. As explained, $1.25/day PPP refers to an amount of income that is equivalent in its purchasing power to having $1.25 in the United States in 2005. Individuals living in extreme poverty could consume no more than an American could buy with $1.25. No one can question that this describes extreme poverty.

In the Millennium Development Goals, the global community set a target of reducing the share of the population living in extreme poverty to half of its 1990 level by the year 2015. As illustrated in Figures 1.3p(10) and 1.3p(11), extreme poverty rates have declined in some regions. Led by China, the rate of extreme poverty in East Asia fell from 55% of the population in 1990 to 17% in 2005 (Table 1.2). This means that there were more than 557 million fewer people in extreme poverty in that region in 2005 than in 1990. However, progress in poverty reduction was uneven. In Sub-Saharan Africa there was little change in the share of the population in poverty. The number of people in extreme poverty actually rose by 92 million.

Figures 1.3p (10) and 1.3p(11) indicate progress that has been made toward the Millennium Development Goals for poverty, regions that are lagging, and places where the prevalence of extreme poverty is exceedingly high. Consistent with the table, the maps show that rates of poverty are extremely high in South Asia and in Sub-Saharan Africa. India has made some progress in reducing the rate of extreme poverty. The poverty rate fell from 53% of the population in 1990 to 42% in 2005 (Table 1.2). Overall, the rate of poverty in the South Asian region fell by 12 percentage points.

The greatest reductions in the $1.25/day poverty rate are found in China, declining from 60% in 1990 to 17% in 2005. Rates of extreme poverty in Pakistan fell from 65% to 23%, while Vietnam registered a decline from 64% to 21% and Indonesia's poverty rate fell from 54% to 22%. In most cases, countries that experienced reductions in poverty combined general growth in the economy (per capita GNI), with wide distribution of that growth.

Despite progress in reducing the rates of extreme poverty in the world, there were still 1.4 billion people living on less than a $1.25 a day (PPP) in 2005. Figures 1.3p (12) and 1.3p(13) show where these people are found. Although poverty rates are falling in India and China, these countries still account for almost half of the people living in extreme poverty, as

TABLE 1.2. Extreme poverty by region, 2005

World Bank Region	Share of population living on less than $1.25/day (PPP) (%)		Number of people living on less than $1.25/day (PPP) (millions)	
	1990	2005	1990	2005
East Asia & Pacific	55	17	873	316
South Asia	52	40	579	596
Latin America & Caribbean	10	8	43	46
North Africa & Middle East	4	4	10	11
Europe & Central Asia	2	4	9	17
Sub-Saharan Africa	58	51	299	391
Low & middle-income countries	42	25	1696	1377

Source: World Bank, PovcalNet, n.d.

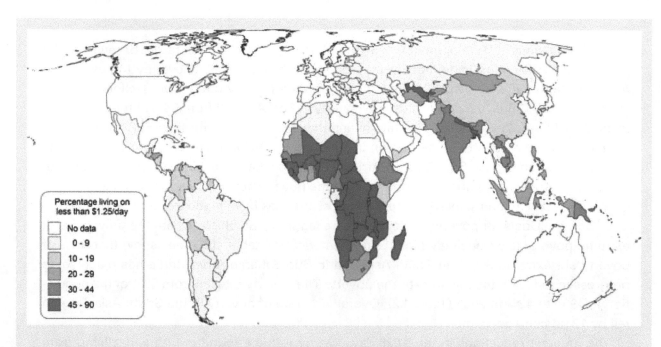

FIGURE 1.3p(10). Percentage of population in extreme poverty, 2005.

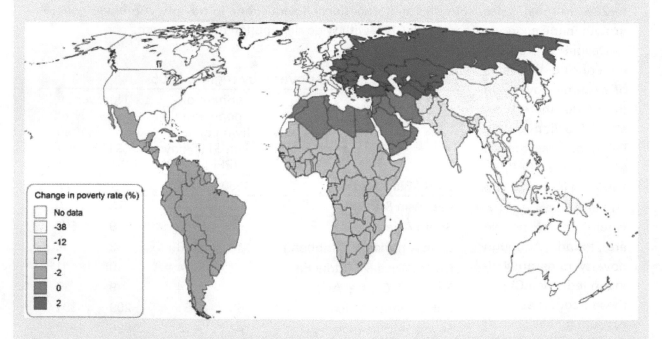

FIGURE 1.3p(11). Change in rate of extreme poverty, 1990–2005. Note: Change measured as the rate in 2005 minus the rate in 1990. Data are for regional aggregates.

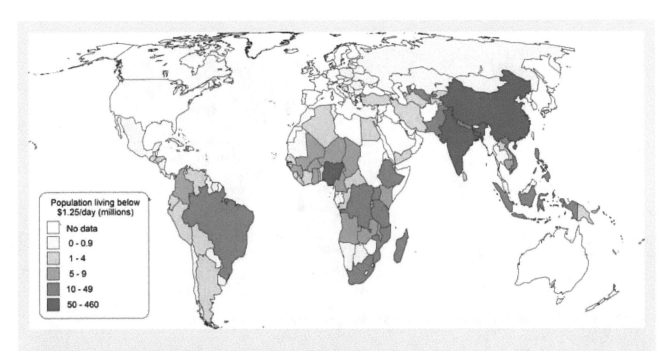

FIGURE 1.3p(12). Population in extreme poverty, 2005.

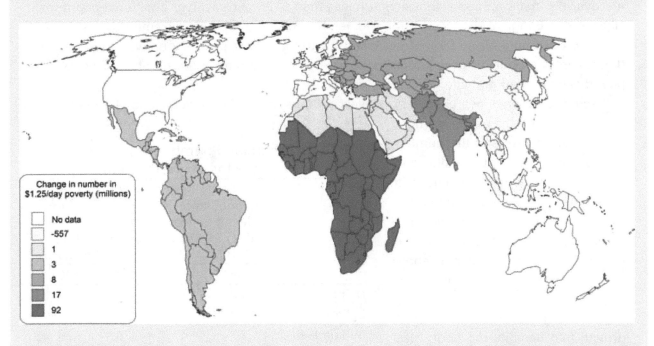

FIGURE 1.3p(13). Change in number of people in extreme poverty, 1990–2005. Note: Measured as the number of people in $1.25/day poverty in 2005 minus the number in poverty in 1990. Data are for regional aggregates.

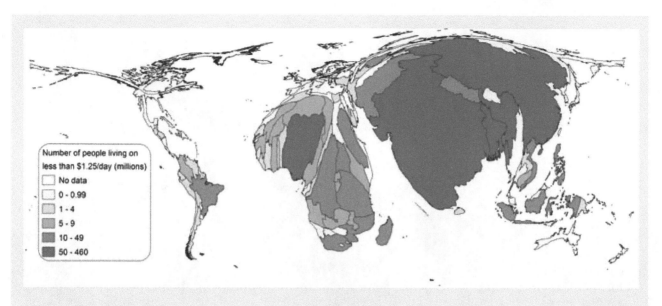

FIGURE 1.3p(14). Number of people living in $1.25/day poverty, 2005 (cartogram).

illustrated in the proportional area map (Figure 1.3p(14)). Between these two countries there are over 665 million people subsisting on less than $1.25 per day. Two additional countries, Nigeria and Bangladesh, account for another 167 million people in extreme poverty. These four countries hold about 60% of the world's extremely poor population. Economic growth that favors the poor in these countries could dramatically reduce the number of people in poverty and hunger globally.

Recent experience has been very uneven in China, India, Bangladesh, and Nigeria (Table 1.3). While China has reduced both the rate of poverty and the number of people in poverty, India and Bangladesh have seen reductions in poverty rates with small increases in the numbers of people in poverty. Meanwhile both the share of the population and the number of people in poverty have risen dramatically in Nigeria. If India, Bangladesh, and Nigeria can stimulate economic growth that benefits the poor, then hundreds of millions of people could move out of extreme deprivation.

TABLE 1.3. Share and number of people living in extreme poverty for selected countries

	Share of population living on less than $1.25/day (PPP) (%)		Number of people living on less than $1.25/day (PPP) (millions)	
	1990	2005	1990	2005
China	60	17	685	213
India	53	42	454	455
Bangladesh	67	50	75	76
Nigeria	49	64	46	91
Average/total	58	31	1261	835

Source: World Bank, PovcalNet, n.d.

DEPENDENCY RATIO

Hunger often occurs in households in which there are few productive workers and many dependents. The dependency ratio indicates how many nonworkers each worker supports. It can be measured for a household or an entire country as in Figure 1.3p(15). The ratio is calculated by dividing the percentage of a population that is unproductive by the percentage that is economically active. The unproductive population refers to people under the age of 15 and over 65. The productive labor force encompasses people between the ages of 15 and 65. This interpretation assumes that children are in school rather than working and that the elderly are retired from fulltime work.

The higher the dependency ratio, the more difficult it is for the workers in a household or country to provide for the population. If the dependency ratio is 1.0, every working-age person in the population must support herself and one other person. A dependency ratio of 0.5 means that there is one dependent for every two workers. In Ethiopia 44% of the population in 2007 was under the age of 15, while 3% was 65 years or older (Table 1.4). In this case, 47% of the population would be viewed as unproductive and 53% as economically active. Ethiopia's dependency ratio of 0.89 (47/53) represents a significant burden for a population with limited incomes and precarious harvests.

If families tend to have more children, the share of the population that is under 15 will be high, causing high dependency ratios. Large families are common among farming households,

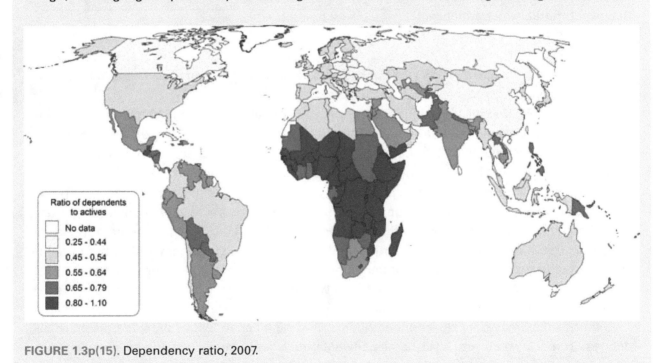

FIGURE 1.3p(15). Dependency ratio, 2007.

since children often contribute labor to farm tasks and may be the sole support of parents in their old age (Figure 1.3p(16)). Parents' anticipation of mortality among children also contributes to high fertility as does poor access to family planning services for families that seek them. Thus, in developing countries that are mostly agricultural, 40% to 50% of the population is under 15 years old and dependency ratios are close to 1 (Table 1.4). In developed countries, dependency ratios are dominated by the elderly rather than the young. For example, Sweden and Peru have comparable dependency ratios, although in Sweden roughly equal numbers of

TABLE 1.4. Dependency ratios and composition of dependents

Country	Dependency ratio	Share of population under 15 years (%)	Share of population over 65 years (%)
China	0.41	21	8
Ethiopia	0.89	44	3
India	0.59	32	5
Malawi	1.00	47	3
Mali	1.08	48	4
Mexico	0.56	30	6
Norway	0.51	19	15
Peru	0.58	31	6
South Africa	0.57	32	4
Sweden	0.54	17	18
United Kingdom	0.51	18	16
United States	0.49	21	12
Zambia	0.96	46	3

Source: World Bank 2008a (2007 data).

people are under 15 and over 65, while in Peru almost a third of the population is under 15 and only 6% is over 65.

As Figure 1.3p(15) indicates, dependency ratios are generally lower in richer countries than in poorer ones. Developing countries that have aggressive family planning programs (China, for example) also have fairly low dependency ratios. Comparison of the map of dependency ratios with the map of hunger vulnerability reveals close correspondence but not necessarily causality. High dependency ratios in poor countries are a product of high fertility rates in rural households that are vulnerable to hunger for many reasons. However, it is not at all clear that high fertility causes hunger vulnerability. Indeed, India, Bangladesh, and Myanmar represent countries that have achieved lower fertility and relatively low dependency ratios, but remain mired in widespread poverty and hunger vulnerability. High fertility, hunger, and poverty are often found in combination, but lowering fertility (and dependency ratios) does not necessarily lead to lower hunger or poverty levels.

While fertility may not cause hunger vulnerability, high dependency ratios do present challenges. In many countries, AIDS has significantly raised dependency ratios by reducing the population of working people. In Zambia, for example, there are 600,000 children orphaned by AIDS, meaning one child in eight is without a birth parent (Table 1.5). Nigeria, South Africa, Tanzania, and Uganda each have nearly a million or more AIDS orphans. Having lost their parents, these children are now dependent on others. The burden on the surviving adults is clearly worsening and not all will cope.

The following comments about a visit to Zambia in 2003 by Stephen Lewis, the UN secretary general's special envoy for HIV/AIDS in Africa, give a clear image of how

FIGURE 1.3p(16). Man with his two wives and nine children in Katiali, Côte d'Ivoire. Seven of the household members are under the age of 15 and none of the adults are over 65. With 58% of the household population classified as unproductive, and 42% active, the dependency ratio is high (1.38) for this rural household. In reality, the children do not go to school and contribute to the household farm economy by planting, weeding, and harvesting crops.

AIDS is affecting the ability of households to provide for dependents.

We entered a home and encountered the following: to the immediate left of the door sat the 84 year old patriarch, entirely blind. Inside the hut sat his two wives, visibly frail, one 76, the other 78. Between them they had given birth to nine children; eight were now dead and the ninth, alas, was dying. On the floor of the hut,

TABLE 1.5. Children orphaned by AIDS

Country	Population under 15 years (millions)	Children orphaned by AIDS (millions)	AIDS orphans as a share of children under 15 (%)
Botswana	0.72	0.10	13
Ethiopia	31.5	0.65	2
Malawi	4.5	0.56	12
Nigeria	59.84	1.20	2
South Africa	14.4	1.40	10
Tanzania	16.2	0.97	6
Uganda	12.5	1.20	10
Zambia	4.6	0.60	13

Source: World Bank 2008a; UNAIDS 2008.

jammed together with barely room to move or breathe, were 32 orphaned grandchildren ranging in age from two to sixteen.[12]

This increasingly common condition of households composed primarily of "dependents" can only result in increasing hunger vulnerability. The members of the household described above, and countless like it, will almost surely face hunger.

DEMOGRAPHY: UNDERSTANDING POPULATION

Understanding human population is a critical component of understanding world regions. Although the breadth and scope of demography cannot be summarized easily, this textbook will provide perspectives and some tools that can be used to understand global population trends as well as regional issues.

Human Population Overview

A good place to begin the discussion of demography is global population trends. Global population is currently at about 7.3 billion persons. This number might seem big when compared to human population norms of the past. Human population remained fairly steady (between a half billion and three-quarters of a billion) from Roman times (AD 1) to Napoleon (1815 CE). Then, in about 1820, the world population finally reached one billion. From there, humans experienced a rapid population increase, to more than seven billion today.

Another good beginning point to a discussion on human population is global *population density*. Where do people live, in volume? Some of this might be common knowledge: China and India, for example, are well known for having large populations. That, however, does not tell us everything. A population density map, for example, shows us population density per square kilometer. This reveals how a country like China holds much of its population in the eastern third of the country. Likewise, it reveals how India has the highest population density in the Gangetic Plain (the region hugging the famous Ganges River).

There are several useful tools that help to illuminate population. One is arithmetic population density, which divides the total population into the land area of a particular state. This can reveal, generally, how dense a particular country is. To continue with China as an example, if you were to divide the enormous population of China into its land area, it would not seem that crowded. The reason is that much of China is not heavily occupied. Bangladesh, on the other hand, has about 160 million people in a country the size of Arkansas. Thus, they have much greater population density, overall, than China.

Another useful tool is physiological population density. This measurement divides total population into arable land (land used for agriculture), and reveals how population clusters around water and agriculture in many world regions. Egypt, for example, has about sixty million people, and most of them hug close the Nile River Valley, Nile River Delta, and reside in Cairo (a city on the Nile). The use of some simple tools opens the door to understanding regional population trends better.

Measuring Population

Demographers use many tools to measure population, from local to global. Some of these tools include:

- **Birth rate:** number of live births per thousand in any given year.
- **Death rate:** number of deaths per thousand in any given year.
- **Life expectancy:** the average number of years a person is expected to live in a particular society (men/women).
- **Rate of natural increase:** birth rates minus death rates.
- **Population growth rate:** $P = (b-d) + (i-e)$, or population equals births minus deaths, added to immigrants minus emigrants.
- **Total Fertility Rate (TFR):** the number of children born to childbearing-age women.

Although these several measurements all reveal something important about a particular population, it could be argued that TFR (Total Fertility Rate) offers the most insight. TFR works in the following way: for example, two parents have two children; because demographers view things generationally, those two parents will die and leave two more humans on the planet. Thus, they have maintained their population at a flat rate. To grow a population, the average must be a minimum of 2.1. This rate, then, reveals something about a particular country or region. Below are characterizations, but they reflect realities.

CASE STUDY 1C

Total Fertility Rate: A Looking Glass

TFR can provide a looking glass into a particular country or region. Although it seems unusual that the number of children being born to childbearing-age women can provide such insight, it actually illuminates several narratives within societies. Below are two lists; one will itemize characteristics of a "wealthy" or "developed/industrialized" society, and the same will be done for a "poor" or "nonindustrialized, developing" society (no country in particular will be used as an example).

Wealthy, Industrialized

TFR Rates: *Typically between 1.5–2.5* or a range that indicates slight population decrease, population flat, or slight population increase.

Access to nutrition: Good to excellent. Most people within society have access to calories and good nutrition.

Access to health care: Good to excellent. Most people in a wealthy society have access to a health care professional to prevent and treat illness and injury.

Access to family planning (birth control): Good to excellent. High percentages of childbearing-age women in developed countries are practicing some form of birth control.

Access to education: Good to excellent. High percentages of the population in developed countries complete their compulsory education (K–12), and many go on to complete undergraduate and graduate degrees. Women, in particular, are highly represented in higher education.

Poor, Nonindustrialized

TFR Rates: *Typically between 3.5–7* or a range that may lead to a population doubling in a single generation *"doubling time"**

Access to nutrition: Poor to fair. Malnutrition is not uncommon in many poor countries. This leads to increased infant mortality rates and lower life expectancy.

Access to health care: Poor to fair. Many living in squalor (slum dwellers) have limited access to health care. When access is available, it is often from a nonprofit organization or NGO (nongovernmental organization).

Access to family planning (birth control): Very poor. Typically, NGOs will use education as a tool to prevent unplanned pregnancies. It is difficult to dispense prescription birth control and the use of prophylactics often conflicts with cultural norms.

Access to education: Poor to fair. This is variable, but the poorest quintile has very limited access to even a low-level grade school education. Like other avenues of service, these are typically schools donated and staffed by teachers paid by NGOs. Lack of funding and political instability often threaten consistent access to these services. Female education is typically even lower, for cultural reasons.

Gender equality: Good and getting better.

Economy: Good to excellent. Despite recessions and economic hard times, many developing nations endure these episodes, keeping 95–96% of the working-age adults employed. Because of greater gender equality, both men and women are part of the workforce (though pay disparities and the underrepresentation of women in high-level positions still persist).

Social outcomes: Marriage delayed by younger generations; the average age of women becoming mothers is increasing, and fewer children are born.

Gender equality: Very poor. Women are still viewed as the property of men in many cultures.

Economy: Largely informal. This means many living in squalor are engaged in activities not counted or measured by their respective economies. People, then, survive on very little (about one-fifth of the world population survives on less than $2 a day).

Social outcomes: High rates of pregnancy in younger women. Each childbearing-age woman having between four and seven children is not uncommon. Because of poor access to health care and nutrition, many lose children. Those who survive likewise have children at a young age, which then increases generational turnover (the time between one generation and the next).

* **doubling time** refers to a society that doubles its population in a measurable time. Typically the result of high TFR.

The "Population Paradox"

The *population paradox* has to do with an earlier discussion about the increase in humanity from one billion in 1820 to more than seven billion today. We learned that population increased after the *First Agricultural Revolution*, about nine thousand years ago, and again after the *Second Agricultural Revolution* during the early to mid-nineteenth century. Thus, it can be concluded that greater agricultural production results in population increases. This is both true and false—hence the paradox. It is true because population increase was indeed measured (archeological records, government data, etc.), and those measurements show us, with certainty, that humanity increased exponentially. It is also *not* true because we see the lowest quintile of humanity (economically)—or those with the least access to calories—growing the fastest. At the same time, we see those with the most access to calories experiencing population stagnation or decreases. How does this happen? This can be partially explained by the discussion in *Case Study 3*. It is perhaps also a reflection of humanity as a whole. Some countries leverage their science, resources, and industry to increase food productivity to levels never seen before. At the same time, not everyone is the beneficiary of this productivity. The food grown by industrialized nations is for markets, not for philanthropic endeavors. Therefore, we see this contradiction in the human landscape.

BOX 1E THOMAS ROBERT MALTHUS: THE POPULATION PROBLEM

In 1798, English cleric and scholar Thomas Malthus wrote *An Essay on the Principle of Population*. In this essay, he wrote a scathing review of humanity's propensity to procreate irresponsibly. His main thesis was that "the power of population was indefinitely greater than the power in the earth to produce subsistence for man." In other words, population increase was "geometric" or exponential, whereas food production was linear. Thus, humanity faced a great conundrum: if humanity were to reach the point at which population exceeded our ability to provide subsistence, then disaster would follow (famine, disease, etc.).

Malthus, viewing this as inevitable, turned his frustration on humanity. He asserted that man was essentially lazy and felt empowered to procreate as long as there were available calories. This human complacency, although it could be interrupted by necessity on occasion, was seen as the norm. Therefore, Malthus did not shy away from population-controlling measures like infanticide, delays in marriage, abortion, celibacy, and others. Although Malthus underestimated how technology, mechanized farming, and more efficient transportation would change the landscape of agriculture, the spirit of his concerns lives on to this day. *Neo-Malthusians* believe humanity is heading for another impasse. During this century, will human population, especially within populations that have poor access to nutrition, increase, bringing about the potential for disaster?

THE HUMAN ENVIRONMENT: MANUFACTURED SPACE

Although natural landscapes can still easily be seen in much of the world, the space that we live in and use for work and resources has been radically altered for human use. Whether subtle or obvious, one does not have to look hard to see manufactured space. Our ability to manipulate space has only improved over time because our technology has improved—particularly in developed states. It is important to keep in mind that human landscapes often reflect the scope and scale of the economies that occupy that space. A developed nation, then, might look and feel very different than developing countries, even though the same sorts of features and activities can be seen. This makes the study of regions a little more difficult, because there are several coeval narratives. By using some of the tools provided previously in this chapter, we can better understand how landscapes have been manipulated regionally.

Agriculture

Agricultural lands, despite their more natural appearance, represent one of humanity's biggest footprints. Agriculture is the practice of growing crops or raising animals for human consumption or other uses. There are essentially three types of agriculture:

- **Croplands:** corn, rice, wheat, and other plants managed in soils.
- **Pastures:** Livestock, like dairy cows, pigs, and chickens.
- **Rangelands:** Large areas used for the movement of animals used for milk, hide, or human consumption.

Although these human activities have been a visible feature of society since the *Neolithic Revolution*, they have never before existed at the scale they do today. Currently, about 38% of the terrestrial surface of the planet (apart from Greenland and Antarctica) has been transformed from a natural ecosystem into an agro-ecosystem (land used for agriculture). This transformation from natural ecosystem to agroecosystem changes how Earth's subsystems converse. Runoff patterns, soil composition, and carbon levels in the atmosphere, to name a few, sometimes radically change. When considering that this occurs at some level over nearly 40% of Earth, it becomes easy to see how land-use change becomes a significant and important discussion.

Modern agriculture in industrialized nations is now scientifically and technologically advanced. Farms in the United States, for example, can be characterized by the following:

- *Large*: The average farm in the United States is about 450 acres.
- *Corporate affiliation:* Many US farms are corporate-owned or are occupied by farmers who are contracted by large companies. This creates reliable channels for many key crops and livestock to travel to processing plants, and then markets, with great efficiency.
- *Scientific farming:* Most commercial farms use GMOs (genetically modified organisms), advanced pesticides, and agrochemical fertilizers, and rely on satellite or aerial remote sensing to provide useful data.
- *Mechanized:* Many farmers and ranchers use advanced machinery to plant, harvest, and irrigate crops or to slaughter and break down livestock.
- *Political Support:* The US Farm Bill provides protections for farmers which often includes subsidies designed to compensate farmers for not producing crops.

FIGURE 1.3q. Agriculture in countries like the United States, is more technologically advanced, scientifically advanced, and more productive than ever before. Copyright © Michael Gäbler (CC BY-SA 3.0) at https://commons.wikimedia.org/wiki/File%3AUnload_wheat_by_the_combine_Claas_Lexion_584.jpg

This level of agriculture can support massive industries like fast food and other food services, grocery chains, livestock feed, food processing, and even energy (ethanol and other biofuels), to name a few. Agriculture changed land use radically in the eastern United States between 1850 and 1920, and the methods and technologies have extended to many parts of the world. Because it remains an important part of national economies, the transformation of natural landscapes to agroecosystems characterizes much of the developed world.

Although commercial agriculture dominates the landscapes of wealthier nations (typically between 20–45%), developing nations' agricultural activities are often more a part of the informal economy. Subsistence agriculture can be defined as individuals farming small plots of land, tending to small numbers of livestock, or fishing for personal consumption. Most of the time, these farmers do not own the land they farm. Instead, they are often poor and squat on lands they believe can yield a small variety of crops for personal use. Numerically, this is the most common farmer on the planet.

Some estimates indicate that about one billion people survive off some form of subsistence agriculture. The methods used reflect the climates in which they reside. For example, subsistence farmers in the subtropics and tropics often deal with soils that aren't ideal for agriculture. The amount of rainfall received in these regions leeches nutrients to lower soil horizons. To replenish nutrients, subsistence farmers sometimes use *slash and burn agriculture* to support several crop rotations (a.k.a. shifting cultivation). Burning the canopy replaces lost carbon and nutrients in the soil, allowing a season or two of crops before they must repeat the burn or move on to another site.

Agriculture, in its various forms and scale, helps define human landscapes. It provides a lens through which to observe the differences between regions, as well as highlighting the common need to feed ourselves. In some countries, you can observe how commercial agriculture supports giant industries like fast food and convenient processed foods, making it easier for a busy population to eat. In others, you see the poorest quintile of humanity planting an acre of corn, beets, and beans just to feed a family. Either way, they are both an important part of the human story and show us how we change the use of land for our needs.

Industrialization

As discussed earlier, some countries have industrialized, and many have not. The types of industrial activities in which a particular country or region engages determines how its landscapes look. Although there are many variables to this, wealthier countries are often characterized by the most robust industries that cover a broad spectrum of commercial ventures. Yet, at the same time, this heavy industry is matched by regulations, policies, and laws that protect society from the heavy pollution, disposal of industrial waste, and obliterated landscapes seen in the past. Germany, for example, was amongst the first nations to industrialize. Areas like the Ruhr Valley act as epicenters for industrial activity. However, cities like Dortmund—despite the obvious industrial features—appear to be pleasant and observably clean.

Oppositely, industrial activities in developing countries often reflect more direct environmental harm to their landscapes. Because many of these nations have valuable raw materials, it is common to see multinational corporations operating in them. Unlike in the countries in which these companies headquarter, the political landscapes (regulation, environmental protection, and sometimes corruption) influence what can be seen. The Niger River Delta in Nigeria, for example, is home to large oil refineries. Much of that oil is pirated on the delta and cooked into fuels on the riverbanks, leaving a devastated landscape. Although developed nations have a much larger industrial footprint, developing countries often deal with aesthetic and environmentally degradative challenges to their landscapes.

The Urban Realm

Whereas agriculture shapes the character of the human landscapes, urbanism defines space through radical transformation. Cities today are the habitat of humanity. Currently, 51% of all humans live in urban areas, and that number is expected to rise in the foreseeable future. Unlike agriculture, cities occupy a very small portion of the terrestrial surface of the planet. If every city in the world (New York, London, and Tokyo, for example) were put side by side, they would together account for less than 4% of the surface of the planet. However, next to war, nothing changes land like the urban realm. Cities tell us a lot about regional culture and society, a nation's economy, and perhaps something about their politics.

Because of the various terms that can be used to describe this topic, a few definitions may help. A city can be described as a politically designated space often characterized by a large number of people, culture, politics, and economic activities. It typically has a border, its own administrative structure, and municipal codes and laws that govern people and commercial activities, and it maintains or partners with other government agencies to maintain infrastructure. An urban area (or metropolitan area) is multiple cities clustered together to form a connected entity with distinct parts. This is becoming increasingly common as more people move into cities.

The origin of a city is a very geographical conversation. The original settlers of a location that would become a city often chose the location for a particular attribute or mix of attributes. This is what geographers call *the why of where*. Cities were often chosen for their site or situation. A site attribute would be a physical feature you can still find within the city. The *fall line*, in the eastern United States, for example, is where the Piedmont succumbs to the coastal plain. In other words, it is where water speeds up or "falls" from a hilly region to a flat coastal plain. This physical attribute allows humans to harness the power of water, thus making it a good place to settle. Another *site* attribute might be a bay. A situation attribute would be proximity to something useful, like timber, coal, or some other natural resource. These features, or a combination of them, help us understand where cities are and why.

Today, cities are the engines of globalization and the vector for humanity. In developed nations, typically 80–90% of the people live in urban areas, as opposed to rural areas. This dictates the location of markets, investments, and infrastructure. Likewise, transportation networks are needed to not only move around not only large populations, but also to transport goods and services in and out of the region. Because products are produced in one part of the world and sold in another, thousands of shipping lanes with thousands of transoceanic liners cross the oceans from one city to another every day.

In developing countries, cities are often beacons of hope for poor rural dwellers seeking more opportunity. Even though roughly four out of ten people in poor nations live in cities, these countries' urban growth rates are amongst the highest in the world. Cities like Lagos, Nigeria and Dhaka, Bangladesh, for example, have very high growth rates. However, much of the growth in cities like these is from the poorest rural communities. Often, migration like this makes their slums larger. Understanding cities and urban patterns helps us understand regions around the world.

1.4 Why Conflict & Cooperation?

This textbook has already informed you, in this chapter, that it will approach the study of world regions in ways consistent with the field of geography. However, it will also infuse a second narrative into the study of world regions: *conflict and cooperation*. This human narrative is critical if we are to understand the complexity of human landscapes. Why?

To begin with, the world has been shaped by humans in almost every way. We change how land is used, we use the world's resources, we have imposed human-constructed borders around every state on the planet, and we have even changed our climate. This is not to say we have excelled at shaping the world. We control or lack control over the landscapes we created. This control and lack of control can best be observed through our conflicts and cooperation with each other at any given time and in any particular region. This approach is rooted in the idea that humans fundamentally have a complicated relationship with each other. This is true of your family at home, and it is also true of the human race as a whole.

DEFINING HUMAN CONFLICT

For the purpose of this textbook, conflict will be defined as a point or episode in time when cooperation ends and transformative changes ensue. This textbook will borrow aspects of *anarchism* to help define conflict. One aspect of *anarchism* is the belief that humans are fundamentally cooperative. Anarchists might argue that we are more defined by episodes of cooperation with each other than by the conflicts that arise. This is likely a difficult concept to grasp, considering we are taught about many famous historical conflicts and are barraged by the media's continuously reporting on hostilities. Although this textbook will not take sides in this debate, it will illuminate regional conflicts while examining how cooperation failed. This approach better illuminates the backstory of regional issues and, sometimes, reveals the scaffolding around regions in the midst of change.

Understanding Cooperation

Cooperation is an abstract concept that characterizes a point or episode in time where people or nations work together. This textbook uses this concept because it frees us from the cultural judgements sometimes embedded in "peace studies." Peace studies, despite using similar methods, often requires a critical approach (from one's own viewpoint), which then runs the risk of having our personal values or perceptions get in the way. This can be a liability when examining other cultures and regions because we are often hardwired to feel certain ways about a certain group, or religion, or event. If we examine world regions through patterns of conflict and cooperation, we can gain a deeper, less biased understanding of them.

Intersecting Themes: A Different Approach

The beginning of each chapter will have a small illustration called an intersecting theme model. This is designed to be a visual reminder of both conflict points and the cooperation that preceded it or followed. Important themes will be preselected from the list below:

- **Historical:** This theme considers historical aspects like rivalries, previous wars, contested territory, etc.
- **Physical/Physiological:** This theme considers resources, raw materials, bodies of water, ports, and other physical attributes that foster cooperation or cause conflict.
- **Social:** This theme looks at society within a region and examines how social structure (class, caste) informs us on potential internal issues.
- **Economic:** This theme explores how the myriad of commercial activities, trade relationships, policy, and competition in markets shape relationships.
- **Cultural:** This theme examines race, gender, divisions, and other features related to groups of people.
- **Political:** This theme examines political space, geopolitical hierarchies, and how political systems are sometimes imposed upon others or desired by some.
- **Demographic:** This theme examines population trends and how they have affected or might impact the future.

Although most of these themes are present in any given region, only several will be carefully chosen for how the intersection between two or three has helped to shape the landscapes we see today. This approach will usually be subtle (by design), and will not interfere with conventional geography this textbook will put into motion. However, the main challenge of a Global Geography course is providing the tools and insights for students to use on their own, after the class is completed. The world is more sophisticated than ever and there is so much more to know than that provided by the media. The intersection model could be that tool that helps you illuminate the complexities behind each region.

KEY TERMS

Geography
Global Geography
Physical Geography
Human Geography
Geographic Information
  Systems (GIS)
Four (4) Spatial Questions
Core-periphery model
Diffusion
Time-distance decay
Mental maps
Cartography
Scale
Environmental
Determinism
Possibilism
System
Subsystem
Four (4) subsystems
Absolute location
Prime Meridian
International Date Line
  (IDL)
Intertropical Convergence
  Zone (ITCZ)
Hadley Cell
Subtropical high-pressure
  zones
Physiography
Human landscapes
First Agricultural
Revolution
Neolithic Revolution
Hearths

Contagious Diffusion
Relocation Diffusion
Cyclic movement
Periodic movements
Migration
Immigrant
Emigrant
Push factor
Pull factor
Forced migration
Refugees
Cultural landscape
Culture
Cultural trait
Cultural complex
Cultural hearth
Identity
Ethnicity
Race
Territoriality
Sovereignty
Nation-state
Economic Geography
Formal economy
Informal economy
Occupational structure
Primary
Secondary sector
Tertiary sector
Stages of growth
Foreign Direct Investment
  (FDI)
World Systems Theory

Gross Domestic Product
  (GDP)
Gross National Product
  (GNP)
Per capita GDP
Growth Rate
Colonialism
Industrial Revolution
Poverty
Corruption
Global Population
Population density
Arithmetic population
  density
Physiologic population
  density
Birth rate
Death rate
Life expectancy
Rate of natural increase
Population growth rate
Total Fertility Rate (TFR)
Agriculture
Croplands
Pastures
Rangelands
Subsistence Agriculture
City
Urban area
Site
Situation
Conflict
Cooperation

CLASS DISCUSSIONS

1. Discuss the *four spatial questions* and how they apply to your city or region.
2. Describe how culture has spread out over time, from core to periphery. Provide examples.
3. Explain the origin of political space.
4. How did the world evolve economically? Explain why the world developed unevenly.
5. Why did the world population go from one billion to more than seven billion in under two hundred years?
6. Have human interactions throughout history been more characterized and/or defined by conflicts or cooperation? Why?

ADDITIONAL RESOURCES

CIA World Factbook:

https://www.cia.gov/library/publications/the-world-factbook/

Free Map Worksheets (AZGA):

http://alliance.la.asu.edu/maps/maps.htm

NOAA Climate.gov:

http://www.climate.gov/

UN Habitat:

http://unhabitat.org/

World Bank:

http://www.worldbank.org/

World Health Organization:

http://www.who.int/en/

World Population Clock:

http://www.worldometers.info/world-population/

BIBLIOGRAPHY

University Readers: s189065, s189068, s189072, s189074

Balter. M. (2007). Seeking Agriculture's Ancient Roots. Science. Vol 316, 29 June 2007, pp 1830–1835.

Central Intelligence Agency. The World Factbook. n.d. Web. https://www.cia.gov/library/publications/the-world-factbook/. 04 Oct. 2014.

Diamond, J. (1999). Guns, Germs, and Steel: The Fates of Human Societies. W.W. Norton. New York, NY.

NOAA Climate.gov/ Science & Information for a Climate-smart Nation. "NOAA Climate.gov Science & Information for a Climate-smart Nation." N.p., n.d. Web. http://www.climate.gov/. 15 November 2014.

"USGS Water Data for the Nation." USGS Water Data for the Nation. N.p., n.d. Web. http://waterdata.usgs.gov/nwis. 04 Nov. 2014.

"UN-Habitat." UN-Habitat. N.p., n.d. Web. http://unhabitat.org/. 04 Jan. 2015.

"World Bank Group." World Bank Group. N.p., n.d. Web. http://www.worldbank.org/. Oct.–Nov. 2014.

"WHO | World Health Organization." WHO | World Health Organization. N.p., n.d. Web. http://www.who.int/en/. 04 Dec. 2014.

CHAPTER 2

Europe

Key Intersecting Themes:

Physical/Physiographic, Historical, Cultural, Political, Economic

Countries discussed:
- Iceland
- Ireland
- United Kingdom
- Portugal
- Spain
- France
- Italy
- Belgium
- Luxembourg
- Netherlands
- Denmark

- Norway
- Sweden
- Finland
- Germany
- Austria
- Switzerland
- Czech Republic
- Poland
- Greece
- Eastern European nations

FIGURE 2.1. Political map of Europe
Copyright in the Public Domain.

2.1 Regional Overview

Many world regional geography textbooks begin with a discussion about Europe. Europe's importance and influence are, in many ways, immeasurable. This textbook will comply with this established trend for the same reasons. Understanding all of Europe's influences is no easy task, as there are many. Of course, not all influences were good. As much as it has shaped the world culturally, economically, or politically, it has also defined us through war, conflict, and atrocities committed at a scale and with a severity rarely, if ever, seen in human history. This is why examining Europe in conventional geographic ways, in addition to conflict and cooperation, is important. Together, these approaches will enable a deeper understanding of the patterns and processes that influenced humanity, as well as how human conflict at this scale, and the episodes and frameworks of cooperation that followed, shaped Europe and the world today.

Europe is composed of more than fifty sovereign and recognized states, spanning from Iceland in the middle of the North Atlantic to Greece in the southeastern extent of the continent. Despite the number of nations, Europe is relatively small, compared to other continents. Its land area occupies approximately 3.9 million square miles, which is about the size of the United States.

Within its space, Europe has a large population. Approximately 742 million people reside there, resulting in a greater population density than much of the world. Because it is an industrialized region of the world, many Europeans (about 83%) live in cities. Several European cities are enormous global centers of economic and political power, whereas others are smaller and reflect more provincial characteristics. These are but a few features of this fascinating region. Although this chapter cannot possibly discuss all of Europe's features and influences, it will use the selected themes above to illuminate important aspects of this very important and interesting part of Earth.

2.2 Europe's Physical Geography

Europe is considered an independent continent, though it is connected by land to the greater Eurasian landmass. This landmass stretches from Portugal, on the Atlantic, to the Pacific Ocean, in the eastern realms of nations like Russia and China. Combined, Europe and Asia make up the largest landmass on the planet. Extending beyond its contiguous lands are islands. The United Kingdom, Ireland, Iceland, Corsica, and the Azores provide a few examples of Europe's island nations.

Because Europe resides on the western edge of this supercontinent and within the middle latitudes, it has the benefit of being within the westerly winds. These winds carry moisture-laden, warmer air over Europe, resulting in ample, steady precipitation over much of its land area (see *Figure 2.2b*). At the same time, Europe lacks the continentality (extreme variation in temperature, seasonal aridity, etc.) that characterizes the Asian realm east of Europe. Thus, from a physical geographical perspective, Europe's climates and topographical features reflect these processes and have provided enough distinction to warrant its classification as a continent.

FIGURE 2.2a. A physical map of Europe, with borders.
Copyright in the Public Domain.

FIGURE 2.2b. The green Irish countryside, shown here, offers evidence of the amount of precipitation Europe receives. Copyright © Gavigan (CC BY-SA 3.0) at https://commons.wikimedia.org/wiki/File:NunsTurgesius_Castle_isles_Lough_Lene.JPG.

EUROPE'S CLIMATE

Europe has several climate types. Climate is defined as an aggregate of environmental conditions (weather patterns, precipitation levels) involving heat, moisture, and motion. It is commonly said that weather is what you get today; climate is what you get over time. Europe's climates, simply put, are reflections of its geography in any given region (see *Figure 2.2c*).

As seen in *Figure 2.2c*, much of Western Europe (Ireland, UK, France, Netherlands, West Germany, etc.) falls within the Köppen-Geiger *Cfb* classification, or a temperate oceanic climate. Further to the east (south of Sweden, central and eastern Germany, Eastern Europe, and Ukraine), Europe's climate becomes more characterized by humid continental/cool summer patterns, thus earning it a *Dfb* climate type. Europe's colder Scandinavian realm is classified as a *Dfc*, or having a cool continental/subarctic climate. In the southern Mediterranean region, Europe becomes a *Csa* climate. This climate type is determined by latitude. Southern Europe (Greece through Portugal), is under the influence of a high-pressure system that influences warmer, drier conditions with seasonal cooling and precipitation events. These climate types help to define Europe, and the patterns within these climate types help to shape physiologic features within the region.

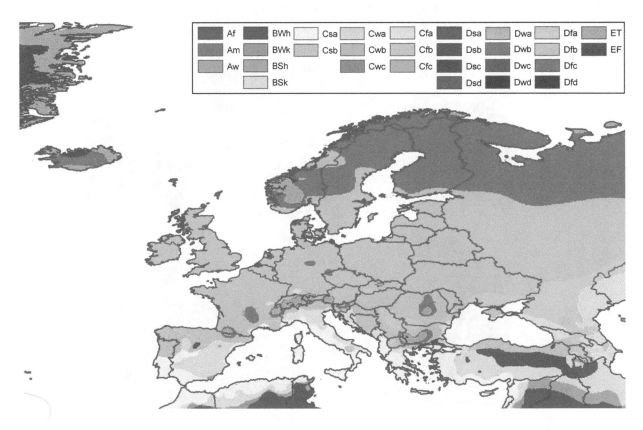

FIGURE 2.2c. Köppen-Geiger climate classification is a widely used tool to spatially identify the spatial distribution of climate types, both regionally and globally. Copyright © M.C. Peel, B.L. Finlayson, and T.A. McMahon (CC BY-SA 2.5) at http://commons.wikimedia.org/wiki/File%3AEurope_Köppen_Map.png.

The amount of precipitation Europe receives helps to define the physical landscapes. As seen in *Figure 2.2d*, much of Europe is under a thick canopy of clouds.

This can be explained by the high-to-low airflow patterns that begin in the middle North Atlantic Ocean and then move east. A stable high-pressure system is parked in the middle of the Atlantic Ocean between Bermuda and the Azores, thus earning its name, *Azores High Pressure* or *Azores/Bermuda High*. As discussed in the Introduction, high-pressure systems are descending air from the *Hadley Cell*, spinning clockwise down to Earth's surface. The high-pressure system inhibits convection, which means it's a storm-free zone. However, the airflow that circles the high-pressure system (in a clockwise pattern) swings around the high-pressure system and keeps flowing in a trajectory that carries it to low pressure. These low-pressure zones exist in the subarctic region (near Iceland) and again over the continent of Asia. This physical dynamic explains the steady flow of marine air from the Northern Atlantic Ocean over much of Europe (see *Figure 2.2e*).

PHYSIOGRAPHIC REGIONS

Europe's physiographic regions are determined by both its climate and topography. Topography can be defined as the physical features that define a landscape. This may be best understood as "what you can describe." For example, describing a landscape as "mountainous," "flat," or "rolling hills" reveals its

FIGURE 2.2d. This image reveals the volume of clouds and potential for precipitation over Europe.
Copyright in the Public Domain.

topography in the simplest way. Naturally, the climate helps to shape the observable topography over time. This textbook will keep it simple by broadly defining Europe in this manner and then discussing specific physiographic features in context later in this chapter.

Europe is topographically divided into (roughly) four physiographic regions. The *(1) Coastal Lowlands* begin on the west coast of France and arc over through southern England, the Netherlands, Northern Germany, Denmark, and on through Poland and the west coast of the Black Sea. This topographic region is characterized by flat coastal plains, rich soils, river systems, inlets, and coastline. Many tourists see this physiographic region and remember Europe this way because major urban destinations like London, Paris, Amsterdam, Copenhagen, and Berlin are all located here.

The *(2) Western Highlands* is a discontinuous region that can be described as hilly, with defined river valleys and some forested lands. Spain, Portugal, and southern Italy are largely within this physiographic region, as well as much of western UK and Ireland. Scandinavia (including Iceland) is likewise a part of this region, with more extremes in both elevation and picturesque fjord valley systems. A fjord is a narrow,

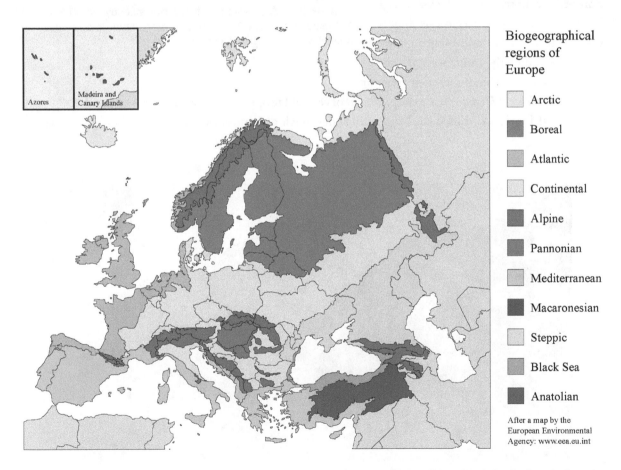

Biogeographical regions of Europe

- Arctic
- Boreal
- Atlantic
- Continental
- Alpine
- Pannonian
- Mediterranean
- Macaronesian
- Steppic
- Black Sea
- Anatolian

After a map by the European Environmental Agency: www.eea.eu.int

FIGURE 2.2e. This map shows Europe's biogeographic regions, which reflect physiological and climatic characteristics. Copyright © Júlio Reis (CC BY-SA 3.0) at http://commons.wikimedia.org/wiki/File%3AEurope_biogeography_countries.svg.

deep inlet between steep mountains and the sea, caused by retreating glaciers (*see Figure 2.2f*).

The *(3) Alpine Region* includes Europe's several Alps ranges, as well as the Pyrenees and Carpathian Mountains. The *Alps* are commonly known as defining Switzerland, southeast France, western Austria, and northern Italy. There is also the lesser-known but equally beautiful *Julian Alps* of Slovenia and the *Transylvanian Alps/Carpathians* of Romania, Slovakia, and other Eastern European countries (*See Figure 2.2g*). Though this Alpine Region is highly variable in elevation and biogeography, it is either directly influenced by the mountains or is influenced by their proximity.

FIGURE 2.2f. A classic fjord in Norway.Copyright © Erik A. Drabløs (CC BY-SA 2.5) at http://commons.wikimedia.org/wiki/File%3ANorwegian_Fjord.jpg.

The *(4) Central Highlands* are the *piedmont* of central Europe, or an area wedged between the *Alps* and the Coastal Lowlands. This inland region includes much of France, Belgium, Luxembourg, Germany's

FIGURE 2.2g. This is the Carpathian Mountains town of Zdiar, Slovakia.
Copyright © AnnetteK (CC BY-SA 3.0) at http://commons.wikimedia.org/wiki/File%3AZdiar1.jpg.

Bavarian region, and parts of Austria and the Czech Republic. This used to be a heavily forested section of Europe and is, incidentally, rich in resources.

WATER & RESOURCES

Europe's abundant precipitation has resulted in a landscape replete with watershed zones, and its geology has provided a patchwork of robust natural resources. The watershed zones are characterized by a complex system of runoff channels, tributaries, and major river systems that have defined Europe. Likewise, Europe's other natural resources (timber and coal, for example) have played a key role in its historical development and industrialization. Although these physical attributes have not "determined" Europe's power and influence, over time they have often been central to the human narrative.

Europe has many important river systems that collect and shed the volume of precipitation the continent receives. Although there are many watershed zones, this textbook will focus on the *four (4) key river systems* that have played, and continue to play, an important role in regional human activities. The (1) *Danube River*, running about 1,700 miles, is the longest river in Europe. It forms in the Black Forest of Germany and flows through major cities like Vienna, Budapest, and Belgrade before reaching its delta at the Black Sea (Romania and Ukraine). The (2) *Rhine River* begins in the Swiss Alps and flows north until it deltas into the North Sea in the Netherlands. This river is Europe's second longest and has played a key role in trade and security for millennia (see *Figure 2.2h*).

The (3) *Rhone River* runs about five hundred miles through France, from the Swiss Alps south to the Mediterranean Sea. Finally, the (4) *River Thames* (pronounced "Tims") is the shortest of the four (about 215 miles) and lies entirely within England, running east to west from Gloucestershire to its delta in Essex. This important waterway links England's interior to London and the sea (see *Figsures 2.2i (1) and (2)*).

The importance of these rivers and patchwork of natural resources and raw materials will be explored further in this chapter.

2.3 Historical Landscapes

The historical landscapes of Europe can take a lifetime to study. The region has been teeming with activity for thousands of years, and has been the site of countless events, many of which have shaped the world beyond its borders. To add more complexity, each era (the Roman Empire, Medieval times, Renaissance, Exploration, colonialism, etc.) has specific narratives that intertwine, scaffold, and layer in important aspects of Europe in ways that stretch well beyond a simple chronological understanding. Rather than attempting to encapsulate and condense the history of such an important and influential region, this textbook will focus in on key thematic concepts that might shed some light on Europe's cultural evolution, decisive economic and political narratives, and conflicts (and the cooperation that followed) that have helped to shape the world we know today.

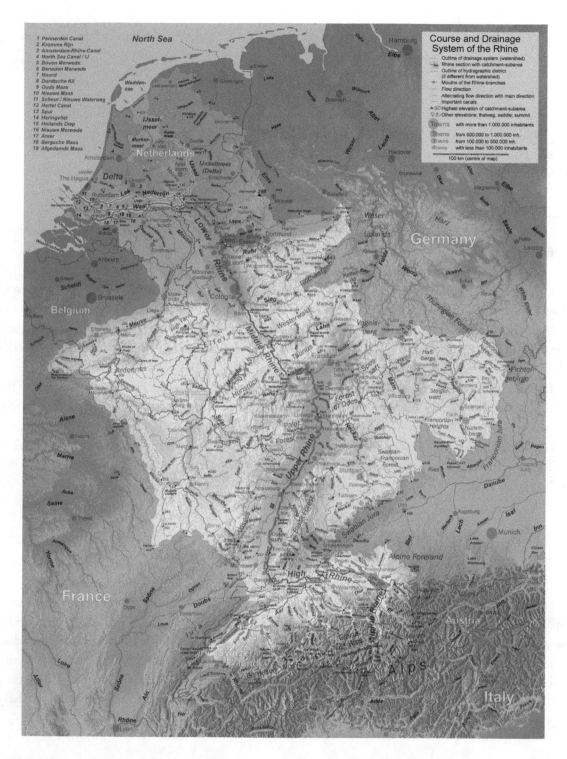

FIGURE 2.2h. The Rhein River begins in the Swiss Alps and deltas in the Netherlands.
Copyright © Wwasser (CC BY-SA 3.0) at http://commons.wikimedia.org/wiki/File%3AFlusssystemkarte_Rhein_04.jpg.

FIGURE 2.2i(1). Locals enjoying the picturesque River Thames as it runs through Oxford, England. Copyright © Zxb (CC BY-SA 2.0) at http://commons.wikimedia.org/wiki/File:River_thames_oxford.jpg.

FIGURE 2.2i(2). The most common association of the River Thames is its association with the City of London. Copyright © Diliff (CC BY-SA 3.0) at http://commons.wikimedia.org/wiki/File:London_Thames_Sunset_panorama_-_Feb_2008.jpg.

ANCIENT INFLUENCES

Just like Europe's overall history, its ancient history can be quite layered. To begin with, one could examine its early settlement patterns by groups that brought language, customs, and agricultural practices to the greater region more than seven thousand years ago. The study of ancient Europe can begin with early civilizations that settled in certain parts of Europe, like the Celts, Anglos, Saxons, or the Jutes, for example. However, to facilitate the understanding of how Europe's ancient history spatially influenced the region—and eventually Western culture in general—over time, we will begin with the Romans (see *Figure 2.3a*).

The Romans were the most powerful and influential presence in Europe and beyond for nearly a thousand years. Rising to power in the fourth century BCE, the Roman Republic established itself as a dominant military and cultural force in southern Europe (modern-day Italy). Eventually, Rome would become an empire that would expand and become practically undefeatable for an extended period of time, then eventually weaken until its fall in 479 CE.

During these various periods, Rome ruled with structure. This enabled them to govern and maintain large areas of Europe in a rather unique way. For example, the Romans used a complex system of roads that linked distant garrison towns and frontier fortifications with Rome. This allowed for faster communication from the emperor and the ability to quickly deploy armies to areas of conflict, and promoted stable trade between various appendages of the realm. The Romans employed laws and local governors

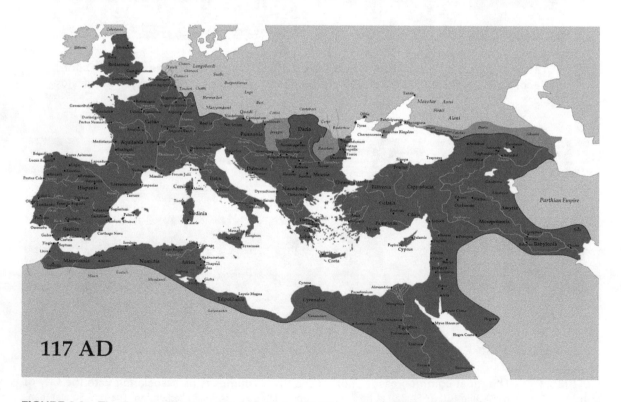

FIGURE 2.3a. The Roman Empire at its height, in 117AD, covered much of Europe.
Copyright © Tataryn (CC BY-SA 3.0) at http://commons.wikimedia.org/wiki/File%3ARoman_Empire_Trajan_117AD.png.

to keep people in diverse geographic areas in order. They employed a naturalization structure that meant conquered or occupied people could become Roman citizens (if they were not used as slaves). Latin was used as a primary language across much of the empire and became a cohesive element in much of Europe. Though Rome fell in the west, its influences would remain and help to shape the Europe of today.

BIRTH OF WESTERN CULTURE

Europe is unequivocally the birthplace of Western culture. Western culture might be broadly defined as the sum of various cultures that trace their origins to Europe and, later, to its colonies in the Western Hemisphere. Although identifying the many influences would be an arduous task, there are *Four Key Influences* that have worked together to shape Western culture:

1. *Greco-Roman Complex*
2. *Germanic*
3. *Gaelic/Celtic*
4. *Islam*

The main influence on Western culture is the *Greco-Roman Complex*. This complex can be described as the various direct influences of Rome (discussed previously) as well as indirect influences from the Greeks. Greek influences would come more into play during the Renaissance (theatre, art, architecture) and Enlightenment (math, science, philosophy), and later, of course, with democracy itself.

Roman law and religion would directly influence Europe. Roman legal structure survived the fall of the west with Justinian in Constantinople. Likewise, various elements of civil law and the language of law are Roman in origin. This legal foundation can still be seen around the world, used by various nations that were once European colonies. Roman religion (adopted) was Christianity. After Rome's fall in the west, the church would slowly regain power and eventually become the most influential institution in Europe. Although only briefly discussed, it is evident that the *Greco-Roman Complex* was the most influential component of European culture.

Another important influence was *Germanic* culture. Although the Romans controlled much of

FIGURE 2.3b. An ancient Roman aqueduct in Vers-Pont-du-Gard, France.
Copyright © Emanuele (CC BY-SA 2.0) at http://commons.wikimedia.org/wiki/File%3APont_du_Gard_Oct_2007.jpg.

Europe directly, they identified that invading *Germania* would have been both costly and perhaps unnecessary. Instead, the Romans elected to "contain" the Germanic tribes by building fortifications along the Rhine River. This largely kept the Germanic tribes (and culture) sequestered, thus allowing them to evolve, in large part, independent of Roman influence.

As these tribes began to exploit Roman internal weaknesses, they would increasingly raid and eventually overthrow the Western Roman Empire. Their influences would become more evident. The distribution of Germanic languages, for example, is evidence of this influence. Languages like German, Danish, Swedish, Norwegian, English, Dutch, Flemish, and more are all from the Germanic subfamily. When Martin Luther split from the Catholic Church in 1516, it would not be long until other Germanic cultures also converted to some form of Protestant faith. Germany, Scandinavia, England, and Denmark, for example, all became Protestant. This would influence conflicts between European kingdoms for centuries and even define cultural landscapes around the world through eras of exploration and colonization.

The next two influences are smaller but important. For much of the same reasons as containing *Germania*, the Romans contained Scotland and, to a lesser degree, Ireland. They lacked the incentive to invest in prolonged military engagements with wild groups like the Picts and Scots, so they built Hadrian's Wall to contain and monitor them instead. Resulting from this posture was a Gaelic culture that evolved fairly independently from Roman influence. Later, traits would be visible in Scottish and Irish culture.

This has indirectly played a role in the relationship between the English and Scottish over time. The Romans occupied and influenced the English landscape for five hundred years, whereas the Scots were essentially removed from that influence. The result is two peoples with very different cultural influences, despite sharing political space. Later, the Irish would extend Gaelic culture to the United States through the emigration of millions between the mid-nineteenth and early twentieth centuries.

Although it may feel counterintuitive to accept Islam as an influence on Western culture, it has been in some specific ways. For example, the Moors (a Muslim people) invaded Spain in 711 CE. This was known as *reconquista*. This occupation of much of the Iberian Peninsula (Al-Andalus) lasted roughly seven hundred years, through various eras. This persistent presence resulted in the rich infusion of Moorish culture into the Iberian Peninsula.

This cultural influence diffused after the Spanish defeated and expelled the Muslims in 1492. The Spanish, having only just gained control again of their country, heard news of Columbus's findings across the Atlantic Ocean and immediately set forth exploring and exploiting the new world. The Moorish-influenced Iberian culture quickly spread from the modern-day southwestern United States to the southern tip of Argentina. Although Spain would lose all these colonies to independence, many aspects of Iberian culture remain visible to this day. Several include mathematics (*algorithm*, *algebra*), physics and chemistry (*alcohol*), mapping and navigation, food, music, currency, and art, and other influences of the Moors can still be seen in many Western cultures.

FIGURE 2.4a. The classic and ancient European city of Brugge, Belgium.
Copyright © Jean-Christophe Benoist (CC BY-SA 3.0) at http://commons.wikimedia.org/wiki/File%3ABrugge-CanalRozenhoedkaai.JPG.

2.4 European Culture

European culture has been forming since the emergence of early agriculture more than seven thousand years ago. As people disseminated across the continent, they carried with them language(s), knowledge, and customs that would alter and morph over time and eventually reflect the geographic areas in which they settled. *Figure 2.4b* illustrates how some groups might have come up the Danube River Valley into central and northwestern Europe, whereas others dispersed from the Mediterranean region into the southern regions of Europe. These groups would eventually take on more local or regional characteristics, distinguishing them from others on the continent. Even within these subregions, more groups would split off or be invaded, thus further diversifying or amalgamating the early cultural landscapes of Europe.

By Roman times, these cultural groups had themselves become societies with well-established customs, languages, and traditions that exhibited regional distinction.

As discussed earlier, the Romans would conquer, subjugate, or absorb many diverse groups into their own and, in doing so, congeal Roman culture in much of the realm. After Roman times, however, the Europeans would endure a lengthy period of collapse and then reemerge under the light of Charlemagne, the Frankish king who would unite Western Europe after the Dark Ages. These kingdoms would fight, compete, or form alliances in ways that continued to shape cultural landscapes well into the sixteenth century.

INFLUENCE OF CHRISTIANITY

Beginning with the *Edict of Milan* in 313 CE, Roman Emperor Constantine declared religious "benevolence" to Christians, leading to a declaration of Christianity as the religion of Rome. This pairing of Christianity with Rome meant the religion would, by association, have great powers. After Rome fell, Christianity

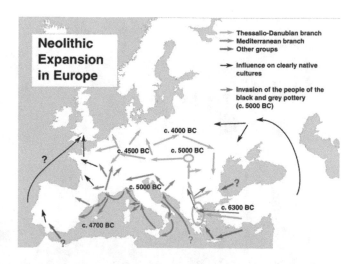

FIGURE 2.4b. One view on Neolithic expansion into Europe. Copyright in the Public Domain.

thrived in Byzantium in the east, but it was greatly weakened in the west. As Europe emerged from the Dark Ages, so too would the Christian church of Rome. In order to once again pair the church's influence with political power, Pope Leo III crowned Charlemagne Roman Emperor, thereby symbolically reviving the Christian-political complex.

As time would pass, the church would grow stronger. Kings would often align their own objectives with those of the pope. As church power spread, so did those who disagreed with that power. By the fifteen hundreds, protests over selling indulgences, corruption, sainting, views on purgatory, and so on were openly expressed by Martin Luther, John Calvin, and others. These "reformers" not only built a following, but the written expression of their views was also more widely spread due to the invention of the printing press (See *Figure 2.4c*).

After the Protestant Reformation, Europe would have to contend with this division of faith. Generally, Germanic-speaking countries would turn Protestant, whereas many Roman-influenced

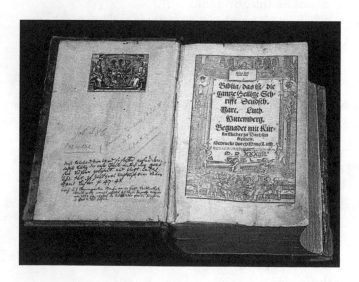

FIGURE 2.4c. Martin Luther's Bible: Printed and distributed in 1534, this version of the Bible helped to share new views of Christianity across German speaking Europe. Copyright in the Public Domain.

countries would remain Catholic and loyal to the pope. This division would create landscapes of conflict for over a century.

EUROPEAN THEMATIC INTERSECTION 2A

Culture and Politics in Seventeenth-Century Europe: Conflict becomes Cooperation

Themes: Cultural/Political

One's faith or belief system is often very personal. When questioned about beliefs, a person of a particular faith can become defensive and even confrontational. The same could be said of how cultures feel about their faith. After the Protestant Revolution, Europeans were no longer under the umbrella of the same

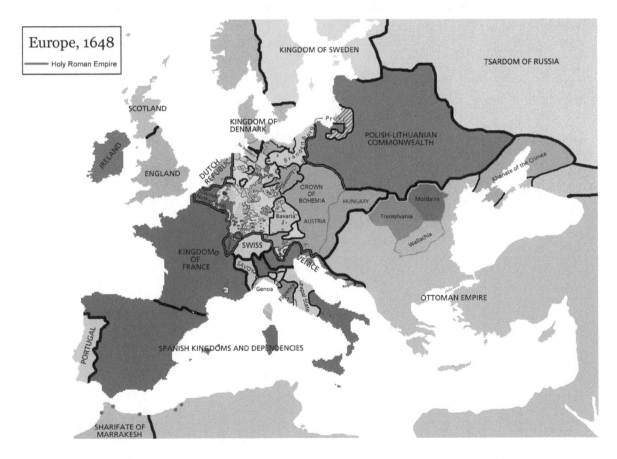

FIGURE 2.4d. New Nation-state system: Following the Peace of Westphalia, a new nation-state system was implemented. The borders you see in this image are not that different from European borders today. Copyright © Roke~commonswiki (CC BY-SA 3.0) at http://commons.wikimedia.org/wiki/File:Europe_map_1648. PNG.

church, and some of the issues that caused the division became irreconcilable. This resulted in great conflicts such as the "Thirty Years' War." This bloody conflict resulted from the Holy Roman Emperor, Ferdinand II, attempting to bring under control the Protestant Christians in Germany. Soon, many countries, both Protestant and Catholic, joined the fight in a bloody engagement that lasted thirty years.

This "cultural" conflict would have a "political" outcome—or the conflict would result in cooperation in a way that defined Europe and later the world. The Peace of Westphalia (1646–1648) was a summit of belligerent nations seeking peace. A key concept to come from this summit was the notion of "sovereignty" in a political rather than religious context. It was recognized that people of similar cultures and belief systems remained together in the same geographical area but were subject to the rules and restrictions of not only local leaders, but external sources of power as well (pope, Holy Roman Emperor, etc.). Political sovereignty meant that the affairs of a nation of people were their affairs to manage. To further define their sovereignty, they would need to mutually agree upon a border that would be recognized and respected by others and define their space internally. Within that space, a country could have its own laws, taxes, and administrative structure. Born from this was the "nation-state" system, which became a standard for political space that was widely used by Europeans, postcolonial independent states, and much of the rest of the world.

2.5 Political Space

The discussion in *Thematic Intersection 1* helps us understand the inception of the *nation-state* system as a response to great conflict. Again, this system can be defined as a cultural group having sovereign political space in which they may govern their own affairs, be recognized by neighbors and other states, and maintain a border or borders that define that space. Although cooperative by design, Europeans would empower themselves to use this system as a platform for defining space around the world, thereby making it a global practice. Today, the world is divided into political space that is rooted in the nation-state system of seventeenth-century Europe.

EXPLORATION, COLONIALISM, AND THE DIFFUSION OF EUROPEAN POWER

As this textbook discusses world regions, European political, economic, and cultural influences will surface as part of the narrative in nearly every chapter. This is because the Europeans—mainly the British, French, and Spanish—explored and colonized much of the world. And if they did not directly colonize a region, they likely played some role in indirectly influencing some aspect of a country's history. Therefore, it is important to understand a little backstory that might help illuminate how they became so influential politically.

Exploration

The first wave of post-Roman European influence beyond its own region can be seen during the *Age of Exploration*. European exploration can be defined as the move by Europeans to establish more direct routes of trade with the Far East. When the knights of Europe warred with Muslim invaders in Jerusalem during the *Crusades*, they were exposed to largely unknown foods, goods, and ideas. See the list below for just a few examples:

FOODS

- Rice
- Coffee
- Dates
- Apricots

- Lemons
- Sugar
- Ginger and other spices
- Melons

GOODS

- Mirrors
- Carpet
- Cotton for clothing and silk
- Compass

- Paper for writing
- Wheelbarrow
- Bed mattresses

IDEAS

- Agricultural irrigation
- Games
- Clocks
- Alchemy
- Arabic numbers

- Drugs
- Mathematics (algebra)
- Scarlet red
- Fortification/castle design

These only begin to describe the broad spectrum of goods and ideas that Christian knights came in contact with while abroad. These products were primarily controlled by land traders and merchants along the *Silk Road*.

Once these goods were brought back to Europe, several countries quickly moved to establish trade routes to the Far East. The Venetians of Northern Italy established themselves along the *Silk Road*, thanks in part to their native son, Marco Polo, and his famous travels to the Mongol Empire in China. Later, the pope granted Portugal the sea routes around Africa. England and France would be delayed in this initial push to explore. Spain, however, was denied a viable trade route. They, instead, would devise a plan to sail west into the unknown. The result of this action is well known.

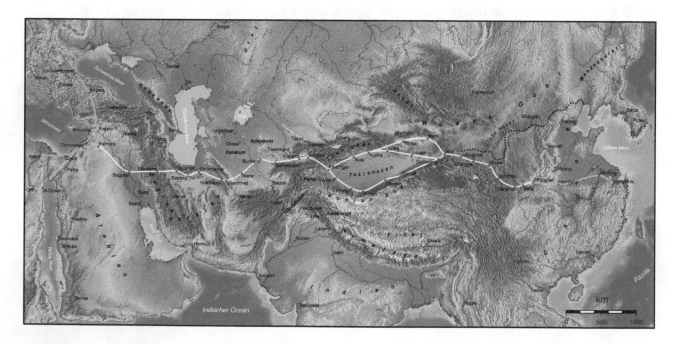

FIGURE 2.5a. The Silk Road: Established in ancient times, the Muslim traders took over old Persian roots, bringing goods from the far east into the Middle East. Europeans would come into contact with these goods, often for the first time, during the Crusades.
Copyright in the Public Domain.

When the Spanish arrived in what would be recognized as the "New World," they quickly declared it for Spain, so beginning a century of exploitation. Gold, silver, and other valuables flooded into Europe. This would have profound effects. These might be best summarized in the four (4) outcomes of exploration:

- *Domestic Inflation:* The amount of riches coming into Europe would drive up the cost of goods and services, putting a huge strain on the common person.
- *Competition:* European nations (and wealthy individuals) would race to claim new lands to compete with the Spanish. This would include fellow Iberian Portuguese claiming Brazil, and the Dutch, French, and English all moved quickly, deploying explorers.
- *Colonization*: In order to maintain the flow of resources and capital from claimed lands to Europe, colonies had to be established and maintained. To attract colonizers, land gifts, royalties, and appointed titles were common.
- *Diffusion*: European power, culture, economic influence, political structure, and disease would spread into lands exploited and controlled by Europeans.

Colonization

European political influence can best be seen through the creation and maintenance of colonies. *Colonialism* can be defined as the direct use of a country's natural and human resources for the benefit a foreign, more powerful country. Additionally, it involves the immigration of people from the colonizing nation to control, maintain, and profit from the colony. Although it can include military action to secure a colony, it is not necessarily a military invasion. Colonies resulted from a combination of political manipulation and intimidation. Europeans' military prowess and capital enabled them to mitigate threats in colonies, but not necessarily with fellow Europeans.

As a result of colonialism and the competition it bred within their community of nations, Europe's political space would expand out well beyond its borders. Because of the global reach of Europeans (especially the British during the Victorian era), European ideas, systems, and economic influences could be seen as "implemented policy" around the globe. Africa, for example, was robustly colonized by the Europeans. Because of conflicts over issues at home and in Africa, the colonizers elected to divide Africa up into political space (See *Figure 2.5b*).

Although the details of the *Berlin Conference* will be discussed in Chapter 5 (Sub-Saharan Africa), it effectively sheds light on how European political systems began to take shape on other continents. For them, political borders helped to distinguish space. Naturally, there will be discussions later in this chapter about the modern political landscape of the European Union. To better understand that complex dynamic, it is best to begin with how European colonialism planted the seed that would grow into the modern political landscape of the developed world.

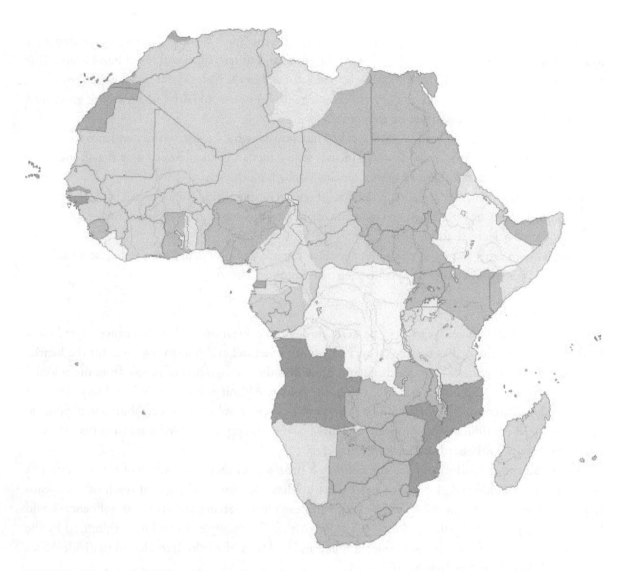

FIGURE 2.5b. Colonial Africa: After the Berlin Conference, Africa was divided into political space that fit the needs of competing European powers. Copyright © Eric Gaba (CC BY-SA 3.0) at http://commons.wikimedia.org/wiki/File%3AColonial_Africa_1913_map.svg.

2.6 Europe's Economic Geography

Europe's economic landscape can be easily characterized as influential and highly relevant. A full exploration of this would fill textbooks because there are so many layers of discussion. Rather than attempt to deconstruct Europe's complex and rich economic story, this section will continue briefly to discuss colonialism and then examine *industrialization* as facilitators of economic growth over the past 150 years. At the same time, this section uses these "facilitators" to pave an understanding of Europe's current economic landscapes. It is important to point out that between colonialism and industrialization and the modern landscapes are two of the largest human conflicts in history. These conflicts that Europe and the world would face in the twentieth century—and the cooperation that resulted from them—were fundamentally economic in nature. In many ways, this is the most important narrative in European history.

LANDSCAPES OF COMPETITION

Colonialism played a central role in the economies of several powerful European nations. Amongst them, the British would become the dominant power in Europe because they had both a sophisticated network of colonies and an economic system that allowed markets to control and resolve many of the regional conflicts that seemed tethered to foreign operations. By the 1860s, the British controlled one-fifth of all global trade. Therefore, maintaining and even strengthening control over their colonies was increasingly important. Likewise, the French had established colonies in Africa and Southeast Asia. These colonies would help Europeans ascend economically but at the same time create tensions between them.

Colonies, as it would turn out, were by nature difficult to maintain. Despite markets resolving many of the issues that arose, European nations would have to periodically show muscle to maintain the *status quo*. This might be best illustrated by the *problems of maintaining colonial operations*. This included (1) *distance*, or the fact that European nations had to not only maintain colonial commercial activities—which involved coordinating the movement of goods and materials thousands of miles—but a host of other issues as well.

Managing colonies from a distance meant local issues had to be resolved by regional authorities who were often themselves removed from the problem. One key issue within colonies was (2) *anticolonial sentiment/solidarity*. Because colonies were, by design, economic appendages of a foreign nation, local

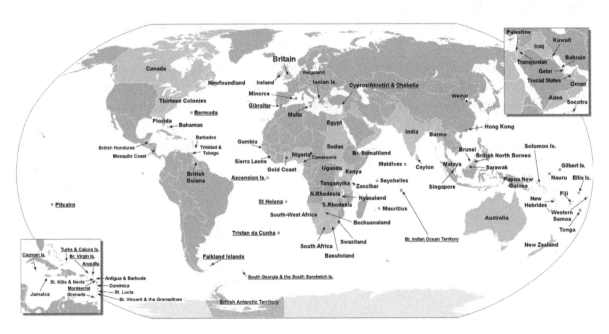

FIGURE 2.6a. The British Empire over time.
Copyright in the Public Domain.

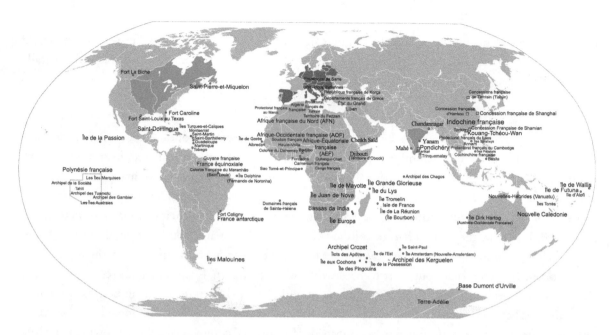

FIGURE 2.6b. The French Empire over time.
Copyright in the Public Domain.

and regional resentment was a constant. To control this, the British, for example, would place limits on access into the cities because they viewed it, pragmatically, as a security threat. If too many disenfranchised citizens gathered in critical mass in a colonial capital or a town with an important economic function, the entire colony could be at risk.

Finally, colonies would be (3) *vulnerable to external threats*. Competition between Europeans would often spill over as conflicts in the colonies. Additionally, the sea lanes that transported raw materials and goods from colonies to Europe were often preyed upon by pirates and other belligerents. Therefore, maintaining a military presence around the world would be necessary, although costly. After the Second World War, Europe would eventually lose its colonies for reasons that will be discussed shortly.

CASE STUDY 2A

The Industrial Revolution: a Nodal Point of Humanity

The Industrial Revolution is likely the most profound and influential "nodal point" in human history. The world before industrialization barely resembled the world that would emerge after. Although this change would not be instant, it would not take long for the industrial landscapes of Europe to form. Britain would be the first to industrialize in the early nineteenth century, and by the 1880s, the Donbas region of the Ukraine would join the rest of Europe in transforming from a traditional economy into an industrial economy.

FIGURE 2.6c. The industrial landscape of Manchester, England, during the late nineteenth and early twentieth centuries. It was locally referred to as "Cottonopolis," for all the textile mills.
Copyright in the Public Domain.

This Case Study will focus on the outcomes of the Industrial Revolution in Europe, rather than its causes and specific inventions. The reason is simple: studying outcomes of industrialization might help us understand the epic conflicts, social divisions, and global changes that would result from them. See below:

1. **Industrial-commercial productivity:** Mechanization in many fields like mining, agriculture, manufacturing, and so on fundamentally changed productivity. Nations that engaged these new technologies and participated in industrial activities (and continued to perfect them) would see a transformation in the scale of their operations. Raw materials could be more effectively and efficiently drawn from Earth. Those raw materials could be commodified with greater speed and into a broader range of products. The products that resulted from these technologies could then be sold in global markets, thus creating wealth and opportunity.

2. **Stronger materials enable advancements in society:** The Industrial Revolution saw a shift from limited, weaker labor and materials to mechanized labor and stronger materials. Steel, for example, would combine with mobility technologies to radically change ship design and speed, railroad networks, and urban design. Steam and, later, coal would more efficiently move raw materials to industrial centers and commodities from industrial centers to markets, not only locally, but globally as well.

3. **Socioeconomic Discourses:** Europe would be the birthplace of divergent social and economic philosophies that resulted from industrialization. On one hand, you would see a Smith-Ricardo-inspired "laissez faire" approach to capitalism which stressed the importance of free markets and low regulation. This led to great divisions in wealth, along with economic disparities (and animosities) between nations. On the other hand, you see the emergence of a Marxist reaction to industrialization. Karl Marx formed his various theses after visiting a

factory in Britain and seeing the atrocious conditions of the working class. These two themes were born from the Industrial Revolution and would evolve into complex, competing social-economic ideologies that play out to this day.

4. **Rise of Urbanism:** Industry often began to operate where the attributes were optimum. This usually meant there was some physical geographical feature (like a river or port), proximity to raw materials, and, eventually, proximity to labor pools. Cities in Europe were often established in areas that met these industrial requirements, thus pairing industrial operations with cities. As industries grew, so did the need for labor. At the same time, agricultural advances meant that farm labor was in decline, and many tens of thousands would trickle from rural communities into European cities.

   Resulting from this rural-to-urban migration throughout Europe during the mid-nineteenth and early twentieth centuries were epic changes. People began living in closer proximity to each other in critical mass. Cities would have the challenges of managing and planning for a more complex anatomy. A growing residential base combined with a greater need for industrial functionality, resulting in new, sometimes troublesome urban landscapes.

5. **Rise of Environmental Issues:** Industry requires not only a change in land use, but also sometimes the obliteration of landscapes. As seen in *Figure 2.6c*, even early industrial landscapes revealed a more sinister reality of smokestacks, clustered buildings, and the reduction of natural habitats. What is harder to see are the effects of pollution on the local biome, human health, and how people view nature. It was more socially accepted to view industry as a creator of jobs and wealth. Thus, industrial activities had to be a priority. The price was paid by the environment, and that is something that Europeans, and the world for that matter, deal with to this day.

6. **Economic Competition:** Not every European nation industrialized at the same pace. The reason for this can be found both in Europe's physical landscape and its political power. Britain's Midlands region, for example, had a plethora of raw materials that easily linked to rivers and ports. This was the birthplace of the Industrial Revolution. Before long, others with similar physical geographic features that facilitated industrial aspirations would emerge. Belgium's Wallonia region, Germany's Ruhr and Saxony regions, Poland's Silesia region, and Ukraine's Donbas region were all centers of industry.

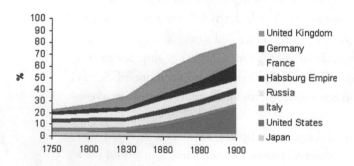

Relative Share of World Manufacturing Output, 1750-1900

FIGURE 2.6d. World Share of Manufacturing 1750–1900: This graph reveals the strength of the British economy, resulting from both colonial operations and industrialization. Copyright © TwoOneTwo (CC BY-SA 3.0) at https://commons.wikimedia.org/wiki/File:Graph_rel_share_world_manuf_1750_1900_02.png.

As it would turn out, industrial productivity did not necessarily equate with power and influence. The British, in securing and maintaining trade routes to colonies and the naval prowess to secure them, became hegemons. Other industrialized nations, like Germany, which both equaled British productivity and exceeded British quality, grew increasingly frustrated about playing a secondary role, at best, in global trade and commerce. This tension would eventually contribute to the ignition of wars at a scale never before seen in human history.

Industrialization and Imperialism

In 1871, Germany finally became a cohesive "empire." Before that, it shared culture but lacked any tangible political organization, due to chronic regional disagreements and post-French Revolution sentiments of

FIGURE 2.6e. German Empire 1871–1918.
Copyright © kgberger (CC BY-SA 2.5) at http://commons.wikimedia.org/wiki/File%3ADeutsches_Reich_1871-1918.png.

freedom competing with more hardline ideals. Under Otto Von Bismarck, this would change. Germany, under the Chancellor, would win several decisive wars and pull under a common umbrella industrial activities and colonial operations in Africa.

Despite these political gains and a marked rise in population, Germany was still a distant second to British imperial power. To complicate matters more, the icy relationship Britain had with its former colony and emerging superpower, the United States, was beginning to thaw. The prospects of a transatlantic super alliance between Anglophone nations suggested that the British would only strengthen their hegemony over global trade and industrial networking. This would be a great source of tension for Germany through the turn of the century. As it would turn out, industrial might combined with imperialistic aspirations would be an explosive combination.

2.7 How Conflicts Defined Europe

The two great wars of the twentieth century were started, both directly and indirectly, by Europeans. By 1914, Germany's economic tensions with Britain were well established but largely unresolved. When Archduke Franz Ferdinand, the Austro-Hungarian heir presumptive, was assassinated, war broke out regionally. Because of alliances, the war escalated into the *Great War*—a military engagement on a scale never before seen by humanity. By the end, the Great War resulted in roughly forty million casualties and devastated the European landscape. Many scholars feel this was a "black swan" event, in that war on this scale should not have erupted as a result of a murdered prince. It might be viewed, then, that the assassination merely pulled the cork out of a bottle filled with decades of economic tensions in Europe between the British, Germans, and others trying to leverage their industry for economic gains on an uneven playing field. Germany and its allies lost this war, and what resulted set the stage for an even deadlier war to come.

After World War I (Great War), Germany was punished and forced to pay enormous reparations. The conditions of the *Treaty of Versailles* were, to the Germans, humiliating, and the cost of the war thrust them into a deep economic depression. Meanwhile, the victors met in Washington, DC in 1921–22 to determine how to avoid future calamities of this scale. It was identified that war itself had changed drastically. Industrialized nations could now leverage their industry to strengthen themselves, prolong war, and ultimately change the scale and cost of war.

To prevent this from happening again, the *Washington Naval Conference* established that the best way to maintain peace was through naval power. Benefiting from this agreement were the British and Americans, who allotted themselves the most tonnage (number of warships that could be built). The Japanese, who reluctantly accepted less naval power, countered by demanding that the British ultimately leave them alone east of Singapore and that the Americans not interfere west of Pearl Harbor, Hawaii. This condition was agreed upon, thus essentially giving the Japanese free rein over East Asia and Southeast Asia. The Japanese would employ aggressive and even inhumane measures to subjugate East Asian nations, thus leading to war.

In Europe, German power was greatly diminished. The British reestablished themselves economically, and, though their colonies were growing harder to manage, enjoyed their hegemony once again. Within Germany, however, was an emerging threat. Germans, already in a postwar economic depression—and then hit harder by the *Great Depression* of 1929—had experienced a 40% reduction in wealth. This fostered political instability. Emerging from this was a young, charismatic politician: Adolf Hitler. Hitler would fan the flames of nationalism while using brute force to mitigate opposition. By 1933, Hitler would take over as Chancellor and Europe would, once again, face war on a scale greater than the last.

THEMATIC INTERSECTION 2B

Political and Economic Themes Collide

Themes: Political/Economic

Following the Thirty Years' War, Europeans turned conflict into political cooperation by laying the groundwork for the "nation-state" system. This allowed them to respect each other's borders while governing their own affairs within their politically defined space. Although this system did not guarantee conflict-free coexistence with neighbors, it effectively helped redefine the nature of conflict in the future.

After Europe colonized and industrialized (and tethered the former to the latter), landscapes of competition created an uneven playing field. Some European nations grew economically while enjoying the benefits of political sovereignty. In other words, they would exploit foreign colonies and leverage natural resources for industry, doing it all within the laws they wrote and the ideological framework they created for themselves. The result was deep economic disparities, not only between nations, but also amongst people. Industrialization required a large, low-skilled, inexpensive workforce to keep the factories productive, the goods and services moving, and the money rolling in. The working class became an increasingly larger segment of society, while the captains of industry became extraordinarily wealthy. As it would turn out, this would become the climate that provided the opportunity for a perfect storm to occur in the 1930s.

Two coeval series of events were unfolding: the consolidation of nationalistic Germany under a charismatic leader and the overly aggressive imperial Japanese economic and military subjugation of the East Asian realm. Germany and Japan became allies, and World War II began. Despite the lethality of both the German and Japanese militaries, they would both lose the war. When examined, it was not only the military prowess of the Allied forces, but also the productivity of their industry. Simply put, the United States and the British outmanufactured the Axis powers. The Americans, for example, converted their giant automotive industries to manufacture war planes, armored vehicles, tanks, and other war machines. By 1944, the industrial might of the United States and Britain outproduced their opponents. Like the Great War, the outcome was significantly determined by industrial production and the ability to leverage it in wartime.

The economic narratives around WWII are directly related to the political outcomes that would result from victory. Not only did the United States leverage their industrial might; they emerged from the war comparatively unscathed. The European and East Asian realms were devastated by war, whereas the contiguous United States remained unmolested by Hitler or the Japanese. The United States, with Britain's support, would become the most powerful country on Earth, both militaristically and economically. Both nations immediately helped to establish a new global political (and by extension, economic) framework that would redefine the world order.

The Bretton-Woods Conference of 1947 sought to construct global cooperation by redefining economic systems in the postwar world. This included supporting development (IMF, World Bank), controlling exchange rates, monitoring aggregate demand and methods to balance it, etc. The result was an economic system that balanced important social systems with economic systems while providing lines of capital for those who sought to develop in a way that reflected this balance. This new socioeconomic framework resulted from the conflicts created by economic social inequalities. Emerging from this was a system that helped, for a while at least, forge cooperation between nations.

THE COLD WAR

After WWII, Europe faced the arduous task of reconstruction. The Germans had essentially been defanged by the Americans, British, and Soviets, and now faced an occupied, divided nation. This division occurred because the postwar relationship between the USSR and the West quickly deteriorated. The Soviet Union, though an ally during the war, rushed to Berlin to grab top German scientists in an attempt to best position themselves against the West in postwar times. This was done with the primary reason of developing nuclear abilities and atomic weaponry. They were successful, and it would soon follow that the Western European nations (with the North Americans) would have to form alliances to counter this resurrected ideological and potentially dangerous rivalry. Multinational alliances like the *North Atlantic Treaty Organization (NATO)* were formed loosely in the late 1940s and then strengthened after the Soviets supported North Korea during the Korean War. From the late 1940s until the fall of the Soviet Union, Europe would be engaged in a chess game of intimidation and show of strength.

Western Europe's economic recovery was quick. Allied-occupied Germany, for example, experienced rapid postwar economic recovery. West Germany rebuilt, reindustrialized, and experienced rapid population growth. In many ways, however, the opposite was occurring in East Germany. The communist economy was abysmal, and their population declined. This helped to showcase the differences between a Soviet-controlled communist system and a western capitalist democracy. Because of this dynamic, Germany would become the epicenter for tensions in Europe that would define the next several decades.

2.8 Europe and the Twenty-First Century

Following the war, Europe experienced tremendous changes and faced some real challenges. These might be best summarized in the four (4) challenges of postwar Europe, below:

1. *Security:* Europeans faced a new threat from the Soviet Union. NATO and other alliances resulted in watchful eyes on the Soviets. This included missile systems, advanced tracking systems, military readiness, and managing a border between the democratic west and the "Iron Curtain."

2. *Interregional Political Division*: Europe's eastern nations were communist and were affiliated with (if not directly controlled by) the Soviets, which kept these tensions within their close. After the fall of the Soviet Union, the independent nations of Eastern Europe (East Germany, Poland, Romania, Hungary, and Yugoslavia, for example) would struggle to build their own economies and, as such, were greatly behind western countries economically.

3. *Recovery:* A devastated landscape made it difficult for Europeans to rebound after seven years of intense warfare. The United States would initiate the *Marshall Plan* to help Europeans recover economically, infrastructurally, and in other ways.

4. *Global Competition:* The United States and Canada, though very helpful to Europeans in the postwar era, would emerge as the dominant economy. Not only did North American industry and infrastructure remain undamaged; the nations also used their victory to propel themselves into the global economy. In order to compete with this, Europe would have to consolidate, cooperate, and compete.

FIGURE 2.8a. The Marshall Plan: Resulting from the Economic Cooperation Act of 1948. This provided about 160 Billion (in today's dollars) to European Recovery efforts. Copyright in the Public Domain. Copyright in the Public Domain.

COMPETING IN A GLOBAL ECONOMY

During the war, exiled leaders from the Netherlands, Belgium, and Luxembourg sought to construct a postwar economic framework that would allow them to better leverage their labor, resources, and geographical features for their mutual benefit. This became a supranational organization, which can be defined as three or more nations voluntarily aligning their economic, political, and cultural interests in a way that requires them to yield some aspects of sovereignty for the benefit of all involved. This Benelux Agreement of 1944 involved the following:

1. Build a joint economic and administrative structure.
2. Provide access to capital and financial aid for development, infrastructure enhancements, and other mutually beneficial endeavors.
3. Allow the free flow of resources, capital, and labor across borders.
4. Regulate restrictive trade tariffs.
5. Maintain strong political cooperation.

This agreement within Europe would combine with financing from the Marshall Plan of 1947–1948 and lead to what would become the European Union.

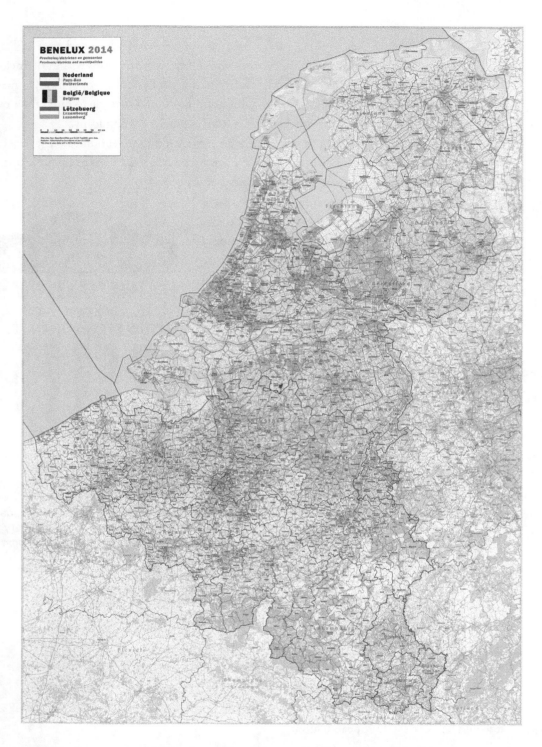

FIGURE 2.8b. Benelux: Belgium, Netherlands, and Luxembourg were amongst the first to form a post-war cooperative agreement that would help inspire the future European Union. Copyright © Janwillemvanaalst (CC BY-SA 3.0) at http://commons.wikimedia.org/wiki/ File%3ABenelux-map-prov-gem-2014.jpg.

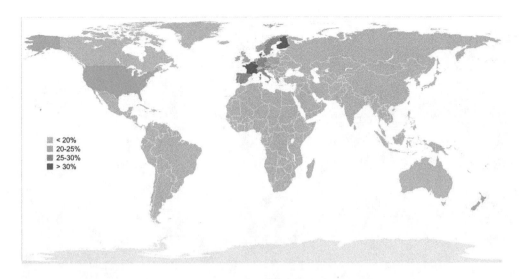

FIGURE 2.8c. Percentage of GDP in OECD nations, 2013.
Copyright in the Public Domain.

SOCIAL WELFARE IN EUROPE

After the war, European nations implemented plans to distribute wealth more evenly. Social welfare can be described as a state's commitment and investment in the well-being of its residents. Although each nation had to define this for itself, the results have been measurable. Many European nations rank high in *per capita* GDP (Gross Domestic Product) and *Standard of Living* indices. This is the product of policies that help build a high standard of living with good working conditions while fostering global trade. Essentially, this system takes *Gross National Income* (all revenues, incomes within and outside a nation) and uses it in a way that betters society as a whole.

This is often paired with a high personal income tax rate. The *benefits of the European social welfare* system are:

- Available and accessible health care: Standard care, hospitalization, family planning, dental care.
- Maintained or cutting-edge infrastructure: Roads, ports, railways, airports, bridges, and so on are well maintained.
- Social inclusionism: There are both direct and indirect investments in child rearing, education, and elderly care. Also, addiction is often viewed as a social issue that requires treatment, as opposed to a crime.
- Education: Compulsory and university education is often free.
- Work-life balance: Europeans typically have more vacation time, longer time off with infants, and more protections and options if unemployed.

These systems were implemented in the postwar era to help maintain balance in society, reduce wealth gaps, and increase cooperation.

FIGURE 2.8d. European Union today: There are currently 28 member nations with several applications under review. Copyright © Alina Zienowicz (CC BY-SA 3.0) at https://commons.wikimedia.org/wiki/File%3A2007_07_16_parlament_europejski_bruksela_26.JPG.

RISE OF THE EUROPEAN UNION AND THE EUROZONE

Europe's need to cooperate and compete in the postwar era led to the creation of the supranational organization known as the European Union (EU). The EU is comprised of twenty-eight member nations that cooperate in almost every way while still maintaining some control over their own internal affairs. Functions of the EU extend into many areas, which include:

- Central European Bank
- European Court of Justice
- European Parliament
- European Council
- Council of Ministers
- Court of Auditors

FIGURE 2.8e. European Union headquarters, in Brussels, Belgium. Copyright © Euseson (CC BY-SA 3.0) at http://commons.wikimedia.org/wiki/File%3AEurop%C3%A4ischer_Rechnungshof.jpg.

Their collective role is to leverage the union's economic power to compete at the global scale. The governing agencies within the EU are comprised of representatives from the various member nations. Together, they strive to reach consensus on strategies, investments, and policies that help them remain competitive in the global economic arena.

Beginning in 1999, the European Union felt its interests would be best served if they united under a single currency. This currency is known as the *Euro*, and nineteen of the twenty-eight member nations dissolved their own currencies and adopted it. Monetary policy is the responsibility of the Central European Bank. Nations that did not join the Eurozone, like the UK, cooperate politically with the goals of the EU, but they have more economic control over their own affairs. In many ways, this unification was successful;

it established the EU as a major player in the global economy. Combined, they are larger than the North Americans (US, Canada, Mexico).

Challenges of Unity

In 2008, the United States fell into a deep recession. Because of the interconnected economies (markets, interest and exchange rates, etc.), the European economy was hit shortly afterwards. The recession in Europe was difficult to resolve for several reasons. First, the *Euro* put many nations under one fiscal roof, and they had to work cooperatively to resolve a broad geographical range of problems. Whereas nations with their own currencies can sometimes have more options available to mitigate the effects of financial crises, the Eurozone nations were like a ship taking on water.

Second, some Eurozone nations fared relatively well through the recession because their economies remained more resilient. Germany, for example, maintained a relatively strong economy, while others, like Portugal, Ireland, Italy, Greece, and Spain (derogatorily referred to as the "PIIGS"), were on the road to

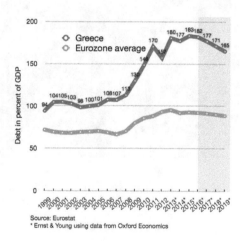

FIGURE 2.8g. Greek debt compared to Eurozone average. Copyright © Spitzl (CC BY-SA 3.0) at http://commons.wikimedia.org/wiki/File%3AGreek_debt_and_EU_average.png.

FIGURE 2.8f. Eurozone: 19 EU nations that chose to unite under one currency, the Euro. Copyright © IgnisFatuus (CC BY-SA 3.0) at http://commons.wikimedia.org/wiki/File%3AEurozone_participation.svg.

FIGURE 2.8h. Syntagma Square, 2011: Over 100,000 Greeks protest the IMF in Athens. Copyright © Kotsolis (CC BY-SA 3.0) at http://commons.wikimedia.org/wiki/File%3A2011_Greece_Uprising.jpg.]

total bankruptcy. Greece, for example, had a rather incendiary combination of robust social welfare and retirement programs and a sharp decline in coveted tourism revenue. The result was extraordinary national debt, which then led to other problems.

Resulting from the uneven impact of the recession were bailouts, the selling of bonds, and agitating austerity measures. Old animosities returned between northwestern and southern-tier Europeans, especially between Germany and Greece. The rise of anarchist movements, social unrest, and protests were common in southern European cities, whereas frustration brewed in Germany over bailouts. Although the Eurozone has not yet resolved its issues, the end of the recession in the United States, combined with a broad spectrum of economic moves, helped to stabilize Europe's economic landscapes.

NEW THREATS TO EUROPE

Europe is currently contending with new issues; some of these may be direct threats, while others may become potential issues in the future. These include Russia's support of Ukraine's civil unrest, climate change, and demographic issues.

Ukraine and Russia

The Ukraine is a European nation on the border with Russia. Russia has long had cultural ties to eastern Ukraine, especially in the Crimea region. When the Ukraine applied to join the EU, eastern Ukrainians protested, as they felt aligning interests with Russia was better. This sparked a great debate in the Ukraine and has since escalated into civil war. Russia, though they are claiming otherwise, is supporting eastern Ukrainians militarily, while Europeans rally behind the legitimate Ukrainian government. This tension over the Ukraine has broadened in scale into yet another political conflict between Europe (and its allies) and Russia. Sanctions have been imposed on Russia, yet its resolve to support eastern Ukrainians seems like an issue far from resolution.

Climate Change

Anthropogenic issues related to climate change are being watched with great interest by Europeans. Lowland coastal nations are already taking steps to mitigate future sea level rise. The Dutch, for example, are very vulnerable to sea level rise and have made heavy investments in levees, dikes, and urban design.

Reducing carbon levels is also a key priority amongst European nations. Germany, Denmark, and Sweden, to name a few, have significantly reduced conventional energy sources and replaced them with alternative energy sources. The Swedes employ a forestry model that is so effective it offsets the carbon footprint from their industry. As the climate continues to change, the Europeans will likely lead the pack with innovative ways to soften the effects and adapt.

FIGURE 2.8i. Muslims protesting in France, 2006. Copyright © David Monniaux (CC BY-SA 3.0) at https://commons.wikimedia.org/wiki/File:Paris_2006-02-11_anti-caricature_protest_bannieres_dsc07478.jpg.

Demographic Issues

Europe faces several population issues. One is purely demographic. Europe is aging, and its younger population is either flat, at best, or shrinking. This means a smaller future workforce, which then challenges notions of revenue supporting robust social welfare systems and future productivity. Both social and economic factors play into this trend. As developed nations engage in global commerce, Europeans tend to be well educated and have good gender equality. Both men and women work, and the cost of living in Europe is high. This usually equates to marrying later and having fewer children (lower Total Fertility Rates). If Europe is to maintain strong social welfare systems and adapt to a more competitive global economy, it will remain focused on demographic issues.

Another demographic issue in Europe is more cultural in nature. Although Europe has long had a percentage of Muslim residents, the Arab Spring of 2007–2012 (or the series of internal revolutions in North Africa) resulted in hundreds of thousands fleeing to Europe. This spiked Muslim populations within cities, especially in France. Although it is illegal to ask someone's religion in France, studies of church attendance and university studies suggest that France's Muslim population is now approximately 10% of its total population. Many of these new arrivals are unemployed or underemployed young men.

In the post 9-11/London Tube bombing era, Europeans have been more suspicious of this new group that resides in cities. Social unrest has resulted from targeted policies against Muslims. For example, in France, a French citizen is entitled to a job before a Muslim immigrant. France has banned the *burka* and discouraged prayer in public areas. The Swiss banned the construction of any more minarets (prayer towers on mosques). The Germans, Danish, and British have all had policies that have ignited resentment toward a new and growing Muslim population. And because TFR is higher amongst Muslim populations, demographers have suggested that Muslim populations will outpace domestic populations into this century. This may continue to result in cultural pushback from Europeans.

CONCLUSION

Clearly, Europe is a fascinating region through almost any lens. Whether discussing the ancient Romans or the modern global political and economic landscapes, Europeans have helped to shape the world we know today. However, as easy as it is to identify European influences that have changed the world for the better, there are likely just as many examples that might illuminate how Europeans have been responsible for some of humanity's darkest events and influences that have had unfortunate outcomes. This makes the study of Europe feel difficult at times.

This chapter has discussed Europe geographically, but it has also shed light on both the good and the bad. This is an important aspect of studying Europe, especially when studying global geography. Europe's influences, simply put, are a part of the narrative in almost every region we study from this point on. They are an inescapable element in global geography because they have touched almost every region and every cultural group, and have influenced how they interact with each other on Earth. Therefore, it could be said that many of the conflicts and the cooperation that followed (or vice versa) have, either directly or indirectly, been influenced by Europeans.

KEY TERMS

Climate
Topography
Coastal Lowlands
Western Highlands
fjord
Alpine Region
Central Highlands
Western Culture
Greco-Roman complex
Germanic
Gaelic/Celtic

Islam
Nation-state system
European Exploration
Four (4) outcomes of
    exploration
Colonialism
Industrialization
Outcomes of
    Industrialization
Bretton-Woods
    Conference

Four (4) Challenges of
    Postwar Europe
Supranational
    Organization
Benelux Agreement
    (1944)
Social Welfare
European Union (EU)
Euro
Eurozone

CLASS DISCUSSIONS

1. How has Europe's geography contributed to its economic success? How has it worked against it?
2. How did the Romans influence "Western Culture?"
3. Describe the relationship between religious landscapes in Europe and language.
4. Describe how Europeans influenced the world through colonialism.
5. What European nations formed an agreement between themselves that would later inspire the European Union? How has the EU benefited member nations? How has it been a problem for them since the Great Recession?

ADDITIONAL RESOURCES

CIA World Factbook Europe:

> https://www.cia.gov/library/publications/the-world-factbook/wfbExt/region_eur.html

History:

http://europeanhistory.about.com/

http://plato.stanford.edu/entries/colonialism/

European Union:

http://europa.eu/index_en.htm

BIBLIOGRAPHY

"Adam Smith Biography." Bio.com. A&E Networks Television, n.d. Web. http://www.biography.com/people/adam-smith-9486480. Nov.–Dec. 2014.

BBC News. BBC, n.d. Web. http://www.bbc.co.uk/history/worldwars/wwone/origins_01.shtml. Nov.–Dec. 2014.

———. http://www.bbc.co.uk/history/british/empire_seapower/overview_empire_seapower_01.shtml. Nov–Dec. 2014.

Central Intelligence Agency. The World Factbook. n.d. Web. https://www.cia.gov/library/publications/the-world-factbook/. Nov.–Dec. 2014.

"The Cold War." John F. Kennedy Presidential Library & Museum. N.p., n.d. Web. http://www.jfklibrary.org/JFK/JFK-in-History/The-Cold-War.aspx. Nov.–Dec. 2014.

"Countries of the Danube River Basin." Countries of the Danube River Basin. N.p., n.d. Web. http://www.icpdr.org/main/danube-basin/countries-danube-river-basin.

Dales, R.C. (1992). The Intellectual Life of Western Europe in the Middle Ages. Leiden: EJ Brill.

Evans, R.J. (2004). Coming of the Third Reich. New York: Penguin Press.

"Islam in France: The French Way of Life Is in Danger." Middle East Forum. N.p., n.d. Web. http://www.meforum.org/337/islam-in-france-the-french-way-of-life-is-in. 03 Jan. 2015.

Official Website of the European Union. EUROPA. N.p., n.d. Web. http://europa.eu/index_en.htm. Nov.–Dec. 2014.

Kennedy, P. (1987). The Rise and Fall of Great Powers. New York: Random House.

Macridis, R.C (1990). Modern Political Systems: Europe. 7th ed. NJ: Prentice Hall.

"Natural Resources." European Environment Agency (EEA). N.p., n.d. Web. 03 Dec 2014.

"Facts about the River Thames & Useful Information." River Thames. N.p., n.d. Web. http://www.visitthames.co.uk/about-the-river. 03 Dec 2014.

CHAPTER 3

Russia and the Central Asian Nations

3.1 Regional Overview

Key Intersecting Themes:

Social, Political, Physical Geographical, Environmental

List of countries:
- *Former Soviet Union*
- *Russia*
- *Ukraine (with Europe)*
- *Central Asian nations*

Russia and the Central Asian nations represent a region typically less known by much of the world's population. Ironically, when examined on a map, it stands out as the largest terrestrial section of Earth. The reasons why some of these lesser-known or poorly understood cultures occupy the largest land area will be discussed in more detail later in this chapter. Generally, many of these reasons have to do with the state that occupies most of this realm: Russia. Russia will be a central focus of this chapter, not because the others lack importance, but because nations like Kazakhstan, Uzbekistan, Turkmenistan, Tajikistan, and Kyrgyzstan have all been, to varying degrees, shaped by the policies of the former Soviet Union, a former socialist republic that was, for the most part, Russian. Additionally, the Russians, and by extension the Central Asian nations, have a history of being viewed as antithetical to western democratic and capitalist ideologies. Their "communist" past and the region's history of internal conflicts have largely defined this realm. Because of this, the region and its people have perhaps been deliberately ignored, but cautiously watched, by outsiders. Despite this unusual combination of characteristics, Russia and the Central Asian nations uniquely offer lenses into a physical geographical

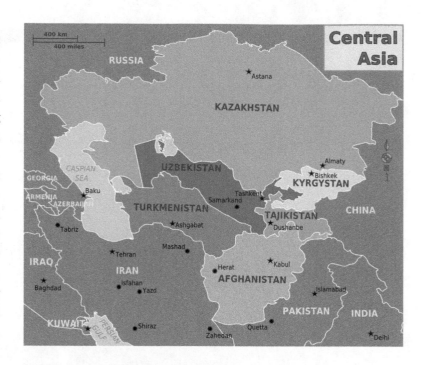

FIGURE 3.1a. Central Asia: Highlighting the "Stans".
Copyright © Cacahuate (CC BY-SA 4.0) at http://commons.wikimedia.org/wiki/File%3AMap_of_Central_Asia.png.

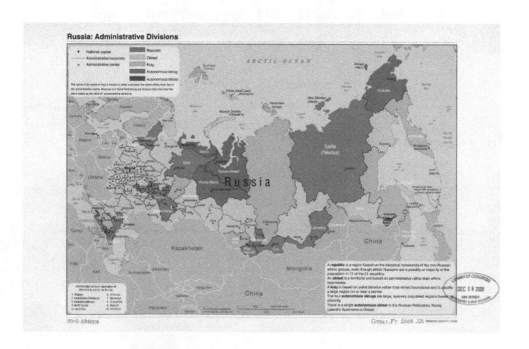

FIGURE 3.1b. Map of the Russian Federation.
Copyright in the Public Domain.

landscape at a scale unparalleled and a human narrative that is complicated and likely not intuitively understood.

PHYSICAL GEOGRAPHY: A LESSON IN SCALE

Central Asia, like Europe, is a part of the Eurasian landmass, or the largest terrestrial surface on Earth. Unlike Europe, this region covers most of this massive area. Its size is unparalleled, in that it stretches approximately six thousand miles in width, east to west, covering nine time zones. From the northern icy shores to the mountainous and desert borders of southwest Asia and South Asia, it stretches about 2,500 miles. This size is a part of this region's narrative. There is so much land that both the Russians and the Soviet Union had vast resources, but they had difficulty reaching them, extracting them, and moving them around. This region is so big that communication and connectivity from one side to the other was always an issue. Managing a broad range of people (cultures and religions) has challenged, and continues to challenge, nations, especially in Russia. In short, keeping this realm's size in mind will provide perspective on almost every aspect of this region.

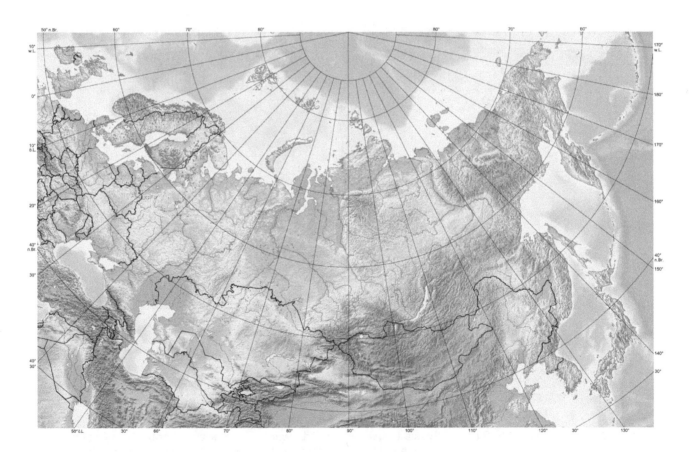

FIGURE 3.1c. Physical relief map of Russia and Central Asian Realm.
Copyright in the Public Domain.

Climate in Russia and the "Stans"

Because of the size of this region, it would be difficult to identify and discuss all the factors that contribute to both Russia's and the Central Asian nations' climates. However, there are *four (4) key climate influences* that help achieve a basic understanding of this realm's climate(s). They are:

1. *Westerly Winds:* The same maritime weather systems that move from west to east over Europe continue on over the Ukraine and start to lose moisture and power over western Russia. This westerly flow of moisture arrives to Russia in the middle latitudes and provides fairly stable levels of precipitation. Because of this, as well as proximity to Europe, most people in Russia live in the Volga River region, roughly between St. Petersburg and Moscow. This is where you find Russia's largest cities and most of its agricultural and industrial activity.

2. *Polar Easterly winds (seasonal):* Much of Russia is above sixty degrees north latitude. This is the subarctic realm on Earth, and during winter in the Northern Hemisphere, these cold

World map of Köppen-Geiger climate classification

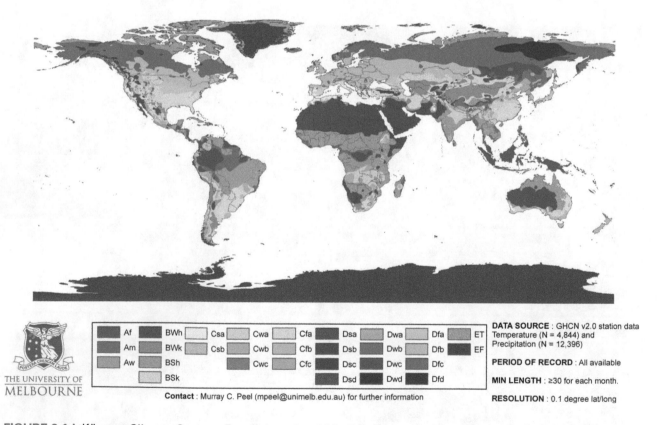

FIGURE 3.1d. Köppen Climate System: Russia largely within Dfb (warm summer continental) and Dfc (subpolar, cold continental). Most central Asian nations have more variety in climate types, based on continentality mixing with altitude and middle latitude location. Copyright © M.C. Peel, B.L. Finlayson, and T.A. McMahon (CC BY-SA 3.0) at http://commons.wikimedia.org/wiki/File%3AKöppen_World_Map_(retouched_version).png.

winds drop down into most of Central Asia. Russia is measurably one of the coldest places on Earth. Several studies show Russian temperatures near those which you would find in Antarctica.

3. *Continentality:* The large terrestrial size of central Asia equates to a greater distance from the influence of oceans. Proximity to water can dictate your climate, but so can lack of proximity. Apart from the western quarter of Russia, most of this region is far removed from any

FIGURE 3.1e(1). Russian winters are notoriously harsh.
Copyright © Arzy Arzamas (CC BY-SA 3.0) at http://commons.wikimedia.org/wiki/File%3ARussian_winter_in_Arzamas.jpg.

FIGURE 3.1e(2). Spring on the Steppes of Kazakhstan.
Copyright © Carole a (CC BY-SA 3.0) at http://commons. wikimedia.org/wiki/File%3ASteppe_of_western_Kazakhstan_ in_the_early_spring.jpg

FIGURE 3.1e(3). Farm in Russia (1909): Western Russia has similar climate as Eastern Europe.
Copyright in the Public Domain.

ocean and is therefore more characterized by extreme annual, and even daily, variability in temperature.

4. *High/Low-Pressure systems:* High- and low-pressure systems determine the flow of air, thus determining climate. Because of central Asia's large land area, it becomes more prone to seasonal energy heating the surface and inducing low pressure. Low pressure, then, becomes the destination for air descending from a high-pressure system far away. Oppositely, when the season is winter, a high-pressure system forms over central Asia, causing the flow of air south and east to low pressure in the Indian subcontinent and East Asia. However, because the air, whether inbound or outbound, is uninfluenced by oceans, it is typically quite dry. This is what characterizes most of the central realm: the dry, *grassy Steppes of Asia.*

Natural Landscapes

Russia and the Central Asian nations have many beautiful landscapes that could be highlighted in this chapter. However, this textbook will focus on several important natural landscapes, mostly because they occupy such large areas. This includes:

- Taiga
- Tundra
- Steppes
-

The *taiga*, or what other nations outside Russia call the *Boreal Forest*, is the largest tree community on Earth. The Boreal forest is a band of coniferous trees (pine trees, spruces, and larches) that rings around Earth, between about fifty and seventy degrees north latitude. Russia is home to the largest section of the Boreal forest on Earth, spanning close to five thousand miles from west to east. This biome is expansive and in many cases remote, but nonetheless provides plenty of forest resources to Russia and, by extension, the world.

FIGURE 3.1f. The great Taiga or Boreal Forest: Sometimes called the "snow forest," this massive community of trees mostly resides in Russia. Copyright © Bartosh Dmytro (CC BY-SA 3.0) at http://commons.wikimedia.org/wiki/File%3AJack_London_Lake_by_bartosh.jpg.

The *tundra* is a biome that is situated north of the *taiga* beyond seventy degrees north latitude. Too cold for trees, this biome is characterized by frozen soils and rocks, with some organic life. Typically, varieties of moss and lichens grow in this frozen ground. One particular characteristic of the *tundra* is that it holds an enormous amount of methane. As the climate changes and this region warms, the methane locked in the frozen ground will be liberated

FIGURE 3.1g(1,2). The Tundra of Russia: Cold, frozen, and treeless coastal realm.
Katpatuka (Copyleft, Free Art License) at http://commons.wikimedia.org/wiki/File%3A800px-Map-Tundra.png.; Copyright © Hannes Grobe (CC BY-SA 2.5) at http://commons.wikimedia.org/wiki/File%3AGreenland_scoresby-sydkapp2_hg.jpg.

into the atmosphere. This is a potential problem because of the nature of methane as a greenhouse gas. It is much more effective at trapping longwave radiation in the atmosphere than carbon. This region within Russia is the most vulnerable to climate change.

The Eurasian and Asian *steppes* is an ecoregion within the drier continental midsection of central Asia. It resides south of the *taiga* and stretches contiguously about four thousand miles within this region. The *steppes* have generally supported more human activities like rangeland agriculture, some farming, fishing, and trade. Likewise, invaders like Gengis

FIGURE 3.1h. Eurasian Steppes: A typically dry series of plains that exhibit great temperature variability, based on the continentality of the ecoregion.
Copyright in the Public Domain.

Khan, Attila the Hun, the Muslims, and even Alexander the Great used the *steppes* as a highway between the east and west, largely because of longer summers, grasses for feeding horses and livestock, and available water.

Although these physiological regions and the key climate types provide an overview of Russia and the Central Asian nations, later discussions in this chapter will highlight resources within this region and how they have shaped modern economic landscapes.

3.2 Economic Causes and Political Effects

In order to understand this region's rather complex economic and political narratives, there must first be a brief exploration of several aspects of Russian history. This will include a survey of the USSR (Soviet Union) as well as post-Soviet independence.

In short, the most definitive thematic intersection of this region is economic and political.

TSARIST RUSSIA

Russia during the nineteenth century was an empire. Much like Europe, Russians were ruled by royals and sought to colonize territories. Beginning with Peter the Great and later Catherine the Great, Russian aristocracy lived in opulence and privilege. Largely based in St. Petersburg, the royals and nobles built palaces that would rival any in Paris or Vienna. However, Russians, unlike the Europeans, never went through the growing pains that often accompanied great divisions in wealth between the ruling class and the commoners. In the late eighteenth century, the French royals learned the hard way that ignoring the needs of the masses—especially when a majority of them lived in poverty—could lead to violent outcomes.

FIGURE 3.2a. St. Petersburg, Russia: Once the seat of royal power in Russia. Many claim it to be amongst the most beautiful cities in the world.
Copyright in the Public Domain.

History shows us that the Tsars (another term for Czar), went too far. Maintaining a system of *serfs*—an agricultural system in which a largely rural population was beholden to rich landowners (who were themselves tethered to the goodwill of the Tsars)—began to erode the entire system. Russia was a country full of peasants. As peasants, they had little, if any, political voice and were often subject to harsh conditions, poor access to resources, and no social mobility. This dire dynamic paved the way to major changes.

INDUSTRIAL REVOLUTION IN RUSSIA

By the 1880s, the *Donbas* region of the Ukraine would finally see the seeds of industrialization. Although late to the game, the Russian aristocracy embraced it because it would become another revenue source for them. However, the burgeoning landscape of mines, factories, and related industrial activities in Russia would, like the rest of Europe, rely on a large unskilled and semiskilled workforce to extract, produce, and move products in and out of the realm. This need for workers sparked a period of rural-to-urban migration. Moscow and St. Petersburg saw significant increases in urban residents. Most of them were poor. Wealthy industrialists would exploit this peasant class, just as the Tsars did. The combinations of Tsarist-induced inequalities and industrial exploitation would result in the Russian people reaching a boiling point during the early twentieth century.

THEMATIC INTERSECTION 3A

Bolsheviks, Lenin, and the Revolutions

Themes: Economic/Social/Political

By the late nineteenth century, the majority of Russians were systemically poor and increasingly agitated. Decades of Tsarist conspicuous wealth were paired with little concern for the masses. While wealth accumulated in the cities, Russia's rural majority often faced poverty, subjugation, and even starvation. With the tide of industrialization came a greater need for a pool of unskilled and semiskilled labor in urban areas. This sparked a massive rural-to-urban migration, and many Russians, for the first time, would learn about the harsh realities of factory work and gritty urban life. This combination became rather incendiary. As if social conditions were not bad enough under nineteenth-century Tsarist control, the industrialists would add a new dimension of abuse. Harsh working conditions, low wages, and abusive treatment were set against a backdrop of wealth and privilege. The majority of Russians within society (the proletariat) would start to reject royal wealth and capitalistic greed and assert themselves more politically.

Beginning with the Social-Democratic Workers' Party (and others), working-class Russians would attempt to reengineer society for the betterment of the people. Using Marxist ideology, the nature of this movement included the dismantling of royal rule and the transfiguration of industry from private to public. This would take time, and there would be a series of conflicts within the movement, particularly amongst its leaders. The Bolsheviks, one party within this movement, would gain the support of the urban working class. Headed by Vladimir Lenin, the Bolsheviks would use Marxism to construct a political framework that could replace the existing system. This would not come easy, as it would require a violent revolution to make a transformation of this size and magnitude.

The result of this revolution was significant not only for this region of nations, but also for the world. The social conditions of Russia were defined by an economic structure that resulted in uneven wealth. The masses were used to create wealth for czars and captains of industry until the people dictated otherwise. This type of political reform was, to this point, unknown. Understanding how these themes intersected in Russia provides perspective into what would come next and, in part, what we see today.

USSR

The USSR (Union of Soviet Socialist Republics) was born from the *Russian Revolution* and politically congealed in the early 1920s. This transfigured nation became the world's first "communist" state, which meant it not only rejected capitalism but also considered democracy antithetical. However, their "ideology" failed to match their actions. The Soviets would justify all actions as "for the people," but they were characteristically "imperial" in motivation.

This became clear, both when the Soviet Union forced former tsarist vassal states behind the *"Iron Curtain"* (controlled by Moscow) and when it developed nuclear weapons after WWII. This made them nontraditional actors on the world stage. What exactly the Soviets were seemed unclear to outsiders. This lack of clarity induced fear, not only in Western nations, but also in industrializing neighbors (Japan, West Germany) and British and French colonial nations with giant poor populations, like China, India, and Indochina. The Soviet Union, in an era that would last from 1917 to 1991, would define Russia and the Central Asian nations, and would shape how outside nations had to work together during a Cold War.

FIGURE 3.2b. Soviet Socialist Republics (SSRs): 1. Russia; 2. Ukraine; 3. Byelorussian; 4. Uzbek; 5. Kazakh; 6. Georgia; 7. Azerbaijan; 8. Lithuanian; 9. Moldavian; 10. Latvian; 11. Kirghiz; 12. Tajik; 13. Armenian; 14. Turkmen; 15. Estonia.

Political Structure

After the Bolshevik and subsequent Russian Revolution (1917–1919), the "communist" party controlled Russia. Prior to the revolutions, the Russians tsars were challenged to maintain a vast empire of vassal states (tsars in other countries loyal to Russia) and more than one hundred ethnic groups. The communists projected the idea of independence and nations run by "the people," but that was not the case.

Lenin, upon assuming control, formed the Soviet Union, a union of 15 "Soviet Socialist Republics." These SSRs were designed to encase various ethnicities in identifiable political units for better control. Thus, the communist Russians never allowed the former tsarist vassal states to return to independence, but instead assimilated them into the collective, with Moscow in charge. Additionally, Moscow would rank each SSR roughly by importance. That meant, for example, a SSR in the "Stans" would have less political voice than white Russians in the Volga River Valley regions (Russian SSR, Ukrainian SSR). These SSRs naturally included Moscow, St. Petersburg, and Kiev. This essentially meant that an SSR's racial and ethnic profile determined its importance. This *internal contradiction* essentially meant the Soviet ideological foundation was flawed and the ethnic issues would erode the "union of nations" they claimed to have created.

To hold these SSRs together, the Soviets would employ *russification*. Russification can be defined as a policy of assimilation, stressing (even requiring) Russian culture and language as dominant, while regional culture and languages were less important. This meant, for example, that Russian should be taught in schools, used in written communication, used on street signs, and spoken casually within the USSR, despite its not being a native language everywhere.

Moscow (more specifically, the Kremlin) was to be viewed as the geographic epicenter of political power as well as the cultural heart of the realm. Likewise, it would use a *command economy* to bring various parts of the USSR together economically. This included redistributing labor and production to where Moscow felt it was needed. This was possible because of collectivization, or the bringing of all productive appendages of society, like manufacturing and agriculture, under government control.

Imperial Behavior: A Russian Story of Defense and Offense

Prior to the Soviet Union, the Russians aspired to be colonizers. Like the Western Europeans, the Russians sought to use lands beyond their realm to secure access to resources, generate revenues, and provide a secondary security protocol in case of invasion. However, they had limits. They lacked warm water ocean ports and had neither a legacy of marine exploration nor the naval prowess that characterized the British, for example. They did, however, have a vast land space between the civilized western realm and the remote eastern half of the Eurasian landmass. This led to an era of land colonizing that, at its farthest extent, included Alaska. Obviously, Alaska was sold to the Americans, but Russia fairly successfully colonized lands that stretched six thousand miles, west to east.

THEMATIC INTERSECTION 3B

Geographic Size Shapes Political Behavior

Themes: Physical Geography/Political

It is important to understand a key motive behind colonizing the Siberian realm to the east. As mentioned, the Russians needed a secondary security protocol in case of invasion. This essentially reflected the Moscow region's lack of geographic barriers that might protect them against invaders. There are no mountains, wide-enough rivers, or inland seas that might protect this political, economic, and cultural heartland against invasion. Because of this, Ivan the Terrible, in the sixteenth century, devised a plan that would give conquered Russians a backup strategy, which would be to retreat behind the Ural Mountains, far to the east, to regroup and continue the fight. This is considered the fallback zone. In order to facilitate this, the Russians (and later Soviets) would have to establish and maintain a string of cities and some form of transportation infrastructure to this frontier realm. The gamble was that if Russians withdrew, they would be able to survive, while foreign invaders were allowed to penetrate deep into Russia only to get caught in a bitter winter with limited resources. This saved the Russians when both Napoleon and Hitler invaded.

Additionally, in order to provide better security, Russia would have to aggressively expand out to where protective geographic boundaries were. This ushered in an era of expansion to the east, southeast, south, and southwest through the Caucasus. Although this would take centuries and seemingly endless wars, Russians would, eventually, have those protective geographic barriers they sought. The only exception was to Moscow's west, which made them vulnerable to European aggression. For this, they had to maintain the fallback zone behind the Urals and spend enormous amounts of money maintaining it.

The Russians have, since Ivan the Terrible, used this paradigm of secondary security protocol to also justify their aggressive, imperialistic behavior. It is not a lone narrative, as there are other factors discussed in this textbook. However, it does reveal a way of thinking that they must conquer or be conquered. So, even though this defensive barrier and fallback zone are an underlying, shadow priority deep in the pathos of Tsarist Russians, the Soviets, and the Russian Federation, it is also an offensive posture. By being assertive, even confrontational, the Russians feel they are—in a way—protecting themselves while serving ulterior economic and political motives.

After the Soviet Union was established, Moscow identified that it needed more than an internal *command economy* could provide, and would again take an offensive posture. It would leverage its large military to help control regions that were prone to internal ethnic conflicts while intimidating western-allied nations on the borders of southern SSRs, China, and East Germany. Still, this did not produce revenue, as the Soviets engaged in minimal outside trade, thus limiting their revenue. The result of this was more aggressive behavior.

The United States supported the regimes in neighboring Iran and Iraq and allied with Turkey, both to protect oil resources and to be a regional presence to keep the Soviets in check. However, after the *Shah* of Iran was exiled and Iran fell into a revolution to refundamentalize under Islam, the region was left in disarray. Other Muslim nations, including nearby Afghanistan, were themselves struggling internally with orthodox Islamists. The Soviets openly declared that they invaded Afghanistan to support one side of a civil war. However, it could be speculated that they had other motives. Their control of Afghanistan would put them closer to the nuclear standoff between Pakistan and India while containing the revolution in Iran and preventing it from spilling over into the Soviet SSRs just to the north. Perhaps, if successful, the end result would be a Soviet-controlled Pakistani coast that would give them a warm ocean port that could house submarines, for example. To stop this, the United States and European nations supplied the Mujahedeen rebels with arms and fostered deeper diplomatic ties with India and Pakistan.

CASE STUDY 3A

The Aral Sea: Soviet Mismanagement and Ecological Disaster

The Soviet "command economy" meant that Moscow could assign revenue-building economic activities to specific geographical locations. The Aral Sea, located on the border of modern-day Kazakhstan and Uzbekistan, became a region targeted by Moscow to grow cotton. Cotton, it was believed, could be easily grown there because of the abundant water supply from the Syr and Amu Darya Rivers. These rivers' deltas were on the Aral Sea and were its main source of fresh water. Because of the continental climate in this region, the dry conditions required robust irrigation systems. Soviet engineers were dispatched to draw water from these rivers, through canal systems, to cultivate thousands of hectares of cotton fields. The problem was that the canals were shabby, and approximately 75% of the water was wasted. With such a reduction in flow, the Darya no longer effectively fed the Aral Sea with fresh water. Evaporation combined with lowering recharge rates, and the fourth-largest freshwater sea on Earth began to disappear.

Meanwhile, the region surrounding the Aral Sea had grown from fourteen million to more than twenty-seven million people. To sustain this large population, the already-healthy fishing industry had to bring in larger hauls. However, the shrinking water levels made it difficult for fishing fleets to access deeper water. Simultaneously, the shabby canals resulted in imprudent agricultural practices, which in turn resulted in a 40% reduction in arable land. The soils were treated with vast quantities of pesticides and herbicides, resulting in both the salinization of soils and the depositing of these chemicals in a disappearing Aral Sea.

The results of the Aral Sea ecological disaster have been:

- Dry sea bed exposes dry pesticides and fertilizers. Windstorms carry this unhealthy chemical-laced dust up to one hundred miles away.
- Fishing industry was annihilated and abandoned.
- Health conditions amongst the worst in the world. Cancer, respiratory illness, chronic bronchitis, kidney and liver disease, and arthritic diseases all contribute to a much higher mortality rate, especially in children, even today.

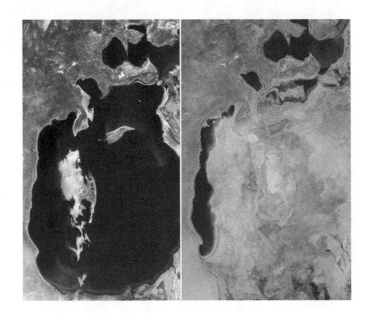

FIGURE 3.2c(1). The former Aral Sea: Between 1960 and 2000, the Aral Sea lost most of its water. Soviet policy created one of the worst ecological disasters of all time. Copyright in the Public Domain.

FIGURE 3.2c(2). Empty Landscape of Ghost Ships: The Aral Sea now is a mostly dry graveyard of fishing ships and camels.
Copyright in the Public Domain.

- Regional growing season reduced from 170 days to about ninety days today, making most crops hard to grow.

After the Soviet Union dismantled in 1991, the independent states of Kazakhstan and Uzbekistan had little or no resources to repair this system. The Russians claim it was the Soviets, not them, and they have no political motive to help. This region remains one of the poorest in central Asia, and the once robust ecosystem is ruined.

Cold War and the End of the Soviet Union

The relationship between the Soviet Union and the Western nations defined the better part of the latter twentieth century. Their communist ideology, imperial behavior, and nuclear arsenal made them an untrusted neighbor to the Europeans, a political and economic concern for the Americans, and a potential security threat to all of humanity should war have broken out. Likewise, the Soviets felt the Western nations were greedy and capitalistic, and that democracy bred corruption and served private interests.

Complicating these tensions were the various supranational alliances that emerged in response to this rivalry. NATO, as mentioned in the second chapter, was a clear move by the Americans and Europeans to stand united, politically and militaristically, in a defensive posture. The loss of China to Maoist forces was considered a major blow to democracy, thus sparking thirty years of western military support and war in Korea and Southwest Asia.

This combined with other actions in the Americas. The Americans had declared over a century earlier that European colonial powers (and by extension, Soviet interloping) would not be tolerated in the Americas (Monroe Doctrine). Thus, actions were taken to thwart socialist regimes in South America, Central America, and Cuba from allying with Moscow. The *nuclear arms race* was a side effect of this tension between the Soviets and the Western nations. Each felt that the size and level of technology of their nuclear arsenals and deployment systems would intimidate the other. Some treaties, like the SALT agreements (Strategic Arms Limitations Talks), helped defuse these tensions by reducing stockpiles and redefining the locations of deployment systems.

The relationship between the Soviet Union and the West changed under American President Ronald Reagan. He not only launched an ideological war against the Soviets, but also openly made it policy to modernize American military power for the purpose of defeating the Soviet Union. The Soviets had difficulty responding to this and entered an era of change, or *perestroika,* which led the end of the USSR.

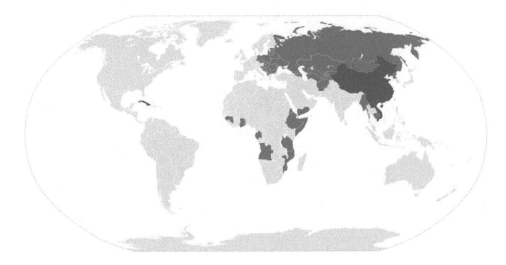

FIGURE 3.2d. The Spread of Communism: Beginning with Russia and the formations of the Soviet Union, much of Eurasian landmass turned communist, after WWII. Copyright © Claritas (CC BY-SA 1.0) at http://commons.wikimedia.org/wiki/File%3ACommunism. svg.

CASE STUDY 3B

President Reagan: an Ideological Warrior

In this case study, you will watch President Reagan speak about the Soviet Union. Pay attention to his tone, how he reflects American ideology, and some specifics about American military operations in the context of a Soviet threat.

1. Using an Internet browser and your favorite search engine, search for "Reagan's Evil Empire Speech" and listen to how he uses American ideology and Christian values.

2. Using an Internet browser and your favorite search engine, search for "President Reagan speaks about Soviets" and select an appropriate speech or news bit. Again, listen and identify his posture towards the Soviet Union.

3. Review the CIA (Central Intelligence Agency) website by searching for "Soviet Deception in the Cuban Missile Crisis, CIA."

This short exercise will provide perspective into why and how western nations, specifically the Americans, helped bring a political end to the Soviet Union.

3.3 Post-Soviet Independence and the Rise of the Russian Federation

After the Soviet Union dissolved, the many states that were once tsarist vassals (and later turned into Soviet "Iron Curtain" states) found themselves free from control. This sparked a period of devolution, or the decentralization of political power into independent nations. Eastern European nations immediately declared independence, as did Central Asian nations. Beyond politics, the absence of the Soviet Union resulted in the reversal of *russification*, and nations brought back their own cultures (languages, customs, religion, etc.).

Like these nations, the Russians had to redefine themselves and eventually try to fit into a world they ultimately did not know. Unlike the West and many Asian neighbors, the Russians had never industrialized in a way that tethered them to foreign markets. They had never gone through the growing pains often associated with capital accumulation (banking and finance systems), like the Europeans and the Americans had. Great gaps in wealth had fostered an era of labor reform and the creation of unions in the West. Struggling to maintain a balance between the needs of industry and social systems was foreign to

FIGURE 3.3a. Moscow's New Business District. Copyright © Kirill Vinokurov (CC BY-SA 3.0) at http://commons. wikimedia.org/wiki/File%3A%D0%9C%D0%BE%D1%81%D0%BA%D0%BE%D0%B2%D1%81%D0%BA%D0%B8%D0%B9_ %D0%BC%D0%B5%D0%B6%D0%B4%D1%83%D0%BD%D0%B0%D1%80%D0%BE%D0%B4%D0%BD%D1%8B%D0%B9_ %D0%B4%D0%B5%D0%BB%D0%BE%D0%B2%D0%BE%D0%B9_%D1%86%D0%B5%D0%BD%D1%82%D1%80_%C2%AB %D0%9C%D0%BE%D1%81%D0%BA%D0%B2%D0%B0-%D0%A1%D0%B8%D1%82%D0%B8%C2%BB_14.07.2014.jpg.

Russians. Therefore, how Russia would emerge from the fog of communism and decades of tensions with the capitalist west is important to understand.

RUSSIA AND THE FREE MARKET

New to world markets, Russia would have to learn how to leverage its resources, manufacturing, and existing infrastructure to engage in global trade. The Soviets had a short list of trade partners (India, Iran, and Syria, for example), but maintained these relationships in a way external to the market systems of the West. Although they had plentiful resources to work with, they faced significant social issues as well. The Soviets invested heavily in certain aspects of their society. The military received the lion's share of funding, and many were employed in the armed services and related industries. But they also maintained a robust health care system, low unemployment rates, and housing programs that accommodated most people. Though the quality of this care might be debated, most Soviet citizens had access to these services, but the independent Russians did not. After the collapse of the USSR, the newly formed Russian Federation had to radically pivot away from the old Soviet sociopolitical model while quickly embracing an independent market economy that was supposed to generate enough revenue to replace these old systems. This never really happened.

Russia indeed embraced a market system and drafted a constitution to support an independent federation. Russia borrowed some aspects of western democracy and government structure. However, especially in the decade following independence, Russians implemented these new systems carelessly. Because the Soviets centralized ownership of everything, the new federation, in order to move forward, would "privatize" almost everything. This bred extreme corruption and cronyism. *Corruption and cronyism* could be seen in the following ways:

- Former Soviet directors of industry became owners of industry because former government officials who knew them occupied new government positions.
- Contracts were awarded to acquaintances, often resulting in lucrative kickbacks.
- Police agency chiefs and mayors were often former KGB commanders, able to mitigate dissent and political competition.
- The constitution is routinely amended to serve the needs of individual politicians.

The result was a new system that shocked their newly formed federation. Money flowed to the few who controlled industry, inflation rates soared, and many investors sought outside avenues for their capital. By the late 1990s, the Russian economy was on the brink of collapse, and civil unrest, crime, and drug and alcohol abuse became commonplace.

Beginning in the early 2000s, a new president, some key political and economic reforms, and changes in global oil prices helped to reverse the catastrophe of the late nineties. Because oil represents about 80% of Russian exports, the price of the commodity directly affects the health of the Russian economy. Soaring oil prices enabled Russians to capitalize handsomely and put the money into a scheme that would bolster trade and reduce debt. This would combine with the stabilization of the *ruble* (Russian currency), a lowering *Perception of Corruption* index, and a subsequent increase in foreign direct investment. Russia was showing signs, for the first time since Catherine the Great, that it was postured to be an important and anticipated part of global trade. By 2008, Russia would have the third-largest *foreign exchange reserves* and ascend to the ninth-largest economy on Earth.

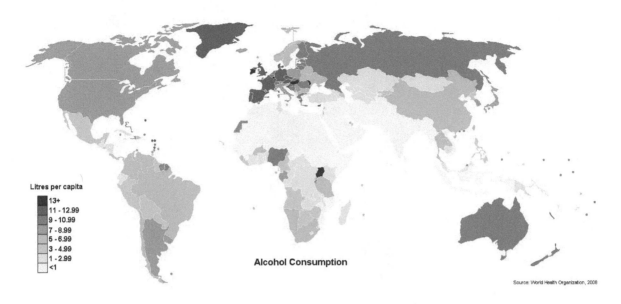

Litres per capita

13+
11 - 12.99
9 - 10.99
7 - 8.99
5 - 6.99
3 - 4.99
1 - 2.99
<1

Alcohol Consumption

Source: World Health Organization, 2008

FIGURE 3.3b. World map of per capita alcohol consumption.
Copyright © Sbw01f (CC BY-SA 3.0) at http://commons.wikimedia.org/wiki/File%3AAlcohol_consumption_per_capita_world_map.PNG.

Despite these changes, the Russian economy is still tethered to global oil prices, and corruption indices remain high. This can be seen in wealth accumulating with a few at the top, while Russia's *per capita* GDP (Gross Domestic Product) remains at about $14,000. Many Russians struggle economically and have limited political voice to persuade changes that might benefit them. This is especially true of Russia's ethnic regions in the south (see *Box 3A*). This has left many Russians disenfranchised or with sustained animosities and has limited, if not prevented, the growth of the middle class and a functional political federation.

THE INDEPENDENT CENTRAL ASIAN NATIONS

This family of nations occupies the rugged mountainous and steppe regions of the central Eurasian

FIGURE 3.3c. Pussy Riot: A feminist Russian punk rock band famous for staging anti-government protest concerts in random public spaces. They stand for human rights, LGBT rights, and view Putin as a dictator. Several of the members have been jailed for extended periods of time, in an attempt to silence them.
Copyright © Denis Bochkarev (CC BY-SA 3.0) at http://commons.wikimedia.org/wiki/File%3APussy_Riot_at_Lobnoye_Mesto_on_Red_Square_in_Moscow_-_Denis_Bochkarev.jpg.

BOX 3A CHECHNYA: CULTURE AND ECONOMY COLLIDE

FIGURE 3.3d. Diverse Ethnic Region of Caucasus: This region is replete with natural resources, like oil, but is also a complicated patchwork of ethnicities. Copyright © Pmx (CC BY-SA 3.0) at http://commons.wikimedia.org/wiki/File%3ACaucasus-ethnic_en.svg.

The southern Russian region of Chechnya lies in the northern Caucasus, between the Caspian and Black Seas. This mountainous realm has, for centuries, been culturally diverse, with a patchwork of ethnicities. The Chechens, a relatively small group within this region, largely converted to Islam during the early formation of the tsarist Russian empire in the eighteenth century. Rich in natural resources, specifically oil resources, the Soviets and later the Russians continually exploited the region's hydrocarbons to fuel the economy. Both the Soviets and the Russians regularly used military force to suppress independence movements, respond to acts of terror in Moscow, and disband radical Islamist factions. Adding to this frustration is that the wealth generated by Chechen oil is not reinvested locally, but is instead funneled to Moscow and investors. This has left Chechnya amongst the poorer oblasts (federal subjects) of the

Russian Federation. Several wars have been waged to keep the Chechens in line. The Second Chechen War (1999–2000) involved eighty thousand Russian troops sent to fight a small militia composed of boys and young men with little training and limited resources.

With an estimated two hundred billion barrels of oil, the Caucasus region and the Caspian Sea will continue to be a source of conflict during this century. Russia needs oil for its economy and seems unwilling and unlikely to ever consider allowing these ethnic groups, like the Chechens, to form independent nations.

FIGURE 3.3e. Chechen Cadets in 1999: Angered Chechens form a militia to fight the Russians in the *Second Chechen War (1999–2000)*. Copyright © Natalia Medvedeva (CC BY-SA 3.0) at http://commons.wikimedia.org/wiki/File%3ACadets_of_the_Ichkeria_Chechen_national_guard_1999.jpg.

landmass. Highly continental, this region is characterized by great distances superimposed over an inhospitable climate. Despite these physical limitations, these newly independent nations have some cultural similarities. The people have a shared nomadic background, similar customs, and histories, and have been touched to various degrees by Islam. As independent nations, they have equally struggled with the ghosts of their Soviet past as well as the growing pains of independence. Finally able to leverage their own resources (oil, gas, raw materials), several of them have made great strides to improve living conditions for themselves. Others, however, like Kazakhstan and Uzbekistan, are amongst the poorest nations in central Asia (*see Aral Sea Disaster in Case Study 4*).

The cities of the region are not well known to much of the world, but can provide an effective looking glass into their societies. Below are five (5) major cities of Central Asia:

- *Ashgabat, Turkmenistan:* The largest city (~one million residents) in Turkmenistan, Ashgabat sits in the Karakum Desert on the border with Iran. Being very dry, the city has long relied on Amu Darya river water, which is distributed to the city by the Garagum Canal. This diversion has contributed to the critical reduction of the Aral Sea, hundreds of miles to the north.
- *Dushanbe, Tajikistan:* With a population around seven hundred thousand, Dushanbe is the largest city in Tajikistan. The city has an unusually pleasant climate, compared to the other four, because its geography (valley orientation and mountain protection) gives it a Mediterranean-like microclimate. Hot and dry summers and cool (but not typically extreme), wet winters makes it feel like a city closer to an ocean in lower latitudes.
- *Tashkent, Uzbekistan:* Tashkent is the largest city in the Central Asian nations, boasting a population of more than two million. Located in the eastern realm of Uzbekistan, Tashkent's juxta-

FIGURE 3.3f. Map of Uzbekistan: Tashkent, located in the eastern edge of the country, sits at the crossroads of neighboring nations.
Copyright in the Public Domain.

position into the multinational border region of central Asia gives it a strategic importance, both historically (Silk Trade) and today (regional economy). To the north is the border of Kazakhstan, to the east is Kyrgyzstan, and to the south is Tajikistan (see *Figure 3.3f*).

- *Bishkek, Kyrgyzstan:* This Central Asian city of Kyrgyzstan is the youngest of the five. With a population of around nine hundred thousand, the city is alive with markets, a significant part of their highly localized economy (see *Figure 3.3g*).

- *Almaty, Kazakhstan:* Also referred to as Kazakhstan City (or the Garden City), this urban center of Kazakhstan is known for its scenic beauty. Once the capital, it is the commercial and cultural hearth of the country. It is also the financial hub of Central Asia, with a significant banking sector. Almaty is known for its colorful nightlife.

FIGURE 3.3g. Dordoy Bazaar near Bishkek, Kyrgyzstan. Copyright © Vmenkov (CC BY-SA 3.0) at http://commons.wikimedia.org/wiki/File%3AE7919-Dordoy-Bazaar-clothing.jpg.

CASE STUDY 3C

Russian Demographic Crisis

Following the end of the Soviet Union, the Russian population began to decline rapidly. The shift from a communist regime to an oligarchy heavy with corruption and cronyism shocked the freshly independent people into a new reality. Most Russians had limited resources, both under Soviet control and as independent citizens. However, the several services the USSR did provide (work, health care, housing) quickly disappeared, and many Russians faced uncertainties in life. This spiked social anxieties and resulted in a sharp decline in the birth rate (number of babies born per thousand) during the nineties.

These political changes and economic uncertainty also exacerbated social trends within Russian society. This includes an increase in alcohol consumption and alcoholism, drug abuse, high cultural tolerance for abortion and divorce, increases in suicide rates, and spikes in homicides and other violent crimes. Hard economic times and social problems also led to an increase in prostitution and the subsequent rise in venereal diseases like HIV. All of these factors played a role in a significant demographic shift within the nation.

Between 2008 and 2014, these demographics characterized Russia:
- Birth Rate: 11.87/1000 or 68th in world
- Total Fertility Rate (TFR): 1.61 (population decline)

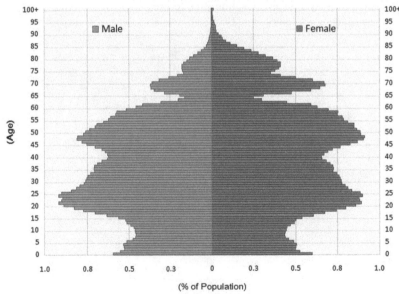

FIGURE 3.3h. Russian Population Pyramid: This graph reveals a downward trend in Russia population, with recent increases being partially attributed to ethnic groups with higher fertility rates.
Copyright © LokiiT (CC BY-SA 3.0) at http://commons.wikimedia.org/wiki/File%3APopulation_Pyramid_of_Russia_2009.PNG.

- Infant Mortality Rate: 7.08/1000
- Population Growth Rate or p = (births - deaths) + (immigrants - emigrants): −0.03, or the 200th worst in the world.
- Death rate: 13.1/1000
- Life expectancy: 71.6 (66.1 for males)

These statistics reveal a grim future for Russians. Their aging population (fifty-plus) is their largest demographic group, and with a lower-than-average life expectancy, they will leave the Russian population significantly smaller by about 2025.

To counter this trend, the Russians have tried to create incentives, both regionally and nationally. Regional incentives have been wide ranging and include offers to pay cash bonuses to couples, per baby. This has not had the desired effect, because the amount offered is often well under the total cost of prenatal care, childbirth, and childrearing. One town offered an SUV or car to any couple that had children. Again, this incentive did not have the desired effect.

Nationally, the Russian government used immigration to bolster population. This was not intended for outsiders to immigrate into Russian, but instead for Russians displaced by Soviet "collectivization" (the distribution of labor where needed). These Russians, who had been deployed and settled in countries like Romania, Poland, the Czech Republic, Ukraine, and so on, could return to Russia with ease. As of 2013, Russia had seen some trends that indicate an improvement in birth rates. The Russian economy had reached a level that supported a larger middle class, thereby raising more confidence in society. Russia's involvement in the Ukrainian civil unrest has, however, led to pinching sanctions, and how this will play out, demographically, is yet to be seen.

3.4 Russian Resources, the Environment, and Geopolitics

Russia's enormous size and physiographic features mean it has a wide range of natural resources and raw materials. Oil and gas resources are plentiful enough to make them an influence in the global calculus of energy consumption. Their raw materials (timber resources and mining, for example) likewise give Russia leverage in global markets and political arenas. Their size also means they are geographically adjacent to several major economic centers on Earth. These include:

- Eastern Europe/Scandinavia
- Eastern Asia (China, Mongolia)
- Northern North America (Arctic Region with Canada, US, and Greenland)
- Southwest Asia (border region with Iran, Iraq, and Turkey)

Because of their proximity to these four important economic regions, they play a role, both directly and indirectly, in economic relationships, security dynamics, and in regional and international alliance diplomacy. However, despite these resources, Russia lacks experience with global trade and does not have the trust of the international business community. Too long have they been the adversary and viewed by much of the world as a security threat, as opposed to a reliable business partner. Therefore, how they conduct themselves is often on terms they manipulate, because they remain external to most multinational agreements and supranational organizations.

FIGURE 3.4a. Heartland Theory (1904): John Mackinder theorized that Russia/Ukraine was a "historical pivot" region and the natural resources and central geography gave them, or whoever conquered it, a chance at world domination. Hitler was greatly influenced by this theory, which led to the largest military engagement in history, on the Eastern Front, during WWII.
Copyright in the Public Domain.

Mining and Minerals

Russia has a tremendous volume of raw materials, putting it in the top percentile in many categories. Minerals from Russia include aluminum, copper, nickel, diamonds, and iron ore. These minerals are extracted via massive mining operations. Because of this, several of Russia's mines rank amongst the largest in the world. However, the distance between mineral-rich regions and markets is often a major obstacle for Russians. Transportation infrastructure and harsh winters make operations difficult and delays constant.

Coal, Natural Gas, and Oil

Russia also has abundant energy fuels like coal, natural gas, and oil. The Caspian region is thought to have approximately two hundred billion barrels of oil resources, while Siberia and the Arctic realm are estimated to have one hundred billion. Russia's coal and oil resources are greatly needed to help fuel the growing economies of Eastern Europe and, potentially, China. Multibillion dollar contracts are under negotiation between Russia and China to construct and move thirty billion cubic meters of gas to China. Lowering prices and Russia's military support of eastern Ukraine have stalled these talks. If this agreement moves forward and the infrastructure is built, Russia could create a new arena of competition in the energy markets.

Despite the volume of resources and potential for lucrative energy agreements, Russia is still subject to global commodity prices set by external organizations like OPEC and market speculators. If fuel costs trend lower, Russian revenue reduces. In 2014–2015, for example, fuel costs reduced significantly from the years prior, thus inducing an economic problem for Russia. Additionally, Russia's involvement in the Ukrainian conflict has brought on further sanctions imposed by the West. These two factors alone have altered, and will continue to alter, Russia's economic trajectory.

FIGURE 3.4b. Yakutia, Russia: This remote federal district of Russia is used for its raw materials. Copyright © Staselnik (CC BY-SA 3.0) at http://commons.wikimedia.org/wiki/File%3AMirny_in_Yakutia.jpg.

FIGURE 3.4c. The "Friendship" Pipelines: These pipelines that cross Russia into Eastern Europe are the largest and longest in the world.
Copyright in the Public Domain.

3.5 Russian Power and the Future

It is difficult to identify how Russia will fit into the global economy and community of nations in the future. The region has plentiful resources to support and even grow their economy, but they lack political trust that may help lubricate economic partnerships. In short, they still behave in ways that make them a security wild card, which forces countries that could do business with Russia to side with those that stand against Russian aggressiveness. They have geographic proximity to major economic zones but remain committed to an assertive posture in their border regions. This fosters conflict with ethnic groups within the region while fanning the flames of civil unrest in nations outside their political space. They have a fascinating culture and a rich history but are suffering from social- and economic-induced demographic trends that will threaten their future, should they continue. These factors and many more make Russia an interesting study but confirm that they are hardly predictable.

PUTIN AND POWER: NEW NATION, OLD WAYS

Vladimir Putin was born in St. Petersburg (Leningrad), Russia in 1952. He was formerly a military officer (Lt. Colonel) in the KGB during the Soviet era. After the fall of the Soviet Union, Putin remained in positions of power by cleverly maintaining relationships with leadership and by adapting to a changing political and economic landscape in Russia. He moved to Moscow during the 1990s to serve on Yeltsin's staff and eventually ascended to Acting President when Yeltsin abruptly retired. He was able to win the presidency in 2000 and has served as both the second and fourth President of the Russian Federation. The Russian constitution limits office terms, so Putin has assumed the role of Prime Minister several times, while the Presidency went to others. Power, however, transferred with Putin. As Prime Minister, his administration dictated national policy, which has essentially kept him as head of state continually since 2000.

Putin is a particularly interesting politician because he both adapts well to change and asserts control in a way consistent with the Russian paradigm discussed in the last *Thematic Intersection*. He captainved reforms that led to more foreign investment and trade, but he has simultaneously silenced opposition and

FIGURE 3.5a. Prime Minister Putin and US President Obama: Outside Moscow in 2009.
Copyright in the Public Domain.

manipulated political processes to keep him in power, and he continues to challenge the West. He subscribes to the *modus operandi* of painting the Americans and Western Europeans as expansionists who must be dealt with sternly and even confrontationally. These actions have made Putin both lamented and respected. Many Russians view his leadership as strong, even if it costs them, while others fear challenging his human rights violations, corruption, and the shadowy governing style he carries with him from his Soviet KGB days.

UNDERSTANDING THE UKRAINIAN CONFLICT

From Russia's perspective, Crimea, the Donbas, and other eastern Ukrainian regions were formerly Russian, culturally, and are still viewed as an appendage of Mother Russia. The Ukraine was able to secure political independence after the Soviet Union dissolved in 1991. About 18% of Ukrainians consider themselves Russian; most of these live in the east, near the border.

The conflict within the Ukraine resulted from the nation's seeking membership in the European Union (EU). This was popular in the central and western regions of the Ukraine, but not in the east, which pushed for tighter political and economic bonds with Moscow. The result was an outbreak of civil unrest and even war. With the shooting down of Malaysian Airlines Flight 17 by Ukrainian "rebels," many questioned the quality and precision of the weaponry used. It raised many questions about Russian military involvement because the hardware used was beyond that which the rebels possessed. It was concluded that Putin was supporting the Ukrainian rebellion, which has been denied by his administration. This alleged Russian intervention was viewed by the West as an indirect act of aggression, and sanctions soon followed.

Beneath the confusion of this civil war and the downed commercial aircraft is some consistency with how the Russians have behaved historically. The Russians have long maintained that the West seeks to assert more political and economic control over Eastern Europeans and, perhaps, even the Russians. This is seen as a geographical threat to Russia (possible NATO military presence closer to Moscow) and as a political threat. Russia views American and Western European interloping in the region as an attempt

FIGURE 3.5b. Pro-Russian demonstration in Donetsk, Ukraine in 2004. Copyright © Andrew Butko (CC BY-SA 3.0) at http://commons.wikimedia.org/wiki/File%3A2014-03-09._%D0%9F%D1%80%D0%BE%D1%82%D0%B5%D1%81%D1%82%D1%8B_%D0%B2_%D0%94%D0%BE%D0%BD%D0%B5%D1%86%D0%BA%D0%B5_022.jpg.

to cultivate democracy and capitalism in the hearts and minds of Ukrainians and, by extension, Russians. Putin, then, is acting in a way consistent with the Soviets, the Tsarists, and even Ivan the Terrible, in that he seeks to protect Russia by being offensive beyond Russia's heartland. This behavior has not typically been easily understood by outsiders but perhaps makes perfect sense to Russians-hence his popularity.

THE BRICS: GAME CHANGING COOPERATION?

BRICS, as mentioned previously, is an acronym for Brazil, Russia, China, India, and South Africa. This community of nations exhibits characteristics of both *Core* nations and *Periphery* nations in several key ways, listed below:

- *High FDI and low labor costs:* These nations have created enough incentives and Special Economic Zones (SEZs)—and invested in enough infrastructure to produce and move products—to attract significant global business (manufacturing, services, etc.).
- *Strong GDP growth, low per capita GDP:* This means the nation is growing and prospering to some degree, but most people still live close or at poverty levels.
- *Corruption high, concessions high:* BRICS, especially Russia and Brazil, have high corruption indices, but have systems in place to protect industry and commercial activities.
- *Wealth generated is invested in foreign debt or stockpiling of foreign reserves:* This enables these nations to have leverage when negotiating with *Core* nations.

They achieved this status because they had a combination of factors that made them attractive to foreign investment, manufacturing, and related industries. The engines of globalization have come to rely on these nations because they produce many of the goods purchased in volume in large consumer markets. Russia, in particular, is not a lead manufacturer like China or a large provider of services like India. As mentioned previously, it provides many of the raw materials, minerals, and energy fuels. Their ability to accumulate wealth from these activities has led to the ability of Russia to effectively manage its debt ratios, as well as stockpiling foreign reserves. The crippling sanctions on Russia, as a response to supporting the rebellion in the Ukraine, has redefined, and will continue to redefine, the health of its economy.

BOX 3B BRICS CHALLENGE WESTERN CHANNELS OF DEVELOPMENT

Following the Second World War, the Bretton-Woods Conference determined that there must be money available for nations that seek to develop and join with a community of nations that trade with each other. This is theoretically a worthy investment because it not only helps a country restructure in a way that may fundamentally change the lives of its citizens (jobs, revenue, education, a growing middle class, etc.), but also fosters political alliances with nations that have enormous consumer markets (US, Western Europe). Therefore, the agencies that would eventually become the IMF and World Bank were set up as sources of development funding. However, by accepting this money from these funding sources, you are ultimately becoming dependent on the nations from where the money is loaned. If you are loaned money in US dollars, you are ultimately tethered to that economy. This is both good and perhaps a liability. If the US economy, for example, goes into recession, if currency devalues, or if interest rates change dramatically, it often becomes the problem of the lendee, too.

FIGURE 3.5c. BRICS Leaders: They are all members of G-20, but also meet at their own summits. Copyright © Roberto Stuckert Filho (CC BY-SA 3.0) at http://commons.wikimedia.org/wiki/ File%3ABRICS_heads_of_state_and_government_ hold_hands_ahead_of_the_2014_G-20_summit_in_ Brisbane%2C_Australia_(Agencia_Brasil).jpg.

The BRICS represent 40% of the world population and together are worth about $16 trillion (~20% of the global economy). They also collectively hold about $4 trillion in foreign reserves. They have set aside $100 billion in capital as a buffer for another global economic downturn. These factors make them appear more resilient and adaptable to fluctuations in the global economy. The BRICS know this and have devised a plan to create the **BRICS Bank**, or another way developing nations can seek financial aid to invest in their futures.

This move challenges the importance and relevance of western sources of capital. Often the World Bank and the IMF will require that "neoliberal" policies be implemented, thus ushering in a western form of capitalism, which then requires some form of democracy as a political framework. The BRICS, who themselves struggle with high corruption indices and are accused of human rights violations, may tend to ask fewer questions when lending money. Some might feel this will become a better option for newly developing nations seeking funding in the future.

CONCLUSION

Russia and the Central Asian nations literally occupy much of the largest terrestrial landmass on Earth. The region's size, however, has not necessarily facilitated their ascension in a globalized world or fostered political cooperation between its many important neighbors. Russia, in particular, has maintained a rather unusual relationship with its adjacent regions (Europe, China, Middle East) and other global powers because its historical fear of invasion has made it adopt a rather offensive, even imperialist, discourse to maintain and expand their interests far from the heartland. It has always been geographically gifted with resources, but has never really understood how to leverage them in global markets through strong trade agreements.

Russia's internal struggles have lasted for decades at a time, and their distrust of outsiders has never waned. Hitler, for example, was a viable military threat, and Russians made great sacrifices to thwart invasion. Millions died on both sides in the deadliest military engagement in the history of humanity. Russia's new perceived enemy is, in short, "Westernization." This threat is not necessarily a military one, but is perceived as a move by expansionist Westerners to assert more control over political and economic affairs in this region while influencing the people in the region to want these changes. This makes this region difficult to decipher. Will the Russians cooperate? Will there be more conflict? Perhaps the answer is to expect both and neither.

KEY TERMS

Eurasian landmass	Steppes	Russification
Polar easterly winds	USSR	Collectivization
Continentality	Bolshevik	Devolution
Taiga	Russian Revolution	BRICS
Tundra	Soviet Socialist Republics	

CLASS DISCUSSIONS

1. Discuss how Russia's geographic size has influenced its views about security and politics.
2. What led to the Bolshevik and Russian Revolution? Discuss how Lenin changed the political structure after the revolution. What did not change?
3. Describe the problems the Soviets had within the SSRs. Why did Moscow use "Russification?"
4. How did the Cold War lead to the collapse of the Soviet Union in the early nineties?
5. Discuss the contradictions of Russian society today. Be sure to address economic successes and political setbacks.

ADDITIONAL RESOURCES

CIA World Factbook Central Asia:

https://www.cia.gov/library/publications/the-world-factbook/wfbExt/region_cas.html

History.com Russia:

http://www.history.com/topics/russian-revolution and http://www.history.com/topics/cold-war/
    perestroika-and-glasnost

BRICS:

http://thebricspost.com/

BIBLIOGRAPHY

"Caspianreport: Russia's Demographic Crisis." YouTube. n.d. Web. https://www.youtube.com/
    watch?v=Y93ip0lMNJ8. 03 July 2015.

Central Intelligence Agency. The World Factbook. n.d. Web. https://www.cia.gov/library/publications/the-world-
    factbook/wfbExt/region_cas.html. Jan.–Feb. 2015.

Hogan, M. (1992) The End of the Cold War: Its Meaning and Implications. Cambridge.

"Putin's Nightmare: Do Population Trends Indicate a Dire Future for Russia?" N.p., n.d. Web. http://www.nation-
    alsecurityforum.org/newsletter/putins-nightmare-do-demographic-trends-indicate-a-dire-future-for-russia/.
    Jan.–Feb. 2014.

"Russian Revolution." History.com. A&E Television Networks, n.d. Web. http://www.history.com/topics/russian-
    revolution. Jan.–Feb. 2015

Ukraine and Russia: War, Not Peace. Economist. August 30, 2014. Vol. 412 Number 8902.

"Perestroika and Glasnost." History.com. A&E Television Networks, n.d. Web. http://www.history.com/topics/
    cold-war/perestroika-and-glasnost. Jan.–Feb. 2015.

"Vladimir Lenin (1870–1924)." BBC News. BBC, n.d. Web. http://www.bbc.co.uk/history/historic_figures/
    lenin_vladimir.shtml. 03 July 2015.

Whish-Wilson, P. (2002). The Aral Sea Environmental Health Crisis. Journal of Rural and Remote Environmental
    Health 1(2): 29–34.

CHAPTER 4

North Africa/Southwest Asia

Key Themes:

Religion, Politics, Economics, Security

List of nations discussed:

- Morocco
- Algeria
- Tunisia
- Libya
- Egypt
- Saudi Arabia
- Sudan and other Saharan nations
- Yemen
- Oman
- United Arab Emirates
- Qatar
- Bahrain
- Kuwait
- Jordan
- Syria
- Palestine
- Lebanon
- Iraq
- Iran
- Afghanistan

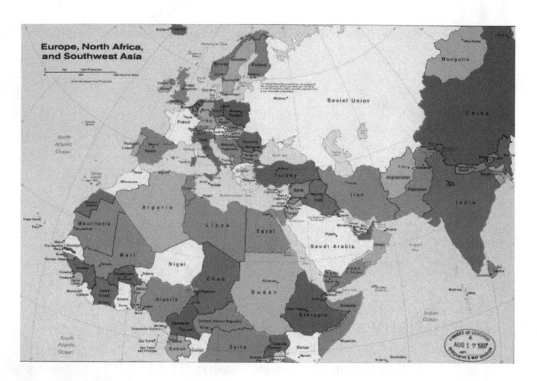

FIGURE 4.0a. North Africa and Southwest Asia extends from Mauritania in western Africa to Afghanistan, on the border of South Asia.
Copyright in the Public Domain.

4.1 Regional Overview

The nations of North Africa and Southwest Asia (NA/SWA), though situated on different continents, together have much in common. This *designation as a region* can be attributed to a number of factors, which include:

- Desert
- Hearths of Ancient Civilizations/Agriculture
- Home to the "Abrahamic" Religions
- Islamic Landscape
- Oil/Petroleum

When examining this region, it becomes clear that the nations within it are either directly or indirectly influenced by all of these attributes. However, beyond these commonalities are also differences. For example, the region may be characterized by a predominantly Muslim population, but is also home to the Jewish state of Israel, located right in the middle of it all. The region has some of the largest oil producers and oil reserves in the world, but not all countries are beneficiaries of its profits. Some nations have deep economic and political ties with the West, while others are embroiled in ongoing conflicts with western nations. In the end, this family of nations has enough in common for geographers to justify its designation as a *region*.

At the same time, especially when examining the complicated landscape of conflicts and cooperation brought on by both internal and external factors to the region, its designation comes more into question.

PHYSICAL GEOGRAPHY OF NA/SWA

Desert

If there is one common physical geographical feature that defines this realm, it would be deserts. A desert is a dry and

FIGURE 4.1a. Sahara Desert of Libya. Copyright © Luca Galuzzi (CC BY-SA 2.5) at http://commons.wikimedia.org/wiki/File%3ALibya_5391_Ubari_Lakes_Luca_Galuzzi_2007.jpg.

often barren region that has become so from either the influence of high pressure, rain shadow, lack of proximity to a large body of water, or a combination of the three. It is a climate type that is not necessarily determined by temperature, but by aridity. In *Figure 4.1b*, the Köppen Climate map shows much of the region as "desert" climates. This is because of both high pressure and lack of proximity to a large body of water.

In North Africa, the massive *Sahara Desert* formed over millennia from a strong combination of high pressure in summer and low pressure (drawing in the dry winds from Asia) during the winter. On the eastern

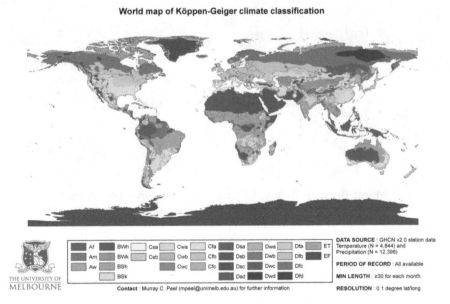

FIGURE 4.1b. NA/SWA Climates: Most of North Africa falls within the BWh Köppen classification, whereas Southwest Asia is more a mix between BWh, BWk, and "Mediterranean" climate type of Csa.
Copyright © M.C. Peel, B.L. Finlayson, and T.A. McMahon (CC BY-SA 3.0) at http://commons.wikimedia.org/wiki/File%3AKöppen_World_Map_(retouched_version).png.

side of this region, Turkey, much of Syria, Northern Iraq and Iran, and Afghanistan are more a steppe desert climate (BWk) and seasonally cold desert with light precipitation (BSk), as seen in *Figure 4.1b*.

Rivers and Water

The role of water in this region cannot be underestimated. The rivers provide a priceless resource of immeasurable importance, as well as scenic landscapes (see *Figure 4.1a.*). Unlike wetter regions in the world, NA/SWA has very limited water resources. Human activity, then, revolves around this resource in much of the realm. This is true of ancient times (Egyptians and Mesopotamians) as well as today.

FIGURE 4.1c. The Murat River in Turkey. This area is a seasonal desert that is both cold and semi-arid, unlike the hot, extremely arid deserts found in the Southwest and North Africa.
Copyright © EvgenyGenkin (CC BY-SA 3.0) at http://commons.wikimedia.org/wiki/File%3AMurat_05.jpg.

CASE STUDY 4A

Physiologic Population Density in Egypt: Understanding Spatial Patterns of Settlement in North Africa

When observing a common satellite image of Egypt, most of the land area would clearly be a giant tan desert. Cutting through this formidable landscape is a thin green line, extending from the south to the north. At the very northern tip, that line becomes a fan that suddenly ends in the Mediterranean Sea. This is the famous Nile River and the Nile Delta (See Figure 4.1d)

The Nile River is the lifeblood of Egypt, in that it has defined human settlement patterns and determined many of the activities of Egypt since ancient times. What you cannot see in Figure 4.1d is where most Egyptians live. If you could pan in closer, you would find that most Egyptians live either near the banks of the Nile or within the Nile Delta region. Why? Water.

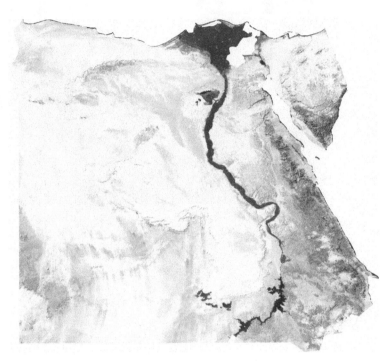

FIGURE 4.1d. Egypt from Space.
Copyright in the Public Domain.

To better understand human settlement patterns in arid environments, demographers rely on a tool called physiologic population density, defined as the total population divided into arable land. For example:

- Egypt Total Land Area: Approximately 1,000,000 sq/km
- Egypt's arable land: 2.81%
- Arable portion of total land area: ~28,100 sq/km of arable land
- Egypt's population: ~87 million
- Physiologic Population Density: 87 million/28,100 = ~3100 people per sq/km.

This is amongst the highest physiologic densities in the world. By comparison, the United States has a physiologic population density of about 156 people per sq/km. This is important to understand, because much of this region exhibits population settlement patterns like Egypt. It reveals how water resources have likely been a major source of conflict and cooperation between tribes, states, and even civilizations.

FIGURE 4.1e. The Nile River of Egypt.
Copyright © Jerzy Strzelecki (CC BY-SA 3.0) at http://commons.wikimedia.org/wiki/File%3ANile03(js).jpg.

FIGURE 4.1f. The Nile: Whether in the narrowest of spaces of the deep desert Nile or the expansive Nile River Delta, you can find human activity. Cairo, one of the largest cities on Earth, is situated within the Nile River Delta region. Beyond the life-providing comfort of the Nile is desert. There is very little settlement in the deep desert.
Copyright © Jawed (CC BY-SA 3.0) at http://commons.wikimedia.org/wiki/File%3ACairo_Nile_River.jpg.

The region's major rivers include the Nile River, the Tigris–Euphrates Rivers, and the River Jordan. The *Nile River* is the longest river in the world. It flows about 4,200 miles from south to north, passing through eleven countries. It deltas in the Mediterranean Sea and has been an important feature of life in North Africa since the ancient Egyptians. The Nile River provides fertile soils and supports robust agricultural activities in Egypt. This has sustained life on its banks for millennia. Occasionally, the Nile has been known to flood severely. Historical accounts have indicated a 25–35 foot rise in water levels during peak flood events. This is both devastating and an advantage. Although floods can devastate lives and crops, the rich sediments deposited from flood events promise a continuation of productive agriculture in the future.

The *Tigris–Euphrates Rivers* are often considered a single river complex, despite the fact that they are two distinct rivers. The Tigris River is about 1,150 miles long, whereas the Euphrates is about 1,700 miles in length. It is considered a river complex because of their proximity to each other and because they, together, form a larger ecoregion. Early civilizations that settled the land area between the two did so because of the soils and resources the lands in between them provided. Both rivers have sources in the

FIGURE 4.1g. The Nile River: The longest river in the world. Copyright © Hel-hama (CC BY-SA 3.0) at http://commons.wikimedia.org/wiki/File%3ARiver_Nile_map.svg.

Taurus Mountains of Turkey and flow down (variably) through Syria, Iraq, Iran, and Kuwait to delta in the Persian Gulf. The rich river soils and climate have made this region one of the most agriculturally productive in Asia.

The *River Jordan* is the shortest and smallest of the highlighted rivers of the region. Its source is high up in the Golan Heights of Israeli-controlled Syria (politics vary), and it flows south 156 miles to

FIGURE 4.1h. The confluence of the Tigris and Euphrates: The Marsh Arabs are located in Southern Iraq. Copyright in the Public Domain.

the Dead Sea. Although this river has been an important source of water, it is also highly significant in cultural ways. In Judaism, this river has great significance because the ancient Israelis crossed the River Jordan into the "promised land." For Christians, this river has great significance because Jesus was from Galilee (a region around the River Jordan), and he was baptized by John the Baptist in the River Jordan.

Ancient Origins: Agriculture and Civilization

The ancient civilizations from this region are well known to the world. However, not all the influential ancient civilizations are from this region. The *ancient Egyptians* were certainly a regional civilization and evolved and ruled in various eras for millennia. This civilization is amongst the most famous and well known, and is commonly taught in grade school curriculums (see *Figure 4.1i*).

Mesopotamians, including Babylonians, Assyrians, and later the Parthians and Persians, were also regional ancient cultures. Babylon was a well-known city in its day and home to the famed Hanging Gardens of Babylon. Along with the Great Pyramids of Egypt, these gardens were one of the *Seven Wonders of the Ancient World*. Perhaps more important is the agriculture that emerged from this *Fertile Crescent* region. As discussed in Chapter 1, the agricultural practices and crops grown there not only diffused outward to much of the Eurasian realm, but the languages, Bronze Age technology, and social systems did as well.

External to the region, but very influential, were the Greeks and Romans. The *Hellenistic Period* followed Alexander the Great's conquests. Not only did he conquer much of this region during the 330s BCE, he also maintained them by setting up cities and administrations to govern them. After his death, his generals divided up his vast territories, continuing the Hellenistic era for a while. The Greeks left both a cultural and architectural imprint on the region. Alexander was famous for having cities built in his honor (or perhaps changing an existing city's name). Alexandria, Egypt is the most recognized, and was home to the *Library of Alexandria*. This was discussed early in Chapter 1 because of Eratosthenes (chief librarian), who is credited as the father of geography.

FIGURE 4.1i. Pyramids at Giza, Egypt. Built during the Old and Middle Kingdoms (~2630 to 2611BCE), these structures were essentially built as elaborate tombs for Pharaohs and their companions.
Copyright © Hamish2k (CC BY-SA 3.0) at http://commons.wikimedia.org/wiki/File%3AEgypt.Giza.Sphinx.02.jpg.]

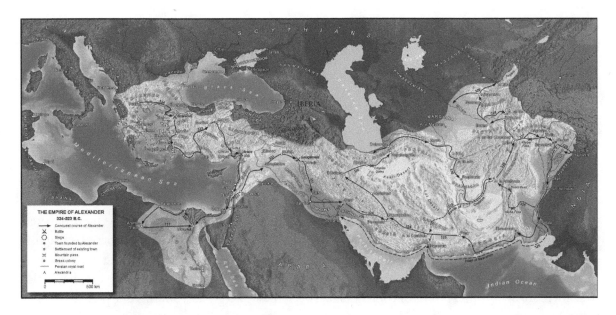

FIGURE 4.1j. Alexander the Great: Much of Southwest Asia and Egypt were conquered by the Greeks, under Alexander the Great. His occupation and later the division of the empire into territories ruled by his former generals, continued the occupation and became known as the Hellenistic Period. Copyright © Captain Blood (CC BY-SA 3.0) at http://commons.wikimedia.org/wiki/File%3AMacedonEmpire.jpg.

The *Roman Empire*, a European power, conquered and occupied most of North Africa and Southwest Asia, extending from the about the third century BCE (with the Roman defeat of Carthage) until the fourth century CE. Although they reigned longer, the Romans ruled with a heavy hand, guided by Rome but executed by a complex system of laws, local governors, and their lethal military when needed. This harsh rule led to a number of revolts and events that would fill history books. An example might be the defeat of Roman general-turned-traitor Mark Antony and Egyptian Pharaoh Cleopatra by Octavian (Augustus Caesar) at the Battle of Actium. Another would be the Roman occupation of Judea at the time of Jesus Christ and his prosecution and crucifixion under Roman governor Pontius Pilate. Rome eventually fell, and the eastern Byzantine Empire could not maintain control over this region after the sixth century CE. Nonetheless, the influence of centuries of rule can still be found today.

Abrahamic Religions

This region is home to the three Abrahamic religions, which include *Judaism*, *Christianity*, and *Islam*. The reason Abraham is viewed as a common thread amongst these faiths depends on which faith is asked. Although they all view Abraham as a beginning point, the context changes amongst religions. In Judaism, Abraham is viewed as the "first Jew," and all Jews born are descendants of Abraham. Christians view Abraham as a biblical figure, but put Jesus Christ at the center of their faith. Islam perhaps highlights the role of Abraham in its faith more prominently than the other two, but not in a way in which he is viewed as a "father" of their faith. Instead, Islam views Abraham as the first in a chain of prophets that led to their

Prophet Muhammad. Because all of these faiths are monotheistic (the worship of a single God) and share a common figure in Abraham, they are called "Abrahamic religions."

ISLAM

Islam, by far, is the most populous and representative religion in this region. Most nations within NA/SWA are Muslim nations. This requires a deeper examination, because not all these nations are united under their religion. Like Christianity and other major religions, there are divisions that ultimately define the region and the relationship between Muslims.

To understand this, it is important to briefly look at the history of Islam and how it diffused. When the Prophet Muhammad died, there was a debate over who would become the *caliph*, or successor. Some of his followers felt his successor should be a member of his family, while others felt his most devoted follower should lead. This debate is the inception point of a division within Islam between Sunnis and Shi'ites. Sunnis, the majority of Muslims, emerged from the camp that believed the most devoted should become *caliph*, whereas the Shi'ites (or Shia Islam) were those who followed the Prophet's relative. There are many other points of contention between these two groups, but this one perhaps defines them the most.

As Islam diffused and expanded, the conquering Muslim armies imported their version of faith. Spatially, more areas were settled by Sunnis. However, some key areas were Shi'ite. An example of this would be the Persian realm, which would become Iran and parts of Iraq, amongst others (see *Figure 4.1k*). These regions and their affiliation to either Sunni or Shia Islam allow a fundamental spatial understanding of the conflicts that characterize the region today.

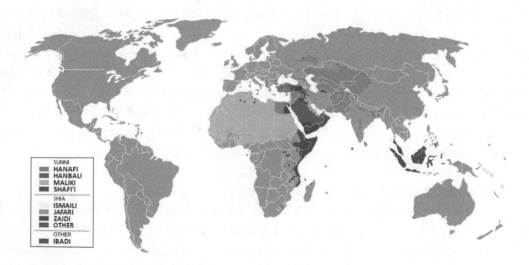

FIGURE 4.1k. Map of Fiqh Law in Islam: Whereas Sharia is the divine law, Fiqh law is how Sharia is interpreted by people. This differs throughout the Muslim regions and even within the subgroups of Islam. This map, then, better reveals both Sunni and Shia regions, as well as subdivisions of Fiqh.
Copyright © Ghibar (CC BY-SA 1.0) at http://commons.wikimedia.org/wiki/File%3AMadhhab_Map_(Divisions_of_Islam).png.

Diffusion of Islam

Islam diffused rapidly, both under the original campaigns of Muhammad and his succeeding *caliphs* (between 632–750 CE) and under the powerful Ottoman Turks (between about 1000–1700 CE). By the end of these periods of expansion, people of Islamic faith stretched from Western Africa and Spain to India and Indonesia and as far north as Yugoslavia and the Caucasus. Much of the region's expansion was culturally Arabic, which may explain the common use of Arabic (a *Semitic language)* in many North African nations as well as in Southwest nations like Jordan, Palestine, Syria, and Iraq. Farsi (non-Semitic) is spoken in the Persian realm, which is now Iran and most of Afghanistan. Although the Ottoman Turks represented the most powerful Islamic *caliphate* known, their general tolerance and system of administration was more important to them than collectivizing and uniting under their culture and language. This may explain why Turkish is not more commonly spoken by Muslims worldwide.

Although the period(s) of Islamic expansion were measurably successful, they eventually stopped. This could be attributed to several factors, but perhaps most important amongst them was European colonialism and the powerful military arm that supported colonial expansion. Europeans would leverage their navies to secure ports and sea routes, while armies would thwart the southbound expansion of Islam into Sub-Saharan Africa and other regions. The Europeans would also begin to colonize whole regions within NA/SWA. For example, between the French and the British, most of North Africa, coastal Arabia, and Palestine through Syria were essentially occupied by the two for decades. This colonial presence will also be an important part of understanding the dynamics of this region today.

4.2 External Influences

Perhaps no other region on Earth has received as much attention from the media, and the watchful eye of the western world, during the last several years as North Africa and Southwest Asia. The problem is that the media often focuses on a single issue and then reports about it in a way that captures the attention of the viewer or reader while failing to provide the much-needed context. At the same time, many westerners have a limited knowledge of this region, but have strong perceptions or biases about terrorism, oil, Islam, or Israel that may get in the way of a deeper understanding. This chapter will provide the various influences, both internal and external, that may help construct a broader perception of the region and a framework for understanding changes that are surely to come.

Although it would seem logical to begin with internal factors, this textbook will first examine external influences, including and since European colonialism. The reason for this is because external influences have helped to shape or exacerbate interregional relationships, which are themselves complicated by interregional conflicts. The *four (4) external influences* are:

- European Colonial Interloping and Alliances
- Oil and other Economic Interests
- Israel and the Creation and Support of a Jewish State
- War and Continued Western Military Action in Region

FIGURE 4.2a. The French arrive in Algiers, in 1857, to establish a North African colony.
Copyright in the Public Domain.

EUROPEAN COLONIAL INTERLOPING AND ALLIANCES

Like many other regions in the world, much of North Africa and Southwest Asia were occupied by European colonial powers. Between the British, French, and Italians, the political landscapes and alliance dynamics of the region were largely influenced by these foreign powers. Europeans, for example, helped to define the region through the creation and international recognition of political borders. These political borders were drawn around cultural or ethnic groups (or resources), thus promoting a western nation-state system. Remember, the "nation-state" is a European concept that diffused around the world over centuries of colonial expansion. These borders, historically, were typically not configured in a way that resulted from consensus amongst natives, but in ways that created advantages for Europeans. This "external influence," then, is important to understand.

One reason for political borders was to distinguish political space from one European colony or colonial occupation to another. For example, the border between Egypt and Libya would reflect an agreement between the British and Italians more than between the Libyans and Egyptians (or Bedouins, for that matter).

Although this may not seem important on the surface, it likely disrupted tribal territories and how internal groups divided space. Part of occupying these countries was dealing with political boundaries superimposed over tribal territories and then dealing with the issues that resulted.

Likewise, European powers often had conflicts with each other, and those problems would often spill over into colonial regions. For example, during the Great War (World War I), the Germans allied with the Ottoman Turks against Britain and its allies. The Turks had railroad lines extending deep into the Arabian Peninsula, which threatened British colonial territories in Palestine, Jordan, and Egypt, not to mention the economically vital Suez Canal. To combat this, the British sent one of their officers who was educated in Arabic language

FIGURE 4.2b. King Faisal of Arabia with British officers (including T.E. Lawrence standing third from the right) and others at a victory celebration in France, after the Great War. This alliance during the war helped to form an Anglo-Arab alliance that continues to this day. Copyright in the Public Domain.

and culture to persuade the patchwork of Arab tribes to unite and ally with Britain. This officer was young, charismatic Lieutenant T.E. Lawrence, who would later become known as "Lawrence of Arabia."

This campaign by the British successfully forged a regional relationship between the Arabs and British that would evolve into an alliance that would include the Americans to this day. This can be seen in oil-based economic relationships and political cooperation. Although this may be viewed as advantageous, especially through an economic lens, it has fostered an uneven economic landscape within the region and alliances with the West that divide countries politically.

OIL AND OTHER ECONOMIC INTERESTS

The British colonial occupation of both Egypt and Palestine came with some economic advantages. One was the Suez Canal. The Suez Canal is a 102-mile-long, human-constructed waterway connecting the Mediterranean Sea to the Red Sea in the south. Because ships do not have to go around the Horn of Africa, this passage reduces the distance travelled between Europe and South Asia by about four thousand miles. Though originally some form of ancient canal, it was later a European construction project, mainly under the French. It took years to construct and more years to fully operationalize, but was completed in 1869. Because the British occupied this part of the region, they considered the canal a strategic asset and protected it accordingly. This protection stretched through two World Wars and, though the Egyptians officially manage its security, its economic importance and proximity to unstable regimes and radical Islamist factions means it has remained under the watchful eyes of both the British and US Navies.

FIGURE 4.2c. American and British naval ships have been, and continue to be, present in this region for decades. This presence is a form of unofficial security in the region. Copyright in the Public Domain.

By far the most significant economic asset of NA/SWA is oil. The British first recognized their vast oil deposits and quickly took steps to ensure access to them. As industrialization advanced in Europe and North America, this regional resource was viewed as critically important to sustaining and continuing industrial activities, enabling greater mobility in Western society and global trade. It could be argued that the Anglo-Arab alliance that formed during the Great War laid the bedrock for economic and political relationships built around oil to this day.

High energy demand over the past hundred years has resulted in a global industry. Because NA/SWA provided much of the oil resources, it would form an international cartel in 1960 to better manage and distribute this resource for global markets. This cartel was **OPEC**, or the *Organization of Petroleum Exporting Countries*. These countries include Algeria, Iran, Iraq, Kuwait, Qatar, Saudi Arabia, and the United Arab Emirates (as well as others outside the region). The objectives of OPEC include the following:

- Coordinate policies
- Ensure a steady supply to markets
- Ensure fair profits for producers
- A fair capital return for those who invest

What this agreement essentially did was empower OPEC to set the "wholesale" cost of oil, or price per barrel. Domestic oil companies were quickly established to facilitate these agreements, and international teams of engineers, geologists, and administrators were deployed to these countries to help develop an enormous infrastructure in the region to extract, refine, and ship oil around the world.

The problem with this dynamic is that it directly linked regional oil production to Western consumer markets. As a result, not only did the producing nations become very wealthy with the steady inflow of western capital, the Western powers also had a vested interest in regional stability. This created an incentive to maintain a strong military presence in the area and nurture political cooperation with producing nations. Perhaps not surprisingly, this both worked and failed. Western powers maintain strong and stable ties to the Saudis, Emiratis, and other oil-producing nations while mismanaging relationships with Iraq and Iran (as discussed in Chapter 2).

Western influences caused a cultural backlash that spread into other countries following the *Iranian Revolution* and the ousting of the Shah in 1979. This fundamentally altered the relationship between the United States and OPEC because some nations began to view the US as antithetical to their belief systems, a threat to their culture, and even a security threat. Likewise, Western powers, especially the US, sought to punish these nations with crippling economic sanctions, severed political ties, and even war (Iraq) or the threat of military action (Iran). Therefore, a Western presence in the region has created a broad spectrum of conflicts.

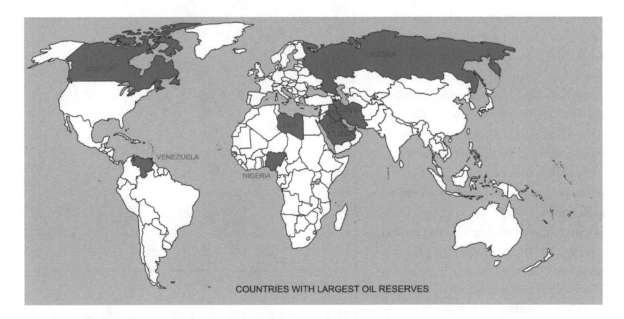

FIGURE 4.2d. NA/SWA is both home to the world's largest oil reserves, but is a top oil producer, as well. This makes the region important to industrial nations and a facilitator of globalization.
Copyright © Roke~commonswiki () at http://commons.wikimedia.org/wiki/File:Top_ten_largest_oil_reserves_by_country.GIF .

ISRAEL: THE CREATION & WESTERN SUPPORT OF A JEWISH STATE

Although the Jewish people have occupied lands in this region for millennia, they have not always had a political state of their own. During the British colonial occupation of Palestine and Jerusalem, it was identified that the cultural and religious tensions between the Arab Palestinians (Muslims) and the local Jewish population was strained and inevitably incendiary in nature. It is important to point out that the Arab Palestinians have also occupied this region since the *Crusades*, and likewise have deep ties to the land.

Beginning in the 1920s, the British drafted the *British Mandate for Palestine*, which determined territories for both Arab Palestinians and the Jewish population. This not only included space for each, but also supported multicultural access to Jerusalem because it was a deeply spiritual and historical site for several groups. As tensions between the two continued, the United Nations moved to create a Jewish state of Israel to take effect in 1948. This led to a war, because the political support for a Jewish state was generally viewed as an outrageous move by Western powers to favor one people over another. This was indeed the case, and the new, heavily armed and supported Israeli military, backed by Western powers, overwhelmed the Arab coalition, resulting in Armistices (1949, 1950) that created new space for Arab Palestinians.

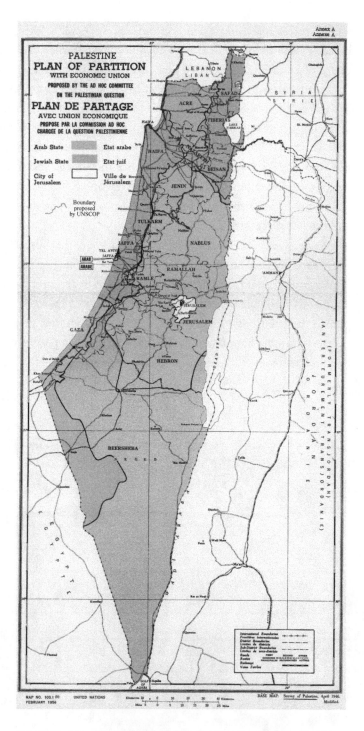

FIGURE 4.2e. This 1947 map of the Palestinian Partition reflected both the original British Mandate and the soon-to-be creation of the Jewish State of Israel, a year later. Copyright in the Public Domain.

The space created for Arab Palestinians remains a major source of tension and conflict to this day. *Three (3) Israeli-occupied or semicontrolled Arab Palestinian areas* are:

- *West Bank:* A landlocked region situated in the eastern half of Israel, bordering the Dead Sea. More than two million Arab Palestinians live there. Because it is essentially Israeli-occupied, about five hundred thousand Israeli Jews also live there.

- Gaza Strip: A small, 6-by-32-mile zone against the Mediterranean Sea. Wedged between Israel and Egypt, Gaza was created as a "nonmember" observer state by the United Nations for Arab Palestinians and some Bedouins. Currently, there are just under two million inhabitants, but that number is growing at a fast pace. Israel allowed some degree of political self-governance, which led to the formation of the Palestinian Authority. However, as tensions grew in the region and more Islamist groups arose, Hamas (a Palestinian Islamist organization related to the Muslim Brotherhood of Egypt) assumed political power for a while. Now, Gaza is a controlled by a difficult-to-define combination between PA and Hamas. The United States and Israel do not recognize any government of Gaza. (See *Figure 4.2f.*)

- *Golan Heights:* The Golan Heights is a mountainous region wedged between Lebanon, Israel, Syria, and Jordan. Because it was claimed by both Syria and Israel, it was fought over in the Six-Day War of 1967. Israel was victorious and justified the conflict and settlement as security necessity to pad them from hostile neighbors. They extended their laws over the land, which was both unpopular with the United Nations and caused internal strife in Syria. Although it is an Israeli-occupied region, there are still Arab Syrians (Circassians) living there.

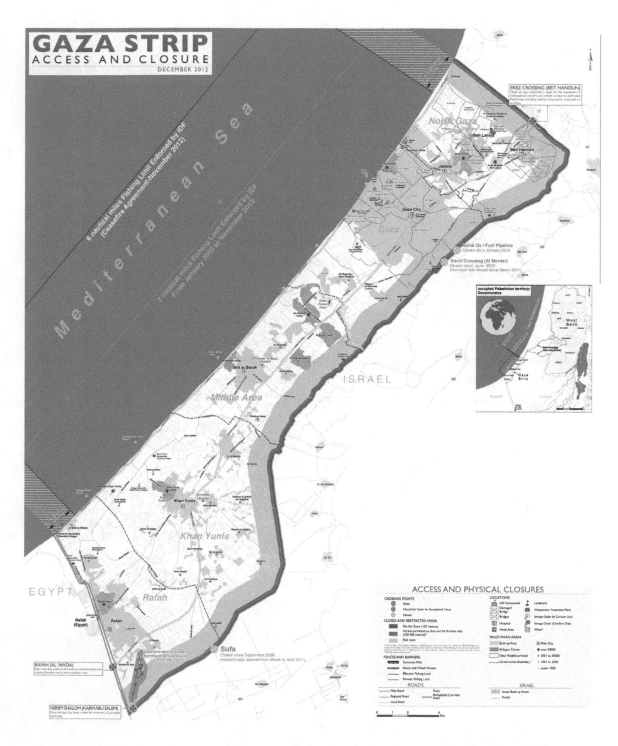

FIGURE 4.2f. The Gaza Closure resulted from violent exchanges between Israelis and Palestinians. Copyright © Wickey-nl (CC BY 3.0) at http://commons.wikimedia.org/wiki/File%3AGaza_closure_December_2012.jpg.

THEMATIC INTERSECTION 4A

Western Support of Israel: a Cycle of Oil and Faith

Themes: Cultural/Economic

Since the creation of the Jewish state of Israel in the late 1940s, Western nations have openly pledged their support. At the core of this support is an intrinsic connection to a region that is widely viewed as the epicenter of Western faith. This support is cultural in origin. Both the Old and New Testaments illuminate the importance of this ancient landscape. The Bible is said to have been authored by Jesus's Apostles, who chronicled his life, teachings, death, and resurrection—all of which occurred in the region that would become modern Israel. Additionally, the United States has positioned itself as an unconditional friend to Israel. This may also be because of the large Jewish community that has thrived in America. Although this Western support of Israel is widely accepted thousands of miles away, it has amplified the tensions between the Jewish state and Muslim nations around them within the region.

The economic theme is related to the high Western demand for oil. Oil is both produced and held in reserve in this region by Muslim OPEC nations. These OPEC nations are key suppliers of global oil, and the United States, until recently, has been their biggest customer. As discussed earlier in this chapter, there is a great tension between the Islamic world and Israel for many reasons (intrinsic connection to region, treatment of Arab Palestinians, war, etc.). However, this mix of Western relationships creates some conflict. Superimposed over the cultural and political support of Israel is an important economic relationship between nations that hate Israel. This is roughly how this plays out:

1. Western nations buy oil from Muslim OPEC nations.
2. Western nations use that oil in military hardware (tanks, war planes, armored transports, etc.).
3. Israel then acquires this military hardware from the West and uses it against Muslim nations in acts of aggression, defense, or war.
4. Muslim nations, including OPEC nations, hate Israel more for leveraging their military strength and resent Western nations more for supporting—even facilitating—this behavior.

An example of the "conflict" that arose from this dynamic is the oil embargo of 1973. Known as the "first oil shock," the Arab OPEC nations elected to punish the West (including the United States) for supporting Israel with arms to fight in the Yom Kippur War. This was part of an ongoing conflict that had raged between Muslim countries (Egypt, Syria) and Israel since the creation of the Jewish state. The Israelis were victorious, in part because they used advanced weaponry and delivery systems provided by the West. Thus, conflict begat conflict, in that the interregional issues between Israel and its Muslim neighbors likewise fostered external resentment and eventual conflict with the West.

FIGURE 4.2g. American-supplied Israeli tank in Golan Heights, 1973.
Copyright in the Public Domain.

It is important to reiterate that external tensions are not exclusively "external." They have also aggravated or fostered cooperation between actors within the region. This is precisely why understanding NA/SWA is often difficult and its issues are easily manipulated by media. External factors have the potential to exacerbate internal conflicts, as this textbook will reveal when examining Islamic extremism.

WAR AND CONTINUED WESTERN MILITARY ACTION

Western military action within the region has never been received well by the community of Muslim nations. Whether these actions are justified or not, Western military operations related to war, continued occupation, or even drone strikes are typically unpopular and foster resentment, if not animosity, towards the United States. Since 9/11, the US and allies have been involved in both direct military campaigns in Iraq and Afghanistan and in more elusive operations related to the "war on terror." Even though these wars are largely over, the United States continues to target potential terrorists and terrorist camps in Yemen, Pakistan, and other locations. The legality of these drone strikes is debatable, and though they often successfully neutralize terrorists, they also kill innocent bystanders, US citizens, and violate the sovereign airspace of nations to do it. This has led to heightened tensions between the US and state governments, and has likely created a generation of people who view the US as evil.

4.3 Internal Agitators

The region of North Africa and Southwest Asia (NA/SWA) has and continues to deal with key internal issues. Although many of these problems are historical, even ancient, in origin, others emerged from changes in regional political and economic dynamics over the course of more recent history. The four (4) key internal agitators are:

- Sunni/Shi'ite Strife
- Economic Disparities from Oil
- Totalitarian Regimes
- The Rise of Islamic Extremism

Although not exclusively internal issues, as recently discussed, these four agitators have measurably and visibly redefined the region.

FIGURE 4.3a. Thousands protest in Yemen, 2011.
Copyright © Email4mobile (CC BY-SA 3.0) at http://commons.wikimedia.org/wiki/File%3AYemeni_Protests_4-Apr-2011_P01.JPG .

SUNNI/SHIA STRIFE: IN A CONTEMPORARY CONTEXT

There have already been discussions about the origin of the religious division within Islam. This section will instead illuminate how this intrafaith tension has shaped the region in ways that have contributed to patterns we see evolving today. First, it is important to reiterate how Iran is an Islamic republic with a majority Shia population. This has made Iran both a feared and lamented nation within the broader community of nations with Sunni-majority populations. For example, states like Saudi Arabia, Turkey, UAE, and Egypt all view Iran as a regional security threat and probably as a source of revenue for terrorism and coercion in certain areas.

The concern that Iran is a security threat stems from its alleged evolving nuclear capabilities. Whether Iran actually has the potential to weaponize its nuclear material has yet to be determined. However, because they are Shia, this uncertainty has led many neighbors to maintain ready militaries and strong political alliances with the United States. The claims that Iran supports terrorism are linked to the imams funding *Hezbollah*, a Shia Islamist political/militant group based in Lebanon. *Hezbollah* has not only been accused of grievous crimes, but it also has and continues to confront Israel, support the Ba'athist regime in Syria, and militarize in wartime. These concerns have fostered intraregional animosity towards Iran, both from Israel and Sunni nations, while drawing the attention of outsiders like the United States, allies, and even the United Nations.

More specifically, the minority *Ba'ath* party of Syria and the minority Shia leadership in Iraq have complicated the intrafaith dynamics of the region, especially in Southwest Asia. The Assad regime in Syria is now in its second generation and has been engaged in violent and seemingly unending civil conflict with its Sunni majority. Iran, via *Hezbollah*, has potentially supported the Assad regime throughout this period. The Shia government of Iraq was put into place by exiting American forces. The problem with this is the majority of Iraqis are Sunni, and the Shia regime has been accused of underserving this majority population, especially in the more tribal, rural areas. This will later help explain the rise of the self-proclaimed "Islamic State," or ISIS.

OIL DISPARITIES

The discovery and extraction of oil resources has made some nations extraordinarily wealthy. This wealth has elevated regions once characterized as tribal desert territories (Bedouin) into world-class epicenters of privilege. *Countries that have directly benefited from oil revenue* by sharing that wealth with its citizens are:

- Saudi Arabia
- United Arab Emirates (UAE)
- Kuwait
- Qatar
- Bahrain

These oil-wealthy nations tend to have significantly higher-than-average *per capita* GDP, capital investment in infrastructure, commercial endeavors, and leisurely activities. In fact, these nations are often recognized for the exclusivity and lavishness of their cities, lifestyles, and tourist destinations.

At the same time, nations with low or no oil resources reflect a very different reality. Poverty rates, rurality, and more traditional Islamic society characterize many nations in NA/SWA. Several nations not directly benefiting from oil wealth are Syria, Yemen, and Egypt. Oman might be an example of a nation with characteristics of both: some oil wealth, but mostly poor.

This oil disparity fosters resentment on several levels. One might be the visible differences between nations. Saudi Arabia, for example, borders Yemen. Both are Arab, both are Muslim, but the economic cleavage is great. The Saudis are generally well off, in that the state invests a lot to elevate the lives of all Saudis, whereas the average Yemeni is poor.

Another source of tension is the economic and political relationships the wealthy oil countries maintain with the West. The oil nations are often heavily scrutinized for their tight bonds with the

FIGURE 4.3b. (and 4.3c below) American Presidents Nixon (1971) and Obama (2014) meeting with Saudi King Faisal and King Abdullah. This show of comradery has become a tradition for both the US and Saudi Arabia.
Copyright in the Public Domain.

United States, for example (see *Figures 4.3b/c*). When the US becomes involved in a military operation or war in a neighboring country, the oil nations often stand mute. At the same time, the oil nations will sometimes leverage their tight bonds to scold the United States over potential deals with Iran or over some affair with Israel. Either way, the "special relationship" with the West has divided the region economically and politically.

FIGURE 4.3c.
Copyright in the Public Domain.

CASE STUDY 4B

Research Exercise: Oil Wealth, No Oil Wealth

In this exercise, you will use the CIA World Factbook to identify some key facts and figures that might reveal how oil has altered the United Arab Emirates and how a lack of oil resources has characterized Yemen. Please follow the steps below and report the findings in a way identified in class:

1. Open the Internet browser and your favorite search engine. Type in CIA World Factbook.
2. Click the website and look for a bar on the right called "Please select a country to view."
3. Scroll down to United Arab Emirates, then click People and Society.
4. Scroll down to Literacy and write down literacy rates for women.
5. Now, scroll to Economy and pan down until you see per capita GDP and record this information.
6. Repeat Steps two through five, only scroll to Yemen instead.
7. What is Yemen's literacy rate for women?
8. What is Yemen's per capita GDP?

FIGURE 4.3d. Ferrari World in Abu Dhabi, UAE illustrates the scale of wealth in this oil-rich nation. Copyright © Aziz J. Hayat (CC BY 2.0) at http://commons.wikimedia.org/wiki/File%3AFerrari_World_Abu_Dhabi.jpg .

This simple exercise can be a looking glass into their respective societies. Oil wealth has had many effects on the UAE, one of which is education. All Emiratis have access to a quality education, whereas in Yemen, only men have some access. This reflects more traditional society. Likewise, per capita GDP is very different. The UAE divides its oil wealth amongst the Emirati families from the seven tribes, whereas the average Yemeni is quite poor. Although they share a similar geography, their lives are very different because of oil.

TOTALITARIAN REGIMES

Beginning in the late 1960s, totalitarian regimes began to form in the region. As European colonial powers withdrew after the Second World War, newly independent nations would leverage their resources (often oil) to establish new republics. In some cases, greedy royals would funnel the generated revenue to themselves, leaving an aggravated, underserved majority living in poverty. These wealth gaps would, in some cases, fester enough to induce a revolt or military *coup d'état*. Many of these revolts created a power vacuum often filled by the commander leading these *coups*. These officers would often conveniently promote themselves to a high rank, eliminate any dissension or threat, and leverage the state military and police to force conformity and provide security. This dysfunctionality ushered in an era of dictators in countries like Libya, Syria, Tunisia, and Iraq.

The main reason these regimes were so oppressive, controlling, and corrupt had to do with maintaining power. A heavy-handed dictator with military support could govern indefinitely. Muammar Gaddafi of Libya, for example, remained in power and maintained a totalitarian regime for forty-two years. In Syria, the Assad regime (father, then son) has and continues to engage in a caustic civil war that has resulted in tens of thousands of deaths, millions of refugees, and widespread homelessness since the early 1970s. Hosni Mubarak of Egypt was in many ways more mainstream in that he maintained alliances and economic relationships with other nations, but was accused internally of corruption, suppression, and other actions that led to his fall. Saddam Hussein of Iraq kept power for decades until he was toppled by Americans. He was accused of countless crimes against humanity as well as the unprovoked attempted invasion of Kuwait. As it turns out, many of these regimes would be overthrown by their own people, thus changing the political landscape of the region in a way that has yet to be defined.

Arab Spring

The impetus for the regional revolution that would change the landscapes of North Africa and parts of Southwest Asia between 2010 and 2013 can be traced to the young generations of oppressed countries. The Arab Spring can be defined as a "youth revolt" because a younger, tech-savvy generation used social media to view the stability and opportunities of the outside world while also documenting and sharing the atrocities from within their own countries. The use of smart phones allowed them to share their frustrations, post unjust actions to websites, and cultivate hope that democracy and freedoms may someday be their reality. However, this would entail dismantling totalitarian regimes that, incidentally, target, imprison, and even eliminate opposition. So they took to the streets, and did so in numbers. Through peaceful protests, violent protests, civil disorder, riots, and even full-blown civil war, the revolution toppled governments in Tunisia, Libya, Egypt (still ongoing), Yemen, Syria (unsuccessful), and so on.

The results of the "Arab Spring," or the revolutions that set out to end oppression, have been mixed at best. Democracy, as it turns out, was not a perfect fit for these nations, and many of them have entered a period of instability that continues to this day. Egypt, for example, has gone through several leaders, one of whom was from an Islamist group called the *Islamic Brotherhood*. Zealots, Islamic extremists, and jihadists have become more assertive now that the powerful dictatorships have dissolved. Because of the continued civil strife, many thousands are fleeing the region in hope of a better future in Europe. This rise of Islamist groups is redefining the region and will continue to be an issue for the foreseeable future.

RISE OF ISLAMIC EXTREMISM

Islamic extremism is a broad term that encompasses fundamentalism, jihadist terrorism, and the new war to create an Islamic State, or *caliphate*. Although these forms of extremism have differences, they all share conservative, even puritanical, Islamic perspectives; they seek, to some degree, a move back to a more conservative society shaped exclusively by their faith (*Sharia* law).

Some conservative Islamic groups are well established. *Wahhabism* and the *Salafi* movement have been in place for some time in countries like Saudi Arabia. Though Saudis are very connected to their Western economic partners and political allies, they are very strict within their own society.

Jihadists are groups that resort to terrorism. *Al-Qaeda*, for example, is an international terrorist organization that has largely functioned in the shadows, and it has planned and executed some of the most terrible acts in America and other regions. This form of Islamic extremism launched a "war on terror" that has had global implications. However, Islamist extremism in its latest form, the *caliphate movement*, is very much in the open. The self-proclaimed *"Islamic State"* or *ISIS* (Islamic State in Iraq and Syria) does not operate in the shadows. Rather, they have openly declared war on all *apostates* and continue to aggressively fight with all who stand in their way. This group has sparked movements in neighboring areas as well, and is now being combated by a coalition of Arab states, the United States, and even the Iranians.

THEMATIC INTERSECTION 4B

Understanding ISIS

Themes: Religion/Political/Economic

ISIS, or the "Islamic State" is a relatively new form of Islamic extremism. They do not hide. They do not scheme. They openly fight. The reason a large number of people (beginning in Syria and Iraq, but now spreading to other nations) have joined this group is important to understand. Why they are so violent and unapologetic about their methods is also important to understand. Rather than chronologically piecing together the formation of this movement, this Thematic Intersection will look at several of the root causes that might explain its rise. These include rather complicated religious, political, and economic narratives. See below for a breakdown of these categories:

1. **Religion:** Both Syria and Iraq have governments that are Shia or related to Shia Islam (like the Syrian "Alawite" Assad regime). The majority of their people, however, are Sunni. Many of these Sunni groups are in more rural areas that are often deliberately underserved, even ignored, by the Shia governments. Likewise, the military is often comprised of commanders that are Shia, thus lacking the will (and resources) to protect and serve these areas. Resulting from

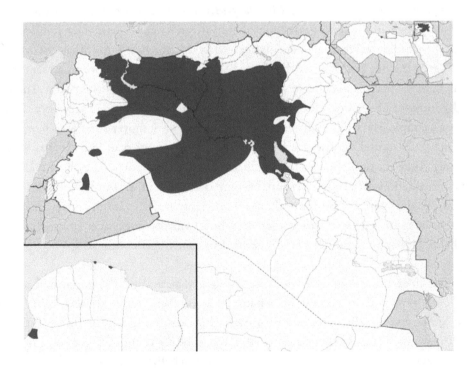

FIGURE 4.3e. ISIS controlled areas in 2014.
Copyright © NordNordWest (CC BY-SA 3.0) at http://commons.wikimedia.org/wiki/File%3ATerritorial_control_of_the_ISIS.svg .

this are entire regions of often uneducated and underemployed Sunnis who, in their frustration, have only their religion to turn to. This may explain the rise of this type of Islamic extremism and the ease of finding recruits to join the movement. It gives them purpose and definition, while they believe they are serving God.

FIGURE 4.3f. Islamic State fighters
Copyright © Menendj (CC BY-SA 2.5) at http://commons.wikimedia.org/wiki/File%3AIraqi_insurgents_with_guns.JPG .

2. **Political:** The reason why these regimes are in place is complicated. In Iraq, for example, ending the war and the withdrawal of troops meant that the United States had to help establish a democratic system (in some form), a functioning government, and a military/security force that could, with the crutch of US troops, prevent the country from devolving into civil war. Because these political systems are new to Iraqis and are fundamentally coerced by the Americans, the Shia government in place is really the one put there by the United States. Therefore, the poor treatment of the Sunni majority, especially in underserved regions, may be a side effect of this political manipulation.

3. Economic: The Sunni militia fundamentalists who joined ISIS are very poor. Eastern Syria, for example, is "Syria" in name only, but is really an impoverished region with little help from Damascus. Likewise, the southern and western frontiers of Iraq are also "Iraq" in name only. They are rural, poor, and have little or no political voice. They have a long history of confrontation with the Kurds and, in some cases, each other, but lack the resources or support to deal with the problems they face. This fosters desperation, and as ISIS formed (and became more aggressive), they went after the all sources of revenue. This included banks, oil fields, kidnapping and ransoms, and even drugs and human trafficking.

None of this offers an excuse for their behavior. The actions and tactics of ISIS have created an atmosphere of anxiety and even infuriated the community of nations around them. They have also gotten the attention of the United States, the Assad regime, and even Iran, which has oddly put the three on the same side. Nonetheless, it may also point out that a group like ISIS may be the result of larger issues that many who joined felt were out of their control. Now they seek control and believe passionately that their actions are both just and the will of God.

4.4 NA/SWA and the Twenty–First Century

Although North Africa and Southwest Asia have ongoing issues that seem regional in scale, they actually influence political and economic trends globally. Some of these issues that will likely remain important well into the twenty-first century are:

- Arab Palestinian/Israeli Relations
- Iran
- Oil Resources and Dependency
- Islamic Extremism

The challenging aspect of these issues is that there is no viable resolution or consensus on the table about how to deal with any of them. The reason for this is that each is complicated and opinions vary significantly. This chapter will briefly examine these conundrums and perhaps provide some insights on how to keep an eye on these important issues moving forward.

ARAB PALESTINIAN–ISRAELI RELATIONS

There is no easy way to discuss this antagonistic, contentious relationship between the Arab Palestinians and Israelis. This textbook has already discussed the formation of the Jewish state, conflicts that defined the space they occupy, and the potential for future issues, but cannot predict how this will play out. Some call for cooperation between the two, which involves the creation of a sovereign Palestinian state. This would enable them to achieve political independence from Israel, create a government of their own, and then contend with Israel as a neighbor rather than an occupation force. This thread of dialogue typically ends with hard-line conservatives in Israel, who claim that a united Palestine is a security threat and annexes lands their faith dictates was given to them by God.

Other threads of dialogue call for a more aggressive Israel. Maintaining peace by force. This approach not only guarantees continued conflicts with neighbors and continued Western military support of Israel, but also seems to fail to address the antagonism and tensions between two peoples who share a home. Because these two narratives exist, it can be easy to identify which voice is louder as general elections in both Israel and the United States occur. This issue has divided Israelis, and has been, and will continue to be, a key political argument for them. Likewise, with such strong support from the United States, it is predictable that presidential candidates will all take a position on what Israel should do.

IRAN

Iran presents an interesting situation that should play out in the next decade. Within the region, Iran is both feared and distrusted. Part of the reason for this is because they have some form of nuclear capability and have a long history of antagonizing both Israel and the United States. This, combined with the Islamic Revolution of 1979, has placed Iran in a category President Bush called the "Axis of Evil."

But this assertion has made the realities of Iran less visible. Iranians, it could be argued, want change. Many Iranians want the opportunity to build a life, open businesses, and travel without the oppressive theocratic leadership. If this is indeed true, then perhaps the relationship with the West—specifically the

United States—will thaw and someday become friendlier. Of course, this will not likely happen if the Supreme Leader and the imams do not wish it and the people fail to overthrow them. However, Iran has been showing little sign that it is adopting a friendlier disposition. At the same time, each positive sign from Iran is matched by a burst of doubt from Israel, the Saudis, and political voices in the United States. How this will play out may also be detected in the American political arena. If the United States accepts these signs as positives and continues to foster more dialogue, the relationship may improve and fundamentally change Southwest Asia. If Iran is villainized, it may lead to a military encounter and even war.

OIL RESOURCES AND DEPENDENCY

As of 2015, the Chinese surpassed the United States as the largest consumer of oil from this region. This is a major shift that reveals several trends occurring outside the region. The United States, though it has been and continues to be a key purchaser of oil from OPEC, has had a decrease in demand and an amplified resolve to wean itself off of Middle East oil. If the Americans continue to leverage their own gas and oil resources, they may very well redefine the economic bonds with producing nations like Saudi Arabia, Kuwait, and the UAE that have been tight for a hundred years. If indeed China builds strong economic bonds with these producing nations, the United States may lose political clout in the region and witness a shift of alliances to the East.

ISLAMIC EXTREMISM

Islamic extremism is likely to continue to be a very real issue for nations within the region and a viable threat to Western nations should this movement expand. If that is the case, the United States' armed forces will likely remain deployed locally and ready to engage these threats as directed. The problem with this form of Islamic extremism is that it is very spread out and grassroots in nature. Identifying exactly who is ISIS and who is not will perhaps be the greatest challenge and greatest handicap, should the coalition forces get it wrong. As discussed earlier, whether justified or not, most Muslim nations lament Western forces fighting in the region and if some form of war were to break out, this might have the potential to erode relationships with the West.

CONCLUSION

Although much of this chapter has been focused on both internal and external agitators that illuminate some key issues of the NA/SWA, it is important to highlight some extraordinary aspects of this region as well. To begin with, incredible ancient civilizations and early cultural hearths of humanity once occupied this region. Nicknamed the "cradle of civilization," North Africa and Southwest Asia have shaped much about the world we know. The *Fertile Crescent* crops are still widely used around the world in numerous cuisines. The *Proto-Indo-European* language that emerged in Anatolia, or modern day Turkey, is the mother language of everything from English to Hindi in India. The religions that trace roots to this region are the largest and most well-known religions on the planet. In many ways, this region is as fascinating as it is concerning.

Superimposed over these wonderful and interesting regional attributes are matters that cannot be ignored. Southwest Asia has become a geopolitical arena, in that the problems found there are potentially problems for all. Likewise, the trends that are still regionally observable can shape, and perhaps have already shaped, international political and economic alliances in ways that will become more visible and defined this century. Whether it's Israel, Iran, oil, or extremism, this region is worth respecting and critically observing.

KEY TERMS

Desert	Islam	Arab Spring
River complex	Suez Canal	Islamic Extremism
Fertile Crescent	OPEC	ISIS
Mesopotamia	Cultural backlash	Oil
Abrahamic religions	Palestine	
Monotheism	Israel	

CLASS DISCUSSIONS

1. Describe early agriculture and the rise of civilization in the region. How did language, crops, and complex society influence regions beyond the "Fertile Crescent"?
2. Discuss the common geography and monotheism of the region's religions. Briefly describe each of the three "Abrahamic Religions."
3. Discuss the spread of Islam throughout the region. Describe why Islam divided into Shia and Sunni.
4. Discuss "external" influences that agitate the region.
5. Discuss "internal" issues they face within the region.
6. Describe the reasons behind the "Arab Spring." Have the revolutions and the attempt at democracy worked? How have they worked, or why haven't they worked?

ADDITIONAL RESOURCES

https://www.cia.gov/library/publications/the-world-factbook/wfbExt/region_mde.html

Ancient Mesopotamia:

http://www.rivervalleycivilizations.com/

Islam:

http://www.metmuseum.org/learn/for-educators/publications-for-educators/art-of-the-islamic-world/unit-one/the-prophet-muhammad-and-the-origins-of-islam

Suez Canal Information:

http://www.suezcanal.gov.eg/

BIBLIOGRAPHY

Central Intelligence Agency. The World Factbook n.d. Web. https://www.cia.gov/library/publications/the-world-factbook/wfbExt/region_mde.html. 03 Jan. 2015.

Crooke, Alastair. "You Can't Understand ISIS If You Don't Know the History of Wahhabism in Saudi Arabia." The Huffington Post. HuffingtonPost.com, n.d. Web. http://www.huffingtonpost.com/alastair-crooke/isis-wahhabism-saudi-arabia_b_5717157.html. 03 Jan. 2015.

Goldberg, Jeffrey. "Israel's Dangerous Predicament." The Atlantic. Atlantic Media Company, 20 Mar. 2015. Web. http://www.theatlantic.com/international/archive/2015/03/israels-and-netanyahus-dangerous-predicament/388315/. 25 March 2015.

OPEC . N.p., n.d. Web. http://www.opec.org/opec_web/en/. 11 Jan. 2015.

Palestine: Revolution in the air at last. Economist. September 15, 2012.

Suez Canal Authority. N.p., n.d. Web. http://www.suezcanal.gov.eg/. 03 Jan. 2015.

Sunni-Shia Strife: The sword and the word. Economist. 12 May 2012.

"The Prophet Muhammad and the Origins of Islam." The Metropolitan Museum of Art (i.e., The Met Museum). N.p., n.d. Web. http://www.metmuseum.org/learn/for-educators/publications-for-educators/art-of-the-islamic-world/unit-one/the-prophet-muhammad-and-the-origins-of-islam. 10 Jan. 2015.

"The River Nile Facts." River Nile Facts. N.p., n.d. Web. http://www.ancient-egypt-online.com/river-nile-facts.html. 03 Jan. 2015.

"TIGRIS/EUPHRATES RIVER VALLEY CIVILIZATION." Tigris-Euphrates Civilization. N.p., n.d. Web. http://www.rivervalleycivilizations.com/tigris-euphrates.php. 07 Jan. 2015.

"Why Are Israel and the Palestinians Fighting Over Gaza?" BBC News. BBC. n.d. Web. http://www.bbc.co.uk/newsround/20436092. 23 Feb. 2015.

CHAPTER 5

Sub-Saharan Africa

Key Intersecting Themes:

Physical Geography, Cultural, Political, Economic

Countries discussed:
- Western African nations
- Sahel nations
- Nigeria
- Congo
- Central African Republic
- Uganda
- Ethiopia
- Somalia
- Kenya
- Tanzania
- Rwanda
- Angola
- Namibia
- South Africa
- Botswana
- Other central and southeast nations

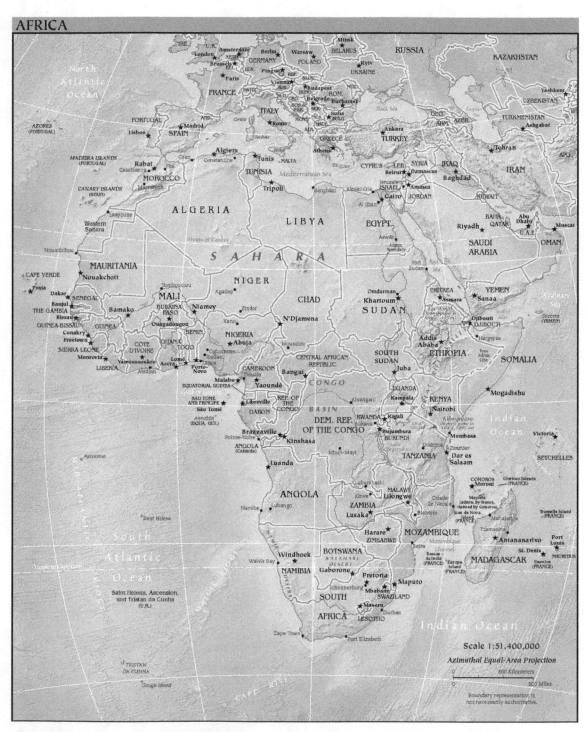

FIGURE 5.0. Sub-Saharan Africa lies south of the Sahara Desert. Some nations, like Mali, Niger, Chad, and Sudan, fall both within the Sahara Desert and in the southern Sahara Desert realm, known as the Sahel. Copyright in the Public Domain.

5.1 Regional Overview

Perhaps no other region on Earth fills the imagination as much as Sub-Saharan Africa. Untamed landscapes, wild and dangerous animals, and its colorful cultures have been portrayed in countless movies, cartoons, and books. At the same time, not many people from developed countries like the United States and Canada have ever travelled there. This may be true because some of the grim realities in the region countervail those that make Sub-Saharan Africa enchanting. Superimposed over a beautiful and awe-inspiring landscape is a region carved into pieces by European colonial powers, vast poverty, environmental and climatic tragedies, and periodic regional violence that can be gruesome in nature. Understanding Sub-Saharan Africa, then, requires a special examination into both.

THE AFRICAN LANDSCAPE

Sub-Saharan Africa's natural landscapes exhibit great diversity. There are deserts, plains, subtropical savannas, tropical rainforests, mountainous realms, thousands of miles of coasts, and even Mediterranean climates that are very much like that found in Southern California. Because of this, Sub-Saharan Africa also has rich biodiversity. Zoo visitors often anticipate the gorillas, lions, hippopotami, rhinos, zebras, and crocodiles—all of which and more are indigenous to Africa. Understanding the region's physical features fosters a better understanding of the human narratives and activities.

FIGURE 5.1a. A farmer in Kenya. Humans and the natural landscape have a shared narrative in Sub-Saharan Africa for tens of thousands of years. Copyright © CIAT International Center for Tropical Agriculture (CC BY-SA 2.0) at http://commons.wikimedia.org/wiki/File%3A2DU_Kenya_86_ (5367322642).jpg .

North–South Axis: A Lesson in Latitude

A continent's axis refers to its east–west or north–south orientation. If a region is more defined by latitude than longitude, like Sub-Saharan Africa, then it has a north–south axis. This is an important physical geographical feature, because a continent with a north–south axis characteristically sees more defined changes in shorter distances, especially if near or on the equator. The reason for this is that Earth receives all its direct energy between 23.5 degrees north and south latitude, but not all in one place or at the same time. Instead, it shifts towards the Northern Hemisphere between September and March and towards the Southern Hemisphere between March and September. This explains the subtropical to tropical climates, both to the north and south of the equator, in Sub-Saharan Africa.

Also, this area around the planet is where the easterly trade winds converge, in the *Intertropical Convergence Zone (ITCZ)*. However, beyond the ITCZ is the high-pressure belt, at about thirty degrees north and south latitude. These climates are typically desert. Sub-Saharan Africa, as seen in *Figure 5.1b*, has a rainy, largely tropical/subtropical climate profile within the range of the ITCZ, but then changes radically beyond that zone. Within the ITCZ, though, is an atmospheric band of rain that advances north with the energy of the sun (albeit at a lag) during their summer months and begins to ebb or retreat as that energy shifts to the south. This diversity in climate, over short distances, sets the pulse of Africa which animals and humans follow.

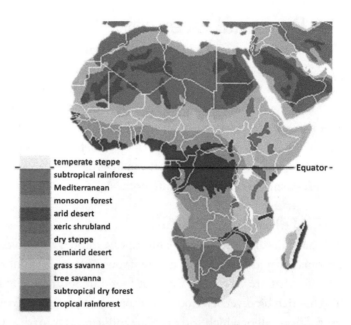

temperate steppe
subtropical rainforest
Mediterranean
monsoon forest
arid desert
xeric shrubland
dry steppe
semiarid desert
grass savanna
tree savanna
subtropical dry forest
tropical rainforest

Equator -

FIGURE 5.1b. Sub-Saharan Africa's north-south axis explains biodiversity in shorter distances.
Copyright © Ville Koistinen (CC BY-SA 2.5) at http://commons.wikimedia.org/wiki/File%3AVegetation_Africa.png .

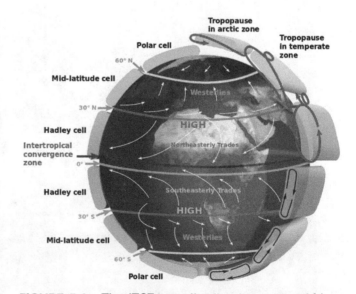

FIGURE 5.1c. The ITCZ actually dips in eastern Africa, because of a high pressure zone forming over the Eurasian continent. This means the easterly winds flowing towards the equator are dry, thus making a part of the world that should be continually wet, seasonally relatively dry. Copyright © Kaidor (CC BY-SA 3.0) at http://commons.wikimedia.org/wiki/File%3AEarth_Global_Circulation_-_en.svg .

Within these climates are subregions that take on their own character; some are unique in the world. Below are *Sub-Saharan Africa's five (5) key subregions,* with brief descriptions.

The (1) *Sahel* is a narrow subregion located on the northern boundary of Sub-Saharan Africa. Because it is situated between about fifteen and eighteen degrees north latitude, it is technically in the subtropics. However, it is also the transition zone that separates the subtropical south and the gigantic Sahara Desert to the north. This means it is the farthest northern reach of the ITCZ (rain bands). The rains in this region have become less reliable and reach less to the north than before, causing *desertification* and increased aridity in the subregion.

The (2) *Savannas* of central east Africa are *transition zones* between woodlands and grasslands. They are defined by their seasonal precipitation patterns. During the rainy season, the savannas turn green, the rivers swell, and life thrives. During the dry season, the savannas turn beige, much of the wildlife leaves to follow the rain or becomes less active, and rivers and other water sources dry out. One unusual aspect of the savannas of Africa is that they are close enough to the equator (on the equator, in some areas) to be very wet and rainy much of the year. However, the ITCZ does something quite different in Africa. As a high-pressure system forms over the Eurasian continent, it sends cold, dry air down to the ITCZ, as opposed to many other places in the world where this is warm, moist ocean air. This makes the ITCZ dip in eastern Africa, resulting in drier, more seasonal precipitation.

The (3) *Valley and Lakes* subregion of Africa is a part of the tectonically active Great Rift Valley, which is itself a part of a larger, more intricate system of divergent faults. These valley systems stretch over three thousand miles, from Mozambique all the way through the Red Sea Rift and on to the Jordan Rift Valley in NA/SWA. Within Africa, this area is characterized by highlands (even mountains), the largest lakes on the continent, and fertile soils. This access to water and fertile soils makes this the most agriculturally productive subregion in Africa. The lakes in the region are some of the largest on Earth and include Lake Malawi, Lake Tanganyika, and the famous Lake Victoria.

The (4) *Tropical Rainforests* can be found in central western Africa in nations like Congo, Central Congo Republic, Cameroon, Gabon, and Equatorial Guinea. This subregion is one of the rainiest areas on the planet and is rich in biodiversity. The *Congo Rainforest,* for example, is the second largest tropical rainforest (a.k.a. jungle) on Earth, next to the *Amazon Rainforest.* These forested areas are home to gorillas, bonobos, and forest elephants. The human inhabitants of this subregion are mostly *Pygmies,* who average in height less than four feet.

The (5) *Desert* subregions are located both in the north (on the southern margin of the Sahara Desert) and in the southern third of Africa (in Botswana, South Africa, and Namibia). In Botswana, the *Kalahari Desert* is seasonally dry and remote. The *Namib Desert* of Namibia is a coastal desert of great aridity. This

FIGURE 5.1d. Tanzania in dry season. Animals forage on grasses and conserve energy. Copyright © Gary (CC BY 2.0) at http://commons.wikimedia.org/wiki/File%3AZebras%2C_Serengeti_savana_plains%2C_Tanzania.jpg .

subregion has been dry for so long, it has epic sand dunes of a size and variety that rivals the Sahara thousands of miles to the north. The *Karoo Desert* of South Africa occupies the southernmost margin of Africa, just inland from the coast. This desert is well known for its many fossils from eras long past.

BOX 5a THE OKAVANGO DELTA: AN UNUSUAL PLACE

In the northern margin of the Kalahari is an unusual geographic feature known as an endorheic basin. Essentially a tectonic trough, or a land area sunken in lower than the broader region, the Okavango River has chosen this to be its delta. Whereas most rivers delta into the ocean, the Okavango swells with seasonal rain in Angola and then flows south, filling this endorheic basin with shallow water (see Figure 5.1e(2,3) below). This water brings all kinds of life, from predators to elephants. Once the rainy season wanes, the river's volume decreases and the water disappears, along with most of animals that came to enjoy the oasis.

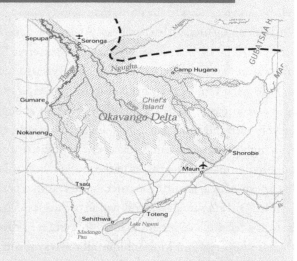

FIGURE 5.1e(1). This map shows the extent of seasonal flooding on the Okavango. During the rainy season, the Okavango becomes lush and full of life. During the dry season, it returns to its desert habitat, dry and unforgiving.

FIGURE 5.1e(2).

FIGURE 5.1e(3).

5.2 The Human Experience

Sub-Saharan Africa has been referred to as the "cradle of humanity" because the earliest archeological remains of common ancestors have been found in this region. However, this textbook will focus more on the cultural landscape that was well established when slavers and Europeans arrived to exploit Africa. It will also focus on the postcolonial era and the struggle of independent nations to establish stable political systems and deal with interregional and civil conflicts. By focusing on these elements of Sub-Saharan cultural landscapes, it becomes easier to understand the conflicts and episodes of cooperation that have together shaped the region.

TRIBAL LANDSCAPES

The very foundation of Sub-Saharan Africa's human landscape is the tribe. Tribal life is a tradition in Africa, dating back to pre-ancient times. Tribal society can be described as traditional societies held together by ethnic and cultural bonds using a simple structure of leadership (a chief), living off the land and its resources, and practicing *animistic* customs and beliefs. It was certainly what foreigners observed upon arriving to Africa and still shapes local, regional, and even national relationships to this day.

FIGURE 5.2a. Young Maasai jumping strengthens social bonds.
Copyright © Bjørn Christian Tørrissen (CC BY-SA 3.0) at http://commons.wikimedia.org/wiki/File%3AMara-Young-Men-Jumping-2012.JPG .

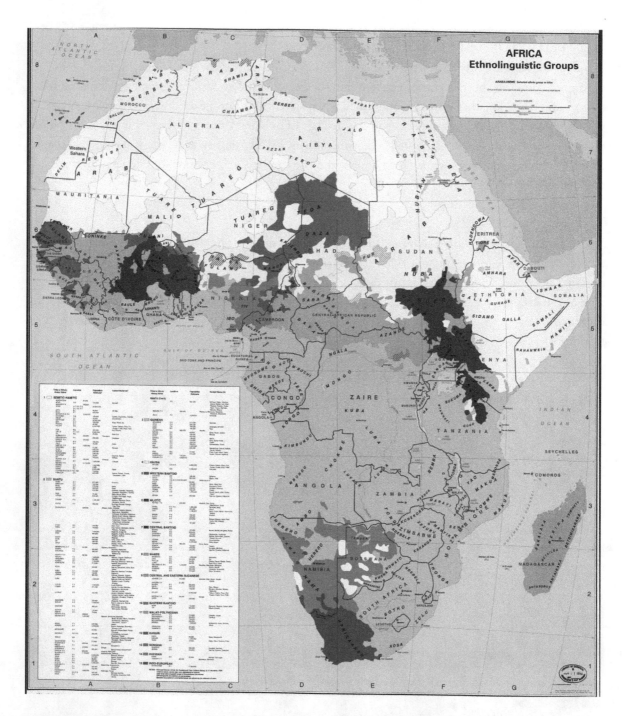

FIGURE 5.2b. This Sub-Saharan African ethnolinguistic map reveals patterns of settlement.
Copyright in the Public Domain.

As with any patterns of human settlement over time, Africa's tribal landscapes took millennia to form. By the time the first slavers and colonial powers arrived, tribal territories were well established. Although there are many, the *seven (7) key tribes of Sub-Saharan Africa* are:

- *Zulu*: This tribe has about ten million members, mostly occupying South Africa.
- *Maasai*: The Maasai were great warriors and skilled herders. Their lands were well dispersed over much of central east Africa (Kenya, Tanzania).
- *San*: The San tribes (many) are from the Kalahari Desert region of Botswana and South Africa. They are known for their survival skills and curious language of "pops and clicks."
- *Ashanti*: An ancient tribal people who still occupy western African nations.
- *Pygmies*: Known for their short stature, these rainforest tribes still occupy parts of the Congo.
- *Hutu/Tutsi*: These tribes are independent of each other but occupy the same areas of Rwanda and sections of Burundi. They are well known for their rivalry that led to genocide not long ago.
- *Dogon*: This tribe occupied a territory near the Mali-Niger border. They are known for their ornate costumes.

Beyond the specific customs and traditions unique to each tribe, they would all have a deep connection to the territory which they occupied. This territorial affiliation, and the tribal activities that occurred on the lands they considered home (herding, hunting, nomadism, etc.), would become a source of conflict with the Europeans attempting to establish colonies. This will be discussed in more detail later in the chapter.

THE SLAVE TRADE

Exploiting human beings in Africa began as early as ancient times. The Egyptians would use tens of thousands of slaves, acquired by military conquest, to build the pyramids and other ancient relics. The Romans would use conquered Africans to build roads, fight in gladiatorial events, or as house servants. However, the era of slave trading really began in the eighth century with the Arab slavers. The *Arab Slave Trade* lasted from the eighth century to as late as the 1880s, in places like Zanzibar. It is estimated that roughly twelve million Africans were enslaved by the Arab slavers. Most of the slaves were Bantu collected from the Swahili Coast and some inland regions of east Africa (Tanzania, Kenya, etc.).

The Atlantic Slave Trade represented the largest, perhaps most organized and horrific slave operation in Africa. Beginning with the Portuguese and later adopted by the Spanish, French, and English, the

FIGURE 5.2c. The Arab Slave Trade was the first wave of commercial slavery in Africa. Approximately 12 million Africans captured.
Copyright in the Public Domain.

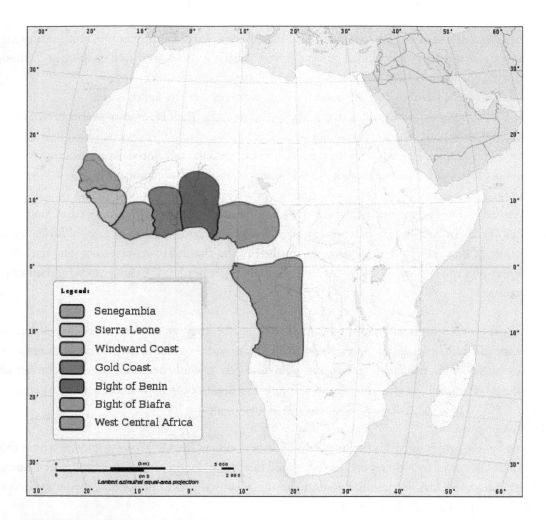

FIGURE 5.2d. The Atlantic Slave Trade used these African regions to capture and export slaves. Copyright © Eric Gaba (CC BY-SA 2.5) at http://commons.wikimedia.org/wiki/File%3AAfrica_slave_Regions.svg .

slaves from West Africa were collected and sent to the New World to be used as labor in colonial economic activities. These included plantations (sugar, cocoa, tobacco, cotton, etc.), mining, and as general help in construction, timber industries, shipping, and domestic services. The Triangle Trade, or the use of African slaves in plantation colonies to grow sugar (which then was used to distill rum, which then was shipped back to Africa to trade for more slaves), helped to keep this industry robust.

The Africans called this slave trade *Maafa*, which is a Swahili word for "great disaster." And indeed it was, in Sub-Saharan Africa. Between the 1600s and the mid-1800s, roughly fifteen million Africans were enslaved. This inflow of slave labor to the New World generated fringe industries that would breed African slaves to be used for future needs, bypassing the direct channels of slave acquisition. Most Africans used as slaves were put through terrible ordeals. These ordeals included:

- Kidnapping or an attack on their village would separate Africans from their family and tribe.
- They were then marched to the coast and held in forts, where they were beaten into submission by slavers waiting to ship them to the New World.
- On the voyage across, they were chained and crammed together in dark cargo holds below deck without fresh air, toilets, or adequate nutrition. Many Africans would contract disease or die en route.
- Once they arrived to the New World, many would be placed in assimilation camps to "break them" and ready them for a life of submission and hard labor.
- They would be sold to plantation owners or assigned to some form of work to live out their lives as possessions. Often, the conditions of their final destination were deplorable.

The British would be the first to outlaw slavery in their empire. The *Slavery Abolition Act of 1833* mandated slavery as illegal, with some exceptions. This began to reduce the volume of slaves exported from West Africa because British naval ships would patrol the African coast and arrest slavers, making it more difficult for plantations to acquire new sources of labor. By the end of the era of African slavery, roughly thirty million Africans were enslaved.

Sub-Saharan Africa, today, is only fractionally shaped by its tribal past. This is largely because the colonial period, and the postcolonial era of independence that followed, redefined the region in many ways. At the same time, many of the conflicts and regional cooperation are, at the core, tribal in nature. Rival groups in countries that have fallen into civil unrest are often affiliated by tribe and cohesive because of tribal loyalties. Because of this, there is a particular brand of loyalty that can be observed by seeing how deep into violence a person will go if his commander is part of the same tribe. This is why it is important to consider tribal dynamics when examining Africa's human landscapes and how Africans interact at various scales.

5.3 European Colonial and Postcolonial Influences

The engine of European imperialism was its colonies. Foreign colonies provided European imperial powers the ability to directly use the human and natural resources of Africa for their own benefit. Because Africa was geographically nearby, the European nations that maintained African colonies could better be supported and supplied, and they benefited from military assistance deployed more expeditiously than colonies thousands of miles further away. At the same time, Sub-Saharan Africa was wild compared to other colonial locations. Oppressive tropical and subtropical heat and humidity, biodiverse landscapes rich in dangerous animals, feared diseases, and hostile natives made Africa a challenge to colonize, despite European power and the colonies' relative proximity to home. In many cases, Europeans—especially the British—would have to fight to stay. Wars in Africa became costly for Europeans. Africans were, after all, savages in the eyes of European imperialists, and therefore had to be controlled (see *Figure 5.3a*).

THE LURE OF AFRICA

As Western Europe industrialized during the nineteenth century, there was a "Scramble for Africa"—a rush by European powers to obtain, secure, and profit from the rich natural resources of the region. This "scramble" led to confrontations between European powers. Likewise, as mentioned in Chapter 1, war back home in Europe spread to the colonies in Africa (and other parts of the world), thus adding regional dimensions to the conflict. In order for Europeans to better define their African colonies and respect the political system they put into place in Europe to solve the same problem, they agreed to partition Africa. The *Great Partition* (not to be confused with the Great Partition of India, to be discussed later), as it was known, divided Africa into political space in a way that served the needs of European imperial powers. This was done at the Berlin Conference of 1884–1885. This meeting in Europe would fundamentally change Sub-Saharan Africa forever.

FIGURE 5.3a. The Battle of Isandhlwana (1879), was representative of the resistance, especially from the Zulu nation, to European imperialism and colonization. Depicted in this painting is a British platoon fighting in close quarters against the Zulu warriors.
Copyright in the Public Domain.

FIGURE 5.3b. Europe colonizes Africa. This illustration of a British soldier with one foot in Cairo, Egypt and the other in Cape Town, South Africa symbolizes Europe's vision of controlling Africa.
Copyright in the Public Domain.

THEMATIC INTERSECTION 5(A)

The Division of Africa: European Politics & Tribal Dynamics

Themes: Political/Cultural

Perhaps no other region on Earth showcases European colonial power and how influential it was than nineteenth-century Africa. The "Scramble for Africa" merely broadened the arena of conflict between European powers. Because the natural resources of Africa were so profitable, Europeans bullied and fought each other over turf. Likewise, any unrelated conflicts in Europe would spill over into the colonies, creating a need for greater definition and, eventually, a mutually tolerated political system that they could all recognize. It was determined in Berlin, in 1884–1885, that Africa should be partitioned into political space that, at least in part, met the needs of the various imperial powers operating colonies. The map shown in Figure 5.3c shows the result of this conference. The political divisions in Africa remain similar to this day.

The **political theme,** then, is a European one. Like other parts of the world, Europeans divided space for both political needs (sovereignty, territorial legality, rights to resources, and security) and economic needs (the flow of capital from these political spaces to home countries, industries operating with protections). However, with political space come political norms within that space. When political space is created, it is often shaped in a way that reflects the norms, values, and practices of the culture responsible for its creation. Because Europeans neither wanted to create a new political system nor cared much what the native Africans thought, they simply adopted systems they knew and put into motion practices they were familiar with. This included:

- Systems of governance: Governor, parliament or council, taxes and revenue, restrictions on mobility, etc.
- Economic systems: Trade and tariffs, banking systems, private enterprise, etc.
- Security: Military operations, ports, fortifications, policing
- Social structures: Land grants, the privatization of land for political and economic purposes, urban design, social stratification
- Judicial/Legal systems: Courts, laws, policies

The issue with these adopted European systems was that they were European, not African, and often collided with well-established tribal dynamics. This would be the *cultural theme.* European political systems superimposed over regional cultural systems created conflicts that can still be seen today.

An example of this would be tribes in Kenya. For centuries or longer, they had used their territories for herding, hunting, and nomadism. After the British helped create political space and defined the laws and social structure of that space, land-use practices changed. Whereas once a tribal herdsman could cross a river, as his father and father's father had, it would now get him arrested. This is because the land on the other side of the river became privately owned by a white English colonist, and that colonist would use the law to keep the herdsmen off his land. This colonial dynamic is still an issue in Kenya to this day. White landowners, now in their third or fourth generation, are still using the law to punish tribesmen who cross onto their lands. This continual conflict has generated the political will to change the laws in Kenya, but how that will play out is yet to be seen.

COLONIAL CITIES AND INFRASTRUCTURE

Sub-Saharan Africa was indeed a land rich in natural resources and tribal culture. In order to leverage these resources while maintaining a strong colonial administration, Europeans would invest in both cities and regional infrastructure. These investments allowed European colonies to remain relatively cohesive as foreigners while exploiting the region around them with greater efficiency.

Larger regional cities would become centers of politics, economic activities, and military operations. They would form (by design) a protective membrane from which Europeans could manage the colony. Cities, then, began to reflect more European characteristics. Buildings, road systems, housing, and social centers would, architecturally, more reflect home (London, Paris, Amsterdam, etc.). Cities were also more secure and allowed more freedom for the families of colonists to enjoy more "European" lifestyles while abroad. To secure cities, colonial powers (especially the British) would use gates or barrier points with armed soldiers to limit and control who could enter the city. They did this because the locals often resented colonists, and if they gathered en masse, it could lead to anticolonial solidarity in places where that could threaten everything. This kept most locals dispersed in the rural areas, while Europeans occupied the cities.

Infrastructure was also a priority for colonial powers. Sub-Saharan Africa was wild and undeveloped. Getting to natural resources often meant long-distance travel to remote and inhospitable places. And once these raw materials and natural resources were obtained, they would have to get them to ships and off to Europe or other destinations. A solution to this issue was infrastructure. Railroads, road systems, and modern ports would help expedite economic activities, move people and supplies around, and enable travelers to explore the continent. Communication networks were constructed. The ability to communicate across great distances provided many benefits. Ports in cities like Durban and Cape Town in South Africa and Dar es Salaam in Tanzania became the crossroads of Africa and the world.

CASE STUDY 5A

The Cape to Cairo Railway: a Strong Vision, a Partial Reality

The Cape to Cairo Railway perhaps best represented Britain's desire to tame Africa by linking its most distant colonial cities together with a single railroad system and communication system. The idea came from British scholar and wealthy businessman Cecil John Rhodes (depicted in Figure 5.3b), who envisioned a tangible link between Cape Town, South Africa, and Cairo, Egypt 4,500 miles to the north. This railroad would mostly pass through key British colonies, thus linking key regions together. Although this transportation artery never fully linked, thousands of miles of railroad lines were constructed and used by the British. Curtailing its completion were competing railroad plans by the French and Portuguese, difficulties with construction (climate, native attacks), and foreign territorial politics. Nonetheless, the British put in thousands of miles of railroad tracks that linked many parts of Africa never linked before.

COLLAPSE OF COLONIALISM IN SUB-SAHARAN AFRICA

Between World War II and the 1970s, European colonies in Africa collapsed. A key exception to this is South Africa, which would become independent in 1910. The reasons for this are largely external to Africa. Colonialism as a system began to wane in the 1930s. This was partially because decades of colonial mismanagement led to independent movements around the world. Likewise, in Europe the threat of war led to a withdrawal of troops and all military resources (ships, tanks, armories, canons, etc.) from colonial outposts back home. With the absence of military, the colonial nations assumed more regional control, thus facilitating a quicker independence.

Sub-Saharan Africa experienced a more spread-out independence movement, as dictated by its unique situation. Africa had to supplement resources the Japanese controlled and could no longer provide from Southeast Asia during World War II. At the same time, they struggled to get those resources to Europe because of German *U-boats*. This made Africans in more direct control of their resources while making them more independent because issues had to be solved locally. However, when decolonization finally arrived, it would again radically shape the region today.

After the war, Sub-Saharan Africa was more independent, despite colonialism lasting longer. The world was a different place after 1945. Europeans had to not only rebuild their devastated landscapes and economies; they also had to subscribe to a new world order of economic systems and the emergence of the United States as a dominant player promoting and safeguarding these new systems. In the United Kingdom, the postwar era was labor unions and welfare systems and more focused on the rising threat of the Soviet Union, communism, and a community economy. African colonies, then, would shift from direct colonial operations to economic partner states with a colonial presence.

To facilitate this transition, European powers would rely on the political elite (who had been born and raised in Europe and educated by Europeans) to inherit and maintain these profitable systems. This, perceivably, would allow Europeans to benefit from the resources while facilitating a peaceful transition to independence. However, Sub-Saharan African nations had little, if any, recognition from the community of nations outside, and Africa was, by and large, considered backwards and unreliable without direct European management. This meant African nations would cling to those revenue sources while failing to ignite their independent economies. Those who assumed control of or inherited these profitable trade contracts with their former colonizers would use the resources to remain in power rather than to invest the revenue in development.

THE ROAD TO CHAOS: POSTCOLONIAL SUB-SAHARAN AFRICA

The withdrawal of the Europeans from Sub-Saharan Africa created a power vacuum filled by the colonial-educated political elite. Because the absence of Europeans also meant nations were responsible for their own security (absence of foreign military), many who took over as leaders of independent nations found themselves in precarious positions. The relatively lucrative flow of resources and revenue turned out to be limited, because a safer postwar world meant that resources could flow from other world regions. Africa, though it remained rich in resources, was viewed

FIGURE 5.3c(1). Map of Africa showing the plans for a Cape Town–Cairo railway.
Copyright © Classical geographer (CC BY-SA 3.0) at http://commons.wikimedia.org/wiki/File%3ACape_to_Cairo.svg .

as backwards, risky, and even a dangerous place to conduct business. Without the Europeans, it fell into disrepair. Before the Europeans arrived, the landscapes of Sub-Saharan Africa reflected tribal, pastoral,

FIGURE 5.3c(2). Uganda Line railroad completed by the British.
Copyright in the Public Domain.

and simple structures. After the Europeans left, the landscape had been fundamentally altered. Land use, urbanism, and economic activities were all Western in influence. Independence, then, meant either maintaining these colonial systems or attempting to return back to simpler times.

Although the region's nations never returned to their simpler tribal format, leaders who inherited this power often found themselves struggling to keep it. Therefore, maintaining tribal alliances often helped. If, however, a leader was from one tribe and underserved another, tensions and even violence would often follow. This translated into high levels of corruption, cruelty against opposition, and the politicization of religion and ethnicity. Ruling groups would blame economic shortfalls on others, sparking violence, military *coups*, rebellions, and, in some cases, genocide. Religious differences, especially in the Sahel, continue to spark atrocities in Mali, Sudan, Chad, and the Central African Republic, to name a few.

Today, many Sub-Saharan African countries are still struggling with corruption, violence, slow and uneven development, and ethnic/racial tensions. South Africa, a nation believed to have shed its past and trounced *apartheid*, seems to have returned in some form. *Apartheid* can be defined as the South African policy or system of segregation and discrimination, based on race, which existed between about 1948 and 1994.

Today, violence against foreigners, especially Zimbabwean laborers and others perceived as taking jobs away from poor South Africans, is on the rise. Additionally, racial divisions and attitudes are still a part of the cultural landscape. However, some positive changes can also be observed. Foreign direct investment, especially from multinational corporations, the Chinese, and the Americans, is on the rise and has begun transforming some of Africa's urban centers (see *Section 5.4*). Likewise, African nations are working together more to form economic alliances that might ready them for a future of growth, on their own terms.

5.4 Poverty and Population

Sub-Saharan Africa has some of the most severe landscapes of poverty on Earth. As the world industrialized, virtually every country in the region was exploited for its resources by other, more powerful nations and then left to fend for themselves. Europeans had the trade networks and access to consumer markets that, within their economic ecosystem, contributed to their ability to generate wealth. Africans were barely allowed into their cities and had little influence in economic matters. Once independent, the nations of the region simply lacked the global connections and camaraderie with neighbors to form an economic nucleus of their own. Revenue streams often funneled to those in political power, thus making top political positions both lucrative and targeted. Beneath the political turmoil, corruption, and lack of social systems designed to distribute revenue into schools, health care, economic activities, and agriculture was a majority simply surviving. This is why Sub-Saharan African nations are still poor and more characterized by their informal economies and landscapes of poverty.

POPULATION TRENDS

As discussed in Chapter 1, demography provides a lens through which one may examine a particular country or region. Although generalizing can often be irresponsible, there are some common features amongst Sub-Saharan African national demographic profiles. These trends are directly related to poverty. Using the

FIGURE 5.3d The political conflicts in Central African Republic are religious. The *Seleka* rebels are muslims fighting the Christian government forces and African coalition forces. As many as 200,000 people have been displaced and made refugees by this series of conflicts.
Copyright in the Public Domain.

Democratic Republic of Congo (DRC) as an example, below are *some common features found in areas of high poverty:*

- *Low per capita GDP*: The average person has an extremely low yearly income because the state does not distribute wealth into education, jobs, or health care. The Democratic Republic of Congo (DRC), for example, has a *per capita* GDP of just $700.

- *High Total Fertility Rates*: TFR is the number of children born to childbearing-age women. In the DRC, the TFR rate is about 4.66, , compared to Sweden's 1.8. This is because the population, especially women, is uneducated and has little or no access to health care or family planning, etc.

- *High Dependency Ratios*: This measures the number of people, per household, under the age of sixteen and over the age of sixty-five that depend on a working-age adult. In the DRC, the

FIGURE 5.3e. Joseph Kony's LRA (Lord's Resistance Army) of the Democratic Republic of Congo and Central African Republic are Christian fundamentalists fighting corruption, cruelty, and child soldier recruitment, but are themselves accused of heinous crimes. Kony is currently wanted by Interpol, but remains at large. Copyright © wapt.com (CC BY-SA 4.0) at http://commons.wikimedia.org/wiki/File%3AInsurgents_of_the_LRA.jpg .

rate is 91.1%. This essentially means that most homes in the country have both children and elderly sharing them and depending on (typically one) an adult to provide.

- *Low Average Age:* If the bulk of your population is young, that typically results from high TFR and low life expectancy. Lack of access to steady nutrition, sanitation, clean water, and medicine results in lower life expectancy. In the DRC, the average age is about seventeen. With the bulk of the national population being seventeen, the generational turnover is much faster.

Beyond what these general demographic trends reveal are aspects of poverty that are less measurable but important to understand. It may be one thing to define, measure, and categorize various characteristics of poverty, but few in the developed world know what it means to live in the kind of abject poverty found in Sub-Saharan Africa. Abject poverty means people living with limited or no access to things like clean drinking water, sanitation, reliable nutrition, health care or family planning, and land tenure. These people often have no political voice and become the lowest, most exploited, and most vulnerable group in society. The problem is that in many countries, a majority of Sub-Saharan Africans live in poverty, with a significant share of them living in slums.

There are also long-lasting cultural customs in the Sahel region that reflect low education levels and gender inequality. **Female Genital Mutilation (FGM)** is the practice of removing part of or all of the

FIGURE 5.4a. Kibera slum in Nairobi, Kenya is amongst the largest slums in the world. It is estimated that between 500,000 and 2 million live here on an income of $1.00 a day. Megaslums are often on railway lines, because it is public land (okay for squatting) and residents can use the train to export their services elsewhere to make money.

female genitalia at a young age. It is estimated that up to 140 million women have gone through FGM. The goal of this practice is to inform a man (future husband) that the woman has waited and not been sullied. The procedure is usually done with dirty and dull tools, but rates of infection or death are not reported because it often happens in remote areas and is illegal in many countries.

CITIES

The city, even conceptually, was relatively unknown in traditional Africa. As foreigners arrived, they would often occupy locations with ports (or some other strategic value) and cluster their activities within that space. For foreign occupiers, this was normal, as they came from regions where cities played a central role in society. In Africa, cities would become epicenters of colonial activities while limiting access to locals.

In the postcolonial era, established cities became beacons of hope. The rural poor would view the cities as place of opportunity and move to them in great numbers. As it would turn out, opportunities would be limited, and the rural poor would essentially become the growing mass of urban poor. This postcolonial flood into cities could be seen around the world, giving rise to the megaslum, or smaller urban slums growing together to make a giant slum occupied by, in some cases, more than a million people. Sub-Saharan Africa has some of the fastest-growing cities on Earth. A majority of their residents are poor.

FIGURE 5.4b Typical family in the DRC. They exemplify larger demographic trends of low *per capita* GDP, high TFR, high dependency ratio, and low average age.
Copyright © Julien Harneis (CC BY-SA 2.0) at http://commons.wikimedia.org/wiki/File%3ACecilia_and_her_family.jpg .

BOX 5B URBAN GROWTH IN SUB-SAHARAN AFRICA

FIGURE 5.4c. Kano, Nigeria is amongst the fastest-growing cities in Sub-Saharan Africa. Today, the metropolitan area is quickly approaching 10 million. Copyright © Shiraz Chakera (CC BY-SA 2.0) at http://commons.wikimedia.org/wiki/File%3AKanofromDalaHill.jpg .

Many Sub-Saharan African cities are growing at a pace faster than the global average. Although the nations of the region are still statistically more rural than urban, that has been changing and continues to change quickly. Below is a list of Sub-Saharan African city populations in 1950 and 2012:

City	1950	2010	2025 (projected)
Lagos, Nigeria	300k	10m	15m
Dar es Salaam, Tan.	69k	4.3m	6.2m
Nairobi, Kenya	120k	3.1m	6.2m
Kinshasa, Congo	95k	8.7m	15m
Johannesburg, SA	200k	3.6m	4.1m

These cities represent just a few in the region. As these cities grow, they also grow together and expand out. Conurbation is two or more cities growing together for mutual benefit over time, whereas urban sprawl is the outward trajectory of cities resulting from urban growth. Urban growth at this rate can be viewed as both good and bad. Growth is good, because a large labor pool might attract foreign industries that rely on it for textiles, manufacturing, or oil industries. On the other hand, much of the urban growth is comprised of poor, rural people seeking opportunities in the cities. They add to the urban poor and do not generate tax revenues that could go into urban infrastructure. Kinshasa, Congo, for example, has about ten million residents today, but it does not have a waterborne sanitation system. This has made the city "ground zero" for many diseases like cholera. Sub-Saharan Africa will continue to deal with rapid urban growth well into this century.

Slums

It is important to remember that many of the world's megaslums exist because of colonial/postcolonial influences. Many cities were founded and governed by European colonial powers, but then became the economic and cultural centers of independent nations after the colonial era. Cities under European rule were often small, grand, and relatively secure. The postcolonial period (1950–1970) was characterized by the uneven distribution of wealth, civil unrest or war, broad malnutrition, and even starvation. This dynamic drives individuals and families to areas where, at least perceivably, they can have greater opportunities. Cities, then, became magnets for millions of rural poor. As decades passed, the colonial cities that once were small and rich became massive, expanded cities of blight and poverty.

The *Kibera* slum of Nairobi (seen in *Figure 5.4d*), is likely the largest single megaslum in Africa. This was originally public land controlled by the British colonial government, adjacent to the railway lines. The British allowed local soldiers to live off this land, in squatter settlements, because it did not cost them anything and enabled the soldiers to easily board a train when needed. In the postcolonial era, *Kibera* swelled with urban-bound Kenyans who sought opportunity in the city. Today, *Kibera* is like a city itself. There are about a million residents, all of whom are quite poor, living on about $1 a day. Although *Kibera* is alive with more traditional informal economic activities, it is also higher in rape, malnutrition, percentage of those living with HIV, and dependency ratios. In Liberia, a former colony of the United States, the Monrovian slum, West Point, is amongst the most disadvantaged urban slums on Earth (see *Figure 5.4e*). This area of Monrovia is dangerous to visit because of the percentage of people using drugs, frequency of rape, and percentages of those living with HIV are very high.

Refugees

Sub-Saharan Africa generates many millions of refugees. A *refugee* is a person forced to leave his or her homeland because of war, persecution, or climate-related catastrophes.

Each of these reasons is present in Sub-Saharan Africa. At the same time, each of these reasons comes with very different narratives. Earlier in this chapter was a discussion about religious violence in the Central African Republic. This generated tens of thousands of refugees. In 2008, the Nord-Kivu tribal conflict in the DR Congo generated thousands of refugees. These people were mainly villagers fearing rape, bodily harm, and the recruitment of child soldiers.

In Dadaab, Kenya, there has been a steady flow of Somali refugees fleeing the violence (religious, political, climate). The *Dangahaley, Ifo,* and *Hayadera* refugee camps in this part of Kenya are very large, with a total of 350,000 living in them. Nongovernmental and international agencies have worked to supply these people with help, but funding is always limited, leaving many to fend for themselves. Sub-Saharan Africa, particularly in the Sahel region, will continue to generate refugees well into this century.

FIGURE 5.4d. Nairobi's Kibera slum is one of the largest megaslums in the world. Estimates suggest the slum has over a million residents living on about $1.00 a day. Copyright © Schreibkraft (CC BY-SA 3.0) at http://commons.wikimedia.org/wiki/ File%3ANairobi_Kibera_04.JPG .

5.5 Climate, Environmental Vulnerability, and Disease

Sub-Saharan Africa's human—environmental dynamic can be defined by two coexisting narratives. One is climate and how anthropogenic change is already impacting, and will continue to impact, the region in potentially devastating ways. The second has to do with the endemic poverty and exploitation of natural ecosystems, in biodiverse areas, for human survival. Both collide in Africa, making it one of the more environmentally concerning regions on Earth.

CLIMATE CHANGE AND AFRICA

As discussed in Chapter 1, climate is established by energy levels received by the sun and the interaction between the atmosphere, hydrosphere, lithosphere, and biosphere in a particular location. The atmosphere, for example, explains wind patterns (Easterly trade winds, Westerlies, etc.) and the hydrosphere reflects the level of precipitation those winds bring (or fail to bring). This particular interaction that helps to shape Africa's climate is important to understand. The reason for this has to do with climate change and how these processes are changing.

Climate change can generally be observed in three ways: sea level rise, sea surface temperature, and high-to-low-pressure wind patterns. Sub-Saharan Africa's climate is heavily influenced by its wind patterns, largely because the equator runs through the central portion of the landmass. This means the winds are flowing from high-pressure systems, situated somewhere around thirty degrees north and south latitude, towards the equator, forming the (before mentioned) Intertropical Convergence Zone (ITCZ). As climate changes, these wind patterns change. This can be observed, for example, in extended periods of dry winds flowing into areas that desperately await seasonal rains. If these intensified episodes of dry deflect or prevent seasonal precipitation, then droughts intensify and famines begin. In other areas, the precipitation may be extreme. This also results from changes in high-to-low-pressure wind patterns. There are signs that the ITCZ is weakening in areas like the Sahel. As the rainy season wanes, millions suffer (see *Figures 5.5b and 5.5c*).

FIGURE 5.4e. The West Point slum in Monrovia is one of the most downtrodden and poor slums in the world. There is no form of sanitation, so residents use the beach as a bathroom. HIV, drug abuse, and rape are common in West Point. Copyright © Rjruiziii (CC BY-SA 3.0) at http://commons.wikimedia.org/wiki/File%3ABushrod_Island%2C_Monrovia%2C_Liberia.JPG .

Broadly, changes in climate will have major effects beyond what was just discussed. The *four (4) impacts of climate change in Sub-Saharan Africa* are:

- *Agriculture*: Changes in precipitation will impact millions of subsistence farmers, or people who squat on lands and grow just enough food to feed themselves. This has induced, and will continue to induce, famines that have the potential to kill hundreds of thousands of people.

- *Ecosystems*: Changes in precipitation patterns directly affect the biome. Food chains start to break down because reductions in biomass and available water resources impact all levels of life.

FIGURE 5.4f. This tribal, ethnic violence in DR Congo has generated the movement of refugees out of the conflict zone by the thousands. Copyright © Julien Harneis (CC BY-SA 1.0) at http://commons.wikimedia.org/wiki/File%3ARefugee_camp.jpg .

FIGURE 5.4g.
Copyright © Julien Harneis (CC BY-SA 2.0) at http://commons.wikimedia.org/wiki/File%3AKibativillagers.jpg .

- *Human Health*: This region already struggles with consistent access to nutrition. In drier conditions, reductions in livestock, water resources, and nutritional resources will continue to combine and affect the human well-being. Disease vectors will continue to shift as well, affecting a larger number of people.

ENVIRONMENTAL VULNERABILITY

There is a direct correlation between regions characterized by poverty and corruption and environmental degradation. This is not just the case in Sub-Saharan Africa, but a theme around the world. Some of the most biodiverse areas on Earth are the precise areas most exploited by people. Simply put, people will do what they must to survive. If, for example, 80 to 90% of the population lives on $3 or less a day, they will likely struggle to survive. If the habitat around them has resources that offer a source of revenue, that revenue stream will be exploited, regardless of the laws, policies, and environmental impacts. This helps to explain the reduction of species like elephants, rhinoceri, and gorillas in the region.

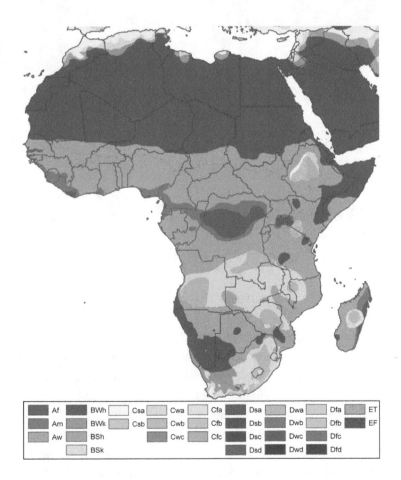

FIGURE 5.5a. Köppen Climate Map of Africa.
Copyright © M.C. Peel, B.L. Finlayson, and T.A. McMahon (CC BY-SA 3.0) at
http://commons.wikimedia.org/wiki/File%3AAfrica_Köppen_Map.png .

FIGURE 5.5b. Drought in eastern Africa is becoming more common and this area already has a high level of refugees from political and religious violence.
Copyright © Andy Hall / Oxfam East Africa (CC BY-SA 2.0) at http://commons.wikimedia.org/wiki/File%3AOxfam_East_Africa_-_A_mass_grave_for_children_in_Dadaab.jpg .

THEMATIC INTERSECTION 5B

The Ivory Trade: Endangering the African Elephant

Themes: Economic/Environmental

The Ivory Trade in Sub-Saharan Africa has been around, in some form, since the colonial era. However, because the impact on the African elephant (both the bush and forest species), had become so severe, an organized international ban on ivory was implemented in 1989. During the 1980s, approximately seventy-five thousand African elephants were being killed each year for their tusks. Of those elephants, about 80% of them resulted from illegal poaching. Although this ivory ban was good on paper, the poaching of elephants never stopped. To better understand this, an examination of two colliding themes is necessary.

The economic theme is complex and multifaceted. One economic narrative is the low-growth economy, political corruption, and lack of resources in many Sub-Saharan African nations. This region literally has millions of hectares of wild habitats, many of which are protected. However, they generally lack the resources to staff an effective number of rangers dedicated to protecting these large areas. More

FIGURE 5.5c. Dead livestock in Somaliland (Northern Somalia). These animals represent how many in the region make a living and survive. The drought of 2011 killed tens of thousands of animals. Copyright © Oxfam East Africa (CC BY-SA 2.0) at http://commons.wikimedia.org/wiki/File%3A2011_Horn_of_Africa_famine_Oxfam_01.jpg .

specifically, the economic recession between 2008 and 2011 reduced significantly the number of tourists, which then hit local economies even harder. At the same time, severe droughts in key habitats in east Africa resulted in the mass loss of livestock. Tribes like the Maasai, who once coveted and lived in harmony with the elephants, turned on them as a source of income.

The other economic narrative is the rise of the Chinese middle class. China has experienced double-digit growth for more than a decade, resulting in the swelling of its middle class. With several hundred million people now earning good wages, Chinese families seek to represent their position with coveted material possessions like ivory sculptures. This demand has created an incentive for poor Africans to turn on their own elephants. This trade is so lucrative, it is not only easy to bribe local officials, but sometimes the local officials are the poachers as well. With this lack of organized security, approximately thirty thousand elephants are still being butchered, despite the ivory ban.

The intersecting theme, then, is the environment. This animal, amongst many others, has been pushed to the brink of extinction. One of the reasons for this is poaching, but another is land-use change and habitat fragmentation. As Sub-Saharan Africa urbanizes and expands its economies, more land must be converted into urban space, agricultural use, mining operations, oil drilling, forest resources and logging, infrastructure, and so on. These land-use changes have reduced natural habitats significantly. This is largely why giant land conservatories have been set aside for species like elephants. But with the lack of proper funding, high corruption, and consistent demand from China, the poaching shall likely continue well into this century and potentially push the African elephant into extinction.

FIGURE 5.5d. The Ivory Trade was well established in Africa, under European control.
Copyright in the Public Domain.

DISEASE

Disease has always been synonymous with Sub-Saharan Africa. This is both because a tropical/subtropical climate is where many diseases fester and because underdevelopment has left many in this region directly vulnerable to the types of diseases rooted in human activity. Although there are many, the *four (4) diseases of Sub-Saharan Africa* highlighted are:

- Malaria
- HIV
- Cholera
- Gastroenteritis

According to the World Health Organization, malaria is caused by blood parasites transmitted from person to person through the bites of infected mosquitos. Africa is a hotbed of malarial activity, in that 85% of world malaria cases and 90% of malaria-caused deaths are in Africa. This disease affects mostly children, which represent about 85% of all malaria cases. Because antimalarial medicine is sometimes ineffective and difficult to distribute, the best approach for controlling malaria in Africa is bed nets. Nets that cover a bed at night reduce the chance of infection significantly.

The impact of HIV in Sub-Saharan Africa can never be fully realized. It has devastated families by the millions and continues to be a major challenge for nations in this region. When looked at broadly, Sub-Saharan Africa stands out as the epicenter of this disease. HIV is sexually transmitted. As discussed earlier, the region is broadly characterized by several key social and demographic trends. The average age of many nations is between nineteen and twenty years old—a very sexually active age. Also, educations levels are very low, especially amongst women. Lack of access to health care and family planning (prophylactics, birth control medication, sex education) has exacerbated the spread of this disease. When looked at compared to the world, 67% of all people living with HIV are in Sub-Saharan Africa. Approximately 70% of all people who die from HIV are in the region. Alarmingly, about 72% of all new infections are also in the region. However, at the same time, nongovernmental organizations have really made strides in educating young Africans about the disease and how to avoid contracting it.

Cholera and gastroenteritis are contracted from poor sanitation and contaminated water resources. Because so many Africans live in either slums or cities with poor infrastructure, outbreaks are common. In Kinshasa, DR Congo, for example, ten to twelve million people live in a city without a waterborne sewer system. This has resulted in regular, deadly outbreaks of cholera. Gastroenteritis is the number one killer of children in the world. The source is unsanitary water, which is typically all slum dwellers have access to. In the water are parasites and the rotavirus, which are contracted and induce water diarrhea. Because so many living in extreme poverty have little or no access to a health care professional, they often dehydrate and die.

CONCLUSION

Sub-Saharan Africa is a fascinating region in many ways. On one hand, the primal landscapes, biodiverse habitats, and colorful cultures are a welcome part of the human and natural landscapes of Earth. On the other hand, the region provides a platform from which to observe human poverty, corruption,

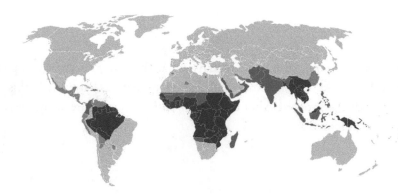

FIGURE 5.5e. This world map of malarial incidence shows that Africa has a major vector of the disease.
Copyright © Percherie (CC BY-SA 3.0) at http://commons.wikimedia.org/wiki/File%3APaludisme.png .

environmental degradation, and the impact of disease on humanity. And to add context to these issues, many of these issues are, at their base, influenced by foreigners. Africa was colonized by richer, more powerful Europeans who exploited the region and then left it underdeveloped. Africa, though it is redefining itself in many ways, is still the poorest region on Earth, and still struggles with its manipulated past.

When examining Sub-Saharan Africa moving forward, it is important to approach it in a certain way. The *four (4) considerations of Sub-Saharan Africa* are:

- *Tribal dynamics:* Even though tribes don't run governments, they are still an important, less obvious element of both conflict and cooperation in the region.

- *Colonial/Postcolonial Influences:* Remember that the Europeans changed many aspects of African life. Cities are colonial, political boundaries are colonial, and infrastructure and resource extraction were originally colonial activities. As nations became independent, many of these systems were grabbed and held onto by corrupt leaders in the postcolonial era. Therefore, these narratives are important to consider.

- *Poverty*: The huge percentage of Sub-Saharan Africans living in poverty allows us to understand their conditions and motives. Environmental degradation, species loss, disease, etc. are all related to poverty.

- *Climate*: Africa's climate is like a clock which hundreds of millions follow. The movement of the ITCZ is a central feature of this region. As climate changes and these climatic processes shift and change, this region will feel it in very measurable ways.

Axis

Intertropical Convergence Zone (ITCZ)

Sahel

FIGURE 5.5f. A group of young Angolans being educated on the dangers of HIV and what precautions can be taken. Education, by NGOs, has been key in reducing infection rates.
Copyright in the Public Domain.

KEY TERMS

Rift Valley	Apartheid	Environment
Okavango Delta	Poverty	Ivory
Tribalism	HIV	Disease
Atlantic Slave Trade	Megaslum	
Triangle Trade	Female Genital Mutilation	
Colonialism	(FGM)	
Berlin Conference	Refugees	

CLASS DISCUSSIONS

1. Describe the role of the "tribe" in African culture. How did this change when the Europeans arrived?
2. Discuss the effects of the Berlin Conference and how this fundamentally altered Africa.
3. Describe slavery in Africa and the slave trade that followed.
4. What happened after decolonization? How did many nations in Sub-Saharan Africa handle independence?
5. Discuss poverty in Africa and how it informs us about such issues as disease, dependency ratios, and the role of women in society.
6. Why does Female Genital Mutilation (FGM) still occur in the Sahel?

ADDITIONAL RESOURCES

African Environment:

http://whc.unesco.org/en/list/1432

http://www.ifaw.org/united-states/our-work/elephants/ending-ivory-trade

https://www.worldwildlife.org/species/

CIA World Factbook Africa:

https://www.cia.gov/library/publications/the-world-factbook/wfbExt/region_afr.html

Economic Growth:

http://www.afdb.org/en/knowledge/publications/african-economic-outlook/

Female Genital Mutilation:

http://www.who.int/mediacentre/factsheets/fs241/en/

Disease:

http://www.afro.who.int/en/health-topics/topics/4337-hivaids.html

Slavery:
http://www.pbs.org/wgbh/aia/part1/1narr4.html

BIBLIOGRAPHY

"The African Slave Trade and the Middle Passage." PBS. n.d. Web. http://www.pbs.org/wgbh/aia/part1/1narr4. html. 22 Jan. 2015.

"A New Chapter in the Battle Against Corruption in Africa." N.p., n.d. Web. http://thecommonwealth.org/project/new-chapter-battle-against-corruption-africa. 14 Jan. 2015.

Central Intelligence Agency.The World Factbook. n.d. Web. https://www.cia.gov/library/publications/the-world-factbook/wfbExt/region_afr.html. 16 Jan. 2015.

Cincotta, R.P., et al. (2000). Human population in biodiversity hotspots. Nature. Vol. 404. 27 April. pp. 990–991.

"Ending the Ivory Trade." IFAW. N.p., n.d. Web. http://www.ifaw.org/united-states/our-work/elephants/ending-ivory-trade. 13 Jan. 2015.

Freire, M.E., et al. "Africa's Urbanization: Challenges and Opportunities." The Growth Dialogue. n.d. Web. http://www.growthdialogue.org/sites/default/files/documents/GD_WP7_web_8.5x11%20(3).pdf. 12 Jan. 2015.

"HIV/AIDS." WHO. N.p., n.d. Web. http://www.afro.who.int/en/health-topics/topics/4337-hivaids.html. 13 Jan. 2015.

"Kenya: Landmark Ruling on Indigenous Land Rights." Human Rights Watch. N.p. 04 Feb. 2010. Web. http://www.hrw.org/news/2010/02/04/kenya-landmark-ruling-indigenous-land-rights. 21 Jan. 2015.

"Okavango Delta." UNESCO World Heritage Centre. N.p., n.d. Web. http://whc.unesco.org/en/list/1432. 15 Jan. 2015.

"The State of African Cities 2014." UN-Habitat. N.p. 13 Mar. 2014. Web. http://unhabitat.org/the-state-of-african-cities-2014/. 13 Jan. 2015.

"Species." WorldWildlife.org. World Wildlife Fund, n.d. Web. https://www.worldwildlife.org/species/. 04 May 2015.

CHAPTER 6

North America

Country List: United States, Canada, Greenland, Caribbean Island nations

Key Intersecting Themes:

Historical, Physical Geographical, Cultural, Political, Economic

Country List:
- United States
- Canada
- Greenland (shared with Pacifica Chapter 11)

6.1 Regional Overview

North America, a region which includes the United States, Canada, and Greenland, is a vast and complex discussion, no matter how it is approached. Although all regions are important in that they have all contributed to the collective narrative and sophisticated landscapes of our planet, North America has, for several hundred years now, played a central role in shaping the world we all live in today. It is important to point out that Mexico, though it is a valued part of a community of nations that occupy the continent of North America, will not be formally discussed in this chapter. The reason for this is Mexico's cultural and economic characteristics seem better represented when discussing the community of nations

NORTH AMERICA

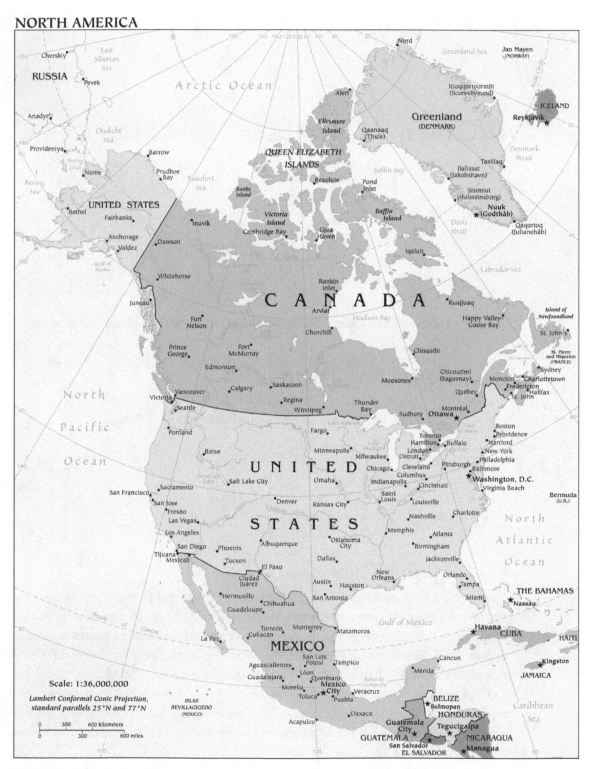

FIGURE 6.1. North America
Copyright in the Public Domain.

in Central and South America. At the same time, Mexico and its deep cultural and economic ties to the United States, as well as the growing political voice of Mexican Americans and other Latino communities within the country, will be highlighted in this chapter. The goal of this chapter is to illuminate some key aspects of this important region while pointing out how the United States, specifically, has been both responsible for vast global cooperation and the architect of many conflicts.

6.2 North America's Physical Geography

CLIMATE

Most of North America is situated in the middle latitudes, between thirty and roughly sixty-five degrees north, or the "Arctic Circle." This position on Earth means much of the region falls within the *westerly winds*. These winds form a band around the planet, both north and south of the equator, between these latitudes. This "westerly" band of wind is caused by air flowing from high-pressure zones (subtropical highs) over the oceans to areas of low pressure, over land (continent). In the case of North America, the high pressure that influences this section of the *westerlies* is in the Pacific Ocean. The region, then, generally receives air from the Pacific Ocean and then distributes it over continental North America, from west to east via the jet stream and an upper atmospheric wind orientation. Understanding wind orientation is a beginning point to understanding the region's climate.

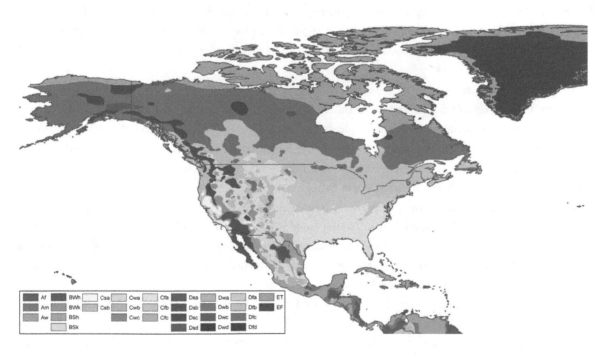

FIGURE 6.2a. Located mostly in the middle latitudes, North America has a wide variety of climates. Copyright © M.C. Peel, B.L. Finlayson, and T.A. McMahon (CC BY-SA 3.0) at https://commons.wikimedia.org/wiki/File%3ANorth-America_Köppen_Map.png.

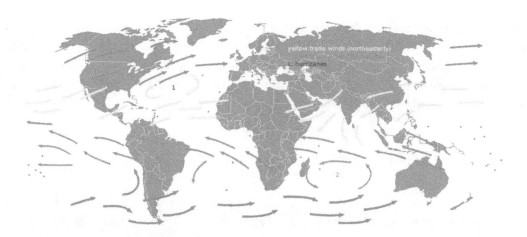

FIGURE 6.2b. Prevailing winds on Earth. North America falls mostly in the westerly winds, flowing from the Pacific Ocean into continental North America, then out into the Atlantic. Copyright in the Public Domain.

Location also plays a key role in North America's general climate composition. Being mostly above the subtropics and mostly below the subpolar latitudes, North America receives an ideal range of oblique solar energy. In other words, the region avoids the direct radiation below 23.5 degrees north latitude and the harsh cold of above sixty-five degrees, making the region seasonal but ideal for a broad range of agriculture. Other factors, like *rain shadow effect* and other climatic and topographical features that influence the diversity of climate types, will be discussed in more detail in this chapter.

Ocean Influences

Although the *westerly winds* seem to explain much about North America's general climate profile, that may not be true at the regional scale. For example, both Santa Barbara, California and Wilmington, North Carolina sit on the same line of latitude (thirty-four degrees north), but if a person in each location decided to go to the beach in mid-December, the two would likely find very different conditions at the beaches, despite latitude. Santa Barbara might be warm enough to wear a bathing suit, whereas Wilmington might be snowy and freezing cold. This can partially be explained by ocean influences. Because California is receiving its wind from the Pacific Ocean (unless there is a Santa Ana wind event), the weather is much more regulated by the ocean. North Carolina, even though it is also on the coast, receives its weather from the interior of the country, rather than the ocean. This mitigates the regulatory influence of ocean and explains how snow may fall at that latitude.

The difference in climate may also be explained by high pressure. Southern California is under the influence of a subtropical high-pressure system. This descending air from the Hadley Cell makes California's climate warmer and drier, on average. The ocean currents, or more specifically the California Current, flow down from the north, carrying cold water by Southern California. This cold water, under a high-pressure system, creates a special climate type rare on Earth: The Köppen "*Csa*" climate (a.k.a. Mediterranean Climate). This climate is generally warm and ocean regulated, with seasonal winter precipitation events.

On the east coast of North America, the Gulf Stream carries warm, tropical water up past the United States and then back across the Atlantic to Europe. This water brings seasonal humidity and subtropical weather to the eastern third of the United States during the summer, but then fades and succumbs to the cold

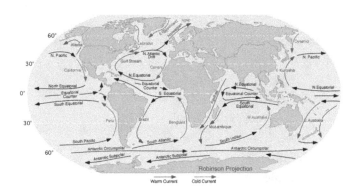

FIGURE 6.2c. Ocean currents in the west generally flow from north to south, whereas in the east currents flow from south to north. Copyright in the Public Domain.

continental trough of westerly air from the western interior during winter. This explains why the eastern third of the United States has a very seasonal climate. These variations are, in part, influenced by oceans.

Topography and Climate

Topography can be described as the arrangement of physical features in a region. Some *key topographical features and how they influence the climates of North America* are:

- *Western mountain ranges:* The coastal ranges, Sierra Nevadas, the Cascade Range, and even the Rocky Mountains create a natural barrier between the ocean-influenced coastal regions and the dry, intermontane realm. Air is forced to rise, release moisture, and then descend, absent most of its moisture, on the other side. These leeward winds are known as the *Chinook* winds. The dry air from the rain shadow is often met by a land area higher in altitude. Much of the intermontane west is between 3,500 and 7,000 feet in average elevation. This makes the climate even drier in many areas.
- *Gulf of Mexico:* The southeast corner of the United States and the Caribbean subregion are within the influence of the Gulf of Mexico. During summer months, the warm, moist air from the Gulf gets caught up in in the westerlies, thus carrying humid air deep into the continental United States through the eastern seaboard. This makes the eastern third of the United States unpleasantly humid between May and September.
- *Great Plains:* During the winter months, cold air troughs down from Canada, unobstructed, making temperatures very cold, even freezing. The extreme nature of this cold seasonal front is enabled by the lack of ocean influence in the most central continental areas. Alberta, Saskatchewan, and Manitoba, Canada, for example, have some of the coldest winters on the planet, because the flat topography and lack of proximity to either the Pacific or Atlantic Oceans punctuates winter temperatures. This cold-air trough often dips deep into the United States, all the way to Texas and the Deep South on occasion.

NATURAL RESOURCES

North America is one of the most resource-rich regions on Earth. The range of natural resources is great, and includes:

- Timber and woodlands resources
- Minerals, metals, and ores
- Oil, natural gas, and coal
- Water (rivers, lakes, deltas)
- Fertile soils
- Grazing lands
- Warm-water ports
- Fish

These natural resources have been the building blocks of both the United States and Canada. Today, they are leveraged in a wide variety of industries that produce countless goods. Because both the US and Canada are key players, even partners, in the globalized economy, these natural resources are distributed around the world.

FIGURE 6.2d. The Mississippi Watershed area is vast and provides water resources, transportation arteries, and fertile soils. Copyright © Shannon (CC BY-SA 4.0) at http://commons.wikimedia.org/wiki/File%3AMississippirivermapnew.jpg .

WATERSHEDS, RIVERS, AND COASTS

Watersheds and Rivers

As seen in *Figure 6.2d*, the Mississippi Watershed is extensive. What it does not show are the wide range of attributes and benefits. A watershed is an area or region that drains precipitation, snow melt, and runoff through a hierarchy of streams and rivers until it reaches the sea. Because the volume of water collected and moved is so great, these systems can be relied on for many things. For example, the silt and sediments carried by the water, over thousands of years, helps to create expansive zones of fertile soils. Therefore, robust agricultural activities can thrive in these zones. The water is often deep enough for barges and even ships, enabling the movement of goods and services from the interior to the ocean. The water can be used broadly for human use, allowing cities with millions of people to live on the banks. The water can be used as a source of energy (hydroelectric power). All these benefits come from watershed zones. At the same time, this resource has been abused in many ways, causing a host of environmental problems like agricultural runoff inducing coastal *hypoxia* and low oxygen zones resulting from the phosphorous and nitrogen in agrochemicals.

Below is a list of **four (4) key watershed zones in North America:**

- *The Mississippi Watershed* (United States): Largest in the region and is one of the largest agricultural hearths in the world.
- *The Columbia River/Willamette Watershed* (United States): Provides very fertile lands in Washington and Oregon, as well as reliable ocean access for larger ships.
- *The Saint Lawrence River Watershed* (Canada, US): This critical watershed zone is Canada's largest and includes the Great Lakes.
- *Hudson River Watershed* (United States, Canada): Though fertile and supports a healthy agricultural region, this watershed is a major artery for shipping.

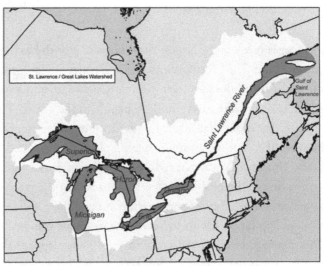

FIGURE 6.2e. The Saint Lawrence River Watershed zone is Canada's most important and includes the Great Lakes, both in the US and Canada.
Copyright © Karl Musser (CC BY-SA 2.5) at http://commons.wikimedia.org/wiki/File:Grlakes_lawrence_map.png .

CASE STUDY 6A

River in Danger: the Colorado River

The Colorado River is the largest river, by volume, in the southwestern United States. It flows about 1,400 miles from the Colorado Rockies to the Gulf of California in Mexico. Because of the rapid growth of California and parts of Arizona and Nevada, the water of the Colorado has been relied upon to provide water resources for approximately thirty million people and more than four million acres of agriculture, including the entire Imperial Valley of California. Because the river flows through several western states, water claims have been a source of tension and legal conflict for decades. Today, the water of the Colorado River is allocated as such:

1. California: 27%
2. Colorado: 23%
3. Arizona: 17%
4. Nevada: 2%

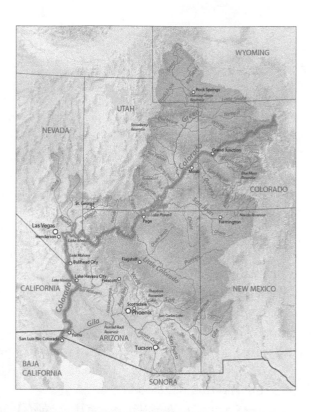

FIGURE 6.2f. The water of the Colorado River is in high demand by California, Arizona, and Nevada. So much is used that the river no longer reaches its delta in the Gulf of California.
Copyright © Shannon (CC BY-SA 4.0) at http://commons. wikimedia.org/wiki/File%3AColoradorivermapnew1.jpg .

California receives the largest share because it both has the largest population (by far) and the most agricultural land. The Metropolitan Water District of California provides water supplies from various sources, including the Colorado River, via an expansive aqueduct system. Arizona has the Central Arizona Project, which canals water to five million people in the greater Phoenix and Tucson metropolitan areas, as well as water for more than eight hundred thousand acres of farmland. Nevada took the smallest allocation because of its robust groundwater supply, but negotiated a large percentage of power from the Hoover Dam. This use of water has reduced the flow of the Colorado River significantly.

Adding to the problem is less snowpack over the past several years. Snowpack acts like a giant natural reservoir. If low levels of snowpack continue, there will be several problems. One is more runoff. Runoff from precipitation events increases the sediment volume, because water moves large amounts of material. This changes the composition of the water and deposits that material in dams while affecting the water's quality. The other is reduced flow volume. Without snowpack, water just flows straight into the watershed. Snowpack holds the water until it is slowly released throughout the year in snowmelt. This water is cleaner and clearer, and provides a steady water supply. Should the Colorado River continue to be overused and the climate continues to change, the people and agriculture that rely on this resource will become more vulnerable to drought, economic catastrophe, and resource conflicts.

Coastline

Coastline, especially coastline with access to warm water, is a beneficial geographic attribute. Canada has the most coastline in the world, measuring about 202,080 km in length. Granted, much of Canada's coastline is seasonally frozen, but the Canadians have good access to the sea, both in the west (Vancouver area) and through the Saint Lawrence watershed region. The United States has about twenty thousand kilometers of coastline, most of which is warm water. This has allowed reliable access to the sea for trade and other commercial, military, and recreational activities.

THE "GREAT BUFFER"

As this chapter shifts to discussions about the human landscapes of North America, a less obvious, but important, aspect of the region's physical geography must be addressed. North America is rather ideally located, in that it has the two largest oceans on Earth separating its mainland from other, older realms. For example, western North America is separated by five to six thousand miles of Pacific Ocean. The eastern coasts of North America have three thousand miles of Atlantic Ocean separating them from more historically hostile, older cultures. This might be considered the "Great Buffer," because the United States and Canada have largely been able to avoid the direct impact of war, political rivalry, invasion, and other caustic aspects of the human landscape, solely because of distance.

Naturally, both the United States and Canada participated in wars, but were never measurably threatened by them at home. Hitler or Napoleon never marched their armies through Times Square in New York City or through the streets of Toronto. The Japanese never invaded Vancouver, Seattle, or Los Angeles. This distance, or "buffer," has allowed North Americans to emerge from two world wars relatively unscathed, apart from the regrettable loss of lives on foreign battlefields. This "Great Buffer" has allowed North Americans to grow their economies without having to rebuild them after atomic devastation or years of carpet bombing. This has contributed to the success of the region, economically and politically.

6.3 Cultural Patterns and Influences in North America

As discussed in Chapter 2, the Europeans, in their quest to establish ocean trade routes to South and East Asia, stumbled upon a "new world" occupied by an indigenous population. The discovery of this new realm would spark an era of European exploration and colonization, fundamentally changing the human landscapes. The colonists made the lands not only political extensions of European nations, but cultural appendages of Europe as well. Centuries of colonization eventually, and in some cases violently, succumbed to a desire for political independence. However, the cultural imprint of European nations remains a part of American and Canadian culture to this day, which makes it important to understand.

NORTH AMERICA'S COLONIAL PAST

As shown in *Figure 6.3a*, the three major European colonial influences in North America were Britain, France, and Spain. Because the British and the French failed to find regions rich in gold and silver, as the Spaniards and Portuguese had, they relied upon identifying lands to be colonized and operated as extensions of their own countries. Measuring how influential these cultures were on the formation of the United

FIGURE 6.3a. Map of European territories in North America (1750). Copyright © Pinpin (CC BY-SA 3.0) at http://commons.wikimedia.org/wiki/File%3ANouvelle-France_map-en.svg .

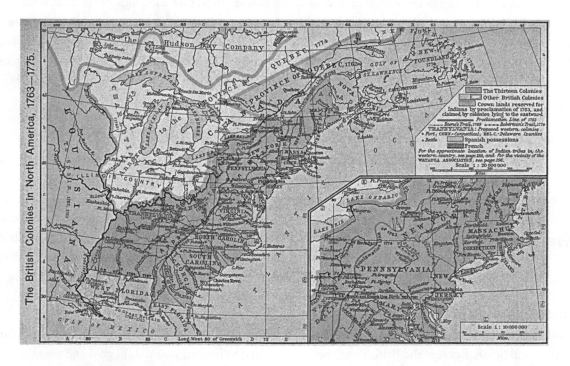

FIGURE 6.3b. Old map of the thirteen colonies in America.
Copyright in the Public Domain.

States and Canada is difficult. However, there are broad discussions that may illuminate the relationship and cultural bonds between Europe and North America.

British Influences

The British colonized the east coast of what would become the United States and parts of Canada. The American colony was composed of people seeking many things, including economic opportunity, social mobility, and religious freedom. These values, aspirations, and opportunities were achievable in the colonies, whereas back in Europe, particularly in Britain, rigid social structures kept people locked into classes. This helped to form an *ethos* amongst colonists that would eventually make them different from their European compatriots.

At the same time, other aspects of the American colonial landscape were patently British. The English language was widely spoken, English common law provided a legal framework, Protestant Christianity formed the spiritual foundation of colonial life, gender inequality and other social norms persisted, and a broad range of economic activities all reflected the British model.

Even deeper, how American colonists viewed other races and ethnicities was characteristically British. The use of slaves in the southern plantation economies, the treatment of Native Americans, and the tensions that accompanied the immigration of people from non-Anglo nations all reflected and echoed British sentiments and paradigms. Even when the Americans achieved independence, their external rejection of Britain concealed their internal predisposition to be very much like them. This "predisposition" would show itself as the United States evolved into a powerful nation.

French Influences

The French not only had established colonies in southwest Canada (later to become Quebec), but also held a vast territory around the Mississippi River, stretching from New Orleans to beyond the border of Canada. Whereas most of the territory was remote and not directly occupied, the colonies In Canada and Louisiana thrived. In southwest Canada and the Ohio River Valley, proximity to British colonies often led to conflicts and even war. The British were not secret about their desire to claim this rich territory, and set up military forts and outposts deep within the realm to maintain a presence.

Down south, New Orleans was a busy colonial city under the French (and briefly, the Spanish). The city was widely used for

FIGURE 6.3c. Quebec City is considered by many the most "European" city in North America. It was established early by the French and is the only city in North America that still has a visible fortress wall.
Copyright © Bernard Gagnon (CC BY-SA 3.0) at http://commons.wikimedia.org/wiki/File%3ACh%C3%A2teau_Frontenac01.jpg .

trade, defense, and as an access point into the wild frontier. French *Cajun* (a derivative of "Canadian") culture is still alive and well, as is French-influenced *creole* culture in the city. In Canada, Quebec has proudly clung to its French past. Although Canada is a part of the British commonwealth of nations, the Quebecois maintain and nurture their French cultural origins, to the point where they have struggled with secession movements over the decades.

Spanish Influences

The Spanish would be influential in many ways, both directly and indirectly, in North America. Because much of the modern United States was once a Spanish territory, their cultural footprint is still quite visible. The Spanish held territories in Florida, the Southwest from Texas to California, and for a while New Orleans, Louisiana. Whereas the Spanish struggled to maintain territories in Florida, the Southwest was fairly well established. It was once the northernmost realm of discovery during the Age of Exploration, and Coronado and his army searched for years for gold, silver, and the type of civilizations found earlier with the Aztecs, Maya, and Inca. His journey ultimately failed, but the Franciscan order of friars traveling with him identified the region as useful for converting natives to Catholicism and establishing agriculture. Santa Fe, New Mexico is the longest continually occupied capital city in North America (1610), and has remained architecturally Spanish for more than four hundred years.

Spanish architecture and urban design is very different from that found in early British colonies. The Spanish would begin with a central *plaza*, or a commons, for all to enjoy. Surrounding this plaza were various accessible services, like a church, a *mercado* (or space for markets), government buildings, schools, and other important civic features. They would also fortify cities, with the entire community's security in mind. That meant both residential and civic space was walled in. The British, on the other hand, would design the town as a place to visit for business and school while allowing people to establish homes outside of town for greater privacy.

Spanish culture and language are an embedded part of American culture. Although Spain lost its colonies long ago, Mexican, Central American, and Spanish Caribbean culture all reflect old Spain in many ways. Approximately 17% of the US population is now Hispanic, and this percentage will likely continue

FIGURE 6.3d. Santa Fe, New Mexico, established in 1610, has been continually occupied, making it the oldest capital city in North America. The San Miguel chapel is also the oldest church in North America.
Copyright © Pretzelpaws (CC BY-SA 3.0) at http://commons.wikimedia.org/wiki/File:Santa_Fe_San_miguel_chapel.jpg .

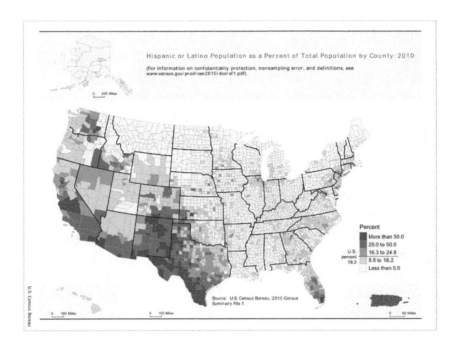

FIGURE 6.3e. The Hispanic population in the US is second only to white, at 17%. This segment of population is growing, as they have higher total fertility rates than Anglo Americans and have formed "minority majorities" in several US states, including New Mexico and California.
Copyright in the Public Domain.

to grow, as fertility rates in the Hispanic community are higher than Anglo-American rates. Hispanic culture is very family focused, generally Catholic, and is highly paternal. Additionally, they tend to occupy important manual labor positions in such sectors as agriculture, construction, textiles, home services, commercial and home gardening services, and so on. This base of labor is important to the economies of southwestern states. There is also a growing political influence of Hispanics, which will be discussed later in this chapter.

Revolution and Independence

The thirteen British colonies of America declared their independence in 1776, thus bringing war to North America. The Americans fought a defensive war, but were able to defeat the British and form a new, independent democracy. Because the United States achieved independence by open war, all political ties with its former colonial master were severed.

Canada, on the other hand, became increasingly independent as a colony of Britain. In 1869, the Canadians were given a form of sovereignty, but really did not achieve full independence from the United Kingdom for decades. This more amicable path to independence kept Canada as a member of the United Kingdom's *Commonwealth of Nations*, which symbolically keeps the Queen (or King) as *head of state*. Despite these separate paths, both the United States and Canada have formed strong cultural, political, and economic bonds with the British to this day.

DEMOCRACY AND THE FEDERAL SYSTEM OF THE UNITED STATES

After achieving independence, the United States became a constitutional democracy. This might be summarized as a political system in which (1) political authority is defined, limited, and balanced by law; (2) political leadership is elected by voting citizens; and (3) a judicial system is maintained to protect the rights and freedoms embedded in the *constitution*. The United States, in adopting a system like this in the wake of a war with a major European colonial power for independence, sparked revolutions around the world and became a model of democracy and freedom.

Despite this achievement, the United States has struggled, and continues to struggle, with how power is distributed. America's political democracy utilizes a form of governing known as a *federal system*. This means the United States, as its name implies, is a union of independent states, each with their own laws, governments, and political sovereignty. This is opposed to a *unitary system*, where power is concentrated in a large central government in a capital city.

America's *federal system* means political power is diffused to state and local levels while maintaining ultimate *supremacy* at the federal level. This legally requires that all state, county, and local laws must align with and not violate any constitutional law. This gives states a lot of power, but when states make laws that violate the Constitution (as determined by the Supreme Court), federal law prevails. In the United States, a vast majority of Supreme Court cases have been over the struggle between federal and state power. Because states often have different interests (ocean access, raw materials, river resources, agriculture, etc.), they do not always align with federal law or policy.

Canada and Greenland

Canada is a parliamentary democracy that utilizes a federal system. The *head of state* is the Queen of England, but political power is divided at the federal level between the prime minister, House of Commons, and the Canadian Supreme Court. Canada has ten provinces and three territories, each of which has its own government that acts in concert with Canada's federal system. Quebec has, perhaps, the most sovereignty. Legally, they still use French civil law, as opposed to a form of British *common law*. They have also been able to require immigrants to speak conversational French in order to be given residency, whereas in the rest of Canada that is not the case. Canada belongs to a community of nations with close alliances, including the United States, the United Kingdom, and several supranational organizations.

After several decades of dialogue, Greenland has nearly achieved full independence from Denmark, in terms of domestic governance. Only foreign affairs and national security remain Denmark's responsibility, as a feature of membership in the Danish Commonwealth. Although Greenland's population is ninety percent Inuit, European influence remains present. Danish and Inuit are both official languages and the economy is evolving in a way that are characteristically western European and North American. Over the past decade, Greenland has been generally welcoming to industries interested in the wealth of natural resources present within their political space. Large oil companies, an aluminum giant, and logistics have all eagerly approached Greenland's newly formed government for rights to survey and even set up operations in their country. This has made Greenland one of the most anticipated new players in the twenty-first century global economy.

THEMATIC INTERSECTION 6A

Special Interests and Politics in America

Themes: Political/Economic

In a democratic system, any citizen who meets some simple requirements can run for public office. Typically, a candidate for office will belong to a political party and will likely use the party's "platform" to convey more regional concerns and potential solutions to regional issues. During this process, they must not only use their campaigns to advertise their positions, but also to compete with candidates for the same seat. This requires money, which is raised by individual, corporate, and special interest donations.

Naturally, if the average voter likes a particular candidate, he or she can contribute money to the campaign. However, if special interests (union, corporation, industry) like a candidate, they see a

FIGURE 6.3f. A caricature of billionaire industrialist, JP Morgan controlling Uncle Sam, during the Gilded Age. Copyright in the Public Domain.

potential political ally who might support their economic objectives. This is potentially very valuable to special interests, hence the sizable donations. The problem is that large special interests donate millions, if not hundreds of millions, to a politician or a political party, with the expectation that their views will be represented if the election is won. Although it is illegal for politicians to promise a particular political favor for a donation received, it is implied that their office or party will generally support the industries or interests that helped them get elected.

Special interests are not a new addition to the American political system. Figure 6.3f is a characterization of the billionaire robber baron J.P. Morgan as more powerful than Uncle Sam. This reflected the truth in those days. Rich, turn-of-the-century industrialists like J.P. Morgan, Andrew Carnegie, Jacob Astor, David Rockefeller, and many others had so much money and power that they were sometimes called upon to help bail out the country from financial ruin. In return, they enjoyed greater freedoms to conduct business in a low regulatory environment.

The way special interests work today, however, is a little different. The Supreme Court ruled in Citizens United v. FEC (2010) that the First Amendment of the Constitution prohibited the government from restricting independent political donations to candidates by nonprofit corporations. The language of the

FIGURE 6.3g. Protests in Wisconsin against Gov. Scott Walker's budget reforms that changed how labor unions functioned in the state. Many believed he was representing special interests.
Copyright © Justin Ormont (CC BY-SA 3.0) at http://commons.wikimedia.org/wiki/File%3A2011_Wisconsin_Budget_Protests_1_JO.jpg .

case extended this ruling to for-profit corporations and other special interests like labor unions. This, in turn, led to the creation of "Super PACs," or "Political Action Committees." These legal entities have become vehicles for the distribution of special-interest money to politicians and political candidates, while donors themselves enjoy the anonymity afforded under the First Amendment. These Super PACs have redefined how candidates are heard, because a campaign with a large purse can hire the best staffs and advisers, and can buy advertisements and run more television commercials while spending less time with actual voters in the field.

This has become a concerning development in the political landscape, because democracy was conceived and designed to give everyone a voice. However, it has been argued that politicians tend to lend an ear to the largest donors (Super PACs), which then gives the largest donors the loudest voice. More broadly, this has generated some criticisms of democracy, both within the United States and abroad. Some economists have accused democracy as being inefficient, in that it creates too many barriers for markets to react effectively. Many people have protested decisions they felt were made for special interests rather than the will of the majority.

Outside the United States, a model of democracy, many countries surveyed have indicated that democracies are not only too bureaucratic and slow to make progress, but are also too tethered to special interests. At the same time, democracy is viewed as the best option for a political system. As it stands, the relationship between the American political system and economic interests is strong, and will likely continue to define how America's democracy works well into this century.

6.4 Industrialization and North American Economic Power

Today, the United States and Canada are key players in the global economy. Not only are the two in alliance with each other regionally, they also stand together as international partners in trade. The United States, specifically, is the largest economy on Earth. With an annual GDP of about $17 trillion and a *per capita* GDP of $54,800, the US has clearly achieved a robust economy and is one of the engines of globalization. Canada, a much smaller nation by population than the US, has an annual GDP of around $1.7 trillion and a *per capita* GDP of $44,500. Understanding how North Americans ascended to this level, and remained there, requires a brief examination of the region's economic history and the evolution of industrialization in North America.

THE RISE OF INDUSTRY IN NORTH AMERICA

Broadly, the North American colonies were political and economic extensions of Europe. As such, they were a part of a larger trend unfolding in Europe that would redefine how the world was viewed. The Scientific Revolution (1500–1750), or the dawn of modern science (resulting from several centuries of scientific and mathematical discovery by scholars in Europe), began to change everything. Understanding science through observation, logic, calculations, and documentation led to advances in engineering and machinery. Various industries, beginning with textiles, would leverage technology to increase productivity, leading to the Industrial Revolution (1760–1800) and the Second Industrial Revolution (1820–1850).

These revolutions would induce a paradigm shift so important, it has been argued to be one of the most critical "nodal points" in human history. Although this began in Britain, the United States and Canada would quickly follow Western Europe into a new, modern world.

Both the adolescent United States and British Canada embraced the Industrial Revolutions. Cities in the east, like New York, Boston, and Philadelphia, all became centers of production, as well as giant markets. Fueling and supplying these industries required both a steady stream of wholesale goods and raw materials, from both distant and domestic sources and from other countries around the world. Likewise, the goods produced needed to be distributed to markets far away. Therefore, *the Industrial Revolution changed the simpler agrarian landscapes in the following ways*:

FIGURE 6.4a. This William Bell Scott painting in the mid-nineteenth century depicts the inertia and transformative power of the Industrial Revolution.
Copyright in the Public Domain.

FIGURE 6.4b. By 1918, the United States had an extensive railroad network connecting major cities to industrial sectors, agricultural regions, and the Pacific coast.
Copyright in the Public Domain.

1. Transportation networks had to expand to facilitate industrial growth. Ships were getting faster and larger, requiring broader, deeper ports.
2. Rivers were used as transportation highways. If not deep enough to be navigable, they were dredged.
3. The invention and use of trains facilitated the movement of raw materials, commodities, and people.
4. Canals, like the *Erie Canal*, were built to connect New York to the Great Lakes, all the way to Chicago.
5. Universities added programs that taught science, engineering, and business to cultivate industrial leaders.
6. Agriculture advanced, and farmers were able to leverage technology to plant, plow, and harvest crops, which then increased yields and expanded the size of farms.
7. Communication networks improved, allowing the coordination of these activities across great distances with greater efficiency.
8. Cities grew, fundamentally changing the environment and lifestyles of millions. Industry was in cities, so people migrated to them for opportunity.

These features radically altered the landscapes of North America over the course of the nineteenth and early twentieth centuries.

SOCIOECONOMIC PATTERNS OF INDUSTRIALIZATION

As seen in Europe, industrial North America would go through several similar stages of growth, resulting in identifiable patterns. Because many giant enterprises were privately owned, they would generate enormous amounts of wealth for individuals. Between about 1860 and 1929, the *captains of industry* (a.k.a. the "Robber Barons") in the United States were amongst the wealthiest people in the world, with billions in assets.

Meanwhile, most people lived modestly and relied on these industries (manufacturing, factories, transportation, etc.) for their livelihoods. While indeed these industries provided jobs, they often viewed their workers as dispensable and failed to address concerns about pay, working conditions, and incentives. In fact, these industries were highly profitable, because wages were low and hours were long. Factory work began to define America's *Northeast Quadrant*, or the belt of manufacturing

FIGURE 6.4c. The Women's Suffrage Movement resulted from social changes like urbanization, socioeconomic trends, and women having no political voice in the American political system.
Copyright in the Public Domain.

between Boston, Massachusetts and St. Louis, Missouri. Cities became grittier and dirtier, communities were largely poor, and the wealth gap in America became wide.

The Rise of Labor, Women, and the Progressive Era

The great division between the super-rich and the rest was largely blamed on the corrupt alliance between wealthy industrialists and politicians. Industry made the United States powerful but undermined the masses doing the work, both in the factories and at home. The working class struggled to have a voice, as did women. The combination between these factors led to the *Progressive Era* in America. The Progressive Era led to:

- *Changes in labor:* Labor Unions, working conditions, working age, education.
- *Education:* Compulsory education and a broad curriculum designed to cultivate a more informed citizen.
- *Family:* The health and well-being of families resulted in better access to clean water sources, safe food, standardized working hours, the creation of Juvenile Courts, etc. Many of these concerns were raised by women.
- *Industry:* Antitrust legislation broke up monopolies.
- *Women's Vote:* The passage of the Nineteenth Amendment in 1920 finally prohibited denying the right to vote based on gender (sex).

Although the *Progressive Era* can be best viewed through social changes, it is important to point out that much of these frustrations were rooted in the economic inequalities and radical changes that resulted from industrialization.

CASE STUDY 6B

Immigration, Industrialization, and Education in America

Between about 1870 and 1920, millions of immigrants flooded into the United States. This flow of immigrants occurred alongside the rise of industry resulting from the Industrial Revolution. Understanding the connection between the two can be explored in a number of ways. A platform to examine this connection may be the changes in the education system during this period; it offers a glimpse into the relationship between the two.

Although immigrants arrived at several key ports for naturalization, different groups settled in ways that formed patterns. Figure 6.4d shows the distribution of major migrant groups in the United States. Germans, as indicated on the map, spread out over much of the upper Midwest, from Pennsylvania to Minnesota. This is because many Germans came to farm. Irish came to America because of political turmoil at home with Britain and economic depression. However, because Ireland had industrialized, they felt more comfortable in big industrial cities like Boston, New York, and Chicago. Whereas Italians arrived by the millions and settled in New York, Philadelphia, and New Jersey for similar reasons, Eastern Europeans (Polish, Lithuanians, and Ukrainians) made Chicago, Detroit, and other cities in the area home. Many of these immigrants would live in American cities and work in the various industries within them.

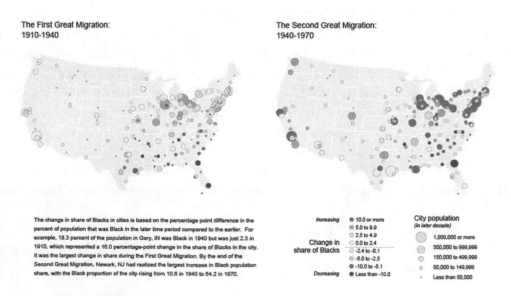

FIGURE 6.4d. Domestic migration of blacks from the south to industrial cities in the north was both social and economic in origin.
Copyright in the Public Domain.

After the Civil War (1865–1940), the depressed postwar economy in the South, hostile racism, and discriminatory Jim Crow laws led to a massive internal migration of blacks to northern industrial cities. This was known as the "Great Migration." Cities like St. Louis, Chicago, Detroit, Cleveland, Buffalo, Philadelphia, and so on saw several waves of migration. Today, many of these cities still have high percentages of African Americans. This reinforced the need for compulsory education, because many coming from the South had no education at all.

Manufacturing operations liked the flow of immigrants because they were cheap and could be worked very hard. However, with so many foreign cultures and southern blacks arriving, there was the issue of cultural conformity. Apart from various languages, each group brought with it its own cultural values. How could foreign immigrants learn English, American values and norms, and the pulses and patterns of urban industrial life in a way that made them more useful in American society? How could southern blacks, many of whom were poor, uneducated, and highly rural, be acclimated to life in the north?

This may have played a role in the transition of the American educational system from the local schoolhouse to the institutional, state compulsory education system in America. If all children between certain ages were required to attend school, and those schools followed a prescribed plan (grade levels, curriculum), then America could "fill the pipeline" with future workers. At the same time, the schools could "condition" students to factory life by structuring the school day like a factory job. A bell would ring in the morning at the same time, another at lunch, and the last to indicate the day was over. Principals were like foremen, handling discipline; teachers would provide instruction, but had some authority to manage behavior, like a floor supervisor. Although there are other reasons that explain the shift to compulsory education, this change did help to acclimate immigrants to life in America and to work in American industries.

INDUSTRY AND WAR

The wars of the twentieth century were different, in that outcomes (win or lose) were determined less by the size of force or the decisive victories achieved through clever strategy, and more by the rate of industrial production. It was identified, during the Great War (1915–1918), that nations that leveraged their industrial might to produce military hardware changed both the scale and lethality of war. More soldiers died in these wars, and more landscapes were devastated, than all wars in history combined.

The Americans, for example, once in the war, would partner with private industry to retask factories to mass produce military hardware. Although both Germany and Japan began the war with much larger arsenals of ships, submarines,

FIGURE 6.4e. During the war, this Niagara Falls factory was re-tasked to produce high-quality fighter planes with great speed.
Copyright in the Public Domain.

tanks, armored transports, cannons, etc., the Americans would quickly outproduce their enemies. Steel production, which is needed to mass produce war machines, increased from thirty-two million tons annually to fifty-one million tons. With available steel and iron, mass production could begin. Between 1941 and 1945, the United States would produce more than 260,000 aircraft, compared to the approximately 110,000 produced by Germany and 70,000 produced by Japan. The United States built around 1.7 million armored military vehicles, compared to Germany's 220,000. The United States built five times as many battleships, eight times as many cruisers, twelve times as many light aircraft carriers, and four times as many destroyers as the Japanese during the same period. This level of production was difficult, if not impossible, to keep up with. This may inform us, at least in part, of how the United States helped achieve victory.

POST WWII ECONOMIC DOMINANCE

If the Industrial Revolution is a critical nodal point in human history, it could also be argued that World War II, and the world that emerged in its wake, is as well. Many things changed after the war, particularly in the global economic arena. The North Americans, particularly the United States, would play a central role in this new world. However, as much as you can find examples of postwar cooperation between nations and a growing global economic system, you can also find many conflicts that still define the world today. How the United States conducted itself, after the war, may provide more insight into the complex landscapes of the twenty-first century.

CASE STUDY 6C

From Globalization to the New Imperialism

By David Harvey

One of the few good things to emerge from the last couple of years of political nightmares is that the seemingly neutral mask of "globalization" has been torn off to reveal the raw imperialism beneath. But imperialisms, like empires, can take many different forms. Our task is to identify more clearly what the capitalist form of imperialism is about in general and what the U.S. form of capitalist imperialism is about in particular, recognizing that there seems to be some momentous shift now occurring as the United States moves from the multilateral neo-liberalism that reached its apogee in the mid-1990s to the unilateral militarism and neoconservativism of the current administration.

FIGURE 6.4f. Presidents Obama, Bush, and Clinton in 2010. Some have criticized the United States for being "neocolonial" or practicing "neo-imperialism" around the world to protect American economic and political interests. This has had adverse effects, in many cases.
Copyright in the Public Domain.

TERRITORIAL VS. CAPITALISTIC LOGICS OF POWER

Capitalist imperialism can best be analyzed as a contradictory fusion of a territorial logic derived from the use of state power and a capitalistic logic that derives from market-driven processes of capital accumulation in space and time. The former stresses the political, diplomatic, and military strategies used by a state as it struggles to assert its interests and achieve its goals in the world at large. The latter focuses on the ways in which economic power flows across and through space, toward or away from territories through the daily practices of production, trade, capital flows, money transfers, labor migration, technology transfer, currency speculation, flows of information, cultural impulses, and the like.

These territorial and capitalist logics are not reducible to each other (Arrighi, 1994; Arrighi and Silver, 1999; Harvey, 2003). The motivations and interests of agents differ. Capitalists place money wherever profits can be had and are usually motivated to accumulate more capital. Politicians and statesmen usually seek outcomes that sustain or augment the power of their state vis-à-vis other states. Capitalists seek

David Harvey, "From Globalization to the New Imperialism," Critical Globalization Studies, eds. Richard P. Appelbaum and William I. Robinson, pp. 91-100. Copyright © 2005 by Taylor & Francis Group. Reprinted with permission.

individual advantage and are responsible to no one except themselves and (to some degree) shareholders, whereas statesmen seek collective advantage and are responsible to citizens or, more often, to an elite group, a class, or some other power structure. Capitalists operate in continuous space and time whereas politicians operate in a territorialized space and, at least in democracies, in the temporality of electoral cycles. Capitalist firms come and go, shift locations, merge, grow phenomenally, or go out of business, whereas states are relatively long-lived entities operating from a fixed territorial base.

The two logics contrast in other ways. State agents arrive at political in the midst of the rough and tumble of a political process where variegated interests clash. Personality conflicts between influential players can sometimes be at the core of decision making. The geographical processes of capital accumulation, on the other hand, are much more molecular and diff use. Many agents bump into each other in the marketplace, counteracting and at other times reinforcing certain aggregate trends. It is hard to manage these processes except indirectly. The institutional arrangements set up by the state are influential, of course, and there are monetary and fiscal levers (of the sort that Alan Greenspan wields as chairman of the Federal Reserve) as well as a range of fiscal and monetary modes of intervention that position the state as a powerful economic agent. But even in authoritarian or "developmental" states, the molecular processes of capital accumulation often escape control. Although separate, the two logics intertwine. The literature on imperialism too often assumes, however, an easy accordance between them: that political-economic processes are guided by the strategies of imperial states that always operate out of capitalistic motivations. In practice the logics frequently tug against and sometimes even oppose each other. The relation between them should be seen as problematic, contradictory, and dialectical rather than as functional or one sided. This sets the stage for a deeper analysis of the nature of capitalist imperialism in general and recent U.S. versions of it in particular.

Imperialistic state practices typically seek to take advantage of the asymmetries that arise out of spatial exchange relations. These asymmetries arise in part because spatial competition is always monopolistic competition and because resources (both naturally occurring and humanly created) are unevenly distributed. The equality condition assumed in perfectly functioning markets is inoperative. The outcome is unfair and unequal exchange, spatially articulated monopoly powers, extortionate practices attached to capital and credit flows and the extraction of monopoly rents. The inequalities that result take on a specific geographical expression with rich regions often growing richer and poor regions often superexploited. One of the state's key tasks is to preserve that pattern of asymmetries in exchange over space in resource endowments that works for its own advantage. If, for example, the United States forces open capital markets around the world through the operations of the International Monetary Fund (IMF) and the World Trade Organization (WTO), it is because specific advantages are thought to accrue to U.S. financial institutions. The state is the political entity, the body politic, that is best able to orchestrate these processes both internally and on the world stage. Failure so to do will likely result in a diminution of the wealth and power of the state. Capitalist imperialism is, then, a property of interstate relations and flows of power within a global system of capital accumulation.

At any given historical–geographical moment, one or other of the logics may dominate the other. The accumulation of control over territory as an end in itself plainly has economic consequences. These may be positive or negative from the standpoint of exaction of tribute, flows of capital, labor power, commodities, and the like. But this looks quite different from a situation in which territorial control (that may or may not entail actual takeover and administration of territory) is intended as a support for the accumulation of capital. But this then poses a crucial question: how can the territorial logics of power, which tend to be awkwardly fixed in space, respond to the open spatial dynamics of endless capital accumulation? And what does endless capital accumulation imply for the territorial logics of power?

Some light is shed on this problem by way of an acute observation made by Hannah Arendt. "A never-ending accumulation of property," she wrote, "must be based on a never-ending accumulation of power." From this derived "the 'progressive' ideology of the late nineteenth century" that "foreshadowed the rise of imperialism" (Arendt, 1968). If, however, the accumulation of power must necessarily accompany the accumulation of capital, then bourgeois history must be a history of accumulation of ever-greater political power. And this scale-shift is exactly what Arrighi records in his comparative history of the shift from the Italian city states, through the Dutch, the British, and now the U.S. phases of global hegemony (Arrighi, 2003). But if Arendt is right, then any imperial state must endlessly seek to extend and intensify its power. There is, in this, an ever-present danger of overextension. Overreach has again and again proven the Achilles' heel of hegemonic states and empires (Rome, Venice, Holland, Britain) (Kennedy, 1990). Since 1980, the United States has extended its powers and commitments remarkably, both militarily and politically, to the point where the dangers of overreach are palpable. This then raises the further question: If the United States is no longer sufficiently large and resourceful to manage the considerably expanded world economy of the twenty-first century, then what kind of accumulation of political power under what kind of political arrangement will be capable of taking its place, given that the world is heavily committed still to capital accumulation without limit? Some argue that world government is not only desirable but inevitable. Others argue that some collection of states working in collaboration with each other (in much the way that Kautsky suggested in his theory of ultraimperialism and as hinted at in organizations like the G7—now G8—meetings) might be able to regulate matters. To this we could add the less optimistic idea that if it proves impossible for some reason to construct this ever vaster accumulation of political power, then endless capital accumulation will likely dissolve into chaos, ending the era of capital not with a revolutionary bang but in tortured anarchy.

THE INNER AND THE OUTER DIALECTIC

In *The Philosophy of Right*, Hegel notes how the inner contradictions of a territorially bounded bourgeois society, registered as an overaccumulation of wealth at one pole and the creation of a rabble of paupers at the other, drive it to seek solutions through external trade and colonial/imperial practices (Hegel, 1967). Lenin quotes Cecil Rhodes as saying that colonialism and imperialism abroad was the only possible way to avoid civil war at home (Lenin, 1965). Class relations and the state of class struggle within a territory clearly affect the drive for imperial solutions. We should, therefore, pay careful attention to the internal circumstances that drive those that command the territorial logic to engage in imperial practices. There are three overlapping impulsions behind this drive.

There is, within capitalism, a perpetual tendency to produce crises of overaccumulation, defined as surpluses of capital and labor, side by side, lacking profitable outlets even in the face of many socially urgent tasks to be addressed (Harvey, 1999, 2001, 2003). The Great Depression of the 1930s was a classic case of this. The problem is, then, to find profitable outlets for surplus capital that accumulates within a given territory. The obvious answer is to export capital (in money, commodity, or production capacity forms) to more profitable locations (or, what amounts to the same thing, procure lower-cost inputs through imports of low-wage labor or low-cost raw materials). This requires that markets for both capital and commodities be open across the world so that surplus capital in one territory can easily circulate into other territories where the profits to be had are greater. If markets and resources are not open, then they have sometimes to be forced open by use of economic, political, or military power (as in Iraq). If profits are still to accrue to the home territory, then asymmetrical power relations through the market or other means of domination must be constructed in relation to other territories. Those in charge of the territorial logic must help to find outlets for surplus capital while striving to retain the benefits to be had from foreign trade, export of capital, or import of cheaper inputs. Imperialist practices of this sort can arise wherever capital surpluses begin to pile up. In the 1980s, for example, South Korea and Taiwan began to experience overaccumulation problems and so started to export their business practices (including vicious labor practices) around the world as subcontractors for multinational corporations. Hierarchical structures of imperialism can in this way be orchestrated; for example, Taiwanese subcontractors do the "dirty work" for U.S.-based multinationals. Seeking outlets for surplus capital is the first aspect of imperial practices that arises out of internal conditions within a country.

A second motivation arises because governments in trouble domestically often seek to solve their problems either by foreign adventures or by manufacturing foreign threats to consolidate solidarities at home. The internal condition of the United States during 2002 was, for example, parlous in the extreme. The recession that began early in 2001 (prodded onward by the shock of 9/11) would not go away. Unemployment was rising and the sense of economic insecurity was palpable. Corporate scandals and accounting failures (as well as cases of outright corruption) cascaded over each other, and seemingly solid corporate empires were literally dissolving overnight. Wall Street fell into disrepute and stocks and other asset values were plunging. Pension funds were depleted (if they did not totally disappear as in the case of Enron employees) and the retirement prospects of the middle class took a serious hit. Healthcare was in a mess, federal, state and local government surpluses were evaporating fast and deficits began to loom larger and larger. The current account balance with the rest of the world was going from bad to worse as the United States became the biggest debtor nation of all time. To top it all, the president had been elected by a five to four vote of the Supreme Court rather than by the people. His legitimacy was questioned by at least half the population on the eve of 9/11. The only thing that saved the Republicans from political annihilation was the intense solidarity—verging on a nationalist revival—created around the events of 9/11. The Republicans used the threat of terrorism to launch into a series of foreign ventures beginning with Afghanistan and then switching to Iraq. The diversionary tactic worked. The American public by and large accepted the idea that there was some sort of connection between Al Qaeda and Saddam. The Republicans were able to consolidate political power through the congressional elections and the President could shed the air of illegitimacy that had hung over his election.

But there is something far deeper than political opportunism at work here. Democracy in the United States has always been chronically unstable. The country sometimes seems impossible to govern except through the corruption of money power. Hannah Arendt observes:

> A community based solely on power must decay in the calm of order and stability; its complete security reveals that it is built on sand. Only by acquiring more power can it guarantee the status quo; only by constantly extending its authority and only through [the] process of power accumulation can it remain stable. Hobbes' Commonwealth is a vacillating structure and must always provide itself with new props from outside; otherwise it would collapse overnight into the aimless, senseless chaos of the private interests from which it sprang. . . . [The] ever-present possibility of war guarantees the Commonwealth a prospect of permanence because it makes it possible for the state to increase its power at the expense of other states (Arendt, 1968).

During the 1990s there was no clear enemy for the United States. The Cold War was over, and the booming economy should have guaranteed an unparalleled level of contentment and satisfaction throughout all but the most underprivileged and marginalized elements in civil society. Yet, as Arendt might have predicted, the 1990s turned out to be one of the most unpleasant decades in U.S. history. Competition was vicious, scams and fraudulent schemes proliferated, scandals (both real and imagined) were everywhere embraced with gusto, vicious rumors circulated about assassinations plotted in the White House, an attempt was made to impeach the president, Howard Stern and Rush Limbaugh typified a media totally out of control, Los Angeles erupted in riots, Waco and Oklahoma symbolized a penchant for internal violence that had long remained latent, and teenagers shot and killed their classmates in Colombine. Civil society was, in short, far from civil. Society seemed, as Arendt would put it, to be collapsing back into the aimless, senseless chaos of private interests. The engagement with Iraq was a grand opportunity to bring the Commonwealth to heel. Criticism was silenced as unpatriotic. The evil enemy without became the prime force through which to exorcise or tame the devils lurking within. If, as Arendt avers, empire abroad always entails tyranny at home then those, like the neoconservatives, interested in establishing order and dominance at home have every incentive to pursue empire abroad as key to their strategy of internal domination. This is central to the neoconservative form of imperialism now emerging in the U.S.

The third major impulsion behind imperialist practices rests on the dynamics of class relations on the home front. The evidence from the end of the nineteenth century is of interest here. Consider, for example, a figure like Joseph Chamberlain ("Radical Joe," as he was known). Closely allied with the liberal manufacturing interests of Birmingham, Chamberlain was initially resolutely opposed to imperialism (in the Afghan Wars of the 1850s, for example) and devoted much of his time to educational reform and other projects aligned to improving the social and physical infrastructures for production and consumption in his home city of Birmingham, England. This provided, he thought, a productive outlet for surpluses that would be repaid in the long run. An important figure within the liberal conservative movement, he saw the rising tide of class struggle in Britain at first hand and in 1885 made a celebrated speech in which he called for the propertied classes to take cognizance of their responsibilities and obligations to society (i.e., to better the conditions of life of the least well-off and invest in social and physical infrastructures in the national interest) rather than solely to promote their individual rights as property owners. The uproar that followed on the part of the propertied classes forced him to recant and, from that moment on, he became the most ardent advocate for imperialism (ultimately, as colonial secretary, leading Britain into the disaster of the Boer War in South Africa) (Julien et al., 1949).

The turn to a liberal form of imperialism in the late nineteenth century arose not from absolute economic imperatives but from the political unwillingness of the bourgeoisie to give up any of its privileges and thereby absorb overaccumulation through social reform at home. Hobson, for one, identified this as the key problem and sought a social democratic policy that would counter it. Both Roosevelts at a certain point recognized that crises of overaccumulation might be off set by domestic reforms (culminating in the weak attempt to construct a "New Deal" as an answer to the 1930s depression). But for this to go far requires that the rich look to their obligations rather than their rights. The internal state of class relations and of class struggle affect the drive towards imperial solutions. It was internal politics of this sort that forced many European powers to look outwards to solve their problems from 1884 to 1945. Currently in the United States the extraordinary growth in inequality and the pressure of the affluent (backed by a media dominated by rightwing business interests) to gain more in the way of rights rather than to concede anything with respect to their obligations makes resort to imperialism almost inevitable as a way to both mask and avert the consequences of the class war they are waging at home.

These three internal impulsions, the first clearly driven by a capitalist logic but the other two far more contingent upon internal politics exist, we may conclude, in a specific relation to the shaping of imperialist practices by state powers.

ACCUMULATION BY DISPOSSESSION

Rosa Luxemburg argues that capital accumulation has a dual character:

> One concerns the commodity market and the place where surplus value is produced—the factory, the mine, the agricultural estate. Regarded in this light accumulation is a purely economic process, with its most important phase a transaction between the capitalist and the wage laborer. . . . Here, in form at any rate, peace, property, and equality prevail, and the keen dialectics of scientific analysis were required to reveal how the right of ownership changes in the course of accumulation into appropriation of other people's property, how commodity exchange turns into exploitation, and equality becomes class rule. The other aspect of the accumulation of capital concerns the relations between capitalism and the noncapitalist modes of production which start making their appearance on the international stage. Its predominant methods are colonial policy, an international loan system—a policy of spheres of interest—and war. Force, fraud, oppression, and looting are openly displayed without any

attempt at concealment, and it requires an effort to discover within this tangle of political violence and contests of power the stern laws of the economic process (Luxemburg, 1968).

These two aspects of accumulation, which I shall term accumulation through expanded reproduction and accumulation by dispossession, are, she argued, "organically linked" and "the historical career of capitalism can only be appreciated by taking them together."

This statement does not fit very well with Marx's general theory of capital accumulation. Marx generally assumes freely functioning competitive markets with institutional arrangements of private property, juridical individualism, freedom of contract and appropriate structures of law and governance guaranteed by a "facilitative" state that secures the integrity of money as a store of value and as a medium of circulation. The roles of the capitalist and laborer are already well-established and "primitive" or "original" accumulation has already occurred. Expanded reproduction (the exploitation of living labor in production) is at the center of the analysis. Such assumptions allow us to see what will happen if the liberal project of the classical political economists or, in our times, the neoliberal project of the economists, is realized. The brilliance of Marx's dialectical method is to show that market liberalization—the credo of the liberals and the neoliberals—will not produce a harmonious state in which everyone is better off. It will, instead, produce greater levels of social inequality (as indeed has been the global trend over the last 30 years). It will also produce chronic crises of overaccumulation, thereby feeding the impulsion to absorb surplus capital by imperialistic expansion or suffer the consequences of crisis and deflation.

The disadvantage of Marx's assumptions is that they relegate accumulation based upon predation, fraud, and violence to an original stage that is considered no longer relevant or, as with Luxemburg, as somehow being outside of the capitalist system. A general reevaluation of the continuous role and persistence of the predatory practices of primitive or original, accumulation is therefore required. Because it seems peculiar to call such an ongoing process primitive or original, I substitute these terms with the concept of *accumulation by dispossession* (Perelman, 2000; Harvey, 2003).

Marx's description of primitive accumulation reveals a wide range of processes that are still with us. These include the commodification and privatization of land; the forceful expulsion of peasant populations; conversion of various forms of property rights (common, collective, etc.) into private property; the suppression of alternative forms of production and consumption; colonial, neocolonial, and imperial processes of appropriation of assets; monetization of exchange and personal taxation; slave trade; and usury, debt, and ultimately the credit system. The state with its monopoly of violence and aura of legality plays a crucial role in both backing and promoting these processes. None of these processes have disappeared and, with respect to privatization and the operation of the credit system, they have arguably moved center stage in the dynamics of capital accuation in recent times. At the same time, wholly new mechanisms of accumulation by dispossession have opened up under the umbrella of neoliberalism. Intellectual property rights and patents preserve monopoly powers and extend corporate rights over genetic materials. Biopiracy is rampant, and the global environmental commons have been degraded in large part through a strategy of privatization. And all manner of fraudulent and predatory practices have sprung up around the stock market, corporate manipulation of accounts, the dispossession of pension rights, and the like.

Neoliberalism—with its dual mantras of privatization and commodification of everything—launched a new wave of enclosure of the commons during the 1980s and 1990s. It used the powers of the credit system backed by state powers to engage in wide-ranging practices of accumulation by dispossession. The financial crises that wracked Mexico (twice), Latin America, Russia, and most of all East and Southeast Asia from 1997 to 1998 facilitated the predation of productive assets by financial powers based in the United States and to a lesser extent Europe and Japan. This was imperialism as accumulation by dispossession. It offered an open field for surplus capitals to play in as assets were released from the public domain into the private realm and as assets already in the private domain were devalued so that they could be bought up at fire-sale prices. The wide swath of resistance to these practices—everything from the Zapatista rebellion to landless peasant movements and protest movements against dam construction, deforestation, and environmental degradation—were largely repressed by state power. The neoliberal state, which largely superseded the social democratic state, withdrew from its social welfare commitments, thus dispossessing populations of their rights even in some of the core capitalist countries. Low-level warfare was waged across the planet as social movements were repressed. A global justice movement arose in response, seeking to reclaim the commons, resist their further degradation, and organize against accumulation by dispossession.

The failure of neoliberalism to deliver on its promises has now produced a crisis within globalization, and it is in that context that we have to interpret the shift towards neoconservative imperialism within the United States (as well as elsewhere, e.g., France, where a president considered illegitimate by many is using his popular stance with respect to the Iraq war to ram through right-wing reforms and build a global coalition favorable to French interests). The United States is currently vulnerable to a capitalistic logic that focuses on international competition. It has lost dominance in most areas of production (with the exception of military, agribusiness, and some fields of advanced technology) and now seems threatened in the realm of finance (its current account deficit with the rest of the world requires over $2 billion a day of capital inflows to be sustained). How can the United States assert its territorial logic to sustain its position in the face of an increasingly unfavorable economic climate? One answer is to use its military superiority to dominate the global economy through control over oil supply. Undoubtedly, it seeks to control OPEC (almost certainly fostering internal discontent in Venezuela and Iran while proclaiming the need to establish democracy in Iraq). That this is yet another form of accumulation by dispossession, but that it has taken a war to accomplish it should be obvious. Oil at $20 a barrel would undoubtedly help revive global capital accumulation while geopolitical control over Middle Eastern oil reserves and oil flow will place the United States in a position to hold competitors (Europe, Japan, Korea, Southeast Asia, and even more important, China) hostage to U.S. control over global oil supplies. Is this what the new U.S. imperialism is about?

FROM CONSENT TO COERCION

The wave of neoliberal globalization that swept out of the United States during the 1980s and 1990s sought to sustain U.S. hegemony and global capital accumulation through a mixture of multilateral consent backed by coercion. Its center lay in an alliance between the financial powers concentrated primarily on Wall Street (but also in Europe and Japan), the policies of a very activist U.S. Treasury (in alliance with central banker committees in Europe and Japan) and the facilities provided by the IMF, the World Bank, and other multinational institutions (such as the nascent WTO) that were dominated by U.S. interests. Culminating in the Washington Consensus of 1995, neoliberalism set in motion wave after wave of accumulation by dispossession across the globe and forced many states away from any social democratic commitments they may have had towards a politics of dispossession. By forcing capital markets open around the world it sought to open the way to financial predation organized largely for the benefit of the main capitalist powers. Financial tribute flowed into the coffers of the main financial centers in vast waves, spawning a speculative boom within the United States in particular (Gowan, 1999; Brenner, 2002). Neoliberalism masked this imperialistic flow of tribute under the neutral banner of financial globalization. But by the late 1990s this project was in crisis. The devastation wrought in East and Southeast Asia from 1997 to 1998 spread to Russia and Latin America, and a major global crisis was narrowly averted. Stresses began to emerge even within the United States.

Vast swaths of resistance welled up around the world in the form of an articulate though fragmented and sometimes inchoate antiglobalization movement. The conversion of that movement into a global justice movement began to shape a politics that focused increasingly upon resistance to accumulation by dispossession as its nexus of action. This politics is very different from the traditional forms of class struggle mobilized around expanded reproduction. But if Luxemburg is correct, and there is always an organic link between accumulation by expanded reproduction and accumulation by dispossession, then there is also an organic link between the two forms of class struggle. That link needs to be affirmed, strengthened, and built upon as the global justice movement gathers strength (Harvey, 2003).

The answer from within the United States has been to convert the low-level global warfare largely orchestrated by neoliberal state apparatuses around the world into a frontal military assault to gain command over a primary global resource. Command over that resource would assure not only the geopolitical power of the United States vs. its competitors but also, if successful, lower the price of a major input into the processes of capital accumulation. At the same time, an imperial venture of this sort helps to secure the internal position of the wealthiest strata within the United States, to evade class struggle at home by appeal to nationalism, and to realize the neoconservative dream of establishing order within the United States by an expanding accumulation of political power in the hands of a well-organized upper class. The neoconservative state is, however, even more fiercely committed to a politics of accumulation by dispossession, both internally and abroad, as was its neoliberal predecessor. But it is prepared to do so through coercion rather than consent, through unilateralism rather than multilateralism, and through militarism rather than through economic and political diplomacy.

Imperialist projects of this sort rarely last. But they can in the short run prove catastrophic if not suicidal for both the countries and the peoples caught up in the turmoil they generate. In this instance it is not even clear that the exercise of this particular territorial logic of power is in any way consistent with the logic of capital accumulation. The latter points increasingly away from the United States toward some broader configuration of powers, with Europe and above all a renascent China leading the way. The East and Southeast Asian regional power bloc will equal if not surpass U.S. economic power in the not too distant future. It is difficult to see how U.S. militarism can provide an effective answer to this, even if it succeeds in controlling a key global resource like oil. And a danger arises, because fiercer interregional competition between Europe, Asia, and North America could plunge the world into geopolitical confrontations that the United States is unlikely to win even by resort to its superior military power.

In the face of this it is imperative that the global justice movement conjoin with an antiwar movement, bridge the gap in both understanding and in politics between movements around expanded reproduction and movements against accumulation by dispossession, and set out entirely different rules of international engagement such that the logic of capital is contained if not displaced and the territorial logics of power are orchestrated to achieve an equality of well-being and of life-chances that has long been realizable but long been frustrated by class-bound politics. Until the inalienable rights of private property and the profit rate are called into question and controlled, there will be no option except to continue the catastrophic consequences of capitalist imperialism, in no matter what form it occurs.

CLASS DISCUSSIONS

1. Harvey distinguishes between "territorial" and "capitalist": logics of power. What does he mean? And how do these two forms of power come together?
2. What does he mean by "imperialism"? How does the current U.S. foreign policy epitomize this?
3. Define "accumulation" as a key part of economic life. What do we mean by "accumulation by dispossession"?
4. How does resistance to imperialism play itself out in today's world?

BIBLIOGRAPHY

Arendt, H. 1968. *Imperialism.* New York: Harcourt Brace.

Arrighi, Giovanni. 1994. *The Long Twentieth Century. Money, Power and the Origins of Our Times.* London: Verso.

Arrighi, Giovanni. 2003. "Tracking Global Turbulence," *New Left Review* 20: 5–72. Arrighi, Giovanni, Beverly J. Silver, and Benjamin Brewer. 2003. "Industrial Convergence and the Persistence of the North–South Divide." *Studies in Comparative*

International Development 38 (1): 3–31.

Arrighi, Giovanni, Beverly J. Silver, and Benjamin Brewer. 2003. "Response." *Studies in Comparative International Development* 38 (1): 39–42.

Brenner, R. 2002. *The Boom and the Bubble: the U.S. in the World Economy.* London: Verso.

Gowan, P. 1999. *The Global Gamble: Washington's Bid for World Dominance.* London: Verso.

Harvey, David. 1999. *The Limits to Capital,* 2nd edition. London: Verso.

Harvey, D. 2001. *Spaces of Capital.* New York: Routledge.

Harvey, David. 2003. *The New Imperialism.* New York: Oxford University Press.

Hegel, G.W. 1967. *The Philosophy of Right.* New York: Oxford University Press.

Julien, C-A., Bruhat, J., Bourgin, C., Crouzet, M. and Renouvin, P. 1949. *Les Poli- tiques d'Expansion Imperialiste.* Paris: Presses Universitaires de France.

Kennedy, P 1990. *The Rise and the Fall of the Great Powers*. New York: Random House.

Lenin, V.I. 1965. "Imperialism: the Highest Stage of Capitalism," in *Selected Works*, Volume 1. Moscow: Progress Publishers.

Luxemburg, R. 1968 edition. *The Accumulation of Capital*. New York: Monthly Review Press, 452–453.

Perelman, M. 2000. *The Invention of Capitalism: Classical Political Economy and the Secret History of Primitive Accumulation*. Durham, NC: Duke University Press.

GLOBALIZATION: THE DIFFUSION OF AMERICAN ECONOMIC INFLUENCE

The transformative power of *globalization* is difficult to measure. Globalization might be defined as the expansion of economic activities, to the global scale, in a way that facilitates supply chains, expands retail operations, spreads popular culture, and leverages advanced technology to orchestrate efficient communication and the movement of goods and capital. The North Americans play a key role in the globalized economy because of their large, collective consumer base, markets, high technology and innovation, and popular culture. Additionally, many of the retail chains around the world are American and Canadian.

Although globalization has been beneficial to Americans and Canadians, it has widened the gap between the developed industrial nations and the rest. The global economy has been able to expand and generally thrive because of cheap labor and incentives to manufacture in poorer countries abroad. At the same time, globalization has induced *cultural homogenization*, or powerful western culture bringing sameness to landscapes that were once unique and regional. The average American, for example, can travel to the other side of the world to enjoy the same cup of coffee or eat the same hamburger as they do at home. A Canadian can travel almost anywhere and find images of their celebrities pasted on foreign billboards advertising a new movie, product, or concert tour. Meanwhile, the majority of the people living in these nations are poor and can be ambivalent about their role in the global economy.

6.5 The Urban/Rural Divide in North America

Cities in North America are influential and well known around the world. They are large, powerful, and important in political, economic, and cultural spheres. At the same time, North American cities, particularly in the West, have been criticized for departing from pedestrian-centered paradigms that once promoted better cultural and socioeconomic interaction, as well as for evolving in ways that accom-

modate continued automobile use. This dual narrative is worth exploring, because how cities interact with the world, and how they are altered to accommodate that interaction (ports, railways, airports, logistics), is often quite different than how locals view their cities. While Chapter 1 provides a sound basic discussion on urbanism, this chapter will first focus on the following *three (3) characteristics of North American urbanism*:

- The rise of the *Metropolitan Complex*
- The suburban habitat
- Infrastructure

FIGURE 6.5a. Los Angeles, California. One of the largest cities in the world, but also a city accused of massive, irresponsible urban sprawl.
Copyright © Remi Jouan (CC BY-SA 3.0) at http://commons.wikimedia.org/wiki/File%3ALos_Angeles_-_Echangeur_autoroute_110_105.JPG .

Then, this section will discuss the growing rift between urban and rural North Americans and address why this matters. It is important to remember that North Americans are predominantly an urban people. In the United States, approximately 80% of the population resides in the urban realm. Canada is even higher, with about 85% living in cities. This essentially means cities are a dominant influence in many aspects of North American society.

URBAN MEGAREGIONS IN NORTH AMERICA

Giant metropolitan areas in North America have both existed and are continuing to form around cities. An urban megaregion can be defined as the expansion of urban space resulting from continued conurbation and sprawl. Conurbation is the growing together of two or more cities in proximity to each other, over time, for mutual benefit. An example of this would be Long Beach, California and Los Angeles, California. Long Beach is situated by one of the largest ports in the world, and Los Angeles is one of the largest cities in the world. Growing together over time had its benefits. Now the two are a part of a metropolitan area and, in some ways, function as a single entity. Sprawl is the outward expansion of a city, typically for residential communities and the services and infrastructure that follow. This makes metropolitan areas geographically larger. The *urban megaregion*, then, arises when these processes reach the outer realm of another major metropolitan area growing in a similar way, thus marrying the two (or more) together and forming an urban area that covers a region.

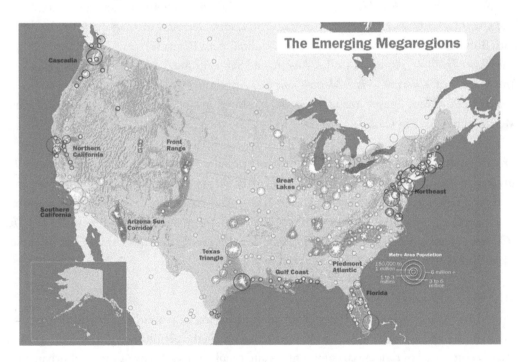

FIGURE 6.5b. Megacities/Megaregions are expected to grow, as North Americans urbanize.
Copyright © IrvingPINYC (CC BY-SA 3.0) at http://commons.wikimedia.org/wiki/File%3AMapofEmergingUSMegaregions.png .

A more established *urban megaregion* in the United States is *Megalopolis*. This is the continuation of urbanization from Washington, DC to Boston, Massachusetts. Locals call it "BOSNYWASH," or Boston, New York, and Washington, DC combined onto one acronym. It includes the cities already mentioned, as well as Philadelphia (PA), Newark (NJ), Baltimore (MD), and dozens of other medium and small cities and towns in between. One in five Americans lives in this this urban zone. When traveling through *Megalopolis*, there are several indicators that these cities have formed an *urban megaregion*. These include:

- Transportation infrastructure connects the cities together with a reliable schedule of operation.
- Communication networks bond these cities together with efficient and reliable connectivity.
- Residential corridors with ample services exist between major cities, so residents can have proximity to more than one.
- Interstate cooperation helps the movement of residents, goods and services, broadens educational and work opportunities across state lines, multi-state licensing, etc.
- Media networks cover and report on the broader region because they recognize that millions move between cities and cross state lines daily.

The formation of *urban megaregions* has been a trend in North America, especially during the last several decades. As seen in *Figure 6.5b*, current urban *megaregions* include:

- *Megalopolis*, mentioned recently as the largest urban megaregion in the US.
- The *South Florida Urban Megaregion*: Miami, Ft. Lauderdale, Orlando, Tampa Bay, etc.
- The *Great Lakes Urban Megaregion*: Chicago, St. Louis, Detroit, Indianapolis, Cleveland, Cincinnati, Buffalo, and the Greater Toronto Metropolitan Area (Canada).
- The *Texas Triangle*: Houston, Dallas, Austin, and San Antonio.
- The *Southern California Urban Megaregion*: Los Angeles Area and Greater San Diego.
- *Cascadia:* Portland, Oregon through Seattle, Washington, and by extension the Greater Vancouver Metropolitan Area in Canada.

These *urban megaregions* work together to coordinate broader regional economic activities while facilitating greater movement and connectivity. Other *urban megaregions* around the world have looked at *Megalopolis* as a template for their own expansion. The Tokyo-Yokohama *urban megaregion*, for example, is now the largest in the world, with around forty-five million residents. The Chinese *Beijing-Shanghai Urban Corridor* is taking shape, as is the *Sao Paulo-Rio De Janeiro Urban Corridor*. All of these urban planners studied North American *urban megaregions*.

THE SUBURBAN HABITAT

In the United States, approximately 70% of all urban residents live in a suburban community, or a "suburb." Suburbs can be defined as smaller cities or townships that are on the periphery of major metropolitan areas and primarily composed of residential communities and retail services. Many of these suburban communities are planned around a particular demographic. Rarely, if ever, are new suburban communities designed for people living in poverty or even for a lower-middle-class base. Instead, they are often meticulously

FIGURE 6.5c. Dallas, Texas is one of the largest cities in the United States and is a regional hub for many businesses. However, it has the type of urban sprawl that invites criticism.
Copyright © Andreas Praefcke (CC BY-SA 3.0) at http://commons.wikimedia.org/wiki/File%3ADallas_skyline_and_suburbs.jpg .

planned with a middle- to upper-middle-class base in mind. If an entire community is designed for a homeowner middle-class resident base, then the many companies that consider them their customers will flock to these communities to do business. The result is communities that are tailored for residential life.

Many of these North American suburbs are designed around the automobile and a commuter resident base. Because suburban communities are often a fair distance from the city center, they know most people will use cars to get around. Also, because public transportation options are often limited (buses, light rail, commuter trains), the majority of suburban residents rely on their cars exclusively. This *automobile-commuter dynamic* has influenced suburban design, in several ways, including:

- Major boulevards that intersect with freeway/expressways are often zoned for retail.
- The retail operations are designed for convenience, which means that ample, accessible parking and drive-through operations are designed into retail space.
- Because the major boulevards have access to freeways, the volume of people passing by each day attracts major companies seeking retail space.
- Major companies tend to occupy these retail spaces because they both have the capital and management chains to move quickly on these locations.

Criticisms of suburban sprawl have been sharp over the past several decades. This *automobile-commuter dynamic* has had what many perceive as negative impacts. The *negative impacts of suburbs* include:

- Large residential subdivisions that cater to a particular economic class that commutes.

FIGURE 6.5d. Suburban boulevard in Jefferson Parish, Louisiana. This major boulevard is clearly zoned for retail operations and big box stores and designed with ample parking for the convenience of a car-dependent community.
Copyright © dbking (CC BY-SA 2.0) at http://commons.wikimedia.org/wiki/File%3AJefferson_Parish_Suburbs_of_New_Orleans.jpg .

- *Facade pedestrianism*, or neighborhoods designed around automobile use but invest in miles of sidewalks that go unused.
- Dividing people geographically by socioeconomic status. High-end and gated subdivisions are often put far away from large apartment complexes.
- Services and urban design reflect socioeconomic divisions. Higher-end subdivisions often have more street lights, larger trees, larger parks, and access to public services (police, fire).
- Destroying the relationship between pedestrian walk space and retail by putting parking lots between them.

Many residents in major North American cities and suburbs have challenged this urban design paradigm. There has been a revival of downtown residential communities, the *urban village* concept, and more pedestrian and activity space. In some cases, the process of *gentrification*, or cities partnering with developers and police to transform areas of urban blight into younger, middle-class residential and entertainment communities, has been successful. Gentrification has changed many parts of Washington DC, Los Angeles, Chicago, and Seattle, for example, drawing in restaurant goers, a younger, more affluent resident base, and entertainment venues.

FIGURE 6.5e. The I35W Mississippi River Bridge collapsed in 2007, killing several commuters.
Copyright © Mike Wills (CC BY-SA 2.0) at http://commons.wikimedia.org/wiki/File%3AI35_Bridge_Collapse_4crop.jpg .

A smaller-scale version of urban renewal is the *urban village* concept. This involves taking older retail space that has largely grown vacant and reviving it with development money, changing zoning and municipal codes to accommodate more street activities, and catering more to local business than to corporate chains. This is accomplished through square footage. Many of the retail pads available are too small to attract large retail and restaurant chains, but they are ideal for small business owners. These urban concepts have offered alternatives to automobile suburbs, but are still niche and have yet to redefine suburban sprawl in North American cities.

INFRASTRUCTURE

This brief section will address how aging infrastructure has become, and will likely continue to be, an issue in many North American cities. North America has many older, colonial-period cities that have evolved and modernized over several centuries. These cities, like New York, Boston, Savannah, Quebec City, and New Orleans, all face the problem of a crumbling infrastructure. Infrastructure includes:

- Utilities
- Roads, highways, bypasses
- Sewers
- Freshwater delivery systems
- Dams, dykes, and levees
- Communication
- Transportation (trains, ferries, ports)

BOX 6A LOS ANGELES AREA PACIFIC ELECTRIC RED CAR (1901–1961)

Los Angeles, California is known for many things like good weather, movie studios, world-class beaches, and, of course, traffic. Less known is that the seemingly endless and notoriously overcrowded freeways were not always how the residents of the greater Los Angeles area moved around the city. Around the turn of the century, the area was experiencing its first population boom, and new arrivals would pour into both Los Angeles proper and peripheral areas like modern-day San Bernardino, Riverside, and Orange counties.

The need to connect these growth areas resulted in a public transportation system like never seen before. Between 1901 and 1961, Los Angeles was home of the Pacific Electric "Red Car" system.

FIGURE 6.5f(1) and **6.5f(b)**. LA's Red Car was the largest and most extensive electric railway system in the world, until it was dismantled.
Copyright in the Public Domain.

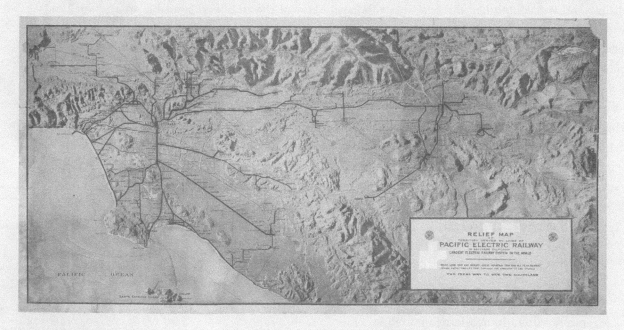

FIGURE 6.5f(2).
Copyright in the Public Domain.

The "Red Car," as it was called, was, at its peak, the largest electric railway system in the world. It was so extensive that it offered regular service to distant communities up to sixty-five miles away, and it stretched from downtown LA to the mountains in the east and the beaches in the west. The PE Red Car was the envy of cities around the world, and Los Angeles, a relatively new city compared to those on the East Coast, was considered a model for public transportation.

In the 1930s, continued growth created a need to connect the San Fernando Valley and Pasadena to downtown Los Angeles. This got the attention of the automobile and oil industries, who lobbied heavily to construct a "freeway" system for cars. Once constructed, the popularity of the "Red Car" began to wane. The postwar population boom of the 1950s was the nail in the coffin, as millions more flooded into LA seeking good weather, new homes, and work opportunities. The car was becoming a coveted part of Southern California culture. Joy rides, cruising streets, and working across town all reflected a collective affection for cars. In Southern California, the car became synonymous with independence and individuality. The Pacific Electric eventually folded, all tracks were removed, and the Red Cars were scrapped.

Many of these forms of infrastructure are publically maintained, and as such are vulnerable to budgetary shortfalls caused by the lack of political will to fund needed repairs, let alone maintenance. Even younger cities like Los Angeles, Denver, Houston, and Minneapolis have all seen problems with their infrastructure but lack the funding to fix them (see *Figure 6.5e*). Although the problem with aging infrastructure is not exclusive to cities, urban infrastructure serves the most people and is relied upon to support the most activity in the region.

THE URBAN/RURAL DIVIDE

The growing rift between the urban and rural communities within North America is essentially the result of economic factors. Cities, since the Industrial Revolution, have been the epicenters of industrial and economic activities, and continue to be so in the globalized economy of today. Although this explains the impetus for the growing rift between the urban and rural realms, it does not necessarily reveal how this growing division can be observed.. The *three (3) ways to observe the urban/rural rift* are:

1. Identify the *percentage of people living in cities, compared to rural areas*, within the same country, state, or province. Between 80 and 85% of North Americans live in cities, but in some states, percentages can reach as high as 95%.

2. What *economic activity* defines the country, state, or province, and where does it go? Whether it's agriculture, mining, timber, fishing, or oil/gas resources, most of what is extracted or produced in rural areas goes to serve large urban populations. This has created a growing interdependence between urban and rural regions while at the same time fostering "culture

clashing." Rural communities tend to be more conservative and religious, and embrace different values than urbanites.

3. *Political polarity* is often rooted in urban/rural differences. Conservative, mostly white communities in rural areas often view urban landscapes as liberal, racially diverse, higher in crime, and perhaps faithless. They may seek politicians that represent the views held in their communities (hard work, fiscal responsibility, Christian values, military strength).

Although the rift this creates is often more subtle in nature and rarely results in civil unrest at the national scale, it is important to understand. Cities are the habitat of most North Americans. As such, if eight or nine out of every ten North Americans live in cities, their perspectives will continue to reflect more "urban" views and support more "urban" political concerns. Likewise, with so many North Americans living in cities, there will be a continued economic reliance on rural resources, fostering more interdependence between urban and rural North Americans. At the same time, many rural Americans and Canadians genuinely feel their lifestyles and values are being overpowered by the big cities. This unusual relationship is becoming a fixed feature in North America's cultural landscape.

6.6 North America and the Twenty-First Century

Although it is difficult to make predictions about the future, there are some key discussions that may illuminate the conflicts or the emerging cooperation that may continue to define North America in this century. These key discussions include:

- Climate change
- Social trends
- Political dysfunction

THEMATIC INTERSECTION 6B

Tar Sands of Canada

Themes: Environmental/Economic

"Tar sands," also known as "oil sands," are essentially bitumen, or heavy crude oil embedded in large fields of sand. Of the estimated two trillion barrels on Earth, Alberta, Canada has the lion's share, with estimates of around 1.7 trillion barrels. The problem with this unconventional type of petroleum deposit is that it requires both extensive and environmentally harmful mining techniques to extract, and has the secondary effect of producing much higher levels of carbon dioxide and particulates when burned, because it is quite literally dirty.

The Canadians, in their own move towards energy independence, embraced this local resource, and have attempted to offer this source of petroleum to the United States via the "Keystone Pipeline." This pipeline would run from Alberta through the Great Plains states to the Gulf to be refined and reserved for domestic use. To date, it has been stopped by President Obama over environmental concerns. So far, just the Athabasca Oil Sands, shown in Figure 6.6a (1), have required the demolition of approximately fifty-four thousand square miles of Earth (forests, peat bogs, and other ecosystems) to reach

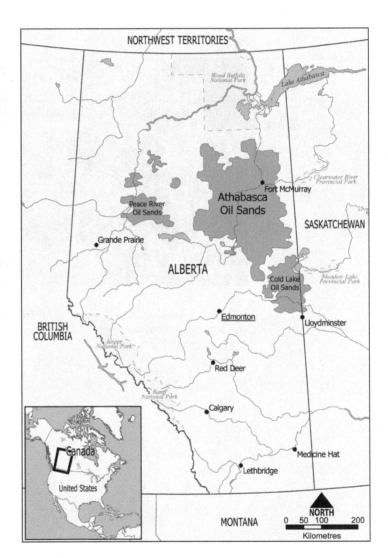

FIGURE 6.6a(1). Canada, once celebrated for its environmental record, has been criticized for mining 54,000 square miles of land to get to 1.7 trillion barrels of heavy crude (bitumen) lodged in surface sands.

Copyright in the Public Domain.

this resource. The large amounts of water and chemicals used to extract tar sands have required the construction of giant tailings ponds to hold the toxic water (seen in Figure 6.6a (2)). These tar sands have damaged Canada's formerly sterling reputation as an environmentally friendly nation. They also showcase how economic incentives can create *environmental* problems. The use of this oil, though profitable for the Canadians and a local source of energy for Americans, is measurably harmful to the environment and potentially devastating for the climate.

FIGURE 6.6a(2). Canada, criticized for mining 54,000 square miles of land.
Copyright in the Public Domain.

Climate Change

Climate change is real and already impacting the planet. North Americans, despite their wealth, are not immune to the effects of climate change, nor can they afford to ignore it. Apart from a small number of wealthy special interest groups and the politicians who support them, the science community and the people of most nations concur that climate change is the most pressing issue we face this century.

The problem is that a growing acceptance of climate change does not necessarily induce radical policy changes or inspire the adoption of new paradigms. Embedded, profitable industries like oil and gas have great inertia, because consumers continue to rely on fossil fuels for mobility, consumerism, energy, and plastics. This stubbornness can be seen with Canada's tar sands, as discussed in *Thematic Intersection 6(b)*. Economic incentives often put the environment at risk in this case, both directly (strip mining) and indirectly (burning oil sands is a huge CO_2 source). This century, **North American issues related to climate change**:

- *Sea Level Rise:* SLR is already causing severe coastal erosion and flooding in North America. Miami is now flooding regularly, and beaches are losing volume. If sea level continues to rise, major cities in the United States and Canada will face critical problems in infrastructure, residential communities, freshwater supply, and property damage in the billions.
- *Frequency & Intensity of Tropical Cyclonic Storms*: Sea surface temperature is rising. In the mid-Atlantic, this is a potential problem because it promotes the formation of tropical storms that have the potential to escalate into hurricanes. Each tropical storm or hurricane that hits the United States has a human and economic cost. In a climate-change scenario, these types of storms are expected to increase both in frequency and intensity. If this combines with sea level rise, the events become more destructive.
- *Drought/Flooding:* Climate change induces a change in airflow patterns from high pressure to low pressure. If high pressure remains intense, the jet stream is deflected, inducing drought over regions like the Southwest, along with cold winters and flooding over more continental zones of low pressure.

Social Trends

Several social trends that will likely continue to redefine the region's cultural landscapes are the rise of *Latinos* in American culture and politics, racial issues, and wealth gaps. Although these discussions are brief, they highlight some of the important social trends following Americans into this century.

As seen in *Figure 6.3e*, the *Latino* population of the American Southwest is significant. In major cities, like Los Angeles, *Latinos* represent approximately 45% of the population, and the number is growing. As this group grows, its political voice gets stronger. Generally, *Latinos* vote Democrat, as seen in the 2012 presidential elections. About 71% voted for Obama, whereas Mitt Romney received about 27% of the vote; many of these voters were the conservative Cuban Americans of Florida.

Racial issues present an internal source of conflict in the United States. The United States was once considered the "Great Paradox" because it was concurrently a free nation and a slave-owning nation. Even after the Civil War and changes to the Constitution, racism and discrimination prevailed in America.

This has been, perhaps, most visibly observable and measurable in poverty levels, incarceration rates, segregation, and even incidents of police brutality.

The *wealth gap* between the richest 10% and the rest has been a growing concern in North America. Some estimates suggest that the richest 1% hold more wealth that 90% of the population combined. This has sparked movements like *Occupy Wall Street* and a call for political reforms to change the tax code, close tax loopholes (domestic and international), and invest in more domestic programs, like infrastructure, that create jobs. This economic imbalance has become very politicized, and whether or not it is an issue is typically debated amongst politicians.

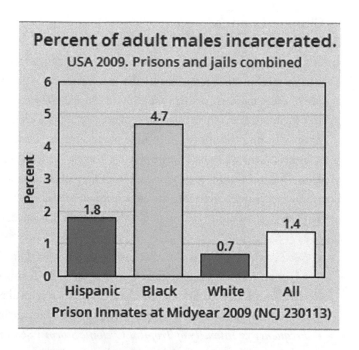

FIGURE 6.6b. Blacks are statistically more likely to be incarcerated than other races.
Copyright in the Public Domain.

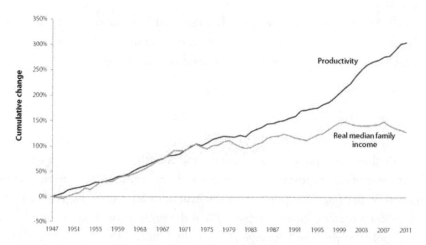

Source: Authors' analysis of Current Population Survey Annual Social and Economic Supplement *Historical Income Tables*, (Table F-5) and Bureau of Labor Statistics, *Productivity – Major Sector Productivity and Costs* Database (2012)

FIGURE 6.6c. The growing division between productivity and real wages. The gap that has been widening between the 1970s and today has been supplemented by credit and the rise of the credit economy. Copyright © (8/14/15 ER: CC BY-SA 3.0. The State of Working America / Economic Policy Institute) at http://commons.wikimedia.org/wiki/File%3AProductivity_and_Real_Median_Family_Income_Growth_1947-2009.png .

Political Polarity and Dysfunction

Politics in the United States has always been an arena of mudslinging. However, the twenty-first century has illuminated a growing trend toward obstructionism and stalemate between the branches of government that has limited the effectiveness of democracy in America. For example, in 2001 Congress had a 56% approval rating, while in 2013 it fell all the way to 14%. Bilateralism has become unpopular, and political parties appear less flexible than before. How this continues to take shape this century is yet to be seen.

CONCLUSION

North America is one of the most powerful and wealthy regions on Earth. The United States and Canada remain one of the largest global economic partnerships, and are still looked upon as beacons of freedom and democracy by many. North American culture has likewise influenced the world. Whether it's movies, music, retail chains, or popular culture, American and Canadian influences are undeniable. At the same time, North Americans inherited a lot from their colonial parents. Not unlike the British, the United States has been an engine of the globalized economy, but has achieved this through economic partnerships that foster uneven development. The United States has a powerful and well-distributed military and uses it to maintain and protect global economic activities, to eliminate threats, and sometimes to wage war. These two narratives have combined to make North America an interesting and influential region historically, and a region to pay very close attention to in the future.

KEY TERMS

Westerly winds	British colonialism	Progressive Era
Middle latitudes	Spanish/French influences	World War II
Natural resources	Independence	Globalization
Watershed	Democracy	Urbanism/suburbanism
"Great Buffer"	Industrial Revolution	Political polarity

CLASS DISCUSSIONS

1. Discuss how European colonial powers shaped the United States and Canada, culturally, politically, and economically.
2. Describe how the United States was like the British, after independence.
3. Discuss key physical geographical features of the United States that have contributed to its ability to grow into an economic giant.
4. How did the role of the United States change after World War II?
5. Describe why the US and Canada are such close allies and economic partners.
6. Discuss North America's urban realm and how it shapes the region.
7. How might *Latinos* change the political landscape of the United States in the future?

ADDITIONAL RESOURCES

CIA World Factbook, United States

https://www.cia.gov/library/publications/the-world-factbook/geos/us.html

United States Census

http://www.census.gov/

United States Chamber of Commerce

https://www.uschamber.com/infrastructure

Canadian Census

http://www12.statcan.gc.ca/census-recensement/index-eng.cfm

CIA World Factbook, Canada

https://www.cia.gov/library/publications/the-world-factbook/geos/ca.html

Physical Geography:

http://water.usgs.gov/watercensus/colorado.html

BIBLIOGRAPHY

Cite: University Readers s1212 David Harvey

"The Ballooning Importance of the 'Latino Vote,' In 3 Charts." NPR. n.d. Web. http://www.npr.org/sections/itsallpolitics/2015/05/20/407954553/the-ballooning-importance-of-the-Latino-vote-in-three-charts. 03 June 2015.

„Canadian Census." Of Canada. N.p., n.d. Web. http://www12.statcan.gc.ca/census-recensement/index-eng.cfm. 13 Feb. 2015.

"Census.gov." Census.gov. N.p., n.d. Web. http://www.census.gov/. 03 Feb. 2015.

"CIA World Factbook United States." Central Intelligence Agency. n.d. Web. https://www.cia.gov/library/publications/the-world-factbook/geos/us.html. 03 Feb. 2015.

"City Mayors: American Megaregions." City Mayors: American Megaregions. N.p., n.d. Web. http://www.citymayors.com/development/usa-megaregions.html. 15 Feb. 2015.

Kron, Josh. "Red State, Blue City: How the Urban-Rural Divide Is Splitting America." The Atlantic. Atlantic Media Company, 30 Nov. 2012. Web. http://www.theatlantic.com/politics/archive/2012/11/red-state-blue-city-how-the-urban-rural-divide-is-splitting-america/265686/. 03 Feb. 2015.

Harvey, D. (2005). A Brief History of Neoliberalism. Oxford University Press. Oxford, UK.

Harvey, D. (2003). New Imperialism. Oxford University Press. Oxford, UK.

Nash, G.B. (2005). The Unknown American Revolution: The Unruly Birth of Democracy and the Struggle to Create America. Penguin. New York.

"National Water Census— Colorado River Basin Focus Area Study." National Water Census— Colorado River Basin Focus Area Study. N.p., n.d. Web. http://water.usgs.gov/watercensus/colorado.html. 03 Feb. 2015.

Page, B. & R. Walker (1991). From Settlement to Fordism: The Agro-industrial Revolution of the American Midwest. Economic Geography. Vol 67(4), pp. 281–315.

Reich, J.R. (2001). Colonial America. 5th ed. Prentice Hall. NJ.

Turnbull, G. (1987). Canals, coal and regional growth during the industrial revolution. Economic History Review, 2nd ser. XL, 4, pp. 537–560.

Weigley, R.F. (1973). The American Way of War: A History of United States Military Strategy and Policy. Indiana University Press. Bloomington.

"Welcome to the Pacific Electric Railway Historical Society." Pacific Electric Railway Historical Society. N.p., n.d. Web. http://www.pacificelectric.org/. 03 Apr. 2015.

"What Are Oil Sands?" Canadian Association of Petroleum Producers. N.p., n.d. Web. http://www.capp.ca/canadian-oil-and-natural-gas/oil-sands/what-are-oil-sands. 03 Apr. 2015.

Wood, G.S. (1991). The Radicalism of the American Revolution. Vintage. New York.

CHAPTER 7

Central and South America

Key Themes:

Environmental, political, cultural, economic

Central American countries:
- Mexico
- Cuba
- Caribbean nations
- Belize
- Guatemala
- Honduras
- El Salvador
- Nicaragua
- Costa Rica
- Panama

South American:
- Colombia
- Venezuela
- Ecuador
- Brazil
- Argentina
- Uruguay/Paraguay
- Bolivia
- Peru
- Chile

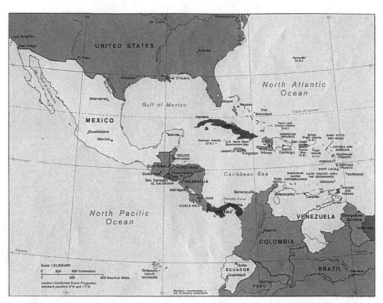

FIGURE 7.1a. Middle America. Copyright in the Public Domain.

FIGURE 7.1b. South America. Copyright in the Public Domain.

7.1 Two Regions

This chapter will depart from convention, in that it will cover two regions, pointing out both similarities and unique physical and human features. This is important, because Central and South America have many distinctions, but also much in common. Formerly referred to as Latin America, or the vast territories within the Americas settled by nations who spoke Latin-based languages like Spanish, Portuguese, and French, this region shares a similar history of conquest, exploration, independence, and culture. However, over time and under various circumstances, these regions (and subregions) have distinctions that must be addressed separately. Therefore, the structure of this chapter will follow a certain formula. First, there will be formal discussions of each region, covering some basic physical geography, population and settlement patterns, regional histories, and then social and economic development. Then, there will be Case Studies and Thematic Intersections that highlight similarities. Finally, the chapter will conclude with a broad overview.

7.2 Central America: Overview

Central America, as the name implies, is a region wedged between North America and South America. Although it is not necessarily a large region compared to others, it has great diversity, both in terms of its physical geography and cultural landscapes. The physical geography includes a large landmass (Mexico, Guatemala, Honduras, El Salvador, Nicaragua), an extended *isthmus* (Costa Rica, Panama), and a splattering of large and small islands stretching approximately 1,700 miles from the Gulf of Mexico to the eastern edge of the Lesser Antilles. This size and diversity, however, is rather compactly wedged between North and South America. Its *north–south axis*—that is, its distance from the southernmost portion of North America (Florida's Keys) to the southeastern edge in the Dutch Caribbean (Bonaire)—is only about 1,100 miles. The region's *east–west axis*, on the other hand, stretches nearly four thousand miles from Tijuana, Mexico to Barbados. This physical profile makes this region quite unique in the world.

Central America: Physiography

The physical geography and physical landscapes of Central America are fascinating. This region has been shaped by (1) tectonic activity, (2) volcanism, and (3) changing ocean levels over millions of years.

1. Plate tectonics is the movement of Earth's lithosphere, in large plates, over time. Central America is one of the most tectonically active regions on the planet (see *Figure 7.2a*). With so many plates interacting, the region is prone to frequent earthquakes, as seen recently in Haiti and Mexico City.

2. Volcanism, or the processes related to the ejection of molten lava, rock fragments, hot vapor, and gas, from Earth's lithosphere onto the surface and into the atmosphere, is another influential force in shaping Central America's physical landscapes. There are both active and dormant volcanoes, both on the mainland and throughout the Caribbean.

Finally, ocean influences, like sea level changes over time, have shaped the many coastal plains of this region. The coastal zones have been smoothed out by changes in sea level during glacial and

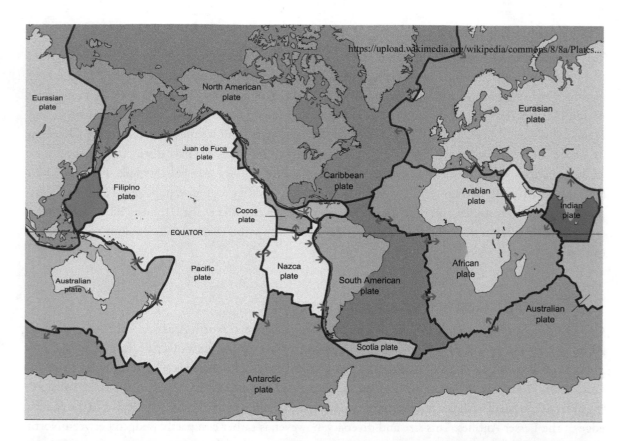

FIGURE 7.2a. Central America is at a dangerous intersection of tectonic plates, which include the Nazca (light blue), Cocos (grey-blue), Caribbean (peach), the North American (brown, and the South American plate (purple). No other region on Earth has this many plates interacting in a single region.
Copyright in the Public Domain.

interglacial episodes (Ice Ages). As an *Ice Age* advances, water on the planet is sequestered in polar ice and glaciers, thus lowering ocean levels. Oppositely, as the ice melts and an interglacial period begins, the oceans rise. This creates coastal plains, and Central America has many important coastal features. One is the Yucatan Peninsula of Mexico and Belize. This giant coastal plain is known for its topographically flat, *karst* landscape composed of soluble limestone. The limestone has formed thousands of *cenotes*, or sinkholes, that provide surface

FIGURE 7.2b. The Haitian Earthquake of 2010 was devastating, because of poor infrastructure and old buildings. Death tolls were estimated to be around 150,000.
Copyright © United Nations Development Programme (CC BY 2.0) at http://commons.wikimedia.org/wiki/File%3AHaitians_pull_out_a_body_from_the_rubbles_of_a_school_(12_january_2010).jpg .

FIGURE 7.2c. The Izalco Volcano of Western El Salvador is relatively new and earned the nickname, "Lighthouse of the Pacific," because it erupted continuously from 1770–1958.
Copyright in the Public Domain.]

access to underground, protected freshwater sources. This enabled the Maya civilization to thrive here for hundreds of years.

Additionally, ocean influence can be seen in tropical storms. This is a particular danger to the eastern realm of this region, or the *Lesser Antilles* (Barbados to St. John) and the large island nations of Puerto Rico, Jamaica, Hispaniola (Dominican Republic/Haiti), and Cuba. Hurricanes have caused great damages in this part of the region.

Subregions

At this point, further discussions about both physical and human features of the region are best addressed in the context of a particular *subregion*. Central America has the following *three (3) subregions:*

1. Mexico
2. Mid-Central America
3. Caribbean Realm

FIGURE 7.2d. Relief map of Mexico. Both the west and east coasts of Mexico quickly succumb to the mountains and high valleys of the interior.

Physically, Mexico is the largest subregion and the most continental. This textbook has given it its own distinction as a subregion because it so large. Although it does share physical and cultural features with neighboring countries, it has both physical features and human narratives that make it better to discuss independently. Mexico stretches from the border of the United States in the north to its interface with the subtropical subregion of Middle America. The northern realm is located around the subtropical high-pressure system, which means it is partly a desert climate. Through the center of Mexico are coastlines that quickly succumb to an interior of mountains and high valleys. Further south, this mountainous realm becomes more volcanic in nature, and dozens of volcanic peaks can be observed from central Mexico deep into Middle America.

CASE STUDY 7A

Altitudinal Zonation in Central and South America

Altitudinal zonation essentially refers to what agricultural activity can occur within certain elevations. This is common around the world, but it is perhaps best observed in Central and South America because the mountains and highlands of these regions are largely within the subtropical and tropical latitudes. A change in altitude in Costa Rica, for example, is not like a change in altitude in Colorado. Colorado is in the middle latitudes, which means changes occur faster over shorter ascensions. For example, a desert climate can change into an alpine climate in just several thousand feet.

In the tropics and subtropics, the atmosphere is a little thicker, warmer (zone of direct radiation), and wetter on average. This means changes in elevation are more subtle, and agricultural activities, then, can stretch from coastal plains at sea level to livestock herding at over ten thousand feet. As seen in Figure 7.2e, bananas grow at the lowest elevation, "tierra caliente." This is a huge industry for countries like Costa Rica, Honduras, and Nicaragua. What Figure 7.2e does not show is that coffee is grown with "tierra templada." This elevation is just right for cultivating coffee because it is characterized by cooler evenings, plentiful seasonal precipitation, and, often, the right soils (volcanic red earth, deep sandy loam, etc.). In South America, growing potatoes and herding alpacas, cows, and other livestock can occur above ten thousand feet. Native Peruvians in the "Altiplano" have engaged in these types of agriculture for many centuries.

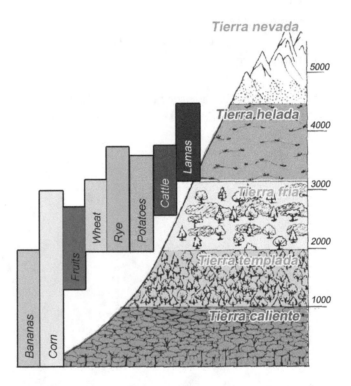

FIGURE 7.2e. In Central and South America, "altitudinal zonation" defines what crops can be grown at a certain subtropical altitude.
Copyright © Chris.urs-o; Maksim; Anita Graser (CC BY-SA 3.0) at http://commons.wikimedia.org/wiki/File%3AHoehenstufen_der_anden.en.PNG .

The second *subregion* of Central America is Mid-Central America. This includes the seven contiguous states south of Mexico to the Colombian border (see *Figure 7.2f*). This part of Central America is an extension of both the coastal subtropical rainforests that start in the Yucatan Peninsula of Mexico and continue through the *Mosquito Coast*, as well as the volcanic mountainous interior that essentially stretches from central Mexico to Panama. This area is classified as having *Af* (tropical), *Am* (tropical monsoon), and *Aw* (tropical savanna) climates. These climates result from direct radiation and wet or seasonally wet precipitation patterns.

The Caribbean Realm *subregion* is composed of thousands of islands, several of which are quite large and populous. The *Greater Antilles* represent the four large islands of the *subregion:*

- Cuba
- Jamaica
- Hispaniola (Dominican Republic/Haiti)
- Puerto Rico

The *Lesser Antilles* include the many small islands of the British and American Virgin Islands through to Barbados, in an arc. Additionally, there are islands that do not fit within either of these classifications, like

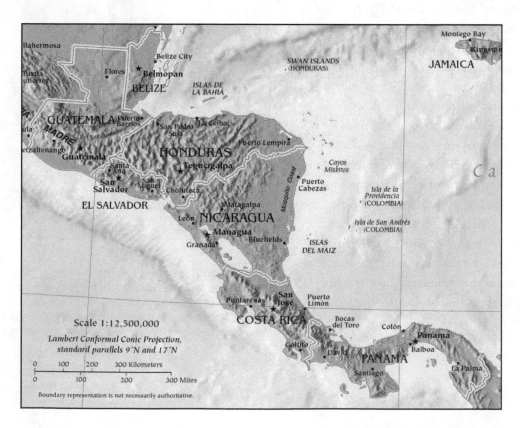

FIGURE 7.2f. The seven countries of Central America's "Middle America" subregion. Copyright in the Public Domain.

the Bahamas, Cayman Islands, and Dutch Caribbean, off the coast of Venezuela. Like the Mid-Central American *subregion*, this realm is mostly subtropical monsoonal. However, its ocean setting and the spread-out topography means not all the islands are the same. Aruba, for example, is so far south that the constant trade winds make the island semiarid, even desertlike. They even have cacti and rattlesnakes, which are typically found in continental North America.

7.3 South America: Overview

South America is a much larger region, with approximately 6.9 million square miles of terrestrial surface. South America is composed of twelve nations, which include Brazil, Colombia, Peru, and Argentina, to name a few (see *Figure 7.0a (2)*). Unlike Central America's mix of continentality, a narrow isthmus region, and the sizable island realm, South America is a continent–region, like Australia. This means it is almost entirely physically independent from any other landmass, apart from the roughly 120-mile long border it shares with Panama. It has a *north–south axis*, which explains the great climatic diversity. The northern two-thirds of the continent fall within the tropical realm. The largest rainforest on Earth, the *Amazon*, is located in the area. The southern third of the continent falls within the *westerlies*, thereby exhibiting seasonal variations not unlike that found in Europe or North America. South America is also remote, in that it is a great distance from the giant economies and population-dense middle latitudes of the Northern Hemisphere.

South America's Physiography and Subregions

South America's physical geography may best be examined in context of its **four (4) subregions**. These include:

- Tropical Realm
- Andes Region
- Patagonia and Plains
- Desert

The Tropical Realm exists in abundance because of several physical factors. A key factor is that the equator runs through South America. This means a significant portion of the region receives and collects direct energy before sharing and exchanging it with the higher latitudes. It is also where Earth's easterly *trade winds* converge, forming the *Intertropical Convergence Zone* (discussed in Chapter 5: Sub-Saharan Africa). Because these winds blow in from the warm Mid-Atlantic, they carry moisture-laden air into the region. This air then rises, condenses, and becomes a frequent source of precipitation for the robust tropic biome below.

The *Amazon Rainforest* is an important part of both this region and the planet. It has been called the "lungs of the world" because 20% of the Earth's oxygen, or one of every five breaths taken, is produced by the Amazon Rainforest. It is the world's largest rainforest, occupying approximately 2.7 million square miles over nine countries, with Brazil having about 60%. Few places on Earth have the biodiversity of the Amazon. There are literally millions of species of insects, about forty thousand species of plants, and thousands of animals.

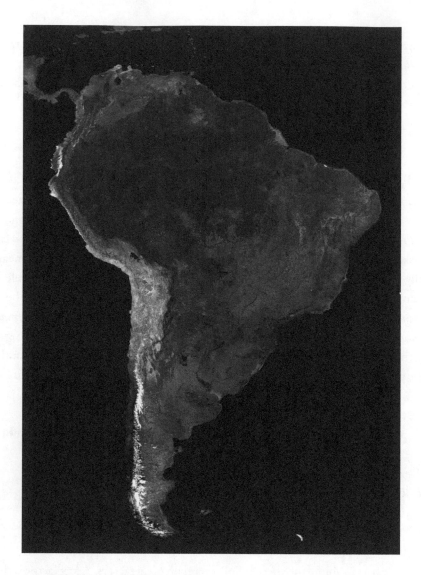

FIGURE 7.3a. This satellite image of South America shows how much of it is tropical.
Copyright in the Public Domain.

The Andes Mountains *subregion* defines the western quarter of the continent. Stretching 4,300 miles, it is the longest terrestrial mountain range in the world and one of the highest. The range extends from Colombia to the southern margin of Chile and Argentina. They define the western quarter of the region because they create a barrier stopping the moist air, moving from east to west over the Amazon, from reaching the Pacific Ocean. When the tropical air mass confronts the eastern slope of the Andes, the air rises, condenses, and sheds its moisture. Because they are so tall, very little moisture makes it to the leeward side, inducing a *rain shadow*. This makes western Peru very dry.

FIGURE 7.3b. The Amazon Rainforest is the largest in the world, covering about 2.7 million square miles.
Copyright © Neil Palmer / CIAT (CC BY-SA 2.0) at http://commons.wikimedia.org/wiki/File%3AAmazon_CIAT_(5).jpg .

FIGURE 7.3c. The Andes Mountains stand tall and in stark contrast to the tropical rainforests that cover much of the region.
Copyright in the Public Domain.

BOX 7A THE GREAT ANDEAN DIVIDE: LIMA OF THE DESERT VS. IQUITOS OF AMAZONIA

The Amazon River is not only one of the longest rivers on Earth; it also has the highest flow volume, depositing four times the amount of water into the ocean than the Nile River in Africa. Much of this water comes from one of the rainiest spots on Earth, the eastern slopes of the Peruvian Andes. Iquitos is the largest city in the Peruvian Amazon. It rains about 222 days a year, totaling around 115 inches annually. The city sits adjacent to the Amazon River, which not only defines the region's landscape but also influences a broad spectrum of economic activities. These include fishing, timber (often illegal), rubber, and tourism.

Lima, Peru is located on the other side of the Andes on the Pacific coast. It is the largest city in Peru, with about ten million residents. This makes it the second most populous city in South America, next to Sao Paulo, Brazil. Lima sits in the rain shadow of the Andes, making it relatively dry. Lima receives about thirteen inches of precipitation annually, mostly falling in spring and autumn months. Although Lima's temperatures are largely regulated by the ocean, it can get humid and foggy. This is because the ocean current off the coast is carrying cold

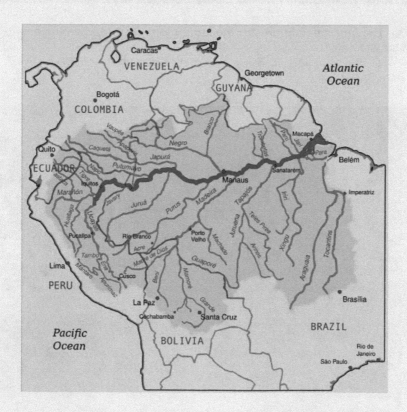

FIGURE 7.3d(1). The Amazon River begins its journey on the wet, windward slopes of the Andes.
Copyright © Kmusser (CC BY-SA 3.0) at http://commons.wikimedia.org/wiki/File%3AAmazonrivermap.svg .

FIGURE 7.3d(2). Iquitos, the largest city in the Peruvian Amazon, sits close to the Amazon River. Here, it rains for around 222 days a year. Copyright © Viault (CC BY-SA 3.0) at http://commons.wikimedia.org/wiki/File%3AIquitos_et_l'Amazonie_983.jpg .

water from the south. Cold water inhibits convection, unless "La Niña" conditions return. The Rimac River is Lima's water source. Unlike the Amazon, the Rimac is more ephemeral in nature, in that its flow volume increases with seasonal precipitation events, but then dries out again. The trickle that remains is heavily polluted with trash, runoff, and sewerage. There have been concerns that climate change may adversely affect the Rimac watershed in the future.

FIGURE 7.3d(3). Lima, the largest city in Peru, is generally dry and getting drier. Its rainfall is only 13 inches a year. Copyright © Håkan Svensson Xauxa (CC BY-SA 3.0) at http://commons.wikimedia.org/wiki/File%3ALima_PuebloJov_4.jpg .

The Andes are not just immensely jagged peaks sometimes reaching well over twenty thousand feet; they are also home to high-altitude, fertile valleys called the *Altiplano*. The *Altiplano* are typically between ten and fourteen thousand feet. They are rich in fertile volcanic soils (enabling agriculture), have reliable sources of water, and are insulated from the bitter cold of the mountains around them. This has made the *Altiplano* habitable for many centuries.

The Patagonia and Plains region is a mixed region that lies in subtropical, fertile savannas south of the rainforests and the middle-latitude, southern continental realm in the rain shadow of the Andes. Although their physical features are each distinctive, they do form a continuum from the Brazilian state of *Parana* all the way to *Tierra Del Fuego* on the southern tip of South America. The *subregion*, known by South Americans as the *Pampas*, is ideal for various forms of agriculture. Like those found in the United States, Mexico, Australia, and New Zealand, the *Pampas* has a long history of cattle ranching. Their cowboys are known as *gauchos*. Many parts of the world rely on agriculture from these areas (including Chile).

Further to the south, the wind orientation changes from easterly *trade winds* (generally an east-to-west flow) to the *westerlies* (generally a west-to-east flow). This means the western side of the Andes is receiving the ocean air from the Pacific, while the leeward side, in Argentina's *Patagonia*, falls within the *rain shadow*.

Patagonia's landscapes are ancient and seemingly untouched. The waters off the coast are cold and the climate is generally chilly with seasonal precipitation. This is not an economically engaged part of the world, and it is too remote to attract or support large numbers of tourists. It does, however, attract many ecotravelers interested in the raw beauty and

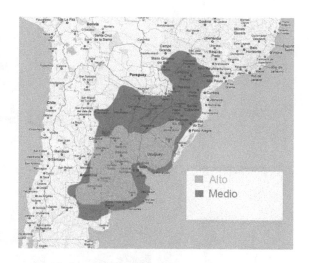

FIGURE 7.3e. This maps shows the "Pampas" of South America.
Copyright in the Public Domain.

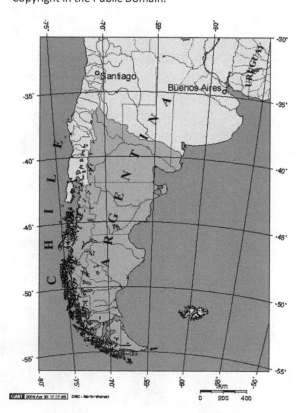

FIGURE 7.3f. Map of Patagonia. Note the latitude and how most of this region falls in the middle-latitudes, are in the *westerlies*.
Copyright © Gi (CC BY-SA 3.0) at http://commons.wiki-media.org/wiki/File:Pat_map.PNG .

nature of the realm. On the western margin of *Patagonia* are glaciers, and, to the south, some of the most feared waters in maritime history. The *Tierra del Fuego* region of South America is known as "The Horn." When ships sailed from the Atlantic to the Pacific Ocean, they would have to travel beneath South America, around "The Horn." This is a hostile shipping route because of the frequent storms. Its latitude is sixty-six degrees south latitude, which means it is a subpolar climate. Countless ships have sunk in those waters.

The final subregion is the Desert. Although South America is broadly not a desert region and the one reputable desert they have is small, it is special. The *Atacama Desert* is wedged between the cold Pacific Ocean and the high Andes Mountains. It is six hundred miles long, north to south, but quite narrow, with a width in some areas not exceeding forty miles. What makes the *Atacama* special is its aridity. Remember that deserts are not determined by how hot they are, but by how dry they are. The *Atacama*, then, is not a hot desert, but it is the driest desert in the world, receiving less than a fraction of an inch of precipitation, annually. Some parts of the desert have not seen any rainfall in over forty years.

Making this desert so dry is an unusual combination of physical features. The wind orientation at this latitude is easterly. This means the moisture gets caught on the eastern slopes of the Andes while inducing a *rain shadow effect* on the west coast of Southern Peru and northern Chile. This area also begins to fall under the influence of a subtropical high-pressure system. This inhibits convection because of descending air from the Hadley Cell. Third, the ocean current in the Pacific is cold at this latitude. Upwelling from the thermocline, it brings cold, nutrient-rich water to the surface. This cold water evaporates, but the humidity is sequestered in the lower troposphere, which produces fog. The *Atacama*, then, is indeed the driest desert on Earth, but has foggy coasts. This fog allows certain plants and animals (and human settlements) to survive, despite the lack of water.

Fishing villages exist along the coast of the *Atacama Desert* because the nutrient-rich waters bring fish. Without reliable water sources and being too remote to build pipelines, the locals rely on *fog fences*. These are net structures that are placed at the top of coastal hills above the villages, where the fog condenses. The fog moves across the fence, forcing it to condense on the net, and is then captured in a trough that leads to a pipe that flows downhill to holding tanks in the village. This fills the tank every day, and villagers get a fixed ration of water for consumption and household use.

FIGURE 7.3g. The Atacama Desert, though the driest on Earth, has abundant fog on the coasts. This allows local plants and animals to survive under these harsh conditions, because the fog condenses and beads on the plants, which then drip down to the roots or is licked up by a local Alpaca. Copyright © Aaron Bornstein (CC BY 2.0) at http://commons.wikimedia.org/wiki/File%3APan_de_Azucar_National_Park.jpg .

It is important to point out that these are all generalized *subregions*. They do not include every climate type, microclimate, and so on. For example, south of the *Atacama* is the beginning of a Mediterranean Climate zone, much like that found in California. It has many of the same features as California, both physical and in terms of human activities like agriculture. California grows a wide variety of crops, as does Chile. California produces wine, as does Chile. In fact, during the winter months in the United States when fresh fruits are out of season, Chilean fruit is often imported because it is summer there (see *Figure 7.3h*). This and other smaller climate regions were either bundled or excluded in the profiles of South America's *subregions*, but not because they lack importance.

In conclusion, both Central America and South America have common features (altitudinal zonation, climate types), but also maintain enough distinction to be addressed separately. Whereas Central America is physically more divided and spread out, South America is a *continent–region*, which means big processes, like wind orientation and latitudinal change, can be observed differently. Superimposed over these physical landscapes are human landscapes. In some ways, these regions share a very similar past and have had very similar outcomes, economically and politically. This is why many geography textbooks, including this one, include Mexico as a part of Central America, rather than North America. At the same time, specific events and activities specific to one region must periodically be addressed.

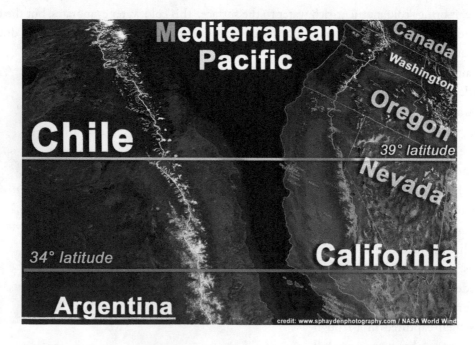

FIGURE 7.3h. This manipulated satellite image of Chile and California show their latitudinal similarities.
Copyright © (CC BY-SA 3.0) at https://en.wikipedia.org/wiki/File:Mediterranean_distribution_in_America.jpg.

7.4 Cultural Landscapes of Central and South America

The early cultural landscapes of both Central and South America can be examined under one roof. The reason for this is that they were both settled by native nomadic peoples, had some groups advance their civilizations by way of agriculture, were both victims of European conquest, and both struggled through periods of independence. This section will platform these discussions as one while pointing out more regional narratives when necessary.

ANCIENT CULTURES

Before Europeans arrived and changed the cultural landscapes of the Americas for good, native peoples occupied the realm. Some of these groups formed more advanced civilizations in ways similar to those found in the early societies of *Mesopotamia* and ancient Egypt. Similar patterns of advancement would unfold. Embracing agriculture resulted in:

- Population growth
- Advances in language

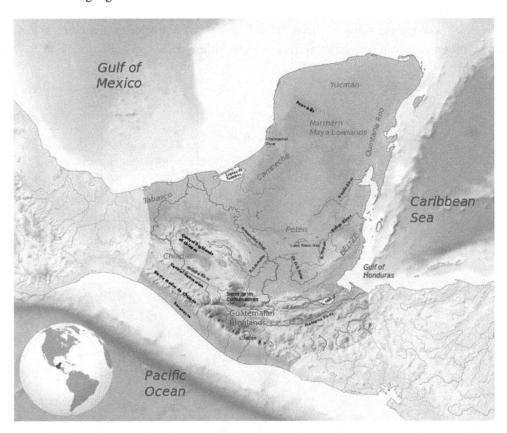

FIGURE 7.4a. The Maya occupied the Yucatan Peninsula through much of modern-day Belize and Guatemala.
Copyright © Simon Burchell (CC BY-SA 4.0) at http://commons.wikimedia.org/wiki/File%3AMaya_civilization_location_map_-_geography.svg

- Specialization
- Administrative structure and leadership
- Organized religion
- Security/military
- Advances in engineering and mathematics

Three regional civilizations that emerged were the *Maya* and *Aztecs* (of Mexico and Mid-Central America) and the *Inca* of the Andes *subregion* (mainly in Peru, Bolivia, and Ecuador).

The *Maya* were located in the modern-day Yucatan Peninsula of Mexico, Belize, and Guatemala (see *Figure 7.4a*). Archeological evidence suggests they advanced as early as the third century BCE and remained cohesive through about the tenth century CE. This makes this the earliest ancient culture in the realm. The Mayan diet was mainly composed of beans, maize, squash, chilies, fish, and cacao. They made many scientific advances, especially in astronomy and mathematics. Competition with neighbors, possible drought induced by the *Medieval Warming Period*, and civil strife led to the fragmentation of the Maya and their eventual collapse.

The *Aztecs* of *Mesoamerica* (Mexico) were formed, through an alliance of several local civilizations, to defeat a common enemy in the early fifteenth century. Although they were hardly the first civilization

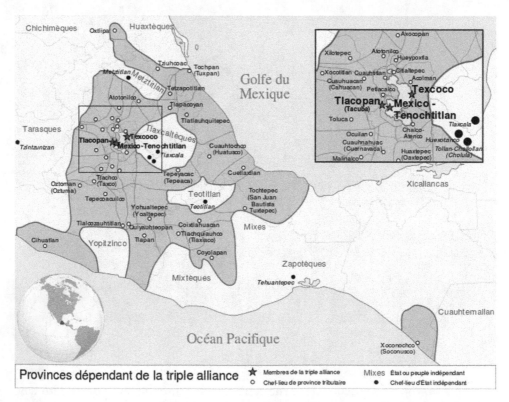

FIGURE 7.4b. The Aztecs at their peak, just before the Spanish arrived.
Copyright © Yavidaxiu (CC BY-SA 3.0) at http://commons.wikimedia.org/wiki/File%3AAztec_Empire_1519_map-fr.svg .

to occupy this region of Mexico, they were certainly the most well-known. Based around Lake Texcoco (now Mexico City), the *Aztecs* built the lake city of *Tenochtitlan* to be their capital. This city was a true marvel of engineering, because the natural protection of the lake helped to make them secure, while long causeways allowed them to move goods, services, and armies to and from the city. The city was close to several of the largest pyramids on Earth. However, the pyramids of the Sun and Moon were built long before the *Aztecs* arrived. The *Aztecs* managed their empire through the placement of local governors, strategic arranged marriages, and a tribute system, as opposed to maintaining military garrisons and ruling with a standing army. Both the *Aztecs* and the *Maya* were known for their religious practice of sacrificing humans atop pyramids (see *Figure 7.4b*). These two civilizations in Mexico and

FIGURE 7.4c. A 16th century illustration of an Aztec ceremony that required human sacrifice.
Copyright in the Public Domain.

Mid-Central America were advanced and powerful, and would astonish the arriving Europeans.

Finally, the *Inca* of South America were the largest of the three main native civilizations, making them the largest in all the Americas. Their territory extended from Ecuador to Chile at its peak, and was interconnected by a system of roads that rivaled those found in the Roman Empire. The Andean terrain which they occupied was rugged and formidable. However, they were able to maintain cohesiveness and unity, despite their physical setting, until civil war broke out over succession.

Based in the Cuzco Valley of the Peruvian *Altiplano*, the *Inca* thrived. They had a powerful and well-trained military, and their king, the *Sapa Inca*, was considered a god. To communicate, they used runners (no horses in the Americas until the Europeans arrived) to carry messages to and from the *Sapa Inca*. These runners would chew coca leaves and sprint for miles, using the network of roads, until they reached another runner at a garrison outpost to carry on. The *Inca* also invented terrace agriculture (step agriculture) to cultivate potatoes and other crops on steep mountainsides. This is still copied today in China, Southeast Asia, and other regions.

These three main civilizations provide a lens into the advanced societies of Central and South America. Not unlike the ancient agricultural hearths of Eurasia and Africa, and the well-known civilizations that followed, the Mesoamerican and Incan civilizations were organized and powerful, and leveraged a deeper understanding of mathematics, physics, and science. This resulted in great cities like *Tenochtitlan*, the

Mayan city temples of *Chichen itza* or *Tulum*, and the Incan city of *Machu Picchu*. At the same time, despite these advancements, they would prove no match for Europeans that arrived. This is not exclusively a narrative about Spanish military prowess. There is much more that might explain how the Europeans were able to, in a short time, completely alter the cultural landscapes that took thousands of years to shape. How did relatively small European countries cause the death of more than twenty million indigenous Americans and claim the lands for themselves with so little resistance? The answer begins with the relationship between the natives and the Iberian invaders.

IBERIAN INVADERS

As discussed in Chapter 2, Spain had little choice but to sail west if they were to secure a trade route to the "Indies." By doing this, Columbus unknowingly, and quite unintentionally, stumbled upon the "New World." His discovery shocked Europe, and soon Spain and Portugal, collectively addressed as the

FIGURE 7.4d. Machu Picchu was an Incan mountain city, built nearly 8,000 feet up in the Andes. Copyright © icelight (CC BY 2.0) at http://commons.wikimedia.org/wiki/File%3AOver_Machu_Picchu.jpg .

FIGURE 7.4e. Columbus landing on Hispaniola in 1492, marking the beginning of the end for native life in the Americas. Copyright in the Public Domain.

Iberians (named after the Iberian Peninsula of Europe), would move fast to explore, plunder, and convert the inhabitants of a seemingly endless land.

Having been at war with the *Moors* for centuries, the first wave of Spaniards, from 1492 to 1550, included experienced soldiers who were clever, manipulative, and cruel when circumstance called. Once it was identified that the natives posed little threat apart from their large numbers, they were expediently exploited as slaves, killed, or used as allies against stronger groups. This "discovery" immediately sparked a rush to the New World. What they would discover would change the world.

The *Iberians* were quick to discover and conquer the great civilizations while easily overcoming more traditional native groups. *Conquistadors* like Cortez defeated the powerful Aztecs with a small army, while Pizarro exploited a civil war to conquer the Inca in South America. The Iberians had advanced weapons made of steel; war horses trained to trample humans in battle; armor; and motive. Silver and gold were abundant, and the Spanish, in particular, amassed a tremendous amount of wealth.

This flow of wealth would change Europe as well. The Spanish, with so much treasure coming in, could not only afford to build a great *Armada* (navy) to protect their interests in Europe and abroad, but could also reinvest in continued explorations and expansions of the crown in other undiscovered territories. As explorers found new areas of the New World, they would claim them for Spain or Portugal. As properties of the crown, they were then obligated to convert the locals to Catholicism and authorized to deal with any threat as a threat against the crown. This contributed to the annihilation of an entire people.

The most effective weapon the *Iberians* had was invisible. As discussed in Chapter 1, the Old World diseases were devastating to the native inhabitants. Whereas Europeans, Asians, and Africans had thousands of years to develop resistance to pathogens that crossed from animals to humans (agricultural society), native peoples died from them. Old World diseases like smallpox, measles, and influenza would devastate entire native communities. Although this was, at first, unintentional, it was quite convenient for the European invaders. By the late colonial period, approximately twenty million native inhabitants had died from disease.

COLONIZATION AND INDEPENDENCE

Most of the contiguous Central American and South American land area was settled by Spain and Portugal. The Portuguese, who had deep cultural and political ties with Spain, were able to independently claim and colonize Brazil. The Spanish had the rest of the realm, stretching from Argentina to the middle of North America.

There were several liabilities that came with maintaining such expansive territories and colonies. In the Caribbean, for example, other powerful European powers moved in aggressively and challenged Spanish hegemony in the region. The British, French, and Dutch would all claim islands and fight the Spanish off to keep them. Likewise, the volume of gold and silver passing through the Caribbean gave rise to piracy. This would, essentially, cut off Spain's revenue source. Back in Europe, the Spanish and English went to war, resulting in the defeat of the Spanish *Armada* (a tropical storm did not help) and the subsequent rise of British naval power. With the British emerging as the dominant naval force on the planet, maintaining expansive colonies and revenue streams was difficult.

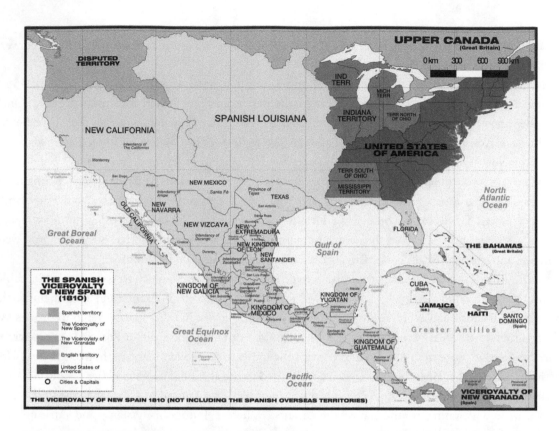

FIGURE 7.4f. New Spain, in 1800, included territories near the United States that would soon be reacquired by the French and sold to the Americans. The lands of New Spain were nonetheless extensive and would shape the cultural landscapes of Central America.
Copyright © Giggette (CC BY-SA 3.0) at http://commons.wikimedia.org/wiki/File%3AViceroyalty_of_the_New_Spain_1800_(without_Philippines).png .

Additionally, the remote geography of South America also presented difficulties. Communication between Madrid, Spain and Lima, Peru, for example, sometimes took a year. The physical landscape of South America made it difficult for more regional colonies to communicate with and support each other. The Andes Mountains, a hot rainforest, or a dry desert often prevented connectivity between Lima, Santiago, Asunción, Cartagena, Buenos Aires, and other Spanish colonial cities. The result was a broad movement towards independence. By the early 1800s, Simon Bolivar, a Venezuelan politician, would take inspiration from the American and French Revolutions and launch a war of independence from Spain. One by one, Spanish colonies would transition and fight their way into independence.

Regional Cultural Patterns

Most countries in Central and South America can be broadly characterized as "Hispanic." Hispanic is a term used to define individuals, cultures, or nations that have Spanish ancestry. Hundreds of millions of people speak Spanish in these realms. However, to claim that the cultures of these regions are exclusively Spanish would be inaccurate. This subsection, then, will explore the cultural patterns that have emerged since independence and briefly identify what traits are more purely Spanish, as well as the local and regional influences that helped form local and regional cultural complexes.

Broadly, there are some aspects of Hispanic culture that were handed down directly from the Iberians. Below are the *four (4) direct Spanish traits:*

1. *Catholicism*: Although not all Central and South Americans are Catholic, the religion is the most popular and has been present since the first Spaniard stepped off his ship from Europe.
2. *Language*: Spanish remains the language of most Latin American countries, and the Brazilians still speak Portuguese.
3. *Architecture*: "Spanish-style" architecture, urban planning principles (where present), and home design still reflect Spanish values.
4. *Social stratum*: European social divisions carried through to the New World, which then fostered the continued separation of privileged and peasant classes.

The later trait, (4) *social stratum*, is more complicated and requires context. This division in society really stems from the Hacienda system put in place by Spanish colonial powers centuries ago. It reflects Europe's old feudal dynamic, in which a landlord (ruling class, nobility, highborn) is master of a large house and expansive lands (typically granted by a monarch or governor with royal authority). These lands (1) are designed to be self-sufficient, in that they grow crops and raise livestock for their own consumption;

FIGURE 7.4g. Old Hacienda in Mexico. The "Don" and his family would typically live in European elegance, unlike the large peasant communities around them.
Copyright © Ruiz (CC BY-SA 2.0) at http://commons.wikimedia.org/wiki/File:Hacienda_San_Gabriel.jpg .

FRANCE MILITAIRE.

Incendie de la Plaine du Cap .   Massacre des Blancs par les Noirs.

FIGURE 7.4h. Slave revolt on French plantation in Caribbean, 1791.
Copyright in the Public Domain.

(2) use peasant labor in exchange for a home or community; (3) are politically powerful, in that they have a voice in regional affairs and enjoy direct lines to the governor or Spain; and (4) typically maintain more purity in their Spanish bloodline.

The goal of the *Hacienda* was not to strategically serve the broader economic goals of the colony (as with the British). Instead, they made the New World more like Spain, culturally. This system, though a colorful part of the cultural landscape, failed to effectively tie distant territories to Spain. If anything, they became too independent and self-sufficient, all while fostering greater social and economic divisions between the landowning ruling class and the growing peasant class. The economies of these nations, as will be discussed in more detail in this chapter, still struggle with remnants of this colonial paradigm.

In the Caribbean, there were other cultures (French, British, Dutch) with different social and economic structures. For example, in British colonies like Jamaica or Barbados, plantations characterized the lands. These plantations were similar to *haciendas* in that the owner often lived in wealth and enjoyed political power, but different in that they used slave labor to produce crops (sugar, cotton, indigo) that were profitable in regional and even global markets. This made the Caribbean more incendiary, because French and English Caribbean colonies were sometimes 90% slave and 10% white colonist. Because the Americans were able to expel the powerful British, other regions under their control fell into active revolt and, eventually, independence.

CASE STUDY 7B

Race and the Americas: Iberian vs. British Culture

How racial and ethnic groups have formed across the landscapes of Central and South America is important to understand. Figure 7.4i is an artist's depiction of an interracial Brazilian family in 1895. Interracial relationships were common in Brazil, as they are today. Currently, more than 50% of Brazilians declare themselves as being mixed race (white–black mix in some portion), or "mulatto."

Likewise, "Hispanic" culture is not exclusively Spanish. It is more "mestizo," or a mix of Spanish and Mesoamerican blood. In fact, much of the culture of Mexico, Mid-Central America, and South America is "mestizo" culture. This can be seen not only in genetic traits, but also in culture. An example might be Mexican cuisine. "Mexican" food is influenced by Spain (beef, pork, chicken, rice) and Mesoamerica (potatoes, corn, cocoa, certain kinds of bean). Tortillas, a Spanish form of flat bread brought from Moorish-influenced Spain, were altered in the Americas by grinding cornmeal with lard into "masa." This "masa" was then used to make tortillas.

Another is religion. Mestizo culture blends traditional Catholic beliefs and practices with native beliefs. Dia de los Muertos (the Day of the Dead celebration) is both a Catholic and native-influenced ceremony.

Unlike the mixed cultures of former Iberian societies, the British deliberately maintained a strong separation between races. The British felt that mixing race was a taboo and was therefore illegal in many colonies. This can still be seen today in former British Caribbean colonies like Jamaica, Barbados, the Bahamas, and the Caymans.

One of the key reasons for this can be found in religion. Both the Spanish and Portuguese were Catholic. Catholicism says that if one converts to the faith and becomes a baptized Catholic, he or she becomes equal in the eyes of God. Once converted, slaves in Brazil or Mesoamericans in Central America could marry other Catholics, with the blessing of the church. This fostered more interracial mixing. Now, it is important to point out that being a Catholic did not smooth

FIGURE 7.4i. A portrait of a mixed race Brazilian family in 1895.
Copyright in the Public Domain.

FIGURE 7.4j. Prince Charles in Jamaica.
Copyright © Mattnad (CC BY-SA 3.0) at http://commons.wikimedia.org/wiki/File%3ACharles_Camilla_Jamaica_2008.jpg .

differences in social class. Those divisions are also deeply embedded in Iberian culture. On the other hand, the Anglican Church, during this period, either reflected or reaffirmed the British racial paradigm of strict separation. An Anglican minister would not typically marry a mixed-race couple, even if one converted.

It is important to point out that the French colonies are unique, in that the French are Catholic, but they shared the British paradigm of strict racial separation during the colonial period. This makes for a particular interesting study: the island of Hispaniola. On one side, you have the Dominican Republic (former Spanish colony) and on the other, Haiti (former French colony). On the Dominican side, they deeply value lighter skin and work hard to minimize any African influence in their looks. Oppositely, Haitians are proudly black and seldom mix with other races (see Figure 7.4k (1,2)).

FIGURE 7.4k(1). Dominican girls all light skinned, which reflects cultural values.
Copyright © Yodanyrd (CC BY-SA 4.0) at http://commons.wikimedia.org/wiki/File%3ADominican_Girls_in_the_N.Y._Parade.jpg .

FIGURE 7.4k(2). Haitian culture is proudly black and seldom sees racial mixing.
Copyright © Alex Proimos (CC BY-SA 2.0) at http://commons.wikimedia.org/wiki/File%3AHaitian_girls.jpg .

7.5 Political and Economic Landscapes

As Central and South America became increasingly independent, the United States was slowly emerging as a new world power. This power was showcased by the Monroe Doctrine (1823), which can be defined as a foreign policy declaring that any attempt by a European nation to colonize or recolonize a nation or island in North or South America would be viewed as an act of aggression, thus requiring prompt intervention. This essentially ended the direct European political and economic influence in the Americas that began with the landing of Columbus in 1492. Although this policy appeared to reflect America's moral objection to European colonialism, it might also have been a move by the United States to have greater control over economic and political partnerships with dozens of nations that share proximity. Likewise, it would later serve to "watchdog" the region's political landscapes to ensure political leaders were not swayed by European creditors or the rise of socialism/communism overseas. Although the United States was not treating Central and South America as the Europeans treated Africa, this policy suggested that they were the new hegemon in the hemisphere.

As already discussed, the Iberian influences left a landscape of social divisions, even after independence. Like Africa much later, the independence movement in Central and South America resulted in a power vacuum. Those who achieved leadership positions often behaved, in many ways, like the Spanish or Portuguese governors before them. They too funneled wealth, lived in privilege and in ways that contrasted the lifestyles around them, and institutionalized corruption. This landscape is still visible in the regions.

THEMATIC INTERSECTION 7A

Understanding Latin America: The Nexus of Economics, Politics, and People

Themes: Political/Social/Economic

To better understand this complicated relationship between the economy, politics, and the people in Central and South America, an examination of intersection points may be a good place to begin. Clearly, this discussion is broad and cannot discuss in detail the specific narratives of each country. Instead, it will provide an overview that may be used or applied to understand a specific country or subregion. This is possible because there are enough similarities to house these three themes in one discussion.

The foundational economic theme has already been highlighted and discussed in the context of European culture. Both the Spanish and the Portuguese had strong cultural complexes that evolved over many centuries in Europe. Europe, in the Middle Ages, was characterized by great divisions in wealth based on class, and the explorers and colonizers employed these paradigms and supported the same social divisions in the New World. As nations gained independence, they maintained many of these systems that generated wealth and power for the few while leaving the masses in poverty. This helps to explain the image in Figure 7.5a (1).

The political theme is more complicated in these regions. The divisions in wealth are well established in both Central and South America, and are even part of the collective history of the realm. Because of this, some political leaders and political movements (even revolutionary movements) challenged this dynamic by pushing for new socialist or communist political systems that might distribute wealth more evenly and end corruption (at least in their rhetoric). This is where the United States comes back into the narrative. Americans, in their quest to influence, secure, and control the region, used many policies and tools to achieve this broad goal. These include, but are not limited to:

- Monroe Doctrine: *already discussed.*
- Roosevelt Corollary: an addendum to the Monroe Doctrine that gave the United States the right to interfere with issues that may affect the economies of Latin American nations.

FIGURE 7.5a(1). Rocinha Favela in Rio de Janeiro, Brazil is old, corrupt, poor, dangerous, and next door to upper-middle class sky rises, housing and the tourist sector. Copyright © Alicia Nijdam (CC BY 2.0) at http://commons.wiki-media.org/wiki/File%3ARocinha_Favela_Brazil_Slums.jpg .

- **Dollar Diplomacy:** Lending money in US dollars to Latin American countries and guaranteeing the loan.
- **Neoliberalism:** Teaching leaders in the two regions to adopt and operationalize free market systems.
- **Military operations:** Which include direct attacks (Panama, Grenada, Cuba), covert CIA operations (El Salvador, Chile, Nicaragua), and law enforcement and the war on drugs (Mexico, Colombia).

Some of these measures have worked, and some have failed. For example, the United States used to educate the wealthy children of Latin American political leaders at American universities, on the assumption they would return to run their countries in ways more economically and politically aligned with the United States. This has fostered some alliances, but has failed to address endemic corruption or reduce poverty levels. Likewise, countries that became socialist or communist have generally failed to fix the issues that sparked the revolutions to begin with.

As you can see in Figure 7.5a (2), the Corruption Perception Index is as high in communist Cuba as it is in neoliberal Brazil. Venezuela, a socialist regime, is perceived as the most corrupt, while US-supported Chile is the least. These mixed narratives make this region difficult to decipher. However, so long as the United States maintains its posture as a regional hegemony, it will likely continue to manipulate, foster, and influence both political and economic outcomes in its favor. Meanwhile, unless the nations of Central and South America tolerate political corruption, many unsavory activities will continue, and wealth will still be grabbed by the few, leaving many in poverty.

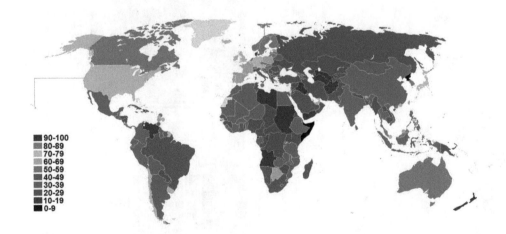

FIGURE 7.5a(2). 2014 Corruption Perception Index: The higher the percentage the lower the corruption (most people feel government officials and politicians are NOT corrupt). Oppositely, the lower percentages indicate higher levels of corruption, because people perceive them NOT to be free from corruption.
Copyright © Ruben.2196 (CC BY-SA 4.0) at http://commons.wikimedia.org/wiki/File%3ATransparency_international_2014.png .

MEXICO AND BRAZIL

Economically, both Mexico and Brazil have emerged as important nations in a globalized world. Though they both continue to struggle with the foundational issues highlighted in *Thematic Intersection 7a* (corruption, divisions in wealth, high percentages living in poverty), they have made great strides to grow and mold their respective economies in ways that have brought them each success.

Whereas Brazil is part of the BRICS (a special group of semi-core nations exhibiting high GDP but relatively low *per capita* GDP), Mexico is considered by the OECD (Organization for Economic Cooperation and Development) as both a regional power and "middle" economy. They both showed some elasticity during the economic downturn of 2008–2011, and show great potential to continue playing an increasingly important role in this century. Perhaps focusing on these two countries might allow us a glimpse into a new breed of economy that is redefining the way business is conducted between nations, as well as how development is financed. This is especially important to do before discussions begin on South and East Asia.

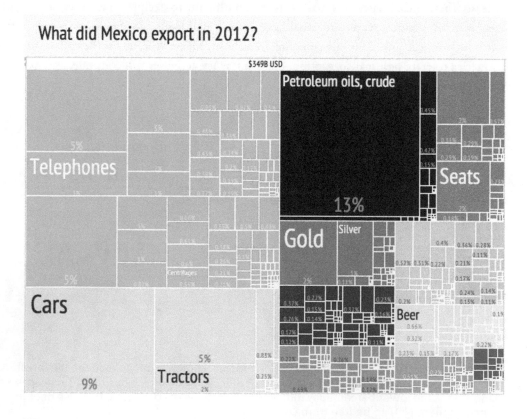

FIGURE 7.5b. Mexico's exports: About 80% go to the United States.
Copyright © Gordon.silvermanaz (CC BY-SA 4.0) at http://commons.wikimedia.org/wiki/File%3A2012_Mexico_Products_Export_Treemap.png .

Mexico

Mexico is indisputably emerging as an industrial giant. It is currently the second-largest economy in Central and South America (next to Brazil) and the eleventh-largest economy (PPP) on the planet. Mexico grew its GDP by 4% in 2014 because of several factors. First, a strong neighborly and economic relationship with the United States has fostered economic growth. The US is Mexico's largest trade partner, representing about 80% of all exports and 51% of imports. Manufacturing remains a top economic activity in Mexico, which has made it the second largest manufacturing nation, next to China. This is because NAFTA (North American Free Trade Agreement) and other economic partnerships have allowed many large companies to operate in Mexico. Secondly, Mexicans are considered by the World Trade Organization (WTO) as the most productive workers on the planet. Proximity to the United States and Canada, high productivity, and relatively inexpensive labor has contributed to Mexico's success.

Despite these successes, Mexico has some barriers to overcome. Although the *per capita* GDP has grown, it remains only a third of that found in the United States. Additionally, a new middle class is indeed emerging, but more than 33% of Mexicans (thirty-eight million) live on less than $5 a day. This concentration of poor can be found in rural regions of the southwest and central mountainous realm (see *Figure 7.5c*). What it fails to show are the growing urban poor of the northern border cities.

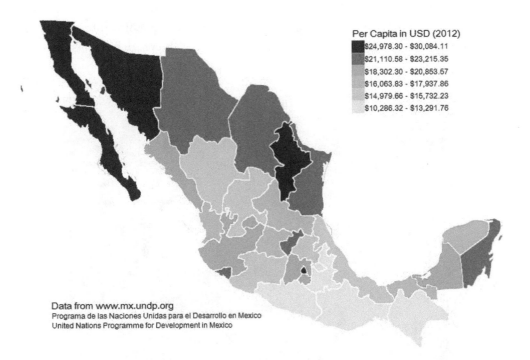

FIGURE 7.5c. Percapita GDP in Mexico. The poorest regions are in the more rural southwest and central mountainous regions. What it does not show are the urban poor in the northern border cities.
Copyright © Cig344 (CC BY-SA 4.0) at http://commons.wikimedia.org/wiki/File%3AMexico_GDP_per_capita_2012.png .

CASE STUDY 7B

Cartel Violence in Mexico

The rise of Mexican drug cartel violence over the past twenty years is connected to economic changes. When NAFTA was signed into policy in 1994, Mexico expanded its manufacturing belt along the border. This is known as the Maquiladora District, the band of manufacturing that stretches along the border of the United States in major cities like Ciudad Juarez and Tijuana. Because the agreement between Mexico, the United States, and Canada liberated many trade restrictions, jobs were created. As a result, many tens of thousands migrated from the south to the north seeking jobs. Many of these migrants were young, unemployed men and women. Not everyone was able to work in the maquiladoras, so they formed large urban camps that became slums.

The drug trade is nothing new. However, the fall of the Colombian drug cartels in the 1990s changed the dynamic for Mexican traffickers. They quickly became the wholesalers of drugs. Today, approximately 80% of all cocaine in the United States was moved in by Mexican drug cartels. In addition to drugs, the cartels pirate oil from Mexican pipelines, kidnap, and have become so influential in the northern half of Mexico that they have created a "narcoculture."

A side effect of this has been the rise in cartel violence along the border. Cartels like Sinaloa, Los Zetas, Tijuana, Juarez, and the Gulf Cartel all compete over drugs, territory, extortion, and other profitable illicit activities. In this war among each other, they seek new recruits. The large flow of young men over the past fifteen to twenty years has given the cartels a recruitment pool. There are literally thousands of grim

FIGURE 7.5d(1) and **7.5d(2)**. Cartel violence along the border has resulted from competition between rival groups.
Copyright in the Public Domain.

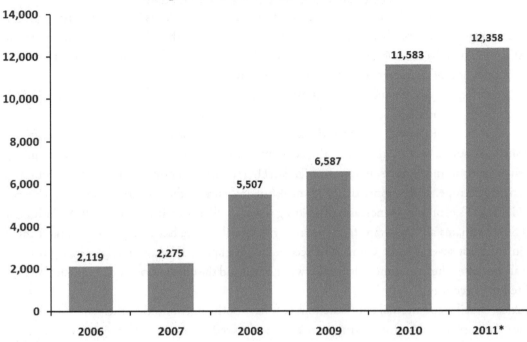

Drug-War Related Murders in Mexico

* Estimated
Source: Reforma Ejecutómetro, Grupo Reforma

FIGURE 7.5d(2).
Copyright in the Public Domain.

murders each year. Additionally, fighting cartel violence is difficult because they bribe or employ many police, soldiers, and politicians. Police on a raid often find a location empty because individual police officers have tipped them off. This drug violence is not related to demand in the United States as much as it is about competition between cartels.

Brazil

Brazil is the largest economy in both Central and South America and ranks as the eighth largest on the planet. Brazil belongs to the formalizing semi-periphery group known as the BRICS. This community of nations, as discussed with Russia and South Africa, are redefining economic landscapes because they have a favorable combination of characteristics. This includes relatively cheap labor, raw materials, large cities with good transportation systems, and incentives for industry, and these nations have thus been relied on by core nations for trade and manufacturing.

Brazil, though its GDP growth has slowed, experienced rapid growth over the last decade. It has well-established economic sectors that keep the economy vibrant. These include agriculture, mining, manufacturing, tourism, and services. In fact, Brazil is largely a service economy, not unlike those found in North America or Europe. Today, more than 71% of Brazilians work in the tertiary sector. As a member of the BRICS, Brazil's economy is increasingly shifting towards alliances with fellow BRICS. Although the United States remains an important trade partner with Brazil, China has emerged as its largest trade partner in just the last several years. China now receives more imports from, and sells more exports to, Brazil than anyone else. The economic alliances between Brazil and the core nations and semi-core BRICS have benefited their economy.

Like Mexico, Brazil faces internal contradictions that have both contributed to their success (cheaper labor, political support [possibly from corruption], etc.) and limited their potential (poverty, corruption). This is the paradox of the BRICS; their ascension into the globalized economy can be attributed to the

FIGURE 7.5e. Downtown Rio de Janeiro: One of many business districts in Brazil.
Copyright © Leandro Ciuffo (CC BY 2.0) at http://commons.wikimedia.org/wiki/File%3ACentroRJ.
jpg .

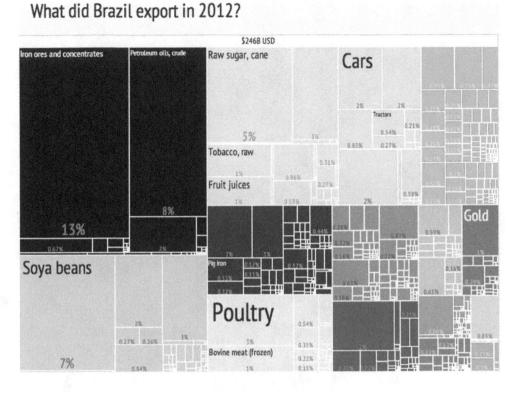

FIGURE 7.5f. Brazil's exports.
Copyright © Gordon.silvermanaz (CC BY-SA 4.0) at http://commons.wikimedia.org/wiki/File%3A2012_Brazil_Products_Export_Treemap.png .

same things that limit their growth. For example, Brazil's wealth disparity is high. As seen in *Figure 7.5a (1)*, giant *favelas* (slums) exist alongside upper-middle-class high-rise condominiums and tourist destinations. Approximately 30% of the country is slum dwellers. Corruption indices are very high as well. Like Mexico, Brazil's *per capita* GDP is only one-third of the United States'. Of course, these economic and social challenges may indeed be surmountable, and Brazil seems postured to do well in the twenty-first century economically. Brazil's most potentially harmful problem, as will soon be discussed, is related to their environment.

7.6 Environmental Problems

The deforestation of the tropical and subtropical biomes of the Amazon Rainforest and surrounding region is one of the most important environmental problems to understand. Although it is not as obvious as the smokestacks of a power plant or the smog over a large city, it is, in many ways, more harmful to remove trees from this region than any other anthropogenic activity. Anthropogenic is a term used to define human-caused environmental problems. Deforestation, or the conversion of forested lands into nonforested land use, is a potentially devastating anthropogenic activity. It is important to point out that

FIGURE 7.6a. Deforestation is one of the most directly harmful environmental activities on Earth, especially in Brazil's southern Amazon region.
Copyright in the Public Domain.

deforestation is often perceived as careless or illegal logging only. This is not the case. Illegal logging and biopiracy are just some of the activities related to deforestation. In Brazil and other parts of the world, licensed logging, land converted for agriculture and grazing, and "slash-and-burn" farming by Native Amazonians can all be considered deforestation because of the immediate effects these activities have on the environment. Brazil is currently one country at the epicenter of this issue.

The reason for this relates to Earth's physical processes. This was broadly covered in Chapter 1. Earth receives its direct energy from the sun between the *Tropic of Cancer* and the *Tropic of Capricorn* (each 23.5 degrees north and south of the equator). This direct energy, before it is exchanged and dispersed around Earth by wind and ocean currents, is mitigated by clouds and used by a robust equatorial biome. As seen in *Figure 7.6a*, the reduction of forested lands leaves the lands exposed to direct energy. This is only the beginning of the problem.

BOX 7B TREES AND THE ECOSYSTEM SERVICES THEY PROVIDE

To explain the effects of deforestation, the scale of the discussion must change. If you picture just one tree and the ecosystem service that one tree provides, the problem can be better highlighted. These are **the ecosystem services a single tree provides**:

- Solar energy is either reflected, absorbed, or makes it past the leaves as fractional radiation on the ground.

- The fractional energy that makes it to the ground supports a more robust ground biome. This, then, enables the ground to retain more water.

- The energy used by the tree is a part of photosynthesis, or the way plants

FIGURE 7.6b. Deforestation in Mato Grosso, Brazil. Copyright © Pedro Biondi/Abr (CC BY-SA 3.0) at http://commons.wikimedia.org/wiki/File%3AMato_Grosso_deforestation_(Pedro_Biondi)_12ago2007.jpg .

eat. This process uses carbon dioxide and produces oxygen. Therefore, a tree "sequesters" carbon dioxide from the atmosphere for this purpose.

- Because the tree is in a warm climate caused by intense solar radiation, it uses a process called "evapotranspiration," or tree sweating. Evapotranspiration, then, releases oxygen into the atmosphere through water, which creates clouds.

- Clouds mitigate the energy received by the sun before it is shared with the rest of Earth.

Removing the ability for a single tree to do this is a problem. **These might be the immediate effects if one tree is removed**:

- Solar energy now reaches the ground directly.

- Intensified energy dries out the ground (evaporating water in soil) and increases albedo (reflectivity), which then puts longwave radiation back into the atmosphere.

- Without the tree, the "carbon sink" it was with the tree (sequestered carbon) is now a "carbon source." This is because the carbon dioxide is now in the atmosphere, where it does not belong, and is being energized by the reflected longwave radiation.

- No evapotranspiration is occurring if there is no tree, which means cloud cover is reduced.

- Because the soils dried, the ground biome is reduced. Soil absorption results in increased runoff. Runoff fills rivers with more sediment, which then destroys estuaries and delta ecosystems downstream (not to mention fish habitats in the water).

This is a major issue in Brazil and Peru. Continued deforestation will not only impact the region, but the planet as well.

Prevalence and Side Effects of Deforestation

It is difficult to measure precisely how much forest in the Amazon has been reduced by human-caused deforestation. The reason is that the region is often covered in clouds, thus making it difficult to rely on satellite imagery to assess changes year to year. However, it is known that the Amazon Rainforest is only 87% of what it used to be, mostly because of land-use change. In some regions of Brazil (Mato Grosso, Rondonia), deforestation has been well documented because much if it has been done with permission. Soybean agriculture and pastures have greatly reduced the rainforests in these two Brazilian states. This area is known as the "Arc of Deforestation."

In the Peruvian Amazon, deforestation is largely done illegally. Companies looking for valuable woods in the rainforest (mahogany, Brazilian walnut, etc.) often fake licensure and bribe local officials to enter forest conservatories. This has led to a poignant response by conservationists. This has led to the murder and disappearance of leaders, without any resolution.

There are indirect effects to reducing rainforest biomes as well. Many of the plants used in pharmaceuticals are from rainforest. Many species have yet to be discovered, and if the forest they reside in is reduced by deforestation, the potential they have to treat illness is removed. Below is a short list of drugs developed from South America and Central America rainforest plants:

- Quinine (cinchona tree): Treats malaria
- Novocaine (cocoa plant): Local anesthetic in surgery and dentistry
- Tubocurarine (curare liana): Muscle issues and Parkinson's Disease
- Cortisone (yams): Birth control

The reduction of the rainforest in this region not only will change, or has changed, more local climatic and weather patterns (cloud reduction, runoff, precipitation patterns, etc.); it may impact, or has already impacted, the rest of the world. If the equatorial region cannot mitigate the energy it receives with a rich biome and cloud cover, the equator will become warmer and drier. This is a problem because Earth is a giant energy-exchange system that shares energy with the rest of the planet through wind and ocean currents. If more energy is diffused, the planet gets warmer. This combines with industrial activities in North America, Europe, and Eastern Asia, as well as land-use change patterns around the world, to increase carbon in the atmosphere. These are the main concerns behind climate change.

CONCLUSION

Both Central and South America are fascinating regions that have a lot in common, and both have nations and people unique to the world. The landscapes include the tropical islands of the Caribbean and the most biodiverse rainforests in the world (in places like Costa Rica Brazil, and Venezuela). The region is home to the longest and second-highest mountain range in the world, the Andes, as well as the driest desert on the planet (Atacama). The Amazon River is the largest river by volume and inspires the imagination with its remote, wild nature.

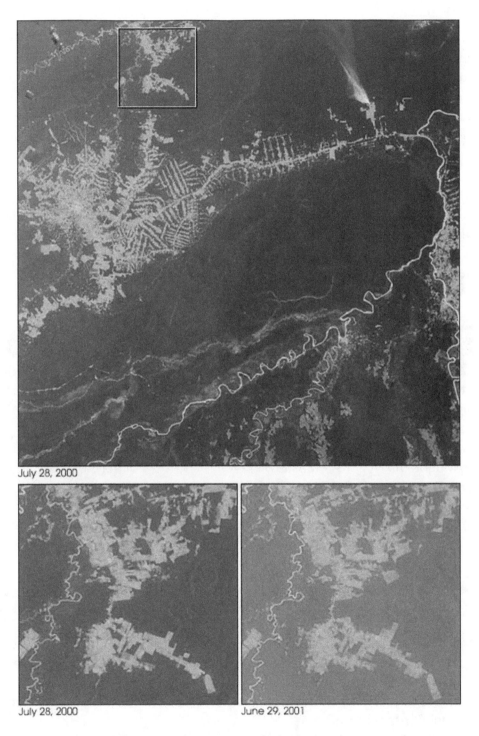

July 28, 2000

July 28, 2000   June 29, 2001

FIGURE 7.6c. Deforestation changes soil into a lighter color, which then reflects more long-wave radiation into an atmosphere with surplus carbon.
Copyright in the Public Domain.

Culturally, these regions share similar backgrounds. They both had advanced civilizations (Maya, Aztecs, and Inca) and were explored and colonized mostly by Iberians (Spanish and Portuguese). The treasures from this region changed the world well beyond its border by shifting power in Europe and creating conflicts that led to independence. At the same time, the cultural imprint of the Spanish, for example, cannot be underestimated. Spanish is spoken from the southwest United States to the tip of South America, and the architecture, family dynamics, and cultural traits remain Spanish influenced to this day.

Finally, these regions are still very poor. Despite some rising stars like Brazil and Mexico, the social landscapes of much of the realm are characterized more by their gaps in wealth than by their economic success. This may change, but so long as there are high corruption indices and social norms that keep groups divided, the people of the region may continue in poverty for some time. Although these brief discussions only highlight several aspects of such a large and diverse region, they effectively illuminate some of the key themes that may allow one to look upon this region in a more informed way as we move further into the new century.

KEY TERMS

Latin America	Iberian Invaders	NAFTA (North American
Plate tectonics	Independence	Free Trade Agreement)
Volcanism	Hispanic	Socialism
Altitudinal Zonation	Hacienda	Neoliberalism
Amazon Rainforest	Plantations	Maquiladora
Andes Mountains	Mestizo	Cartel Violence
Atacama Desert	Monroe Doctrine	BRICS
Maya, Aztec, Inca		Deforestation

CLASS DISCUSSIONS

1. Describe the diverse physical geographic landscapes of Central America.
2. Compare and contrast the Spanish "Hacienda" and the Caribbean "Plantation."
3. What is Mestizo culture?
4. Discuss the differences between British and Spanish colonies. How did religion shape racial interactions?
5. Describe the Amazon Rainforest. Why is it so green, wet, and biodiverse? What problems are associated with deforestation and land-use change in the region?
6. How did the Iberians influence modern-day social dynamics in South America?

ADDITIONAL RESOURCES

CIA World Factbook:

https://www.cia.gov/library/publications/the-world-factbook/wfbExt/region_noa.html

https://www.cia.gov/library/publications/the-world-factbook/wfbExt/region_soa.html

NAFTA (North American Free Trade Agreement):

https://ustr.gov/trade-agreements/free-trade-agreements/north-american-free-trade-agreement-nafta

World Bank:

http://www.worldbank.org/en/region/lac

BIBLIOGRAPHY

"Bernard Elissalde." Altitudinal Zonation. N.p., n.d. Web. http://www.hypergeo.eu/spip.php?article308. 12 May 2015.

"Brazil." Brazil World Bank. N.p., n.d. Web. http://www.worldbank.org/en/country/brazil. 24 May 2015.

"BRAZIL." The Amazon Rainforest. N.p., n.d. Web. http://www.brazil.org.za/amazon-rainforest.html. 11 May 2015.

Central Intelligence Agency. n.d. Web. https://www.cia.gov/library/publications/the-world-factbook/wfbExt/region_noa.html. 04 May 2015.

Central Intelligence Agency. n.d. Web. https://www.cia.gov/library/publications/the-world-factbook/wfbExt/region_soa.html. 04 May 2015.

Deforestation: Chopping Down the Amazon. Economist. May 26, 2011.

Diamond, J. (1999). Guns, Germs, and Steel: The Fates of Human Societies. W.W. Norton. New York.

Marrin, A. (1989). Inca & Spaniard. Atheneum. New York.

"Mayan Civilization." Mayan Civilization. N.p., n.d. Web. http://www.aztec-history.com/mayan-civilization.html. 04 May 2015.

"Mexico." Mexico World Bank. N.p., n.d. Web. http://www.worldbank.org/en/country/mexico. 24 May 2015.

Mexico's Maquiladoras: Big Maq Attack. Economist. October 26, 2013.

"North American Free Trade Agreement (NAFTA) | United States Trade Representative." North American Free Trade Agreement (NAFTA) | United States Trade Representative. N.p., n.d. Web. https://ustr.gov/trade-agreements/free-trade-agreements/north-american-free-trade-agreement-nafta. 16 May 2015.

"Peru: Environmental Profile." Peru: Environmental Profile. N.p., n.d. Web. http://rainforests.mongabay.com/20peru.htm. 05 May 2015.

Shukla, J., et al. (1990). Amazon Deforestation and Climate Change. Science. Vol. 247. pp. 1322–1325.

"Species." WorldWildlife.org. World Wildlife Fund. n.d. Web. https://www.worldwildlife.org/species/. 04 May 2015.

Wikipedia. Wikimedia Foundation. n.d. Web. https://en.wikipedia.org/wiki/Iquitos. 04 May 2015.

CHAPTER 8

Indian Subcontinent

Key Themes:

Political, cultural, economic

Countries Discussed:
- Pakistan
- India
- Nepal
- Bhutan
- Bangladesh
- Sri Lanka
- Maldives

8.1 Regional Overview

The Indian Subcontinent region is a land of extremes. Physically, the Himalayas are the tallest, most "extreme" mountain range in the world, with Mt. Everest towering over the landscape at 29,028 feet. The region also has "extreme" demographic profiles. India, though it is not yet the most populous nation on Earth, will be; China is still ahead by several hundred million people, but India's fertility rate will outpace their population growth in the next decade or so. Pakistan is a Muslim nation, with many who have "extreme" views. Internal problems of Islamic extremism and external diplomatic issues with India and the

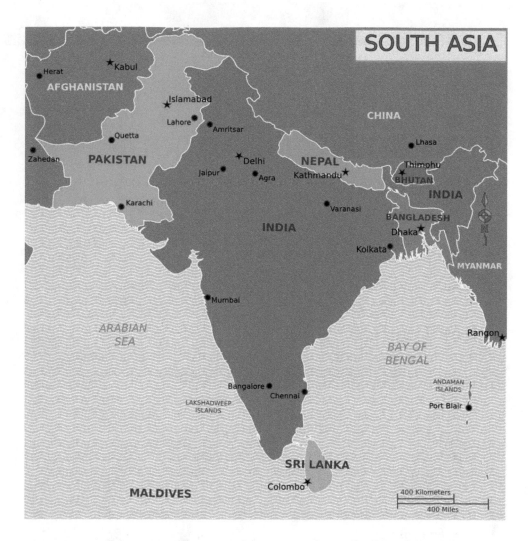

FIGURE 8.0a. The Indian Subcontinent is also referred to as South Asia. This region includes Pakistan, India, Nepal, Bhutan, Bangladesh, Sri Lanka, and the Maldive islands. Copyright © Cacahuate (CC BY-SA 4.0) at http://commons.wikimedia.org/wiki/File%3AMap_of_South_Asia.png .]

United States make Pakistan one of the most-watched countries on the planet. Bangladesh is a nation at the crossroads of nature's fury. They are densely packed into a coastal plain that is vulnerable to tropical cyclonic storms (typhoons) and devastating river floods. Just one event often results in tens of thousands of casualties.

The region is home to the highest concentration of "extreme" poverty on Earth. There are more than a billion people living in squalor (and the number is growing). India has the Hindu religion, which has formed the longest, continually practiced (2,500–3,000 years) cultural complex on Earth. The Maldives, an island chain in the Indian Ocean, is disappearing from the effects of sea level rise brought on by climate change. All these "extreme" features of the Indian Subcontinent will be addressed in more detail in this chapter, but they effectively highlight the nature of the region.

Beyond the "extreme" nature of the region are the very important narratives it has and continues to form. The region, perhaps, provides the greatest political lens for examining the successes and failures of European colonialism, socialism, and borders based on ethnicity and religion. The region may provide the best social lens to examine the dynamics of a well-established caste system, endemic poverty and, perhaps ironically, the level of cooperation between such diverse groups.

The region provides an excellent economic lens into India's path of development and membership in the BRICS. Perhaps most importantly is how the region showcases how these themes have crossed and collided to shape the landscapes we see today.

PHYSICAL FEATURES OF THE INDIAN SUBCONTINENT

As the name implies, the Indian Subcontinent is a contiguous part of the greater Eurasian landmass. Because, geologically speaking, it is a late addition, it has earned the distinction as a "subcontinent." This can be explained by plate tectonics.

Between seventy million years ago and today, the Indian Plate broke off from a larger landmass centered around Africa, moved north, and collided with the Eurasian Plate. Over millions of years, subduction (one plate sliding under another) has created the Himalayas. This mountain range is so high, it has physically made the Indian Subcontinent distinct and largely isolated from the rest of Asia.

Subregions

The Indian Subcontinent has a dynamic climate and a diverse topography. These features and distinctions might best be discussed in the context of subregions. Below are the *four (4) subregions of the Indian Subcontinent:*

- *Himalayan Realm*
- *Deccan Plateau*
- *Subtropical Coastal Realm*
- *Desert West*

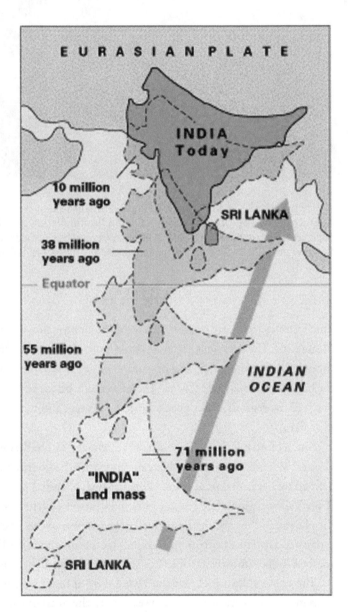

FIGURE 8.1a. It took tens of million of years for the Indian Subcontinent to crash into the Eurasian Plate. This resulted in the Himalaya Mountains forming a natural wall between the region and Asia.
Copyright in the Public Domain.

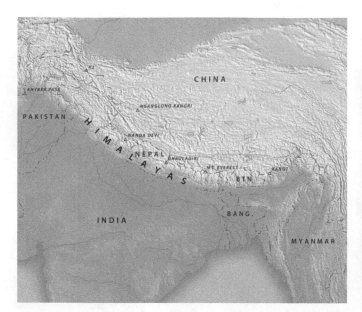

FIGURE 8.1b (1) & (2). The Himalayas are the tallest mountains in the world and cover the northern quarter of the region, including Pakistan, India, Nepal, and Bhutan.
Copyright © Mapbliss (CC BY-SA 4.0) at http://commons.wikimedia.org/wiki/File%3AHimalaya_Map.jpg . Copyright © Carsten.nebel (CC BY-SA 3.0) at http://commons.wikimedia.org/wiki/File%3ACrows_Lake_in_North_Sikkim.jpg .

The Himalayan Realm includes the foothills, slope regions, and high-altitude peaks of the greater Himalayan Mountains. The *subregion* stretches from northern Pakistan through Nepal and northern India to Bhutan. Mount Everest, the tallest and one of the most formidable mountains on Earth, sits atop the Himalayas on the border of Nepal and China. The mountains play a key role in shaping the region's climate and provide much of the region's water needs. Both the Ganges and Indus Rivers originate in the glacial highlands of the Himalaya.

Much of mainland India, south of the Himalayas, is either within the Deccan Plateau or the Subtropical Coastal Realm. The Deccan Plateau represents the continental midsection of much of India. This area is defined by a seasonal *monsoonal* climate. Much of India's agriculture occurs here, particularly in the Ganges River Valley region. The coastal mountain ranges (Ghats) capture much of the moisture, leaving parts of the plateau in the rain shadow. Much of the *subregion* can be characterized as volcanic, though there is little activity today. The Subtropical Coastal Realm surrounds the Deccan Plateau, both to the east and west. The coast of India is mostly a tropical or subtropical climate because of the ample rainfall during the monsoon.

The Desert West includes the *Thar Desert* of India west into southern Pakistan. Although parts of this subregion receive monsoonal rain seasonally, the heart of the desert region is dry. The Thar Desert has sand dunes, camels, and other features that make it resemble the Sahara (see *Figure 8.1e*).

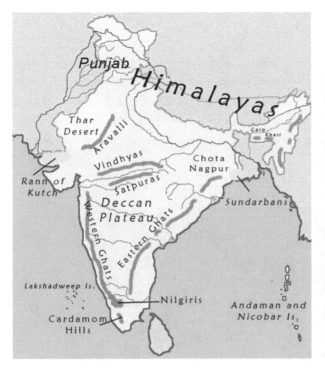

FIGURE 8.1c (1) & (2). The Deccan Plateau is a seasonal highland region that covers much of central India.
Copyright © Nichalp (CC BY-SA 3.0) at http://commons.wikimedia.org/wiki/File%3AIndiahills.png .; Copyright © GFDL (CC BY-SA 3.0) at http://commons.wikimedia.org/wiki/File%3AMonsoon_clouds_near_Nagercoil.jpg .

FIGURE 8.1d. Goa, India is part of a long, tropical and subtropical coastline that receives plentiful seasonal rain.
Copyright © Soman (CC BY-SA 3.0) at http://commons. wikimedia.org/wiki/File:Goa_(44).jpg .

FIGURE 8.1e. The Thar Desert, on the border of India and Pakistan, is a subtropical desert, but because rains are so seasonal and don't always reach this area, it is quite dry.
Copyright © Flicka (CC BY-SA 3.0) at http://commons.wikimedia. org/wiki/File%3AThar_Khuri.jpg .

Monsoon

The Indian Monsoon is a seasonal rainy season that is dictated by changes in airflow from high to low pressure. During the summer months (July to October), a low pressure forms over continental India and/or Central Asia. At the same time, a high-pressure system forms over the Indian Ocean to the south. Air flows from "high pressure" to "low pressure," and because the "high" is over the Indian Ocean at lower latitudes, the moist, warm ocean air flows towards the low-pressure zone over the continent, bringing enormous amounts of precipitation (see *Figure 8.1f*).

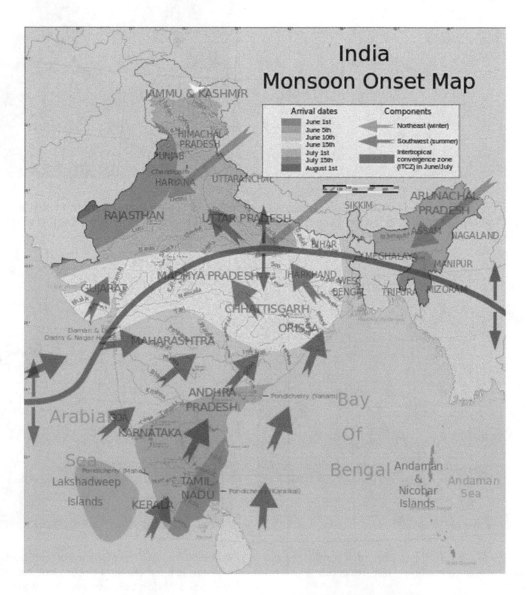

FIGURE 8.1f. The Indian Monsoon is one of Earth's most reliable weather patterns. Copyright © Saravask (CC BY-SA 3.0) at http://commons.wikimedia.org/wiki/File%3AIndia_southwest_summer_monsoon_onset_map_en.svg

The *rainy season* roughly lasts about four months and, like Africans, the people of the Indian Subcontinent rely on them for crops, water, and as a welcome break from the heat. As the season changes, a high-pressure system forms over continental Asia, and a low forms over the Indian Ocean. The air reverses course and flows from north to south, bringing dry and hot conditions into the region. This *dry season* lasts between about January and June, during which parts of the region can experience, at times, a month of temperatures over one hundred degrees. Lands dry up, ephemeral streams dry out, and people survive until the monsoon returns.

Major Rivers

Two of the most significant and important rivers in the world are located within this region. The Ganges River originates with the meltwater of the Satopanth and Gangotri glaciers, as well as the runoff and snowmelt from the various peaks of the Himalayas. The river runs about 1,600 miles from twelve thousand feet to its sea level delta into the Bay of Bengal (Bangladesh). This river supports more than six hundred million people by meeting their water needs. Likewise, the river has great spiritual significance for Hindus. The Ganges is fed by, and combines with, many other rivers before it deltas. These include the Brahmaputra, Meghna, and Yamuna Rivers.

The Indus River resides in the western part of the region, mostly within Pakistan. It is amongst the longest rivers in Asia, flowing nearly two thousand miles from the Tibetan Plateau to the Indian Ocean. The river supports the water needs for between three hundred and four hundred million people, as well as a robust agricultural sector. The river, ironically, was the birthplace of Hinduism, even though Islam defines the region now. It also plays a role in the region's history, which will be discussed in more detail in the next section.

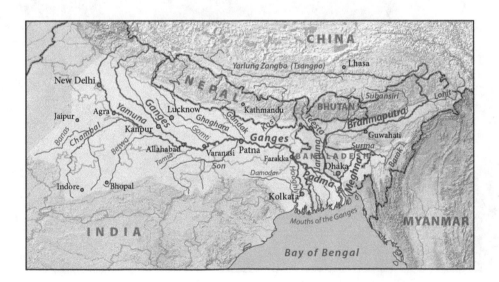

FIGURE 8.1g. BMG River System is one of the planet's largest river complexes. Copyright © Pfly (CC BY-SA 3.0) at http://commons.wikimedia.org/wiki/File%3AGanges-Brahmaputra-Meghna_basins.jpg .

DIVERSE CULTURAL LANDSCAPES

The Indian Subcontinent is home to a diverse population. This includes dozens of ethnicities, several major religions, languages, and a broad range of socioeconomic backgrounds. Although some tensions exist between these groups, much of the region, particularly in India, has generally exhibited great cooperation. When looked at historically, the greater cultural complex of the region is ancient in origin. In fact, many scholars point out that there is a continuum of culture that dates back about three thousand years. In other words, the culture that Alexander the Great briefly experienced in 326 BCE was much the same of today, without the technology.

Religion and Culture

Understanding the rich and complex cultures of the Indian Subcontinent begins with an examination of the main religions, as well as some fundamental ethnic divisions within the region. Key ethnic groups include Indo-Aryan (72%), Dravidian (25%), and Mongoloid (3%). The Dravidian group represents the indigenous Indians that occupy the southern third of the region. The Mongoloid group is an anthropological term for the people with more traditional Asian/Chinese features in the far eastern realm.

FIGURE 8.1h. A bride in India follows customs sometimes thousands of years old.
Copyright © Prakhar Amba (CC BY 2.0) at https://commons.wikimedia.org/wiki/File%3ABride_by_prakhar.jpg .

Several of the religions in the region are eastern religions, thus requiring some context. Western religions, typically associated with one of the Abrahamic religions (Judaism, Christianity, and Islam), have the common thread of being monotheistic, or the belief in one God that is divine, omnipresent, and even powerful. They also have a founder, a narrative, and a theology that binds or divides them. Eastern religions tend to have belief systems that bridge the worship of many gods within a complex framework of customs and practices. At the center of eastern religion is not a deity, but the soul. This is different, in that there is more of a focus on a "way of being" than following the well-articulated, though often debatable, path defined by a sacred text like the Bible or Koran. This region has both eastern and western religions, along with one that exhibits a little of both. The *four (4) main religions/ways of being of the Indian Subcontinent are:*

1. *Hinduism*
2. *Islam*
3. *Sikhism*
4. *Buddhism*

Hinduism is not only the largest religion in the region; it is the third largest on Earth, next to Christianity and Islam. It has shaped culture in India more than any other *religion/way of being*. It originated in the Indus River Valley of modern-day Pakistan around four thousand years ago. Locally, the inhabitants of the area practiced *Vedism*, the local ethnic religion that contributed to the formation of Hinduism. These early belief systems included such values as nonviolence and the prohibition of eating meat.

FIGURE 8.1i. Hindu temple in Delhi, India.
Copyright © Kapil.xerox (CC BY-SA 4.0) at https://commons.wikimedia.org/wiki/File%3AAkshardham_angled.jpg .

About 3,500 years ago, the *Aryans* either invaded or migrated into the area (disputed). They came from the *Caucasus* region of central Asia (northern Persian realm) and brought with them the practice of rigid social stratification, their language (early Hindi), their written form of language (Sanskrit), and various creeds. They mixed with the local culture to form what would become *Hinduism.*

Hindus focus on the soul but also believe many (hundreds) of gods watch over adherents. How people conduct themselves determines not only their *karma*, but also their fate after reincarnation. Reincarnation is the transfer of the soul, up or down, depending on one's conduct. This helps to understand the prohibition of eating meat. The cow is a sacred beast because it is ultimately viewed as a vessel of a reincarnated soul. Hindus also believe in the caste system, or the inflexible system of social stratification based on birth. The four main castes, from high to low, are: Brahmins, Kshatriyas, Vaishyas, and Shudras. Below them were the outcaste "Dalits," also referred to as "untouchables." The caste system in India will be discussed in other contexts later.

Islam is the second-most populous religion in the region. Whereas India is roughly 14% (~180 million) Muslim, Pakistan is over 95%, and Bangladesh is over 90%. This is the result of the *Great Partition* and

FIGURE 8.1j. The Taj Mahal is the most famous and visited sites in India. It was built by a Mughal emperor in the mid seventeenth century.
Copyright © Dhirad (CC BY-SA 3.0) at https://commons.wikimedia.org/wiki/File%3ATaj_Mahal_in_March_2004.jpg .

Bangladesh's independence. Islam arrived to the region through invasion over the course of hundreds of years. The Delhi Sultanate was established in 1206 and lasted through the mid-1500s. At first, the Delhi Sultanate was able to repel the Mongol Invaders who served under Genghis Khan. However, the Islamized Turkic/Mongol Empire, known as the Mughal Empire, replaced the Delhi Sultanate until Hindu-Muslim violence and the arrival of the British marked the end of Muslim rule in India.

Both the Sikhs and Buddhists represent much smaller numbers in the region, as a whole, than either Hinduism or Islam. There are technically more Christians in the region than either, but

FIGURE 8.1k. Sikhs form a proud culture in India and have struggled to define their distinction from muslims. Though Sikhs are not supposed to cut their hair, younger generations have tolerated hair cuts over the past decade or two.
Copyright © KaurArt.com (CC BY-SA 2.0) at https://commons.wikimedia.org/wiki/File%3ASikh_people.jpg .

their narrative with the Indian Subcontinent does not inform us about the region's culture. The Sikhs are a monotheistic religion/way of being that originated in the *Punjab* during the fifteenth century.

Literally wedged between the Islamic west and the Hindu east, the Sikhs have elements of both in their own culture. They believe in one god, but not like the Abrahamic religions. The "One Immortal Being" is spiritual in nature, and the power of that one immortal being manifests itself in the teachings of the ten gurus. Today in India, there are roughly twenty million Sikhs, most of whom live in *Punjab*. They are an ethnic religion, in that they rarely seek converts, but they are open to converts who are willing to adopt the principles of the faith. Their independent faith would later come into use by the British, who would use Sikhs in their colonial army, within India and around the world.

Buddhism is an offspring of Hinduism, dating back about 2,500 years. The nontheistic religion (no deity) is based on the teachings of the "Buddha," or Siddhartha Gautama. These teachings frame a path to enlightenment through knowledge, tolerance, and overcoming cravings. Enlightenment is achievable by way of a self-guided path. Bhutan is largely a Buddhist nation.

Although the distribution of ethnic groups and examination of the largest religious groups do not completely define the region, they do effectively provide a backdrop for understanding the people better. The conflicts and cooperation between groups within this realm are often rooted in these basic human features of the landscape.

8.2 Colonial/Postcolonial Past

This textbook indicated early on that the Europeans, through colonialism, shaped much of the world. Therefore, each region has a colonial and postcolonial narrative that must be highlighted. The very nature of colonialism is conflict. Remember, it is the direct extraction and use of a country or region's natural and human resources for the benefit of another, more powerful foreign nation. This created problems. Therefore, colonial powers often had to mitigate the inherent problems of colonial occupation by either forcing cooperation or compromising to achieve cooperation. The Indian Subcontinent is replete with these narratives. Although this subsection will not delve too deeply into the complicated history and countless issues surrounding Britain's "Crown Jewel" colony, it will point out aspects that helped to shape the region today.

THE BRITISH EMPIRE

By the early nineteenth century, the British fundamentally reengineered the way in which they conducted colonial operations around the world. Under a *laissez-faire* economic model, any nonproductive

FIGURE 8.2a. The East India Company establishing control in India.
Copyright in the Public Domain.

appendage of the economy must not be a priority for investment. Thus, government was smaller, and private enterprise, which had to be highly productive, would be allowed to manage colonies using free-market principles. This market freedom essentially formed the basis of Britain's colony in India. Keep in mind that India included Pakistan and Bangladesh at that time.

East India Company

Beginning as a royal charter in 1600 by Queen Elizabeth, the British *East India Company (EIC)* grew into the largest company ever known. By the mid-nineteenth century, some estimates suggest they singlehandedly controlled about a third of the global economy. They traded conventional commodities like cotton, sugar, salt, spices, and timber, but also controlled the opium trade in East Asia.

In addition to strictly economic activities, they also managed colonies. Remember, the British, after losing the American colonies, replaced the old mercantilist economic model with a free-market model of *minarchism*. This included the reduction of government to what they began calling a "night-watchman state." With nonproductive appendages of the economy minimized, Britain put its economy in the hands of the free market. In India, the EIC would manage the affairs for a century and a half.

THEMATIC INTERSECTION 8A

The British East India Company and the Use of a Private Military

Themes: Cultural/Economic

Although allowing the East India Company to govern the affairs of India was ultimately profitable for the British, the management of such a large and diverse colony had its challenges. The EIC, because they often meddled in the affairs of local and regional leaders while poorly understanding their cultures, periodically encountered conflict and even hostility. To deal with these issues, the EIC had a military branch that grew larger over the years. Ships trading commodities and opium would fall prey to pirates, so war ships and naval captains and officers had to be retained. They had conflicts with local rulers, which periodically required an army. Military forces were often composed of local soldiers trained in British military techniques. However, how the EIC handled these issues sometimes created larger problems. Failing to understand local culture complicated their ability to conduct economic activities in the region. Several examples include:

FIGURE 8.2b. East India Company soldiers were trained at their own academy, by real British military officers. Local soldiers were likewise trained in British military techniques. Copyright in the Public Domain.

- The promotion of lower-caste, noncommissioned officers to command higher-caste soldiers.
- Limiting the rank an Indian officer could reach. Indian officers could never outrank white British officers, even newly commissioned Lieutenants, despite experience and tenure.
- The required use of pig and cow fat to lubricate and polish service weapons was forbidden by Islam and Hinduism.
- Restricting access to temples because they were within secured urban areas.

Decisions like these contributed to the tensions already imposed by a colonial dynamic. In 1857, India fell into open rebellion, which required British military intervention. This was the beginning of the end for the East India Company in the region. In 1858, an act was passed in London transferring power from the EIC to direct British control, largely over these matters.

British Raj

After the transfer of power to the British government, the Indian colony was managed with a firm hand. British governors had military envoys, cities were fortified and restricted, and Indians were used throughout the world to help establish, maintain, and serve in other British colonies like Singapore, Kenya, South Africa, and so on. Queen Victoria declared herself Empress of India in 1876, thus adding legitimacy to Britain's strategy of incorporating the region into the empire. The British Raj ("Raj" means rule in Hindi) lasted from 1857 to 1947.

The administrative structure in India changed under the British Raj. The governor-general was appointed directly by the Crown. This representative would have power over the Indian empire and the military in the region, giving him a coeval distinction as "Viceroy," and chaired a chamber of secretaries, each assigned to a particular area (i.e., transportation, education, agriculture, internal affairs, etc.). This system of governance improved communication and helped coordinate infrastructural improvements (railways, ports, roads), but put into place stronger legal systems (courts, arbitration). The trouble was that the Indians themselves were not necessarily the beneficiaries of these new systems, nor was their voice always heard. Growing concerns over labor issues, religious violence, political representation, and other concerns for Indians often fell on deaf ears.

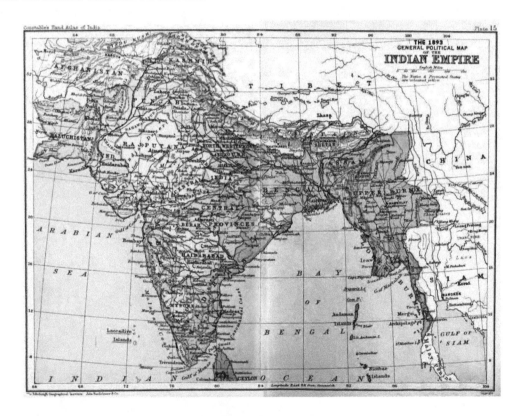

FIGURE 8.2c. Map of India under British Raj, 1893. During this period, Pakistan and Bangladesh were states within India.
Copyright in the Public Domain.

GANDHI AND THE DECLINE OF BRITISH RULE

Many books have been written about Gandhi's extraordinary life and his commitment and sacrifice to make all Indians equal. Perhaps less of a focus is how his story illuminates broader narratives about the British Empire and Islam, around the world and in India. The two are interconnected in this case, and Gandhi was at the center of it all.

CASE STUDY 8A

Gandhi's Influence

Gandhi was born into a well-respected Hindu Indian family of a high caste. He did well in school and sought a law degree in London, despite threats that he would lose his caste affiliation and be excommunicated if he went. Upon his return, he attempted to practice law but had limited success. When given the opportunity to take a legal position in South Africa (a British colony), he did so, and ended up spending more than twenty years there.

In South Africa, Gandhi experienced several things that would shape his perspectives. One was that in South Africa, unlike India, Muslim Indians were the dominant group, and Hindu Indians were servants to them. Gandhi worked as a lawyer for a large Muslim Indian firm and began to view all Indians as the same (what he called "Indianness"), rather than as factions or groups of different kinds of Indians.

Second, he saw how racial lines were drawn and maintained by the British. Although he found it

FIGURE 8.2d. Gandhi with Nehru, a politician and first Prime Minister of an independent India. Copyright in the Public Domain.

unsettling and vowed to address it, he still supported the British at that time. Third, he served in two wars on the British side. He was an ambulance driver during the Boer Wars, and again during the Zulu War. This experience taught him that a direct attack on Britain's powerful military was futile, thus leading him to adopt a nonviolent approach to change by using the law and organizing. He used these experiences to help all Indians in South Africa to have a greater voice, regardless of religious background or caste. This gave him a reputation, both in South Africa and in India, as a proud nationalist and activist.

Upon returning to India, he was able to enter politics. It was not, however, until World War I that conditions changed and allowed him to have a much larger voice in India. The defeat of the Germans also meant the defeat of their allies, the Turks. The Ottoman Turks, for hundreds of years, represented the global Islamic caliphate. After their defeat, the world's Muslims lost their caliphate, which meant there was no longer a powerful empire supporting them. This changed the treatment of Muslims in many countries, especially in India.

Sectarian violence between Hindus and Muslims erupted in India and the Khilafat Movement of 1919. This was a global protest against the dismantling of the Caliphate in Turkey. Because Gandhi worked with Muslim Indians and viewed their concerns as concerns for all Indians, he became their voice, as well as a voice for all Indians (women, untouchables, etc.). Once he achieved a loud political voice in India, he preached nonviolence, cooperation, and equality.

Gandhi's position on equality, nonviolence, and cooperation was successful in that it influenced more Indians to peacefully speak out against rigid British laws and other concerns. However, the British often responded to these changes harshly. Gandhi was not only arrested several times, but the British would also break up peaceful protests and address political dissent with force. This strengthened the growing animosity the Indians had toward their European colonial administration. Gandhi eventually changed his posture with the British by supporting independence and the "Quit India" campaign. When the British became embroiled in World War II, they unilaterally involved India in the war, without the consent of the Indians. Having to pour so much attention and resources into fighting Hitler, India was able to collectively, albeit with great internal strife, stand up to London and usher in a period of transition that would include the partition of Pakistan and Indian independence.

PARTITION AND INDEPENDENCE

There are many circumstances that led to the division of India in 1947. The British knew they had lost the colony, and a component of decolonization was the promise that religious violence between Hindus, Muslims, Sikhs, and Christians would stop if a partition was granted. This proved not to be the case, at least during the process. In 1947, India's total population was about 390 million. The partition would draw a border around a new state of Pakistan for about thirty million Muslims and East Pakistan (later Bangladesh) for thirty million Muslims in the east. Out of fear, millions of Hindus living in the new political state of Pakistan moved across the border to India. Likewise, many millions of Muslims living in India crossed into Pakistan (including East Pakistan). In the process, riots and fighting between religious groups killed more than a million people, women were raped by the tens of thousands, and up to seven million Hindus and Sikhs were displaced in Punjab because it was split by a political border. All in all, this was the

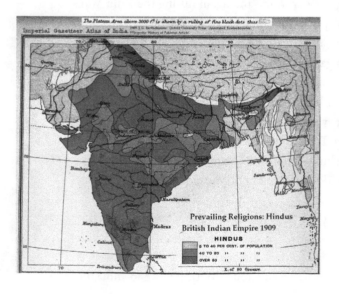 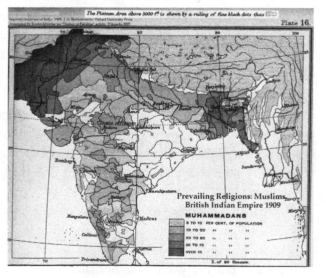

FIGURE 8.2e(1) & (2). India, in 1909, was mostly Hindu, but had a large Muslim population in the west. Copyright in the Public Domain.; Copyright in the Public Domain.

largest and perhaps most violent migration of humans in history, and millions of
refugees resulted from this partition.

After the partition, Pakistan and a new
India had to create and operationalize
new political systems. Although they both
became federal republics, Pakistan's system
was and remains influenced by Islam.
For example, they adopted an English
common-law system with a Supreme
Court, but integrated elements of *sharia
law*. They have administrative provinces,
but also a tribal territory governed more
by principles of their religion than the
constitution.

FIGURE 8.2f. The last Viceroy of India, Lord Mountbatten,
sits on a committee in 1947 to draw new political lines for
the new Muslim state of Pakistan and a revised India.
Copyright in the Public Domain.

India, also a federal republic, adopted a *socialist democracy* at first. This likely resulted from their colonial
past and a general distaste for western forms of capitalism. The idea was that socialism could temper the
economic disparities between Indians and allow them to cultivate a domestic economy. However, giant
social systems resulted in giant bureaucracy, leaving many Indians, and their needs, buried in paperwork.
This became known as the *license raj* and would result in a depressed economy.

A great political tension continued between India and Pakistan after partition. The six (6) sources of
continued tension between India and Pakistan are:

- *Post-partition violence:* The hostile
  interactions between Hindus and
  Muslims were epic in scale. About
  a million were killed, fourteen
  million were displaced, and tens of
  thousands of women were raped.
  Many remaining Muslims in India
  ended up in slums.
- *Political alliances with superpowers:*
  Pakistan allied with the United
  States, and India, being a socialist
  democracy, allied with the Soviet
  Union. These two superpowers
  were in a cold war with each other
  and heightened the tensions
  between India and Pakistan,
  especially concerning the political
  separation of East Pakistan.

FIGURE 8.2g. The Jatiyo Sriti Shoudho in Bangladesh,
commemorates all who served and those who died in the
Bangladeshi Liberation War of 1971.
Copyright © Luthador (CC BY-SA 3.0) at https://commons.wikime-
dia.org/wiki/File%3ASriti_shoud.jpeg.

- *Indian support over East Pakistan independence:* The growing political will of East Pakistan to separate from Pakistan was supported by India. This led to war, and India was able to achieve victory and took about ninety thousand Pakistani prisoners of war (see *Figure 8.2g*). Even more, the United States was afraid that the Indian-supporting Soviets would use this as a chance to establish themselves in modern-day Bangladesh, resulting in the US cultivating alliances with China.

- *Disputed territories in Kashmir and Jammu regions:* In some cases, the British asked local leaders in border regions which nation they wanted to be a part of. Despite the majority of Kashmiris being Muslim, their Hindu leader decided to remain with India. This sparked an internal conflict that was quelled with the help of India. When Pakistan moved its capital city to Islamabad, which has proximity to Kashmir, Pakistan reasserted its domain over the realm, and India bolstered its

FIGURE 8.2h. Contested space in Kashmir and Jammu. This region has been among the most tense in the world.
Copyright in the Public Domain.

military presence to counter that assertion. War and skirmishes have broken out, and tensions continue. China, also with claims in the region, has gone to war with India and had conflict with Pakistan.

- *Nuclear arms race:* Being allied with rival Cold War superpowers led to nuclear weapons in the region. The Americans and Soviets each viewed nuclear arsenals as diplomatic necessities. After the Soviets dissolved, the United States formed new diplomatic bonds with India. Nonetheless, both India and Pakistan have proactively reminded each other, on many occasions, that they have weapons ready, as seen in frequent nuclear testing.
- *Continued terrorism:* There have been many terrorist attacks on India by Islamists. In 2008, the terrorist organization *Lashkar-e-Taiba*, under the premise that Kashmir-Jammu should be Pakistan, bombed a hotel in the business district of Mumbai. Although those responsible were captured and executed, the tensions still exist.

8.3 Social Patterns

The social landscapes of the Indian Subcontinent create a foundation for understanding broader economic narratives that define the region today. After decolonization, the nations of the region were struggling to identify a functional structure that would create economic momentum. This would be difficult, considering that, for the past several hundred years, the British had managed economic affairs in the region. Apart from India and the newly formed Islamic state of Pakistan, nations remained much the same after the British left. Nepal, Bhutan, and Ceylon (Sri Lanka) all had diplomatic agreements with Britain indicating that they were not a part of the British Empire (though they cooperated with them). That meant they had little to reengineer after 1947. India and Pakistan would see fairly radical changes, in certain ways.

POVERTY

As mentioned in Chapter 5 (Sub-Saharan Africa), colonial powers were responsible for the evolution of cities. Because colonial powers needed access to the sea and/or a place to both conduct the affairs of the colony and create residential sectors for European residents and officers, cities would be planned in ways that reflected London. Most Indians were rural, living in countless villages and towns throughout the country. Under a colonial regime, cities were quite exclusive, in that the British restricted access to locals and nationals. Indians living near or in colonial cities were often allowed to reside in government housing projects or on empty government land. In Mumbai (formerly Bombay), for example, the area designated for locals was called "Native Town." After decolonization, the cities opened up, and millions of people flooded into them from rural areas. Driving this rural-to-urban migration was the perception that cities were places of opportunity. This was typically not the case. Resulting from this dynamic was the rise of urban populations around the world and in India, as well as the formation of the *megaslum*. Today, in Indian cities, urban slums grow much faster than the cities around them.

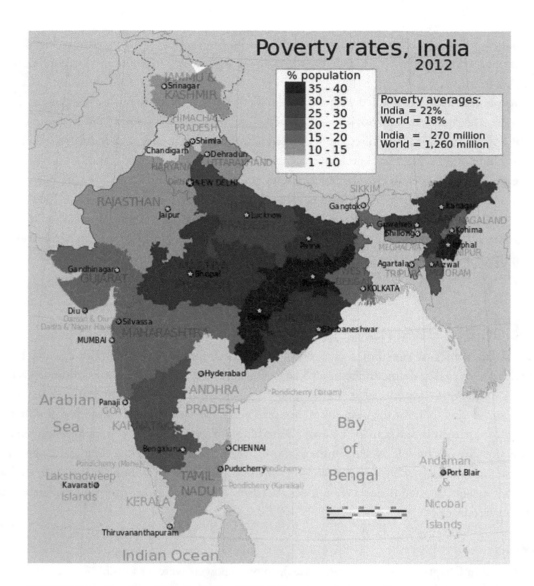

FIGURE 8.3a. Poverty rates in India, 2012. What they do not tell us are poverty rates within cities, which is much higher but not well censused.
Copyright © M Tracy Hunter (CC BY-SA 3.0) at https://commons.wikimedia.org/wiki/File%3A2012_Poverty_distribution_map_in_India_by_its_states_and_union_territories.svg .

Slums and the Informal Economy

The rise of urban slums opens discussions about how so many people in the region live, day by day, and fit into the larger society and economy of the region. For example, approximately five hundred thousand people a year migrate to Delhi from rural areas. Of them, about four hundred thousand end up in slums. The scale of poverty in India and the greater region is often underestimated. The *per capita* GDP of India is about $5,500 annually. This is less than half of that found in Brazil and is roughly one-third of the number that represents the *poverty line* in the United States—a country with a *per capita* GDP about nine times larger than India. Approximately eight hundred million Indians live in poverty.

People *living in poverty* typically lack access to some fundamental resources. These include poor or no access to clean drinking water, emergency services, utility infrastructure (plumbing, sewerage), land tenure, nutrition, education, and health care (family planning). However, to assume all poor are the same would not be accurate. The poverty line in India is about fifty-three cents per day. Many millions of Indians are poor but make significantly more than that amount. So, a classification system may help. There are *three (3) classifications of poverty* in the Indian Subcontinent, which include:

1. **Chawls:** *(upper poverty or >$3 per day)* as seen in *Figure 8.3b (1)*, are the shabby government housing units for native Indians, built in haste after 1900 for the growing colonial industries in cities. They do not appear to be slums from the outside, but residents are often very poor. Each building has between ten and twenty units, and each floor shares one restroom. Each unit is typically small and is ill equipped with running water, but is home to large families with eight to ten people.

2. **Bustees:** *(mid-poverty or between $1 and $2 per day)*, as seen in *Figure 8.3b (2)*, are also known as *JJ clusters* and represent the more typical slum. They are often squatter settlements on low-use government lands (near railroads or public trash dumps) and are composed of makeshift housing, using materials like corrugated metal, burlap, plastic sheets, and anything else one can acquire from refuse. These settlements are vulnerable to floods and landslides and can be home to more than one million people.

FIGURE 8.3b(1). Chawl in Mumbai (upper poverty)
Copyright © Abhinav Saxena (CC BY-SA 2.0) at https://commons. wikimedia.org/wiki/File%3AChawl_-_Mumbai_2006.jpg .

FIGURE 8.3b(2). The Dharavi slum of Mumbai (mid poverty). Some estimates suggest this slum has a million residents.
Copyright © Kounosu (CC BY-SA 3.0) at https://commons.wiki-media.org/wiki/File%3ADharavi_Slum_in_Mumbai.jpg .

FIGURE 8.3b(3). Street dweller (low poverty) without a home.
Copyright © Augustus Binu/ www.dreamsparrow.net (CC BY-SA 3.0) at https://commons.wikimedia.
org/wiki/File%3APoor_woman_in_Parambikkulam%2C_India.jpg .

3. ***Street dwellers:*** *(low poverty or < $1)* as seen in *Figure 8.3b (3)*, are often the poorest of
    the poor. They have no home and sleep directly on the streets. This makes them even more
    vulnerable to natural disasters, disease, and crimes.

The region's poor, or about two-thirds of the entire population, typically earn a living from *informal economic activities*. Informal economic activities, to review again, are not counted or measured in a country's GDP. They include a wide range of activities like selling goods recycled from trash dumps, cooking food on the street, fixing and repairing, begging, construction and labor, and sometimes illegal activities. If you consider the informal economy and then identify the number of people engaged in these sorts of activities or living on these daily rates, it may bring into question how countries in this region truly measure their economies.

CASE STUDY 8B

Land use in India's Cities

The best way to see how poverty is superimposed over the Indian landscape is by using satellite imagery. Google Earth is an excellent tool for this purpose. Follow the directions below:

1. Open Google Earth, or, if you do not have the program, go to your favorite Internet browser and type in Google Earth. Or, load free app onto your smart phone.
2. Once program or app is opened, type in: **Lajpat Nagar, New Delhi, Delhi, India**.
3. Pan out until you see New Delhi to the north, the Indira Gandhi International Airport to the west, and Noida to the east.
4. Pan in, in different areas, and then out until you see grey blotches in the middle of the city. These are slums.
5. Note the erratic nature of the location of slums in Delhi.

This is how land is used in India. There may be a Five-Star hotel with acres of lush grounds, catering to foreigners and wealthy Indians. Next to or all around that hotel may be slums. This is not uncommon in not only India, but Bangladesh, Pakistan, Nepal as well.

DEMOGRAPHIC TRENDS

Roughly a quarter of the world's population lives on the Indian Subcontinent. This area has traditionally been a high- growth region. For example, in 1947, when India was facing partition, it had a combined population of about 139 million people. After the partition, this was reduced by approximately sixty million, leaving India with a total of about 330 million. Today, India has about 1.3 billion people. In other words, they added one billion people in less than one hundred years alone. Likewise, when Pakistan became a state, it had a new population of about thirty million, but has nearly two hundred million today. Bangladesh jumped from thirty million in 1947 to 180 million today. This has a lot to do with fertility, rather than immigration or economic success. India's fertility rate (number of children born to childbearing-age women) has indeed been quite high, but now seems to be slowing (2.5). And like India, both Pakistan (2.9) and Bangladesh (2.4) seem to be flattening out. Remember, two parents having two children have a TFR of 2. In order for population to grow, TFR must be at least 2.1. Therefore, each of these regional nations is still growing, but not as aggressively as the past fifty years.

However, there are inherent problems with statistics from regions like this. Because there is really no reliable data on slum populations, these numbers cannot reflect the "true" numbers. Remember, slums have little or no access to services, infrastructure, or land tenure. With squatters, a census worker may not understand who to poll or whether those polled are truthful about numbers per household. Sometimes,

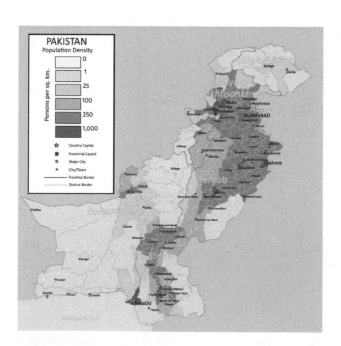

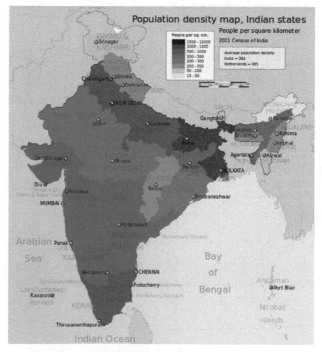

FIGURE 8.3c(1). Pakistan has approximately 196 million people.
Copyright © nomi887 (CC BY-SA 3.0) at https://commons. wikimedia.org/wiki/File%3APakistan_population_density.png .

FIGURE 8.3c(2). India has around 1.25 billion people and should surpass China in the next 10–15 years.
Copyright © M Tracy Hunter (CC BY-SA 3.0) at https:// commons.wikimedia.org/wiki/File%3A2011_Census_India_ population_density_map%2C_states_and_union_territories. svg .

as in the *Orangi* slum of Karachi, Pakistan, a slumlord charges rent, collects for pirated utilities, and bribes local government officials to be left alone. Therefore, people try not to talk, out of fear. Also, rural areas do not measure and record regional migration patterns that show who is leaving and why. Likewise, cities like Dhaka, Bangladesh or Bangalore, India are not accurately measuring the number of inbound rural Indians. When they do collect census information, it usually gives indications of trends, but not comprehensive facts.

One trend is the region's *dependency ratio* and how it is quite high. Data suggests that Pakistan, India, Bangladesh, and Sri Lanka all report ratios above 50%. That means more than 50% of all households polled in these countries reported having either children or elderly adults living in a household and depending on the income of a working age adult. This suggests that even the seemingly better-off, lower-middle-class Indians are taking on the added cost of providing for both children and grandparents. At the same time, *contraception rates*, that is the number of childbearing-age women using some form of birth control, are on the rise. This helps to inform us of a growing middle class that is getting better access to health care professionals (see *Figure 8.3d*). These trends, though they can be a little confusing, illuminate much about the region.

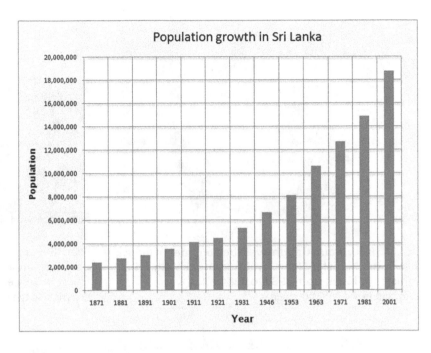

FIGURE 8.3c(3). Sri Lanka has about 22 million people, but growth is slowing.
Copyright in the Public Domain.

FIGURE 8.3d. Doctor educating the public about malaria prevention in Delhi slum.
Copyright in the Public Domain.]

FIGURE 8.3e. Indira Gandhi was the daughter of India's first Prime Minister Nehru and became the 4th Prime Minister of India, from 1980 to 1984.
Copyright in the Public Domain.

FIGURE 8.3f. Benazir Bhutto was from an upper-class political family and served as Prime Minister of Pakistan, twice.
Copyright in the Public Domain.

WOMEN ON THE INDIAN SUBCONTINENT

Women have and continue to play an important role in the history and politics of the region. For example, Indira Gandhi (see *Figure 8.3e*), the daughter of India's first Prime Minister, Jawaharlal Nehru, served as head of several important ministries before being elected Prime Minister in 1980. Pakistan, despite cultural and social gender inequalities, saw the ascension of Benazir Bhutto to the office of Prime Minister twice before she was assassinated during a campaign (see *Figure 8.3d*).

At the same time, there are alarming inequalities that continue to characterize the region. Bangladesh and Sri Lanka, for example, have some of the highest indices of gender inequality. Bangladesh is poor and predominantly Muslim, and has not indicated that it might embrace a future of greater equality for women. Alarmingly, a sign of this might be how Bangladesh ranks first in the regionally-centered crime of acid throwing. Acid throwing is a "crime of passion," and young women are typically the target. There are several reasons for this, which include denying a marriage proposal, jealousy, denying sex, not properly pleasing a man during sex, and so on.

FIGURE 8.3g. Acid attack survivor helping other survivors in Bangladesh.
Copyright © Narayan Nath/FCO/Department for International Development (CC BY 2.0) at https://commons.wikimedia.org/wiki/File%3ASupporting_acid_attack_survivors_in_Bangladesh_(6395599437).jpg .

Gender preference, a culture placing a greater value on a boy at birth, has long been a part of the culture in the Indian Subcontinent. Since these are *patriarchal societies*, men have always been viewed as dominant. Additionally, a *dowry* culture (which practices transferring property or money from the daughter's family to the new husband as a condition of marriage), creates an incentive not to have a girl (or want one). These are only surface explanations, and the way this is exhibited within the region can be identified demographically. In *Figure(s) 8.8h (1), (2), and (3)*, the national census in 2011 reveals gender-related issues in India.

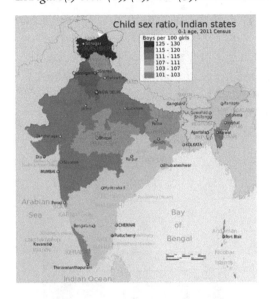

FIGURE 8.3h(1). Child sex ratio in Indian states, based on 2011 national census.

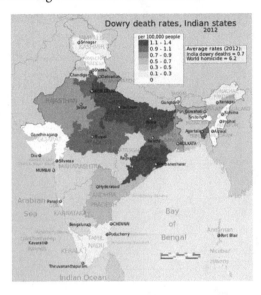

FIGURE 8.3h(2). Dowry death rates in India, based on 2011 census.

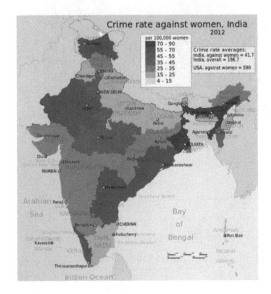

FIGURE 8.3h(3). Crime against women rates, based on 2011 census.

BOX 8.A THE ISSUE OF RAPE

What demographic trends do not address is the apparent rise in rape in slums and gang rapes in India's cities. In 2012, for example, a woman was raped on a bus by five men, and she later died from those injuries in a hospital. This, along with other terrible cases of rape and gang rape, has sparked national conversations and protests around India. Part of this conversation includes challenging how women are viewed and treated in society. In Pakistan, studies suggest that women in slums have a higher incidence of bladder infections than middle-class women in surrounding neighborhoods. The reason for this is fear of rape. Women who leave their domiciles at night to use the restrooms (which are often in dark, private areas) become vulnerable to rape. Because this happens, women in the slums hold it in all night, thus elevating the probability of infection. These crimes are reflections of patriarchal social norms and, perhaps, economic factors. High rates of underemployed young men result in more idle time. However, at least in India, there are tough conversations on the table.

FIGURE 8.3i. In 2012, a young woman was raped by five young men on a bus in Delhi. Copyright © Nilanjana Roy (CC BY-SA 3.0) at https://commons.wikimedia.org/wiki/File%3ADelhi_protests-India_Raped%2C_says_one_young_woman's_sign.jpg .

Social trends within the Indian Subcontinent can be very revealing. They are reflections of a postcolonial era combined with well-established cultural complexes. The people and cultures of the region are some of the oldest on Earth, but the division of the region into religious-political fragments, just decades ago, has altered their landscapes. For example, poverty has always characterized the realm, but not precisely like it does today. Resulting from decolonization was the rise of urban poverty. This form of poverty really did not exist before the British.

Demographic trends have likewise shifted and morphed over time. Whereas between 1947 and 2015 Indians added a billion people to the planet, they are now showing signs of reduced fertility rates. This is, at least in part, because of a postsocialist economic boom and a rising middle class, as well as a growing number of Indians living in cities. Yet there are still unknowns. Because census information about slums is not always accurate, if it occurs at all, we cannot accurately measure the region's "real" demographic trends. Slums are growing in India, Pakistan, and Bangladesh, and the larger they get, the more difficult they are to measure.

Another consideration is that the region was experiencing internal religious conflict. Hindus and Muslims were politically standoffish; they rioted, fought, and killed each other, despite pleas from leaders like Gandhi. The British, in support of the *Muslim League*, arranged the "partition" on the assumption that it would resolve the issues and quell the violence. This could be a *thematic intersection* itself, because the religious tensions, crossed with the political solution from the British (who practice neither religion) inadvertently produced an outcome that was catastrophic. The paper lines the British drew (in good faith) on maps resulted in the murder of more than a million people, the displacement of millions, and the mass migration of nearly fifteen million people. And even after the partition was completed and the nations stood independent, the conflict continued in the political arena, and even that led to war. Today, these tensions continue, despite a more neighborly stance.

8.4 Economic Changes

Perhaps no other region on Earth, apart from East Asia, has transformed so radically over the past twenty-five years. Although there have been some measurable economic successes within Pakistan and Bangladesh, this subsection will focus on India. India provides a looking glass into how nations develop, what problems and challenges accompany development, and some concerns with neoliberal policy. In other ways, India and its BRICS partners highlight a larger paradigm shift in the global economy. Much of the world conducts business in ways that transcend political boundaries and distance. Because of technology (communications, GPS, electronic capital), the relatively low price of oil and natural gas (transportation), trade organizations like WTO and OECD, and typically safe ocean routes (US and other naval forces), the world can rely on the flow of products and services around the world. India, like other nations, combines low labor costs, a robust semiskilled workforce, and enough economic incentives to become an increasingly important part of the global economy.

ENDING THE LICENSE RAJ

The License Raj can be described as the hyper-bureaucracy that resulted from the democratic socialism that arose after India's independence. Because Indians fundamentally believed that a large, orderly government could best serve the nation, layer after layer of government was added. Each stratum of government, from local to national, required endless forms, licenses, permits, and documentation before individuals could start a business, build a structure, file a legal suit, or sell products abroad. This had a direct impact on India's economy between 1950 and 1990. When Indians sought to stimulate their depressed, internally imploding economy in 1990, they would have to rethink and reengineer their bureaucracy in a way that made conducting business easier, especially for foreign firms.

TURNING TO THE WEST: INDIA'S ECONOMIC TRANSFORMATION

A combination of factors led to India's political will to modernize and liberate its economy. By the 1990s, India was struggling with labor unions, politically charged strikes, and a decaying British colonial infrastructure. Additionally, the *Green Revolution* was supposed to help stimulate the economy, but it failed as much as it succeeded. There were also growing demographic concerns, as discussed earlier. India was growing exponentially in population; most of these people were poor, hungry, and would not grow up with an education that might make a better worker in the formal economy. The rational next step was to leverage India's giant labor force, raw materials, and good geography to engage in global trade.

FIGURE 8.4a. Many Indians earn a living in the informal sector, which is difficult to measure. Wages are determined by the worker and money is typically raised to simply survive. Copyright © Sayamindu Dasgupta (CC BY-SA 2.0) at https://commons.wikimedia.org/wiki/File%3AFruit_seller_in_Kolkata.jpg .

BOX 8.B WALT ROSTOW'S 1960 MODERNIZATION MODEL

As discussed in Chapter 1, Walt Rostow's 1960 Modernization Model (a.k.a. "stages of growth") offers an effective platform for discussing India's economic transformation. It suggests that nations seeking to modernize and engage in more global trade, if successful, go through five stages of growth. These five (5) stages are:

1. Traditional Society
2. Preconditions to Take-off
3. Take-off
4. Drive to Maturity
5. High mass consumption

It is important to point out that this model has its criticisms and is interpreted in different ways. However, if kept simple, it can be useful for framing India's economic transformation as well as illuminating the stage they are having difficulty surpassing.

INDIA'S ROAD TO RECOVERY

When India elected to reform its economy, it needed outside development money to put a plan into effect. The way development funding typically works (and still does) is that a nation solicits money from a development bank like the IMF or World Bank. The bank would loan the government a large sum of money (mainly in American dollars), on the grounds the lendees would modernize their country, liberalize their economy, and ultimately attract foreign investment. *IMF and World Bank conditions for loans* often involve:

- *Modernizing infrastructure:* Reliable electric utilities, communication networks, improved roads, ports, and light rail/railway lines.
- *Labor reforms:* Fair wages, arbitration systems to quell labor disputes between workers and companies, etc.
- *Reduced bureaucracy:* Streamline governmental systems, making it easier to conduct business in India.
- *Soften foreign trade policy:* Work with trade organizations and other political and economic parties to make the country more permeable.
- *Invest in education and housing services:* Education allows a nation to grow a semiskilled or skilled labor force. Once educated and working, they need housing.
- *Create incentives to attract foreign investment:* This might include creating *Special Economic Zones*

In India's case, they were a *traditional society* in the 1990s. They applied for development monies and received them, with a long list of conditions. They accepted the conditions and made necessary changes as a part of the *preconditions to take-off*. By 2000, India was ready to attract FDI (foreign direct investment) investment or *take off*. To date, India has generally succeeded. Despite some episodes of slow growth, they have been one of the fastest-growing economies on Earth. Between 2013 and 2015, India surpassed China as the fastest-growing economy (6–7.5% annual GDP growth). Their national GDP is about eight billion a year, making them the seventh-largest economy on the planet. India also has the second-largest, but youngest, workforce on the planet. This would seem a successful *drive to maturity*, and that would be both correct and incorrect.

If examined independently, India is indeed a success story. It has transformed its economy, elevated millions out of poverty, and is beginning to show signs of social change. However, if examined in the context of Walt Rostow's *modernization model*, India has failed to achieve the final stage of *high mass consumption*. To achieve this stage, India must ignite a large enough middle class to fundamentally shift its economy into a *tertiary sector* (service economy) that fuels its own economy. The North Americans, Europeans, Australians–New Zealanders, and several East Asian nations (Japan, South Korea, Taiwan) have all done this. India simply has not. Therefore, the model reveals something requiring further examination. What is standing in the way of the fastest-growing economy on Earth reaching the fifth stage of development?

INDIA'S STRENGTHS

India has had many successes since 1991. It has been the recipient of billions in *foreign direct investment (FDI)*, it has grown its service economy, and it has improved its education system in a way that produces more skilled labor. FDI does not typically occur at this level unless companies have incentives to operate in the country, can rely on the infrastructure, and have a semiskilled and skilled labor pool. As you can see in *Figures 8.4b (1) and (2)*, India's workforce is still primarily engaged in agriculture. This is because approximately 65% of Indians still live in rural areas, and agriculture is the primary activity of rural India. However, technology, education, and the teaching of English in schools have resulted in a fairly large pool

FIGURE 8.4b(1). Cities like Bangalore and Gurgaon (outside Delhi) have become centers of India's valuable service economy.
Copyright © Srisez (CC BY-SA 3.0) at https://commons.wikimedia.org/wiki/File%3AllabsCentre.jpg .

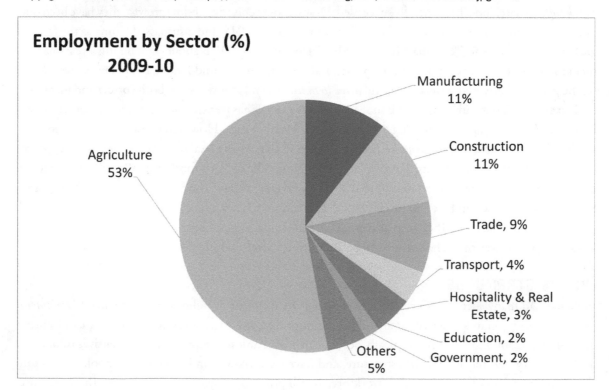

FIGURE 8.4b(2). India's labor by sector. What this pie chart does not reveal is that the agricultural sector is shrinking, while services are continuing to rise.
Copyright © M Tracy Hunter (CC BY-SA 4.0) at https://commons.wikimedia.org/wiki/File%3A2010_Percent_labor_employment_in_India_by_its_economic_sectors.png .

of labor that can be used as "tech support" around the world. These types of economic activities have been quite successful for India.

LIMITS TO GROWTH

There is no easy explanation as to why India is having difficulty growing their middle class to the point where they might ignite their own robust service economy. The answer is essentially interwoven into economic, cultural, social, and political narratives, and is therefore hazy at best. It is also important to point out that one of the criticisms of Rostow's model is that it is too "Western" and that India's inability to take the next step is perceived as some kind of failure. This is a valid concern. However, India's economy does appear to have some limitations, despite its growth. As long as the global economy operates in ways consistent with the past several decades, India's impressive growth could potentially slow.

There are several barrier points worth exploring. Although they cover neither the myriad of discussions nor the depth of issues in areas like economics, they may illuminate what limitations India faces. In a *macroeconomic* context, India's economy is now part of the global economy, which is tethered to markets and reliant on giant consumer nations to purchase goods and services. During episodes of recession, the consumers become squeamish and buy less, thus affecting the nations that either produce goods or provide services. The *Great Recession* (2008–2011) is an example of this.

In a *microeconomic* context, most Indians are poor and continue to engage in informal economic activities. That means they make money in ways not counted into the economy. So, despite the great gains in India's economy, four hundred million Indians are still living in abject poverty, another four hundred million are living just a step or two up from "lower poverty" or "middle poverty," and the final four hundred million are competing for a limited number of positions in the healthier economic sectors, many of which operate in cities.

Because there are not enough "desirable" jobs to go around, underemployment is a big issue in India. Unemployment is less than 4%, but that does not inform us much if you factor in the four hundred million or more working in the informal sector (not measured). Underemployment, which is a real issue in India, can be defined as "qualified" workers taking whatever job they can get (security guard, retail, restaurant, etc.). India has the second-largest workforce on the planet (about five hundred million), but they are youngest workforce. Yet, if the right jobs are not there, many of these workers will be not be used in ways that might grow the economy.

There are also cultural factors to consider. Remember that the culture of this region is three, or even four, thousand years old. This means there are some things in place that are not likely to change. One is the way Indians shop (see *Figure 8.4c*). In India, hundreds of millions walk through dozens of little family-run shops, side by side, to buy things they need. They have rejected attempts by "big box" retail and grocery stores to enter India and revitalize their retail structure. Another cultural feature that limits growth is the embedded caste system. The lowest quintile of society (economically) is going to remain poor because they are either low caste or poor Muslims. Society generally neither cares about them nor is willing to make investments to elevate them out of poverty. In the context of Walt Rostow's model, these economic and cultural characteristics may contribute to India's inability to ascend to the fifth stage of *High Mass Consumption*.

FIGURE 8.4c. Small "Mom and Pop" shops are how Indians do business. They have rejected attempts by Walmart and other "big box" chains, because they prefer shopping this way.
Copyright © Ask27 (CC BY-SA 3.0) at https://commons.wikimedia.org/wiki/File%3AGrocery_Shop_in_a_small_Town_in_South_India_(1).JPG .

THE BRICS

The BRICS, as discussed in previous chapters about Russia and Brazil, are slowly redefining the global economic landscape. Core economies, like the North Americans and European Union, rely on these nations to produce goods and provide services at competitive prices. An ideal combination of relatively cheap labor and the various characteristics that incentivize industry to invest in and conduct business in those nations have made Brazil, Russia, India, China, and South Africa

FIGURE 8.4d. The leaders of the BRICS nations have formed tight enough bonds to build a powerful alliance. Copyright © Roberto Stuckert Filho (CC BY-SA 3.0) at https://commons.wikimedia.org/wiki/File%3ABRICS_heads_of_state_and_government_hold_hands_ahead_of_the_2014_G-20_summit_in_Brisbane%2C_Australia_(Agencia_Brasil).jpg .

very relevant and powerful. United, these nations can even redefine large economic and development systems created after World War II.

India and China are the two largest economies in the BRICS, and together represent about one-third of the total global population. The two have the largest workforces and seem fairly pliable through downturns in the economy. At the same time, India and China are competitors. China, although it is five times the size of India economically, keeps a close eye on India, and vice versa. Should Indian labor remain cheaper than China's increasingly more expensive workforce, then manufacturing could begin to swing toward India. This is already happening in Bangladesh. Also, if the BRICS move forward with forming a BRICS Bank, this channel of development funding could change alliances and loyalties away from North American and Europe to BRICS.

8.5 The Indian Subcontinent and the Twenty-First Century

The Indian Subcontinent will face some important, even critical, challenges this century. These challenges are internally created, externally created, and geographical in nature. Because of the scale of humanity that resides in this region, the effects of these issues may be severe. At the same time, the region is also expected to see some great successes. If the economy continues to grow, more people may be elevated out of poverty. If there are enough conversations about social issues, then women could see more equality and greater safety in the future. This section, though brief, will explore the more critical of the two.

Urban Growth

Cities on the Indian Subcontinent are amongst the fastest growing on the planet. The first stage of population growth occurred after decolonization. However, rural-to-urban migration, though difficult to measure, seems to be spiking. Although rural communities poorly measure who comes and goes and urban census studies often poorly measure demographic trends in slums, satellites can reveal how a city's morphology changes over time. Below is a list of cities in the region growing at a rate of about 3% annually:

- Ghaziabad, India (5.2%)
- Sarat, India (4.99%)
- Faridabad, India (4.44%)
- Chittagong, Bangladesh (4.29%)
- Nashik, India (3.90%)
- Dhaka, Bangladesh (3.79%)
- Delhi, India (3.48%) *now India's largest city, with an urban area population of about twenty-five million.
- Gujranwala, Pakistan (3.49%)

THEMATIC INTERSECTION 8B

Poverty and Development: a Conflict over Space in Delhi, India

Themes: Social/Economic

About a half million Indians migrate each year into Delhi. Of those, about four hundred thousand end up in slums; this then enlarges the megaslums that circle the city. These megaslums grow in an outbound trajectory, because the inner city and historic cores of New Delhi are already densely populated. This social theme, then, intersects with the progressive economic growth of the cities close to Delhi. Gurgaon,

FIGURE 8.4e. Gurgaon, India is one of the most progressive and modern cities in India, yet is still in the trajectory of outbound poverty from Delhi.
Copyright © Pithwilds (CC BY-SA 3.0) at https://commons.wikimedia.org/wiki/File%3AGurgoan5.JPG .

for example, is a progressive satellite city of Delhi. Corporations like Siemens, Coca-Cola, Pepsi, IBM, American Express, Bank of America, and Microsoft have all made Gurgaon their headquarters in India. As such, Gurgaon needs infrastructure and access to Delhi's labor pools to thrive. This gives them an inbound trajectory towards Delhi, because all of this new infrastructure (tollways, light rail system, Dwarka subcity's two million apartment flats) provides better connectivity and access to the global city just miles away. The problem in India is that one will not eliminate the other. Instead, they coexist, though not harmoniously. Poverty in Gurgaon is continuing to push outwards, while Gurgaon adds malls for middle-class patrons. Dwarka subcity (a neighboring residential suburb) added two million flats, a light rail system, universities, and sports complexes—all designed intentionally for the emerging middle class. To date, this city is only roughly 30% occupied, and the slums continue to grow. Now the landscape is both impressive by Western standards, but it also has a growing patchwork of slums between the fancy high-rise buildings.

CLIMATE CHANGE AND THE MALDIVES

Climate change will pose many serious problems for the region in this century. The Himalayan glaciers that feed both the Ganges and Indus Rivers are melting fast. Runoff from precipitation events is adding sediment to both rivers. If these trends continue, these river systems will change in character for the first time in recorded history. Flow volume, mineral content, and other factors may adversely affect the billion people who rely on these rivers. Changing monsoonal flows will likely continue to impact the region. If air flows from high pressure to low pressure differently, patterns of precipitation change. Some areas will be more vulnerable to drought, whereas others will be flooded. Finally, the Maldives, an island nation in the Indian Ocean, is already feeling the effects of sea level rise (see *Figure 8.4f (1) and (2)*).

Former President of the Maldives, Mohamed Nasheed, went on a world tour to address carbon emissions in wealthy industrial nations. His premise was that they were inadvertently sinking his country, and he urged them to rethink their reliance on fossil fuels. Apparently, this was not popular in the Maldives; a *coup* occurred, and he was removed from office.

FIGURE 8.4f(1). Malé (pronounced: Mal-lay) is the Maldives' largest city island. It was only 1 meter above sea level, but now it is less each year, because of sea level rise.
Copyright © Shahee Ilyas (CC BY-SA 3.0) at https://commons.wikimedia.org/wiki/File%3AMale-total.jpg .

FIGURE 8.4f(2). Male after tsunami in 2005. Today, streets are flooding like this, simply because of the rising tide. Copyright © Oblivious (CC BY-SA 3.0) at https://commons.wikimedia.org/wiki/File%3AMal%C3%A9_after_tsunami_(cropped).jpg .

BANGLADESH: IN THE CROSSHAIRS OF NATURE'S FURY

As discussed earlier, Bangladesh has a concerning geography and an enormous, densely-packed population. With a population above 150 million (mostly residing on coastal plains with an elevation less than ten meters above sea level), the people of this nation already suffer from a combination of issues. Of these are tropical cyclonic storms that often have ten-meter storm surges, river flooding and "backwater effect," and a reducing mangrove barrier in the Sunderbans. However, if you add climate change into the equation, matters worsen for Bangladeshis. Sea level rise will further erode their coasts and salinize their fertile soils, intensify the reach of storms, and induce greater flooding. Sea surface-temperature increases may increase the frequency and intensity of tropical cyclonic storms in the region. More runoff from reduced glacial melt will deposit more sediments in Bangladesh, which may be a long-term positive, but it will affect water quality in the short term. Bangladesh, this century, will likely face all these issues.

CONCLUSION

The Indian Subcontinent provides a fascinating study of both physical and human landscapes. Physically, it is a landmass that had been traveling for tens of millions of years until it crashed into the Eurasian Plate about fifty million years ago. This slow, but impactful, collision created the Himalayas, which are the tallest and most formidable mountains in the world. Perhaps it could be said that the human landscapes are equally as interesting. The nations of the Indian Subcontinent showcase a wide variety of cultures, provide an excellent lens to study colonialism and decolonization, and reveal landscapes of both intense poverty and great development and modernization. This region is also home to some of the greater conflicts and attempts at cooperation. The "Great Partition" showed us that sometimes regional conflicts that are internal by nature can be mismanaged by outsiders, with catastrophic results. The political division of Pakistan, though done as a solution, sparked one of the largest regional migrations in history, and more than a million died, violently. We also see a region perhaps not ready for climate change. It is still poor, and hundreds of millions live in ways and in areas more vulnerable to flooding, drought, and disease. It is important to keep in mind that the region has not, by any means, concluded its story. It is still shaping and forming, both in positive ways and in ways that require deeper observations.

KEY TERMS

Plate tectonics	British Empire	Population
Indian monsoon	Gandhi	Gender preferences
Ganges River	Great Partition	Industrialization
Hindu culture	Decolonization	Services
Caste system	Pakistan	Urbanism
Islam	Poverty	Climate change

CLASS DISCUSSIONS

1. Describe Hinduism and Indian culture.
2. Discuss how the British managed the Indian colony differently than others before. How did it work better? Why did it eventually led to decolonization?
3. Describe Gandhi as a person and as an activist.
4. Discuss the Great Partition. Why did they divide India by religion? What were some of the problems associated with partition?
5. Describe the relationship between India and Pakistan.
6. Discuss poverty in the region. Why are the people so poor? What are the slums like?

ADDITIONAL RESOURCES

CIA World Factbook:

https://www.cia.gov/library/publications/the-world-factbook/wfbExt/region_sas.html

Economic:

http://www.worldbank.org/en/country/india

Environment:

https://www.worldwildlife.org/species/

Gandhi:

http://www.biography.com/people/mahatma-gandhi-9305898

Indian Monsoon:

http://www.imd.gov.in/section/nhac/dynamic/Monsoon_frame.htm

Rivers:

http://www.eoearth.org/view/article/173762/

http://geography.about.com/od/culturalgeography/a/Ganges-River.htm

BIBLIOGRAPHY

Central Intelligence Agency. Central Intelligence Agency, n.d. Web. https://www.cia.gov/library/publications/the-world-factbook/wfbExt/region_sas.html. 04 June 2015.

Davis, M. (2005). Planet of Slums. Verso. London.

"Has India's Southwest Monsoon Collapsed?" Al Jazeera English. N.p., n.d. Web. http://www.aljazeera.com/news/2015/06/india-southwest-monsoon-collapsed-150630100226092.html. 01 July 2015.

"India." India World Bank. N.p., n.d. Web. http://www.worldbank.org/en/country/india. May–June 2015.

"Indus River." eoearth.org. N.p., n.d. Web. http://www.eoearth.org/view/article/173762/. May–June 2014.

Kennedy, P. (1987). The Rise and Fall of Great Powers. Random House. New York.

"Mahatma Gandhi." Bio.com. A&E Networks Television, n.d. Web. http://www.biography.com/people/mahatma-gandhi-9305898. 04 June 2015.

Margolis, E.S. (1999). War at the Top of the World: The Struggle for Afghanistan, Kashmir, and Tibet. Routledge. New York.

"The Mutual Genocide of Indian Partition." The New Yorker. N.p., n.d. Web. http://www.newyorker.com/magazine/2015/06/29/the-great-divide-books-dalrymple. 09 June 2015.

Olney, J. (2009). The Raj Reconsidered: British India's Informal Empire and Spheres of Influence in Asia and Africa. Asian Affairs. 40(1). pp. 45–68.

Rosenberg, Matt. "Geography of the Ganges River." N.p., n.d. Web. http://geography.about.com/od/culturalgeography/a/Ganges-River.htm. 23 May 2015.

Shaw, A. and M.K. Satish (2007). Metropolitan Restructuring in Post-liberalized India: Separating the global and the local. Cities. 24(2). pp. 148–163.

CHAPTER 9

Southeast Asia and the Island Realm

Key Themes:

Environmental, political, cultural, economic

Countries discussed:
- Myanmar
- Laos
- Thailand
- Cambodia
- Malaysia
- Indonesia
- Philippines
- Brunei
- Singapore (city-state)

9.1 Regional Overview

When looking at a map of Southeast Asia/Island Realm, it immediately reveals a scattered landscape of islands and peninsulas. In fact, no other region on Earth, apart from the massive Pacific Ocean realm, has so many islands. If you were to take just two of the eight countries of focus in Southeast Asia, the Philippines and Indonesia, they have a combined 24,615 islands. That is nearly four times the number of islands in the Caribbean. The region is also

SOUTHEAST ASIA

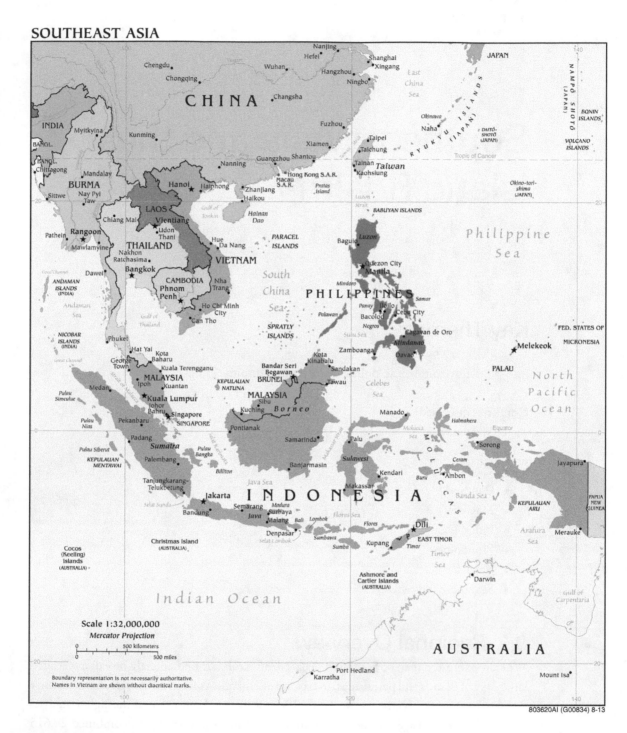

FIGURE 9.0. Southeast Asia: A geographically discontinuous region characterized by peninsulas and island nations.
Copyright in the Public Domain.]

composed of nations that are geographically connected to the expansive Eurasian landmass. Contiguous nations include Myanmar (a.k.a. Burma), which shares a border with both India and China, as well as Laos and Vietnam, each of which shares a border with China. The *peninsular region* begins with Thailand and generally narrows in the south, where Thailand shares a border with Malaysia. The physical geography, then, is an interesting study on its own.

The human landscapes of the region reveal a broad spectrum of ancient cultures, ethnicities, and political histories. Naturally, the Europeans established colonies there, but the narratives are a little different.

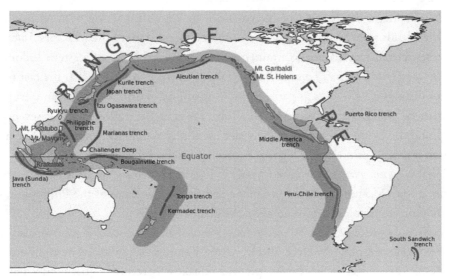

FIGURE 9.1a(1) & (2). Map of volcanoes in Indonesia, alone. Many of these are active. The region's volcanoes are a part of a larger physical realm known as the "Ring of Fire," which essentially arcs around the entire Pacific Ocean.

Copyright in the Public Domain.; Copyright in the Public Domain.

FIGURE 9.1b(1) & (2). 2004 Indonesian earthquake and tsunami. This seismic event was one of the largest ever recorded and triggered one of the most devastating tsunamis in history, killing over 230,000 people in 14 countries.
Copyright in the Public Domain.; Copyright in the Public Domain.

Likewise, this region has a fascinating economic history which includes discussions about the Japanese and their imperial expansion in the realm, as well as the current partnership between key countries to compete on the global stage. Although this chapter will be more brief than most, the region presents a unique combination of traits that help us understand the world today.

PHYSICAL GEOGRAPHY: THE RING OF FIRE

The physical geography of the region is largely defined by volcanism, along with seismic and tectonic activities. All the islands were formed by one or a combination of both of these factors. *Volcanism*, or any physical processes related to volcanoes, certainly defines the island realm of western Indonesia through the Philippines (see *Figures 9.1a (1) and (2)*). The volume of volcanoes, as well as the fact many of them are active, helps distinguish this area as part of the "Ring of Fire." Historically, volcanic eruptions in this region have changed global climate patterns. Mt. Toba, for example, exploded about seventy-four thousand years ago, and this is listed as the most explosive event on Earth in the last twenty-five million years. It is theorized that this eruption was so big that it covered much of Asia in ash, killing the vegetation and inducing a global *volcanic winter* that lasted nearly a decade. Humans were nearly made extinct by this single eruption. Today, Mount Merapi in Indonesia and the Taal volcano of the Philippines are listed as two of the most dangerous volcanoes/calderas on the planet.

Seismic activity, or processes related to the movement of Earth's crust (tectonics), also characterizes this region's physical geography. On December 26, 2004, a *megathrust* subduction event occurred off the coast of Indonesia. This triggered the third-largest earthquake ever recorded (between 9.1 and 9.3 on the Richter scale). This event generated enough energy to power the entire United States for approximately 370 years. The *megathrust* of one plate under another pushed up an enormous amount of water, causing one of the deadliest *tsunami* events in recorded history. The *tsunami* spread out at a speed between three hundred and six hundred miles per hour and at heights of, in some cases, about thirty meters (one hundred feet). By the time this seismic event and tsunami diffused its energy, about 230,000 people had died in fourteen countries.

TROPICAL CLIMATE

Southeast Asia and the Island Realm fall neatly within the tropical latitudes of Earth. The entire region fits between the *Tropics of Cancer* and *Capricorn*, with the equator running almost evenly through the middle. However, unlike South America or Africa, the equator runs mostly through an ocean segment of the realm, apart from the large island of Borneo. This means plentiful rain, heat, and humidity. However, this can change, periodically, with ENSO (El Niño Southern Oscillation) patterns. During *El Niño* events (specifically in 1997–1998), the region can and has become more dry and prone to massive forest fires. Because of the tropical climate, this region is highly biodiverse and has some of the oldest forests on Earth. The biodiversity of the region means it has become nature's grocery store, providing tropical fruits, spices, rubber, and medicinal plants, to name a few.

THEMATIC INTERSECTION 9A

Palm Oil: Global Demand, Habitat Destruction

Like the Amazon Rainforest, deforestation has been and continues to be a problem in Southeast Asia. The rise in demand for palm oil over the past several decades has resulted in the radical transformation of biodiverse regions in Indonesia and Malaysia. Although unlicensed palm oil plantations are illegal in Indonesia, it still occurs in abundance. Some estimates suggest that 60–80% of all palm oil on the market is grown illegally. If you look at Indonesia's ten million acres or more that have been converted from rainforest into palm oil plantations and then consider the amount grown illegally, it leads to the conclusion that corruption is present. Today, Indonesia is the largest producer of palm oil in the world and, as seen in Figure 9.1d, the region as a whole produces most of the palm oil used.

This highlights the intersection between economic demand and political corruption, as well as how it has resulted in environmental conflict. This is a conflict that may affect all of humanity. As mentioned in discussions about Amazon deforestation, the removal of native forests for palm oil plantations can have extraordinary effects. Not only does land-use change affect how carbon is stored and oxygen is produced, but the burning of rainforest (a common way to convert natural habitats into agricultural land), causes pollution, reduces natural habitats in ecologically diverse regions, and adds unusual amounts of carbon into the atmosphere. The reason this is unusual is because many areas converted into palm oil plantations occur in areas rich in peat soils. Peat soils are highly organic soils that take thousands of years to form. Because they are organic, they sequester much more carbon per hectare than traditional tropical soils. When a hectare of peat soil or peat bog is burned, it releases six times the carbon into the atmosphere. This contributes to climate change.

FIGURE 9.1c. Palm oil plantations in Malaysia.
Copyright in the Public Domain.

Other conflicts resulting from often illegal plantations include the destruction of natural habitat, which impacts species like the orangutan, Sumatran tiger, and Asian elephant. Likewise, these plantations displace local villagers, and those who remain are often left impoverished, homeless, and suffer from health problems induced by the continual smoke from burning rainforest. As can be seen in Figure 9.1e, the burning of peat soils in Borneo produces enormous clouds of smoke, which both is bad to breathe and adds millions of tons of surplus carbon into the atmosphere annually.

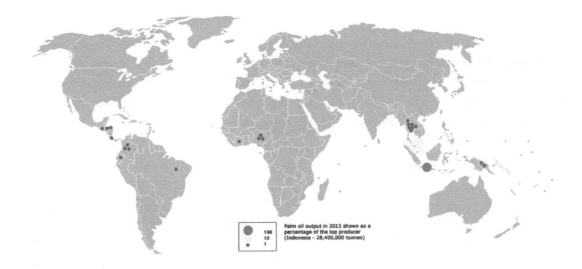

FIGURE 9.1d. 2013 Palm oil map.
Copyright © Swidran (CC BY-SA 4.0) at https://commons.wikimedia.org/wiki/File%3A2013palm_oil.png.

FIGURE 9.1e. Borneo fires, October 2006.
Copyright in the Public Domain.

RIVER SYSTEMS

The mainland of Southeast Asia is a sprawling landscape of tropical forests, rolling hills, coastal plains, and several rivers that run through them. Some of these rivers, like the *Mekong River* and *Red River*, originate outside of the region on the Tibetan Plateau of China. The *Mekong River*, the longest in Southeast Asia, runs through China, Myanmar, Laos, Cambodia, and finally deltas in southern Vietnam. This river has been a vital artery for trade, agriculture (especially rice), and fishing.

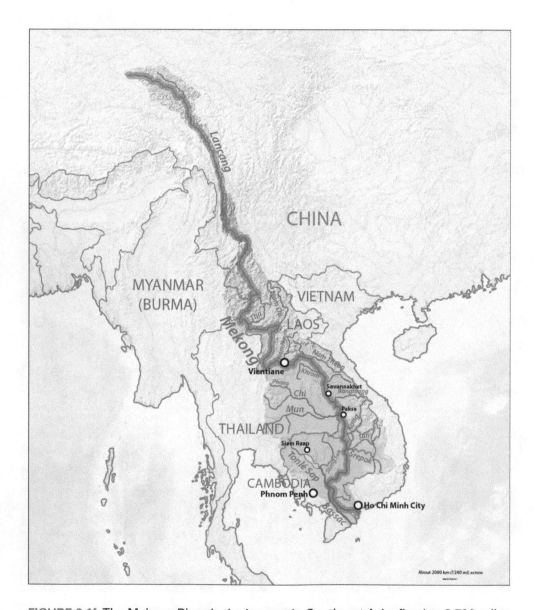

FIGURE 9.1f. The Mekong River is the longest in Southeast Asia, flowing 2,700 miles from China to the South China Sea, in southern Vietnam.
Copyright © Shannon1 (CC BY-SA 4.0) at https://commons.wikimedia.org/wiki/File%3AMekongbasin. jpg .

FIGURE 9.1g. A water taxi in Bangkok, along one of the many canals fed by the Chao Phraya River ferrying about 60,000 people daily around the city.
Copyright © BrokenSphere (CC BY-SA 3.0) at https://commons.wikimedia.org/wiki/File%3AWatertaxi_on_the_Khlong_Saen_Saeb.JPG .

The *Red River* also originates outside the region, in China, and runs about seven hundred miles to the Gulf of Tonkin in Vietnam. This river, though shorter, is important for trade, and links Hanoi with both the interior and the ocean. Two rivers that originate inside the region are the *Irrawaddy River* of Myanmar (Burma) and the *Chao Phraya River* of Thailand. Each of these rivers offers important functionality in economic, agricultural, and transportation sectors.

9.2 Cultural Patterns

The cultural landscapes and patterns of Southeast Asia and the Island Realm are so diverse and incorporate so many narratives that they could easily fill a textbook. Likewise, understanding population dynamics, the rise of cities, and the cultural composition of these population clusters involves examining a rather

FIGURE 9.2a. A Buddhist ceremony in Northern Thailand
Copyright © Takeaway (CC BY-SA 3.0) at https://commons.wikimedia.org/wiki/File%3AChan_Kusalo_cremation_04.jpg .

complex web of migration patterns over time. However, a good place to begin is to highlight several key narratives that might allow a general understanding of the region. These *key cultural narratives* are:

- Ancient culture and early external influences
- Religion
- Regional Ethnicity
- Colonies and Diasporas

ANCIENT CULTURE AND EARLY EXTERNAL INFLUENCES

Although the history of the region dates back to the Bronze Age, this section will focus more on the early empires, including the conflicts with the Chinese, to better illuminate the cultural landscapes of today. During the Han period (206 BCE–220 CE), China united and expanded. Although a Chinese general crossed into modern-day Vietnam and conquered it just prior to the rise of the Han, the realm was incorporated into the Han Dynasty in the early 200s BCE and remained under Chinese control for more than a thousand years. The consolidated empire, with Chinese support, acquired lands all the

FIGURE 9.2b. Traditional Vietnamese music echoes Chinese culture.
Copyright in the Public Domain.

way to the Khmer Empire of modern-day Vietnam, Cambodia, Laos, and parts of Thailand. This lengthy Chinese presence influenced Vietnamese culture in many ways. The Vietnamese are considered "ethnic Chinese" because they formed a southern province of China for so long. They, like the Chinese, celebrate the Chinese New Year, and they share many customs, social philosophies (Confucianism), and Buddhism. Likewise, as will be discussed later, they shared a political and economic trajectory similar to the Chinese during the twentieth century.

The ancient Khmer Empire of modern-day Cambodia was powerful at its zenith, and controlled much of region. It originally began as a Hindu empire, but changed to Buddhism. The cities of the Khmer Empire were some of the most impressive in the world, especially *Angkor Wat* (see *Figure 9.2c*). The *Khmer* employed sophisticated engineering in both buildings and waterworks. Their temple cities required that tens of thousands of tons of stone be mined, cut, transported over significant distances, and constructed into buildings that held thousands and survive to this day. Likewise, they constructed great water reservoirs and canals. The empire faced challenges from Chinese-controlled Vietnam and the growing Ayutthaya Empire of Siam (Thailand), which would eventually overwhelm and sack the empire.

FIGURE 9.2c. Buddhist monks in front of Angkor Wat. Angkor Wat was once one of the largest cities on Earth, but was built for a Hindu god. The Khmer were originally Hindu before becoming Buddhist. Copyright © Sam Garza (CC BY 2.0) at https://commons.wikimedia.org/wiki/File%3ABuddhist_monks_in_front_of_the_ Angkor_Wat.jpg .]

CHINESE MIGRATION

The Chinese have a long history of migrating into this region. Because of proximity, opportunity, and colonial networks, the Chinese have emigrated into the realm in great numbers. Below is a list of nations with Chinese diasporas:

- *Singapore*: Currently, about 74% of Singaporean residents claim Chinese ancestry. Chinese migration to this city resulted from the city being under British control. Hong Kong, also a British colony, had tight economic bonds with Singapore, and therefore the movement of goods, services, and people between the two was common.
- *Thailand*: There are about 9.3 million Chinese and people of Chinese ancestry in Thailand. This was not a case of colonialism, but opportunity. The powerful Ayutthaya Empire was highly tolerant of foreigners conducting business in Siam. This led to an initial *diaspora* and strengthened over time.
- *Malaysia*: Malaysia has a Chinese population of about seven million. Like the *diaspora* in Singapore, the move to Malaysia, specifically Kuala Lumpur, was colonial in origin. The British controlled much of the country as a colony, and the Chinese went for economic opportunities.
- *Indonesia*: Actual numbers of Chinese in Indonesia are obscured because of consistent ethnic tensions, racism, and racial mixing. However, the reasons the original Chinese migrated to Indonesia

FIGURE 9.2d. Anti-Chinese sentiments reach fever pitch in Jakarta, Indonesia in 1998, when looters destroyed Chinese businesses.
Copyright in the Public Domain.

were colonial in nature. Indonesia was a Dutch colony, and they needed workers, thus leading to recruitment efforts in China. The Chinese who arrived were considered foreigners and treated poorly. Although there are roughly 2.8 million Han Chinese, there are estimates that suggest about 6% of the total Indonesian population has some Chinese ancestry.

RELIGION

The religious landscapes of the region can also be very informative, culturally. This discussion fuses several historical narratives together. The four (4) main religions of focus in the region will be:

- *Hinduism*
- *Buddhism*
- *Islam*
- *Catholic Christianity*

Hindus and the "Indianized" Empires

Beginning in ancient times, Hinduism spread outward to the Southeast Asia region. As it became the predominant religion of the region, large "Indianized" empires would institutionalize the religion and build large temples of worship in the name of one god or another. The *Khmer Empire,* as previously discussed, "Indianized" much of the continental, and some peninsular, areas of the mainland, whereas the *Majapahit Empire* of Indonesia held vast territories from Java to the Philippines. They were Hindus, and "Indianized" the territories they occupied.

FIGURE 9.2e. Hindu temple in Bali, Indonesia, which remains a Hindu stronghold. Copyright © Spencer Weart (CC BY-SA 3.0) at https://commons.wikimedia.org/wiki/File%3AKunigan2.JPG .

Buddhism

The Hindu presence in the region waned as a result of several factors. On the mainland, Buddhism was spreading into Hindu regions. Because the Indian Hindus viewed Southeast Asians as a low caste of people, the Buddhist teachings of self-guided enlightenment, tolerance, peace, and the rejection of material wealth were well received. Before long, much of the population, including the "Indianized" *Khmer*, converted to Buddhism. Buddhism is the dominant religion in countries like Thailand. Because Buddhism is "self-guided," there is a greater tolerance within society, unlike that seen in Hindu, Islamic,

FIGURE 9.2f. Statue of Buddha in Thailand. Little shrines of Buddha are everywhere in Thailand and people leave food and milk as offerings. Copyright © Pawyi Lee (CC BY-SA 3.0) at https://commons.wikimedia.org/wiki/File%3AHotei_in_Thailand.JPG .

or Christian areas. This helps to inform us of Thailand's tolerance of the sex trade and other factors that will be discussed later.

Islam

In Indonesia, the *Majapahit Empire* was facing the rising power of the *Damak Sultanate,* who was a Muslim. Because the islands of what would become Indonesia were regional hubs of international trade, many Muslims from Arab ships interacted with locals. Islam caught on and spread fast. Today, Indonesia has the largest Muslim population on Earth, though it still has pockets of Hinduism, Buddhism, and Christianity. Islam also spread to the Malay Peninsula and into the Philippines. Today, not only is Malaysia predominantly Muslim, so is Southern Thailand. There exists an invisible line in Thailand, between the Buddhist north and central sections and the Muslim Malay Thais of the south.

Catholic Christians

The Philippines were explored by Ferdinand Magellan (who, incidentally, died there) and were later established as a Spanish colony. The Spaniards set up the city of Manila to be a key trading post for goods and silver coming across the Pacific from New Spain. This was quite successful, and the Spanish built what was, for a time, the largest trading center in Asia. The Spanish quickly executed their strategy of concurrently establishing a trade and converting locals to Catholicism, especially those on Luzon (largest Philippine island and location of Manila).

The Spanish had difficulty maintaining this colony and had to fight off the Dutch, suffer a British occupation of Manila for several years, and lose to the Americans in the Spanish-American War. The Treaty of Paris, however, dictated that the Americans must pay twenty million dollars for the Philippines, with which they complied. The Americans, after a successive war with the Filipino revolutionaries, would become a colonial power in the region. Nonetheless, the Spanish influence was well established, and the nation remains about 83% Catholic today.

FIGURE 9.2g. Fort Santiago was built near Manila by the Spanish in 1590.
Copyright © Gerswin (CC BY-SA 3.0) at https://en.wikipedia.org/wiki/File:Intramuros_002.JPG .

COLONIALISM

As seen in most parts of the world, the Europeans sought to leverage the geography and resources of the area for their own benefit. Because much of the region is archipelagos, a strong naval presence and naval conflicts would help define the realm through World War II. On land, the dense rainforests and formidable coastal marshes made managing conflict in colonies difficult. Nonetheless, the following Europeans colonized the region:

- *British*: Singapore, Malaysia, Burma (Myanmar), Brunei, and the city of Manila, Philippines for several years. The British also surrounded the region with colonies in India, Hong Kong, and Australia.
- *French*: The French created colonies in several parts of a broader region known by them as "Indochina." This included Vietnam, Cambodia, and Laos.

THE "OLYMPIA" AT MANILA.

FIGURE 9.2h. US Navy defeating the Spanish in Manila, leading to a US take-over. Some argue that the battle was staged as an agreement by the US and Spain, because Spain knew they would lose against American warships.
Copyright in the Public Domain.

- *Dutch*: The Dutch colonized the Indonesian archipelago, with the exception of Portuguese-controlled East Timor. This was the largest European colony in the region. The Dutch attempted to invade the Philippines and take the colony from the Spanish, but were not successful.
- *Spanish (later Americans)*: The Spanish controlled the Philippines and made Manila a key trading port for goods and precious metals coming in from "New Spain" (Mexico) and Peru. The British would seize Manila for a few years, but then lost it back to Spain. American involvement in a Cuban revolt against Spain led to war. The Americans sent their navy to the Philippines and defeated the Spanish. The *Treaty of Paris* gave the US control of the Philippines, Guam, and Puerto Rico, but required that the US pay Spain twenty million dollars to recover the loss of Spanish infrastructure in the Philippines.

The cultural landscapes of the region have been shaped by many factors. The ancient civilizations reveal how Chinese power and a thousand years of occupation influenced much of the continental cultures bordering them. The Vietnamese, for example, are still considered "ethnic Chinese" because they were, essentially, a part of the Han Chinese for so long.

Religion informs us about the distribution of culture and cultural traits as well. Although it was formerly a Hindu region, maintained by powerful "Indianized" empires, the spread of Buddhism quickly changed things on the continent. In the island and peninsular realm, Hinduism succumbed to Islam. Both Indonesia and Malaysia remain predominantly Muslim to this day. In the Philippines, the Spanish converted mostly to Catholicism, and though there are portions of the population claiming ties to Protestant Christianity and Islam, the nation remains mostly Catholic.

Finally, it is clear by this point that the Europeans had the ability to control entire regions with a relatively small number, compared to the local population. That is because they operated under economic incentives and had powerful military and lethal naval capabilities to support their claims. So, like the much of the world, they would move in, control, and change the character of the region. It is also clear that European colonialism did not last.

9.3 Political and Economic Conflicts

Southeast Asia and the Island Realm, because of proximity to East Asia and a wide range of natural resources, would be thrown into a broader arena of conflict during the mid-twentieth century. These conflicts were extensions of economic factors and political movements. The economic narrative begins with a discussion about the Japanese and how they were able to imperialize most of the region, as well as how, upon their defeat, the region continued on under American *hegemony* after World War II. The political narrative is the expansion of communism into Southeast Asia at a time when the West was in a "Cold War" with the Soviet Union and China. Both of these factors led to conflicts that have shaped, and continue to shape, the region today.

FIGURE 9.3a. Japanese occupation of the Philippines resulted in the cruel treatment of Filipinos. Here, an Imperial Japanese soldier looks at propaganda put up in secret.
Copyright in the Public Domain.

IMPERIAL JAPANESE

As briefly discussed in Chapter 1, the victors of World War I met in Washington, DC in 1922 to discuss how to prevent a war of that magnitude from occurring again. They concluded that naval power was the best guarantor of peace and, to better secure the world, subsequently allocated the number of warships each victor could build. The Americans and British took the highest allotment while leaving the Japanese (who fought on their side) with the smallest. The Japanese found this disagreeable and even insulting, so they countered with the proposition that they would accept it if the British promised not to mingle in their affairs east of Singapore and the Americans left them alone west of Pearl Harbor, Hawaii. They agreed, and in doing so, essentially allowed the Japanese to reign free in the region. The highly militarized and imperialistic Japanese took advantage of this by bullying their way into Southeast Asia without European or American military intervention.

The Japanese used their growing military might to expand economic interests in in the region. Their lack of raw materials at home (oil, rubber, etc.) made Southeast Asia a necessary appendage of their empire. However, their occupation of much of the region was accompanied by the harsh treatment of locals (see

Figure 9.3a). Eventually, Japan's behavior began to threaten interests in the region, and they waged war in East Asia against the Chinese, violating the spirit of the agreement in Washington. The United States responded by intervening with blockades, leading to the attack on Pearl Harbor. The Japanese were defeated after a long and costly war. Upon Japan's defeat and the end of World War II, the Americans remained in the region, both as a protective force and to conduct trade with the same nations that fell to the Japanese. The US military still has a regular presence in the region, which has generated growing resentment in China.

COMMUNISM AND WAR

After the *Second World War*, communism expanded, first with China and then Korea. The fall of China into communism was viewed as a huge loss by Americans and other Western nations. When the communist regime in Korea became hostile, the Americans became involved and helped the South Koreans maintain security and democracy. Southeast Asia, in the wake of European colonialism and Japanese imperialism, began to see communism rise. The French, in trying to restore their colonies after the war, were the first to fight the communists in "Indochina," unsuccessfully. By the 1960s the Americans were becoming increasingly involved, because stopping communism had become a moral imperative for the United States. Soon, the United States would become embroiled in a war that would last years and cost more than fifty thousand lives.

Vietnam War

The Vietnam War (1964–1973) was an armed conflict fought by the communist regime in North Vietnam and their South Vietnamese allies (the *Viet Cong)* against the Americans and South Vietnamese coalition. The war was an extension of the broader "Cold War" between Soviet communism and American democracy and each of their imperialistic incentives in the region. The geography of the region, poor execution, and lack of political support for the war in the US resulted in a political defeat and a US withdrawal in 1973. However, the human cost was high. Whereas the Americans lost about fifty-eight thousand soldiers,

FIGURE 9.3b. Casualties from American bombing in Vietnam, following the Tet Offensive, 1968.
Copyright in the Public Domain.

there were an estimated three million casualties in Vietnam, resulting from the persistent carpet bombing, use of chemicals like *napalm* and *Agent Orange*, and ground combat.

CASE STUDY 9A

Sex Tourism in Thailand and Southeast Asia

Sex tourism, as seen in Southeast Asia today, can trace its origin to the Vietnam War. Soldiers and sailors would be granted "shore leave" to "rest and relax." During the Vietnam War, many service personnel would choose Bangkok, Thailand and the surrounding beaches as a destination. Thailand is safe, close, and offered a reprieve from combat. "Red-light districts" emerged, and Thailand remained a destination for sex after the war. Although prostitution has been technically illegal in Thailand since 1960, the industry thrives and represents billions in revenue. The Thais are generally very tolerant of prostitution, unless poor character is exhibited. Child prostitution is not tolerated and can lead to severe punishment. More conventional prostitution occurs in certain beach towns or "red-light districts" in the cities. Prostitutes are not permitted to solicit from the streets, but can, as bar employees, solicit a person to join them in the bar for games, drinks, and to negotiate an exchange of money for sex. Some prostitutes are hired for extended periods by older men seeking companions.

FIGURE 9.3c. Thailand is a destination for sex tourism, or traveling with the intention of engaging in some sexual activity.
Copyright © moomoobloo (CC BY-SA 2.0) at https://commons.wikimedia.org/wiki/File:Soi_Cowboy_night.jpg .

The Philippines also has a large sex industry. Some estimates suggest there are approximately six hundred thousand sex workers in Manila and in cities near military bases. Like in Thailand, prostitution is technically illegal but tolerated. Political corruption is strong in the Philippines, and many officials (police, local politicians) likely allow it to occur because they are paid off. Cambodia has a problem with the child sex trade. This is illegal, but because of the percentage of Cambodians living in poverty, parents sometimes sell their daughters to brothels or to pimps. This has sparked an international response, and Cambodia is trying to control this problem.

Sex tourism comes with great risks. Thailand has the highest incidence of HIV infection amongst adults in Southeast Asia. It is estimated that there are more than six hundred thousand people living with HIV in Thailand today. Sex tourists are often more likely to be victims of crime, as well: prostitutes have been known to drug an inebriated customer so they can take personal items and cash; girls promise to leave prostitution if foreigners send them money every month; and so on. Despite these risks, sex tourism in Southeast Asia is strong.

A NEW ERA

Today, countries that were formerly torn by war have reformed, modernized, and joined a global community of nations. Their status as emerging economies, or countries that have made necessary economic and political reforms in order to participate in the global trade, can be traced to larger regional changes occurring in East Asia and India. Beginning with Japan in the 1970s and 1980s, and then China in the 1990s and South Korea in the 2000s, East Asia experienced radical political and economic transformations that facilitated real growth. Likewise, India's market liberalization and development also sent a loud signal that they were embracing changes and reforms. Because of proximity to both of these regions and, in some cases, cultural and political ties, Southeast Asia began its own metamorphosis. This regional will to change was not necessarily a result of failed communism or some western victory to spread capitalism around the world. Instead, it was, and remains, a more pragmatic response to a globalizing economy and their ability to adapt to change.

The New Vietnam

Vietnam has experienced tremendous economic reforms and has one of the fastest growing economies on Earth. In 2014, their GDP grew by nearly 6%, with roughly two-thirds of the growth coming from manufacturing and service industries as well as a globalized agricultural sector. Tourism has returned to Vietnam, and this is quickly fueling growth in their service sector. The communist regime in Vietnam has reaffirmed their commitment to economic liberalization and growth, despite 40% of all industries being state owned. Vietnam has increased their exports and has been an active member of the World Trade Organization.

FIGURE 9.3d. Tourism in Vietnam has been growing steadily, apart from 2009 (peak Recession). It is still relatively cheap and has a wide variety of natural sites and urban destinations.
Copyright in the Public Domain.

Malaysia

Malaysia has seen tremendous growth since 2000. Over the past three years, Malaysia has grown their GDP by more than 6%. Their economy is diversifying, and they have a firm goal of elevating their *per capita* GDP significantly by 2020. Malaysia grew aggressively in part because of their oil exports, which account for about a third of their revenues. An inflated price per barrel provided a positive cash flow, but then prices dropped. Malaysia, though it has suffered budget shortfalls and the reduced tourism from the fallout of two Malaysia Airlines commercial aircraft going down, the nation should continue to strengthen.

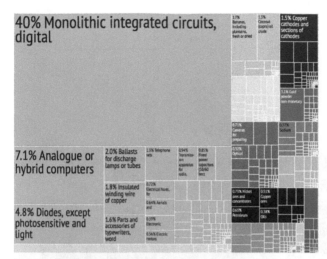

FIGURE 9.3e(1). Philippines exports.
Copyright © R. Haussmann, Cesar Hidalgo, et.al. (CC BY-SA 3.0) at https://commons.wikimedia.org/wiki/File%3APhilippines_Export_Treemap.png .

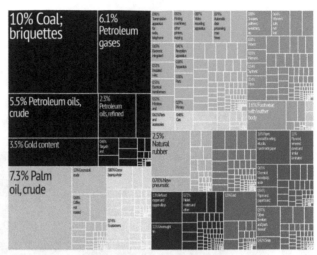

FIGURE 9.3e(2). Indonesian exports.
Copyright © R. Haussmann, Cesar Hidalgo, et.al. (CC BY-SA 3.0) at https://commons.wikimedia.org/wiki/File%3AIndonesia_Export_Treemap.jpg .

Philippines and Indonesia

Both the Philippines and Indonesia have been able to grow their economies, as well. Indonesia has the largest economy in the region, by far, and has experienced a steady growth rate of more than 5% annually, even during the global recession. Their economy is driven by exports in petroleum, rubber, and palm oil, and they have strengthened their manufacturing sector. The Philippines, though their economy is only a quarter of Indonesia's, has seen higher GDP growth. A robust agricultural sector and the assembly of electronics have helped growth. The Philippines have also emerged in tech services and support, and now compete with India.

BOX 9.A MYANMAR: A FUTURE IN TROUBLE?

Until recently, Burma (Myanmar) has been a shadow of Southeast Asia. Unlike its neighbor, Thailand—a nation that has always exhibited tolerance and a willingness to cooperate (even with colonial powers and the Imperial Japanese)—and its more distant neighbor Vietnam (a communist regime that has politically adapted and economically reformed itself to join the world), Myanmar has been fraught with internal strife brought on by a hardline military regime. The systemic cruelty of this military junta led to protests, revolts, death, and displacement. The United States and the United Kingdom, with the support of the United Nations, have imposed severe economic sanctions and political pressures on Myanmar's government, with limited success. In 2010, however, the people were finally able to achieve a transition to an elected government. For the first time in decades, American President Obama sat with

FIGURE 9.3f. Protest against violence in Rangoon, Myanmar.
Copyright © racoles (CC BY 2.0) at https://commons.wikimedia.org/wiki/File%3A2007_Myanmar_protests_7.jpg .

President Thein Sein in 2010 to discuss their path of reform. Following this meeting, economic sanctions were loosened, and Myanmar began restructuring its economy.

There are still concerns with how Myanmar treats its minority religious and ethnic populations, especially the Rohingyas and the Karen. The Rohingyas are Burma's Muslim minority and are considered one of the most persecuted minority groups on the planet. They are from the coastal region of Rakhine and have been treated as an unwelcome guest, despite their long history in the realm. Currently, 1.2 million Rohingyas within the country are not eligible for citizenship, nor do they have any political representation. The Buddhist majority has shown tendencies that some have considered pregenocidal, like systematic stigmatization, constant harassment, isolating them in camps, and weakening them by ignoring their basic human rights. Although there has not yet been an attempt to annihilate them, several hundred thousand have fled to Bangladesh, Thailand, and Malaysia on the assumption that they will. The Karen is an ethnic minority that has likewise been treated poorly. Many of them have fled to neighboring Thailand. It may be that Myanmar's economic future depends partly on how they treat minorities in their own population.

FIGURE 9.3g(1). Rohingyas displaced by a Buddhist majority who hate them, in Rakhine.
Copyright © Foreign and Commonwealth Office (CC BY-ND 2.0) at https://commons.wikimedia.org/wiki/File%3ADisplaced_Rohingya_people_in_Rakhine_State_(8280610831).jpg .

FIGURE 9.3g(2). A refugee camp in Thailand for Burmese Karen, a persecuted ethnic group.
Copyright © Mikhail Esteves (CC BY 2.0) at https://commons.wikimedia.org/wiki/File%3AMae_La_refugee_camp2.jpg .

9.4 Cities and Population

Southeast Asia and the Island Realm have some of the most populated countries, islands, and cities in the world. Although, with one exception, the majority of people in this realm still live in rural areas, the cities are huge and continue to grow. Singapore, the exception, is a rare political entity known as a "city-state." At the same time, the region has some sparsely populated areas. The rainforests of Borneo, for example, are occupied in small numbers by indigenous groups. Likewise, the rainforests of Cambodia, Vietnam, Laos, Thailand, and Myanmar are still quite remote and thus have low population density. This remoteness in Thailand and Myanmar helps us understand how their mountainous region forms the "Golden Triangle;" a regional nickname for the opium agriculture and production (currently second in the world, next to Afghanistan). The islands in the region are very population dense. Half of the top fifteen most-populated islands are here. They include (~ means approximately):

- Java, Indonesia: ~140 million (largest in the world)
- Luzon, Philippines: ~50 million
- Sumatra, Indonesia: ~47 million
- Borneo, Indonesia: ~21 million
- Mindanao, Philippines: ~20 million
- Sulawesi, Indonesia: ~17 million

POPULATION DISTRIBUTION

The distribution of population in the region is not dissimilar to other developing areas. The combination between large and growing cities and a predominantly rural population tells us something. As the economies grow, cities will continue to play an important role. Meanwhile, like in India, as economies grow, agriculture becomes a part of that growth and creates (some) opportunities in the fertile river deltas and valley regions. However, because of a rise in service and industrial/manufacturing sectors of the economy, cities become a destination for those seeking opportunities, or at least the perception of opportunity.

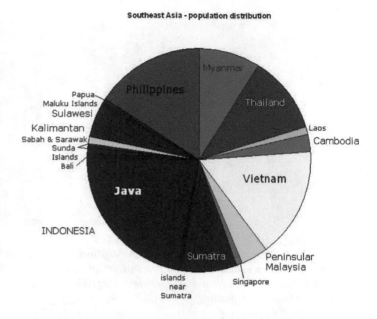

FIGURE 9.4a. Southeast Asian population distribution graph. Copyright in the Public Domain.

However, the distribution of the nation's population is not always so plainly rural or urban. Instead, populations shift to where opportunity exists. It is important to remember that economic incentives have the power to influence demographics and population distribution. The BRICS informed us that sometimes respectable economic growth, at the national level, obscures and masks the poor distribution of that wealth to the average person, as seen in *per capita* GDP. The three largest Southeast Asian nations—Indonesia, Vietnam, and the Philippines—despite strong growth, still have *per capita* GDPs that are only a fraction of those found in industrialized nations. For example, the *per capita* GDP in the Philippines is about $6,000 per year, as opposed to Singapore's $82,000. That low average income informs us of population patterns. People move where they must for economic reasons. If protected rainforests need to be cut down for palm oil plantations in Indonesia, people will go. If tourists start showing up to beach towns in Vietnam, people will move there to find work. If sex tourism in Thailand's "red-light districts" is strong, girls from poor, rural farming communities will go there to make money. This region is exhibiting a general rural-to-urban migration pattern, but also the opposite, because of economic opportunities.

MAJOR CITIES

Southeast Asian cities are interesting in that they provide a platform from which to view the rich culture of their country. The giant temples, traditional architecture, and various festivals reflect the many traits that characterize who they are. They also provide a glimpse into the future through the modern landscape of skyscrapers, light rail systems, new universities, and giant bridges. There are also contrasts and contradictions within Southeast Asian cities. They often have effective new expressways and commuter trains, but

FIGURE 9.4b. Typical day in Bangkok, Thailand.
Copyright © Khaosaming (CC BY-SA 2.5) at https://commons.wikimedia.org/wiki/File%3AScooters_Bangkok_Nana.jpg .

the cities are some of the most crowded and chaotic in the world. On any major boulevard is a rogue orchestra of crisscrossing scooters, tuk-tuks, cars, buses, and nervous bicyclists.

Another contrast is the volume of poverty that makes up a significant portion of cities, despite their increasingly modern look. This section will briefly examine the largest cities in the region and highlight some their features. These *Southeast Asian cities* are:

- Bangkok, Thailand
- Ho Chi Minh City (Saigon), Vietnam
- Manila, Philippines
- Kuala Lumpur, Malaysia
- Singapore
- Jakarta, Indonesia

Bangkok, Thailand

Bangkok, Thailand is the nation's largest urban area, with roughly fourteen million people. Bangkok is located on the transition zone between the central plains and the Chao Phraya River Delta. Although not directly on the coast, Bangkok is still vulnerable to coastal flooding and the backwater effect. The city serves as both the capital and the home of their royal family, and is where most business is conducted. As discussed earlier, the city is also well known for its red-light districts and sex trade industry.

FIGURE 9.4c. Bangkok, Thailand.
Copyright © Terence Ong (CC BY-SA 3.0) at https://commons. wikimedia.org/wiki/File%3AAerial_view_of_Lumphini_Park.jpg .

Ho Chi Minh City (Saigon), Vietnam

Ho Chi Minh City is Vietnam's largest metropolitan area. Conurbation has resulted from suburban growth, and the city has about eleven million people. The city was formerly known (and still is, by locals) as Saigon, but lost that distinction after the American withdrawal and the collapse of the South Vietnamese regime.

Ho Chi Minh City, the oldest of the large regional cities, was an important port for the *Khmer*. The city was then the seat of French colonial power for a long time, and reflects its French past. Within the city, for example, is the Notre Dame Basilica. This closely resembles the original one in Paris. Ho Chi Minh City is also a seat of political power and a center of economic activities. Many factories and manufacturing operations line the city's periphery. Finally, the city is more tourist friendly now, with hotels, resorts, and tours for a wide range of travelers.

FIGURE 9.4d. Traffic in Ho Chi Minh City.
Copyright © Ngô Trung (CC BY-SA 3.0) at https://commons.wikimedia.org/ wiki/File%3AXe_bu%C3%BDt.JPG .

FIGURE 9.4e(1). Manila skyline.
Copyright © mjlsha (CC BY 2.0) at https://commons.wikimedia.org/wiki/File%3AMakati_skyline_mjlsha.jpg .

Manila, Philippines

Manila is the largest city in the region, next to Jakarta, Indonesia. It was formerly a colonial city and major trading port for the Spanish. Old Spanish architecture (forts, plazas, cathedrals) can still be visited in the city. Manila is the epicenter of activity in the Philippines. The majority of Filipinos live on Luzon, and even if they do not live directly in the city, they rely on it for goods, services, and work. Manila is both a bustling global metropolis and a landscape replete with poverty. Some of the largest slums in Southeast Asia are here.

FIGURE 9.4e(2). Slums in Manila are more vulnerable to flooding and landslides. Copyright © SuSanA Secretariat / Sustainable Sanitation Alliance (CC BY 2.0) at https://commons.wikimedia.org/wiki/File%3ASlum_in_Manila_during_flooding_(4046572466).jpg .

Kuala Lumpur, Malaysia

Kuala Lumpur is the largest city and capital of Malaysia. Formerly a British colony, Kuala Lumpur began as a diverse city of trade. It has maintained its diversity and has become an important hub for national and global business. The city's diversity can be seen in its religious and ethnic composition. About 46% of the city's residents are Malays, but their Chinese population is huge and represents 43% of the population. Malaysia is predominantly a Muslim nation, but they only make up 46% of the city's population, whereas Buddhists make up about 35%. There are also significant numbers of Hindus and Christians. It is one of the smaller cities, by population (seven million in greater metro area), because it does not have the giant poor population of Manila or Jakarta. In fact, the city is more middle class in character, with relatively inexpensive housing, lots of shopping, and a large service-sector economy. This has created a visual landscape of both beautiful buildings and ubiquitous advertisements (see *Figures 9.4f (1)* and *(2)*). The city is

FIGURE 9.4f(1). Kuala Lumpur at night.
Copyright © naim fadil (CC BY-SA 2.0) at https://commons.wiki-media.org/wiki/File%3AMoonrise_over_kuala_lumpur.jpg .

FIGURE 9.4f(2). Kuala Lumpur's landscape of advertisements put there to reach the city's large middle class.
Copyright © EurovisionNim at https://commons.wikimedia.org/wiki/File%3AMonorail_Kuala_Lumpur.jpg . Reprinted with Permission.

also home to *Petronas Towers*—formerly the tallest buildings, and still the tallest towers, in the world.

Singapore

Singapore, or the Republic of Singapore, is unique in the region and the world. It is, by far, the wealthiest nation in the region, adjusting for size. It is an island just off the coast of Malaysia, located on the southernmost point of the Malaysian Peninsula. It was originally a British East India Company site, chosen specifically for its pivotal location between India and East Asia. Although it has gone through episodes of political change (British colonization, Japanese invasion and occupation, and Malaysian territory), it gained independence in 1965 and adopted a political system similar to that found in the United Kingdom.

FIGURE 9.4g. Singapore from expensive high rise condominium.
Copyright © William Cho (CC BY-SA 2.0) at https://commons.wikimedia.org/wiki/File%3AView_from_UOB_Plaza_1%2C_Singapore_-_20091211.jpg .

It is unique in that it is a sovereign city-state. The nation is the city, and it has approximately 5.9 million residents, of which about three million are citizens. Those who claim Chinese ancestry compose the largest group, at about 73%. Malays, Indians, and others compose the rest. Singapore has the largest *per GDP* in Southeast Asia (and one of the largest in the world), at just over $81,000. It is considered one of the freest market systems in the world, and has one of the lowest tax rates.

It is also one of the least corrupt nations on Earth because of a rather rigid common-law (English) system that no longer uses trials. Judges determine each case, and they still incorporate more local traditions of corporal punishment (caning, mandatory death penalty for heinous crimes). Because of this, Singapore has been criticized for not allowing due process or the right to a trial, but it is also celebrated for being one of the safer—if not the safest—cities in the world. Singapore's economy is largely services, in particular what is known as the *quinary sector* economy. They essentially are the financial hub of Asia and move money around the world. Singapore also has one of the largest transoceanic shipping ports in the world.

FIGURE 9.4h(1). Jakarta, Indonesia is the largest city in the region and one of the largest in the world.
Copyright © Sanko (CC BY-SA 3.0) at https://commons.wikimedia.org/wiki/File%3AJalanJenderalSudirmanJakarta.jpg .

Jakarta, Indonesia

Jakarta, Indonesia is by all accounts a *megalopolis*. It is the largest city in not only Southeast Asia and the Island Realm, but the world as well. In the greater metropolitan area, there are nearly thirty million people. The city is located on the coastal plain of Java (Jawa). Because of its proximity to the ocean and its low elevation, there are concerns that climate change and sea level rise can be catastrophic for such a large population. There are currently plans to construct a giant dyke-levee system around Jakarta. The city itself is a giant economy.

FIGURE 9.4h(2). Jakarta has some of the largest and poorest urban slums in the world.
Copyright © Jonathan McIntosh (CC BY 2.0) at https://commons.wikimedia.org/wiki/File%3AJakarta_slumhome_2.jpg .

Various services and manufacturing sectors dominate the economy. Jakarta, like large Indian cities, struggles with its image. It has fancy shopping malls, hotels, and business plazas, but also megaslums that literally hold millions of people living in squalor. It has been celebrated for its potential and growth, but has yet to deal with the inequalities that define its landscapes.

9.5 Standing Together: Economic Cooperation in the Twenty-First Century

The final discussion about Southeast Asia and the Island Realm is about regional cooperation. As discussed in Chapter 2, the origin of the European Union was partially born between the BENELUX leaders during their wartime exile in England. They agreed that their proximity and shared interests would be better served by an agreement that could help them align their shared goals and circumvent the barriers that inhibited trade. These included addressing labor issues, trade tariffs, various disputes, finance and capital needs, and softening borders. This "Benelux Agreement" provided the DNA for what would become the European Union. Southeast Asian nations watched how Japan, India, China, and South Korea all transformed into globalized economies and wanted to follow suit. Apart from Singapore, each nation had to make necessary political changes and create economic incentives to attract FDI. Although they have generally had some success, there were still barriers, and the nations of Southeast Asia, like the Europeans (EU) and North Americans (NAFTA), would form a cooperative community of nations to stand together in their push to develop.

ASEAN

ASEAN, or the *Association of Southeast Asian Nations*, started in 1967. As the world globalized and nations in the region began their own paths to development, the association has grown to ten member nations. These include the *core ten:* Brunei, Cambodia, Indonesia, Laos, Malaysia, Myanmar, Philippines,

FIGURE 9.5a. ASEAN is Southeast Asia's supranational organization to promote economic, political, and environmental cooperation between the ten member nations.

Copyright © Gunawan Kartapranata (CC BY-SA 3.0) at https://commons.wikimedia.org/wiki/File%3AASEAN_HQ_1.jpg .

Singapore, Thailand, and Vietnam. ASEAN seeks to facilitate economic growth, maintain a platform for peaceful disputes, soften borders, address cultural and environmental problems, and strengthen the region's economic and political voice within a larger community of nations and supranational organizations. ASEAN is headquartered in Indonesia and has enabled the region to collectively ascend to the eighth-largest (collective) economy in the world. Their collective GDP is about $3.6 trillion, and they represent about 9% of the global population. ASEAN is widely accepted as a supranational entity and should continue to shape the region in the future.

CONCLUSION

The Southeast Asian and Island Realm is indeed intriguing, in many ways. It is a rather geographically discontinuous region that includes continental Eurasia, a peninsular region, and archipelagos that have not only literally thousands of islands, but some of the most populated islands on Earth. Geologically, few places on Earth, if any, are as active. Volcanism and seismic activities have and will continue to shape the landscape. Sometimes, catastrophic events occur, like the 2004 earthquake and tsunami. The region has roughly 650 million people, many of whom live in some of Earth's most important and biodiverse "hotspots." And this biodiversity is threatened by human activities like deforestation and land-use change for palm oil plantations. When forests are burned in this region, they sometimes release six times the carbon into the atmosphere than in the Amazon. Additionally, natural habitats for many species are threatened by these activities.

Perhaps no other region has the religious landscape of Southeast Asia. As discussed earlier in the chapter, much of the region was once predominately Hindu. But those "Indianized" cultures of mainland Southeast Asia eventually succumbed to the rising popularity of Buddhism. In other parts of the region, Islam and Catholicism became well established." Indonesia has the largest population of Muslims on Earth. The region has also been a hotbed of war and military action. The Imperial Japanese took the region for a decade, and then the Cold War turned hot in Vietnam when the French and then Americans fought for years to keep communism at bay. Despite these conflicts, the nations of the region cooperated and changed to join the globalized economy. Many of them have been able to elevate many out of poverty and raise the quality of life for their people, while others, like Myanmar, are still struggling with the past. Although these countries have some contradictions to address, they have joined together in a supranational organization

KEY TERMS

(ASEAN) and are facing the future together.	Chinese and Indian influences	Vietnam War
Islands and Peninsulas	Buddhism	Sex Tourism
Ring of Fire	Islam	Emerging economies
Tsunami/Earthquake	Colonial landscapes	Palm oil
Tropical climate	Imperial Japanese	Major cities
Ancient cultures	Communism	Capitalism

CLASS DISCUSSIONS

Association of Southeast Asian Nations (ASEAN)
1. Describe the religious landscapes of Southeast Asia and the Island Realm.
2. Discuss the problems associated with the production of palm oil in the region.
3. Describe any three of the region's major cities.
4. Explain why the nations of the region formed ASEAN.

ADDITIONAL RESOURCES

ASEAN:

http://www.state.gov/p/eap/regional/asean/

Ring of Fire:

http://geography.about.com/cs/earthquakes/a/ringoffire.htm

River:

http://www.greatriverspartnership.org/en-us/asiapacific/mekong/pages/default.aspx

Vietnam War:

http://www.history.com/topics/vietnam-war/vietnam-war-history/

BIBLIOGRAPHY

"Association of Southeast Asian Nations (ASEAN)." US Department of State. US Department of State, n.d. Web. http://www.state.gov/p/eap/regional/asean/. June–July 2015.

Clyde, P.H. and B.F. Beers (1975). The Far East. Prentice Hall. New Jersey.

"The Economics of Commercial Sexual Exploitation." Pulitzer Center. N.p., 25 Aug. 2009. Web. http://pulitzercenter.org/blog/untold-stories/economics-commercial-sexual-exploitation. May–June 2015.

Harvey, D. (2003). The New Imperialism. Oxford University Press. Oxford, UK.

Karnow, S. (1991). Vietnam: A History. Viking. New York.

"Khmer Empire." Ancient History Encyclopedia. N.p., n.d. Web. http://www.ancient.eu/Khmer_Empire/. May–June 2015.

"Largest Cities in Southeast Asia." Largest Cities in Southeast Asia. N.p., n.d. Web. http://www.mongabay.com/igapo/Southeast_Asia.htm. June–July 2015.

McKeown, A. (1999). Conceptualizing Chinese Diasporas, 1842 to 1949. The Journal of Asian Studies. Vol. 58. No. 2. pp. 306–337.

"Mekong River Basin." Mekong River Basin. N.p., n.d. Web. http://www.greatriverspartnership.org/en-us/asiapacific/mekong/pages/default.aspx. May–June 2015.

"Myanmar Profile—Overview—BBC News." BBC News. N.p., n.d. Web. http://www.bbc.com/news/world-asia-pacific-12990563. June–July 2015.

"Palm Oil." WWF. N.p., n.d. Web. http://wwf.panda.org/what_we_do/footprint/agriculture/palm_oil/. June–July 2015.

Rosenberg, Matt. "The Pacific Ring of Fire." N.p., n.d. Web. http://geography.about.com/cs/earthquakes/a/ringoffire.htm. May–June 2015.

CHAPTER 10

East Asia

Key Themes:

Political, cultural, economic, environmental

List of countries:
- China (including Hong Kong)
- Japan
- Mongolia
- North Korea
- South Korea
- Taiwan

10.1 Regional Overview

In many important ways, East Asia represents more than just a region. It has been argued that economic and political power is perhaps shifting away from Western epicenters to the East. Western powers have shaped and controlled much of the world over the past several hundred years through centuries of European colonialism and decades of American economic, political, and military dominance. Today, China has become a primary node of production, has the potential to build a middle class that would dwarf that of the United States and Europe, and has the capital and an unencumbered political system to fundamentally influence the way the

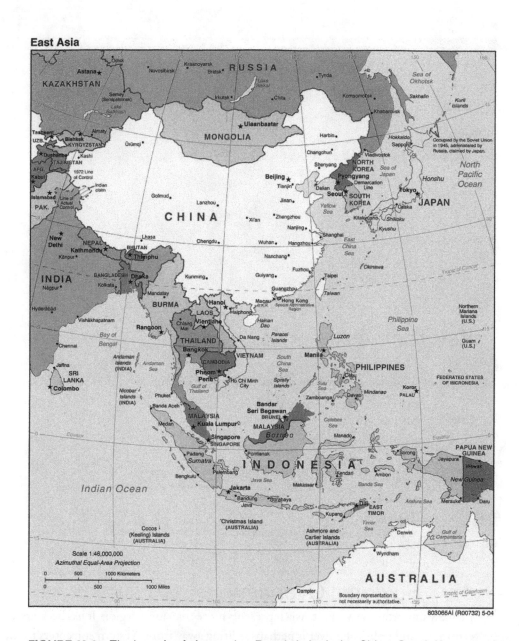

FIGURE 10.0a. The broader Asian realm. East Asia includes China, South Korea, and Japan, to name a few.
Copyright in the Public Domain.

world works. The Chinese are already buying more oil than the United States. They have altered the global flow of commodities and raw materials. They are currently, along with their BRICS partners, redefining how development and emerging markets are financed, which would then alter political allegiances. And, alarmingly for the United States and Europe, they are posturing themselves to assume a more active role in regional security matters in the Eastern Hemisphere. These shifts are more than just regional characteristics; they are signs that the world is potentially changing.

East Asia is important to understand in other ways. Many of the products we buy and use every day are made by East Asian companies and built and shipped around the world from their ports. Also, cultures from the region are often present in communities around the world. The United States, Canada, Southeast Asia, Europe, and so on all have significant Chinese populations. Tens of thousands of Korean and Chinese college students are attending American and European universities. Food from the region is easily found in the biggest cities down to the smallest towns. This cultural ubiquity all has origins in East Asia.

PHYSICAL REALM

Understanding East Asia's physical geography is an important part of understanding the human narratives and activities of the region. The region can roughly be divided subregions. The four (4) subregions of East Asia are:

- *Plateaus and Steppes:* Including the massive Tibetan Plateau and the Eurasian Steppes of the eastern realm.
- *The Gobi Desert:* Covers much of northern China and southern Mongolia.
- *Eastern Realm*: Includes China's populated eastern region.
- *Jakota Triangle*: Includes the maritime peninsula and islands.

The (1) *Tibetan Plateau* is a large, yet remote, part of China, located on the northern slope region of the Himalayas. The subregion is generally high altitude, but has plentiful water. Not unlike the *Altiplano* of South America, the Tibetans have thrived in the harsh condition of the area for centuries, if not longer. Many of Asia's important rivers (Ganges, Indus, Mekong, Red, and Pearl) headwater in this region. Conditions make life hard, but it is home to some hardy species like yaks, hawks, and even a high-altitude jumping spider that can live at twenty-two thousand feet.

The (2) *Gobi Desert* is a cold desert. Remember, deserts are determined, not by their temperature, but by their aridity. Although it can reach unpleasantly hot temperatures during summer, that is due more to the broader region's continentality and the absence of a large body of water to mediate the energy. Generally, a high-pressure system forms over the region during the winter months, which makes the Gobi and surrounding areas cold and dry. Winds descend in a counterclockwise motion during these months, sending the cold, dry air to eastern China and

FIGURE 10.1a. The Tibetan Plateau is high in altitude, remote, but has water. This subregion is home to the headwaters of many major rivers in South Asia, Southeast Asian, and East Asia.
Copyright © Reurinkjan (CC BY 2.0) at https://commons.wikimedia.org/wiki/File%3ANamTso_scene.jpg .

FIGURE 10.1b. The Gobi Desert is a cold, dry desert. Copyright © Severin.stalder (CC BY-SA 3.0) at https://commons.wikimedia.org/wiki/File%3AKhongoryn_Els%2C_Gurvansaikhan_NP%2C_Gobi_desert%2C_Mongolia.jpg .

North Korea. During summer, a low forms over the Gobi, but the air it draws is low in moisture, thus maintaining enough aridity to keep it a desert climate. The Gobi will be discussed in more detail later, because it is currently a major region for mining.

The (3) *Eastern Realm* and the (4) *Jakota Triangle* will together be the most-discussed subregions. The reason is both geographical and demographic. Geographically, China's eastern third is similar to the climate and patterns of the United States. The latitude is similar, which means the south is more subtropical

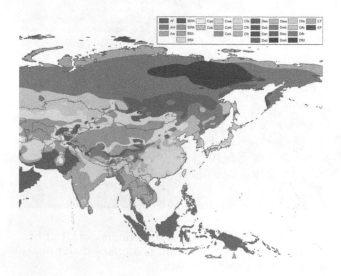

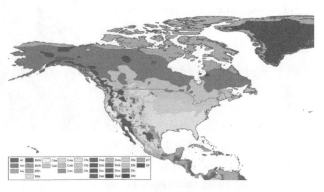

FIGURE 10.1c(1). Köppen Climate map of Asia reveals how China and the United States (Figure 10.1c) have similar climate types.
Copyright © M.C. Peel, B.L. Finlayson, and T.A. McMahon (CC BY-SA 3.0) at https://commons.wikimedia.org/wiki/File%3AAsia_Köppen_Map.png.

FIGURE 10.1c(2).
Copyright © M.C. Peel, B.L. Finlayson, and T.A. McMahon (CC BY-SA 3.0) at https://commons.wikimedia.org/wiki/File%3ANorth-America_Köppen_Map.png .

FIGURE 10.1d. Japanese landscapes are shaped by a temperate climate, which includes good average precipitation. Copyright © 663highland (CC BY-SA 3.0) at https://commons.wikimedia.org/wiki/File%3AWakayama_Yosuien07bs4272.jpg .

and the north is more seasonal. In other words, whereas the south is generally wetter, more humid, and sometimes vulnerable to tropical storms, the north can be cold and snowy (see *Figures 10.1c (1) & (2)*).

Like the United States, most Chinese live in the eastern third of the country, with a majority living within three hundred miles of the ocean. Unlike the US, China does not have a west coast. Instead, it has the formidable *steppe* region of central Asia. The Eastern Realm has fertile soils provided by large river systems, good average rainfall, and a generally pleasant temperate climate. This is due to proximity to the ocean. The *Jakota Triangle* is the maritime subregion. It includes South Korea, which sits on a peninsula juxtaposed into the ocean, and the island nations of Japan and Taiwan. As *Figures 10.1c (1) and (2)* reveal, Japan has a similar climate to the northwestern United States.

Major River Systems

The Eastern Realm subregion is home to three major river systems. The *Huang He River*, also known as the "Yellow River," headwaters in the northern extent of the Tibetan Plateau and loops around the Ordos Desert and deltas in the Bohai Gulf of northern China. In total, this river flows 3,395 miles, making it the second-longest river in East Asia. This river system plays an important role in agriculture and industrialization, and is a key water resource for Beijing, other cities, and the surrounding provinces. The river has great anthropological importance, because it was the site of the earliest civilizations in China. The first signs of agriculture and early society were found in the river's delta region, giving it the distinction as the "cradle of Chinese civilization." Today, the Huang He, despite its size, is unable to support China's growing cities and industrial needs alone. Projects to take water from the Yangtze River, hundreds of miles to the south, are already being planned. Likewise, the river flows through the western city of Lanzhou, which, as part of the state's "Go West" campaign, has become a destination for

FIGURE 10.1e. Lanzhou, China is a "western" city with the newest Special Economic Zone. This will attract more industry and increase water use from the Huang He.
Fig. 10.1e Copyright in the Public Domain.

manufacturing. Water needs are increasing in this region, which will then reduce what can be used further downstream in densely populated and industrial areas.

The *Yangtze River* is not only China's longest river, but Asia's as well. It runs nearly four thousand miles from the Tibetan Plateau to the East China Sea, near the megacity of Shanghai. The Yangtze is a critical feature of middle and eastern China, providing water needs for hundreds of millions of people, agriculture, hydroelectric power, transportation, and tourism. In 2006, the *Three Gorges Dam* was completed, which significantly changed the river system and caused environmental problems (see *Thematic Intersection 10b*).

FIGURE 10.1f. Cargo ship on the Yangtze River.
Copyright © Photnart (CC BY-SA 4.0) at https://commons.wikimedia.org/wiki/File%3AA_container_carrier_on_yangtze.jpg .

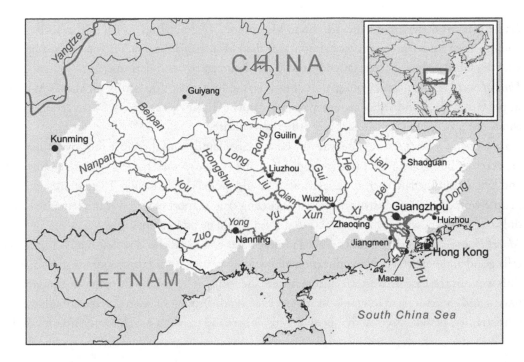

FIGURE 10.1g. Map of the Pearl River complex.
Copyright © Kmusser (CC BY-SA 3.0) at https://commons.wikimedia.org/wiki/
File%3AZhujiangrivermap.png .

Finally, the *Pearl River* complex is China's third longest, but it has the second-highest discharge, next to the Yangtze. The river is fed by dozens of other rivers (like the Dong River) which span from the Tibetan Plateau to rivers in the east. The Pearl is very important for global trade because it links major industrial and manufacturing cities, like Guangzhou and the Special Economic Zones of Shenzhen, to the delta-coastal urban complexes of Hong Kong and Macau.

10.2 Historical and Cultural Influences

A discussion about historical and cultural influences on East Asia must begin by examining an ancient paradigm that is fundamentally different from those which shaped Western cultures. Eastern philosophies, centered in China, revolved around several basic notions or *early eastern social philosophies*. These included:

- *Status*: Man was believed to be born into a particular social level, and was generally expected to remain there. This should not be confused with the Hindu caste system in India; it is more a strong belief that one's path is clear and, to a degree, predetermined. For example, if a father was a fisherman, then it was expected that his son would be as well. This promoted unity between father and son, and was an effective way to pass skills down from one generation to another.

- *Duty*: A man's duty, it was believed, was to his "station." One's station, or his role in society and his commitment to that role, was more important than his personal "rights." This may shed light on why the Chinese have been accused by the West of human rights violations.
- *Unit of Society*: The primary obligation of man was to his family. The family (or clan) was more important than an individual, country, or government. This helps explain why rugged individualism is not a virtue in China like it is in American culture.
- *Nature of Government*: The state was viewed as a large family, and therefore the government was expected to be a good parent to the people. If people were expected to be good citizens, neighbors, and live within the law, then the government should model that behavior. To guarantee the best people would serve in government posts, a grueling examination system was implemented, and only the most knowledgeable, moral, and dutiful would be offered positions.
- *Moral Foundations*: Early Chinese social philosophies embraced the idea that man is fundamentally good and believed that an education allowed a man to cultivate the goodness in his nature. This was not the case in Western culture, where the Romans believed that man was fundamentally flawed and therefore had to employ a strong, even rigid, system of laws to coerce compliance. Christianity, as well, asserted that people were sinners and they must seek forgiveness for their sins.

FIGURE 10.2a. Taoist Temple in Southern China.
Copyright © 江上清风 (CC BY-SA 3.0) at https://commons.wikimedia.org/wiki/File%3AGolden_Lotus_Taoist_Temple_on_Jingshan_top%2C_in_Lucheng%2C_Wenzhou%2C_Zhejiang%2C_China.jpg .

Ways of Being

Confucianism, or the social philosophies of Confucius, embraced and expanded upon these early notions. Confucius was a teacher and philosopher in China around 500 BCE. Less a religion and more a code of ethics and social philosophy, Confucian teachings were officially sanctioned by the Han Dynasty and became a deeply rooted aspect of Chinese culture. He stressed the importance of good moral character, education, and the *Five Relationships*, which included (1) prince–minister; (2) parent–child; (3) husband–wife; (4) elder–younger brother; and (5) friend–friend. Through these relationships came strength in society. Arguably, Confucius would be the most profound influence on Chinese culture.

Buddhism and *Taoism* (Daoism) were and remain important influences on Chinese culture. Although the origin of Buddhism in China is debated, it is known that it eventually became adopted by many Chinese around the third century CE. The Chinese did not see Buddhism so much as a replacement for Confucian philosophies, but as having spiritual appeal. This informed Chinese architecture, customs, and complemented more Taoist philosophies.

Taoism is a "way of teaching" or way of being that is sometimes considered a religion. It is viewed as a "path" for understanding balance achieved through simplicity. Nature, it is viewed, is the simple and natural state, and humans and our activities must therefore seek to achieve greater balance with nature's primordial state. This has influenced various aspects of Chinese culture like *feng shui*, or the practice of achieving natural harmony in urban planning, building design, and even interior decorating. Architecture firms in Hong Kong and Taipei, Taiwan specialize in this skill. These three ways of being are considered the DNA of Chinese culture.

CHINESE REGIONAL DOMINANCE

With the consolidation of the various empires under the Han, the Chinese were finally able to establish a powerful and influential empire in the region. This empire was very large, stretching from the northern realm in Manchuria to modern-day Vietnam in Southeast Asia. The Han Dynasty embraced Confucian political philosophies, which meant it had effective leadership, from the village level to the capital city. It embraced Buddhist and Taoist ways of being, which meant architecture and other aspects of culture would spread throughout the region. In the end, the Chinese would begin to influence the broader region. Koreans and even the Japanese, who were visited early on by Chinese traders and Buddhist monks, would adopt aspects of Chinese culture.

As time went on, the Chinese would become a great naval power, during the fifth century CE, under Admiral Zheng He. Zheng He was commissioned by the Emperor to go on a number of voyages, reportedly with a fleet of giant, well-armed ships. These voyages would reduce piracy in the region and travel far enough (Africa, Middle East) to show the world the power of the Chinese. Europe had yet to become a maritime power. However, this would come to an end, and the Chinese would assume an isolationist posture until the British arrived centuries later.

JAPAN: ISOLATIONISM TO IMPERIALISM

Until the 1860s, Japanese history is more removed from the rest of East Asia than a part it. Although early Chinese traders were able to enter and influence Japanese culture (Buddhism, architecture, written characters, etc.), Japan deliberately remained isolated for centuries, with few exceptions. Portuguese Jesuits were able to enter Japan in the 1500s and introduce their *Samurai* culture to more modern European weapons. The Japanese used these weapons to invade Korea. But that was short lived. Within Japan was a strong feudal system headed by regional *daimyos* who answered to *Shoguns*, or emperors. Each *daimyo* (noble) had his own *samurai*, who followed a strict code that required him to pledge his life and loyalty to his *daimyo*. This **samurai** **code** was known as *bushido,* which included:

- Frugality (a Buddhist ideal)
- Loyalty (Japanese ideal)
- Martial-arts mastery
- Honor until death
- Wisdom (early eastern philosophy from China/Korea, possibly Taoism)

Eventually, the Americans, under Commodore Perry, would bully their way into Japan and influence a restoration and period of modernization. The Japanese would adopt a constitution and begin the process of industrialization. However, having been a *samurai* culture, they militarized quickly and went to war with both China and Russia to expand their interests.

The Japanese continued to militarize and eventually negotiated not to be interfered with by the British or Americans, leading to a hostile military expansion all over East Asia, Southeast Asia, and the Pacific Realm.

FIGURE 10.2b. Chinese surrendering to modern fighting force of Japan in 1894.
Copyright in the Public Domain.

CASE STUDY 10A

Japanese Cruelty and the Legacy of Regional Resentment

Japan today is generally a peaceful nation with a rich culture, strong heritage, and fascinating history. However, during the era of imperial expansion into East Asia and World War II, some Japanese officers and soldiers exhibited unspeakable cruelty towards the Chinese, Koreans, and Southeast Asians, as well as Allied combatants, including American soldiers. Their strategy to overwhelm an enemy with military force was often supported by a drive to shatter the hearts and minds of the enemy as well. Below are some examples of Japanese cruelty:

- Rape of Nanking: Japanese combat troops attacked the capital city of Nanking in 1937. The brutality of the event has been widely reported to include the random beheading and bayoneting of thousands of Chinese troops, the systematic execution of citizens, and the rape of thousands of Chinese women by Japanese soldiers.

- Distribution of Opium: The Japanese were accused of using morphia, an opium derivative, to help subjugate the Chinese people in populated areas through coordinated distribution systems.

- Bataan Death March: After losing a battle over Bataan, Philippines in 1942, the POWs (Filipino and America) were marched in harsh conditions over miles of rainforest, resulting in the death of thousands of Filipino soldiers and hundreds of US soldiers.

- "Comfort Brigades": Japanese soldiers would often have access to what they called "comfort brigades," which were composed of women and children from occupied China, Malaysia, and the Philippines. These women were raped by Japanese soldiers at will.

FIGURE 10.2c(1). Japanese soldier about to behead an Australian soldier.
Copyright in the Public Domain.

FIGURE 10.2c(2). Japanese soldiers would practice bayoneting with dead bodies in China.
Copyright in the Public Domain.

FIGURE 10.2c(3). Japanese "comfort brigades" were composed of Chinese, Malay, and Filipino women and girls, who were forced to have sex with Japanese combat troops.
Copyright in the Public Domain.

This is not to say these behaviors were exclusive to Japanese soldiers. Reports of misconduct sometimes followed Americans and Chinese troops during this period as well. However, the scale of these atrocities left an indelible stain on history, and the Chinese and Koreans, to this day, still exhibit cultural animosities towards the Japanese.

EUROPEAN COLONIALISM

Although both the Japanese and Chinese showed isolationist tendencies and a standoffish posture towards European and American attempts to exert control, they both ultimately succumbed. China maintained a firm position about isolationism but allowed the Portuguese to conduct trade on Macau. The British EIC, under similar dynamics, was eventually able to convince the Chinese to allow trade on China's islands in the southern Canton region (Hong Kong, today).

BOX 10.A THE OPIUM WARS (1839–1842)

The East India Company was both powerful and influential. It not only held a monopoly on trade in South Asia; it was also able to challenge local monopolies that existed in East Asia. Because opium was so profitable, the EIC began shipping it to markets in Canton. Because they could not, themselves, sell it within mainland China, they employed middlemen to carry the product within the reclusive nation. When the Chinese learned of this and saw the effects of opium (addiction, wealth generation), the Emperor appointed an officer to confront the British and abolish the trade. The Chinese seized and destroyed a giant cargo of opium without consulting the British or offering a settlement. Although the EIC knew they had no legal standing, they called in naval warships to quickly and decisively attack and defeat the Chinese. The British victory led to new negotiations that ultimately resulted in a second war. The British proved to be too powerful, despite being grossly outnumbered. The treaty that followed would include the legal use of Hong Kong as a British colony. This would become part of the larger narrative about how the Chinese have become one of the largest economies on Earth.

WORLD WAR II

World War II was arguably the most transformative human event in world history. It touched, either directly or indirectly, almost every region and resulted in the emergence of a different world. East Asia was a part of the war arena and struggled through years of occupation, epic battles, and catastrophic loss of lives. The Chinese, having endured the longest-lasting hostilities from Japan, immediately shifted into a civil war after the Japanese surrendered. The Americans, as an alternative to a full invasion, elected to use new atomic (nuclear) weapons on Japan. Two bombs were dropped on Japanese cities, and they surrendered quickly in the wake of the destruction. This fundamentally changed the way conflicts would be viewed in the future.

If both sides had nuclear weapons, then total annihilation was possible. Nations like the Soviet Union, UK, France, and China all developed nuclear weapons immediately after the war. The war also induced an epic global demographic phenomenon. Within fifteen years after the end of the war, many countries had giant "baby booms." East Asian countries would all experience radical shifts in their populations.

Finally, the American occupation of Japan was largely uncontested. Unlike other countries, the Japanese accepted defeat in a fight they viewed as fair. This reflects the *bushido* culture. Instead of fighting from the underground, they worked with Americans to rebuild a modern Japan. This gave the Japanese an edge during their path to reindustrialize. Not only did they have new infrastructure and modern factories, they also had ties to the giant consumer markets of the United States, who would become a close ally. Terrible conflict between Japan and the United States resulted in a lasting cooperation and political friendship that continues on today.

FIGURE 10.2d. Atomic explosion over Nagasaki, Japan in 1945.
Copyright in the Public Domain.

10.3 Political Conflict

COMMUNIST REVOLUTION IN CHINA

Following China's united effort to defeat the Japanese, communist and nationalist factions within the country refocused on each other after the war. Mao Zedong, as communist leader, had inspired millions of rural poor Chinese to join his cause. He militarized them and then began to reassert himself politically after the war. The National Party, known as the *Kuomintang*, formed the National Revolutionary Army (1928), headed by Generalissimo (and later President) Chiang Kai-shek, and was wrought with corruption and dysfunction. Mao was able to secure a victory on the mainland, and Chiang fled to the island of Taiwan to rule from Taipei. The Chinese, now communist, rejected his claim to the presidency, and thus began decades of tension between Taiwan and China. In China, the communists consolidated under Mao, and by the 1950s, they once again became isolationists.

FIGURE 10.3a. Communist Chinese soldier in front of a giant portrait of Chairman Mao, at the Forbidden City. Copyright © Christophe Meneboeuf (CC BY-SA 3.0) at https://commons. wikimedia.org/wiki/File%3AForbiddenCity_ MaoZedongPortrait_(pixinn.net).jpg .

THEMATIC INTERSECTION 10A

Hong Kong: a Template for Change

Themes: Political/Economic

Hong Kong had become a sovereign British colony, as a condition of a treaty signed with the Chinese, after their defeat in the Opium Wars. As the region grew, more territories would be added to the British colony, eventually leading to the formal area known as Hong Kong today. Because the British did not treat this as an invasion, they negotiated with the Chinese to have full economic control and exercise security for the territory as conditions of an agreed-upon one hundred-year lease. This was signed in 1898 and expired in 1997. However, China changed over the course of those hundred years.

First, the Japanese defeated the British and occupied Hong Kong for about four years. After the war, the British had to reclaim and reoperationalize the territory. During this time, the Chinese Revolution was in full swing, and the communist People's Liberation Army was victorious. The British feared Mao would not honor their lease, so they reinforced the borders around Hong Kong and strengthened their

FIGURE 10.3b. Hong Kong was a British colony between the mid-nineteenth century and 1997. Copyright © chensiyuan (CC BY-SA 4.0) at https://commons.wikimedia.org/wiki/File%3A1_hongkong_panorama_victoria_peak_2011.JPG .

garrison in case of confrontation. This did not happen, and Mao honored the lease. However, as the date approached, the PRC (People's Republic of China) and British signed the Sino-British Joint Declaration that the Chinese would peacefully reacquire Hong Kong under the conditions that it remain "capitalist" for fifty years beyond the expiration of the lease. The Chinese agreed, and in 1997, they embraced the spirit of the agreement with what they referred to as "one country, two systems," and made Hong Kong a "Special Administrative Region of the People's Republic of China."

This political narrative of leases and agreements was really about facilitating economic activities. The British made Hong Kong a vibrant and typically profitable territory. When the Chinese took it over, it was as if they were given New York City. It had modern infrastructure and engaged in a broad range of economic activities like manufacturing, services, trade, and tourism. The Chinese, who would allow a high degree of sovereignty, realized that they could maintain their political system while allowing "special" areas more freedoms. Thus, Hong Kong's "Special Administrative Region" became the template for the "Special Economic Zones (SEZs)" that have attracted so much FDI and enabled China to become one of the largest economies on Earth.

TWO KOREAS

Korea had been occupied by the Japanese for almost a half century. Immediately following their defeat in 1945, the Soviet Union declared war on them. The United States was in the process of occupying both Japan and Japanese-controlled Korea, but it allowed the Soviets to occupy northern Korea, above the 38th parallel (latitude), as a concession. This became a mistake, because the Soviets supported the spread of communism and declared that the North Korean government was the legitimate government. South Korea, with the support of the United States, declared itself the legitimate government.

In 1950, North Korea, with the support of the Soviets and Chinese troops, invaded the southern peninsula and drove the Korean army all the way to the sea. The United Nations responded by sending troops, with limited success, so the United States went to war. The ground battles were ferocious, and many on both sides were lost. However, the Americans used jet aircraft to "carpet bomb" the North Koreans and Chinese units while engaging in "dogfights" with jet fighters. The war ended with an armistice that recognized a "demilitarized zone," or DMZ, and established the 38th parallel as the border between two nations.

10.4 The Economic Rise of the East

Discussions about the rise of East Asia as a "collective" economic superregion must include "Western" narratives. In *Thematic Intersection 10a*, the influence of the capitalist British colony of Hong Kong was highlighted as an inspiration for the Chinese to create

FIGURE 10.3c. North and South Korea at night reveals a lot. The two countries evolved very differently, after the Korean War. North Korea remained totalitarian-communist, while South Korea embraced industrialization. The two nations, apart from a shared past, have little in common, today.
Copyright in the Public Domain.

other "special zones." These SEZs, as they are called, are engines of the Chinese economy today. Likewise, the American occupation of Japan led to the United States, through the Marshall Plan, supporting their reconstruction efforts. Japan got new factories, new infrastructure, and a new alliance that would eventually foster one of the largest trade partnerships in world history. While these "Western" narratives help explain the foundation of change, they do not address other internal and external factors that explain their ascension. Several of these are directly related to the West.

THE RISING SUN OF JAPAN'S ECONOMY

Japan was the first East Asian economy to grow and eventually surpass every nation in the world, except for the United States. Japanese industrialization was swift and efficient. Their economic model was quite different, in that large family corporations, like Mitsubishi, were inflated into huge conglomerates that included banks and subsidiaries while receiving full governmental support. Beyond that, the several giant family conglomerates purchased interests in each other on the assumption that it would strengthen Japan's overall economy and foster economic stability. This economic model would likely have been deemed illegal in the United States because of legislation preventing monopolies.

Japan had limited natural resources, which made them focus more on innovation and high-technology goods. They became an automobile giant because they were the first to use robotic automation, lighter materials, and higher-quality electrical infrastructure in cars. This would directly compete with Detroit, which was still building cars by hand on assembly lines. Also, the energy crisis of the 1970s made big American gas guzzlers less appealing and the lighter, more energy-efficient Japanese cars more desirable.

Japan, in addition to changing the automobile industry, changed home entertainment as well. They developed VCRs, stereo systems, DVDs, CDs, and other devices that would find their way into homes around the world. American business schools started studying Japanese business models, and though they were a top trade partner, they also became a threatening competitor in the free market. The Japanese "bubble economy," however, would burst, and though the Japanese have remained a top producer, their strengths remain in high technology, innovative technologies, and financial endeavors.

SHIFTS IN GLOBAL PRODUCTION

Japan's automation outcompeted human productivity in the United States, and many factories closed. At the same time, union labor agreements were increasingly expensive in a more competitive global arena. Industry, then, sought new avenues—or more accurately, locations—of production. *Least Cost Theory* helps us understand this shift of manufacturing from the factories in America's northeast quadrant to places like Taiwan and China. If the right incentives are present—like low labor costs, lower tax rates, low cost of fuel to offset shipping costs, and available unskilled, semiskilled, and skilled labor pools—then manufacturing could be outsourced. Asia offered these incentives, and manufacturing, as well as industries that support manufacturing (agglomeration), made it more profitable to leave the United States. Between the 1970s and 2015, manufacturing has declined significantly, and the manufacturing that is returning is typically fully automated and does not require armies of machinists, as they once did.

THE CHINESE "MIRACLE"

China's ascension to economic dominance is complicated, but can be fairly easily contextualized through the examination of several key factors. One is the failure of the *Great Leap Forward,* or Mao's attempt to collectivize the nation's human and natural resources into a strong internal economy. He sought to do this by forming people into "communes," or units of people that give up everything for the community. Ultimately, he felt this would grow the economy until it reached and exceeded that of the United States. This failed, and millions of Chinese died from starvation. In the mid-1960s, Mao believed capitalist sentiments were returning and launched what he called the "Cultural Revolution," which was little more than reasserting rigid communistic ideology. This also failed, and by the time Mao passed in 1976, China was dysfunctional, starving, and backwards.

Although it took time, the Chinese would implement many reforms to modernize and industrialize in ways that could strengthen their economy. President Nixon's visit in 1972, though it was done for political reasons, helped to soften relations between the US and China. A series of pacts made between the two paved the way for more risks to be taken in China to bolster an increasingly open economic system. By the time the Chinese reacquired Hong Kong, a modern and global city that generated great wealth, China was readying itself to use this as a platform for expansion in the mainland. Special Economic Zones (SEZs) were created in cities like Shenzhen, Shanghai, and Guangzhou, for example, and they offer several important incentives for foreign business within that space. These include:

- Low taxes
- No or light import and export regulations
- Simplified land leases
- Power for foreign firms to negotiate labor contracts
- Profits can go back to home country of manufacturer

FIGURE 10.4a. Port of Shanghai's Special Economic Zones and ports are amongst the largest in the world.
Copyright in the Public Domain.

The creation of SEZs proved to be a huge success for the Chinese. They experienced more than a decade of double-digit economic growth. They became the number one exporter on the planet. They passed the Japanese as the second-largest economy on Earth, and they are moving towards more state control of production, for economic stability. Currently, China has a GDP of seventeen trillion and is still growing their economy by about 7% each year. It has been speculated that China may surpass the United States, economically, in several measurable ways in the near future.

Appetite for Energy

China's appetite for energy has grown with its economy. When examining China's energy production versus consumption (and, in some cases reserves), and then comparing that to those of the United States, interesting patterns are unveiled. For example, in 2012 the United States produced (extracted) 1,016,458 thousand short tons of coal, whereas the Chinese produced 4,017,920. In terms of consumption, the US consumed 889,185 thousand short tons of coal, or about 87% of that produced, whereas the Chinese consumed 3,887,264 thousand short tons, or about 96% of what they produced. The United States also has roughly twice the reserves, which means stock is growing.

Natural gas, on the other hand, has become an increasingly important part of America's energy budget. For example, the United States produced 24,058 billion cubic feet of natural gas in 2012, but used 26,037 billion cubic feet. The US had to import the difference. China only produced 3,666 billion cubic feet of natural gas and used 5,707 billion cubic feet. Like the US, they also had to import the rest. This reveals two things: one is that the Chinese rely largely on coal energy, which produces much more pollution and particulates; and the US is trying to pivot away from coal, despite high reserves, to natural gas. China recently surpassed the US as the top contributor of carbon dioxide on Earth.

FIGURE 10.4b. A coal barge in China.
Copyright © Rob Loftis (CC BY-SA 3.0) at https://commons.wikimedia.org/wiki/File%3ACoal_hopper_with_barge_Rob_Loftis.jpeg .

THEMATIC INTERSECTION 10B

The Three Gorges Dam: Politics and the Environment in China

Themes: Political/Environmental

The Three Gorges Dam, built in China's midland east on the Yangtze River, is the largest hydroelectric generator in the world. During construction, the Chinese used more concrete than any other project in history, inducing a global concrete shortage. The dam, though not a new idea (Mao originally considered a similar project), was hastily conceived and quickly executed. Despite warnings about potential environmental problems, the Chinese government disregarded them and moved forward. To facilitate the dam, approximately 1.2 million people would have to be relocated, which included more than one hundred villages. Many dislocated Chinese were compensated about $7 per year for their troubles. The goals of

FIGURE 10.4c. China's Three Gorges Dam is the largest hydroelectric dam in the world, but inflicts many environmental problems. Copyright © gugganij (CC BY-SA 3.0) at https://commons.wikimedia.org/wiki/File%3ADrei-Schluchten-Damm_(Jangtse).jpg .

the dam were to provide energy for a growing economy and control flooding, which has the potential to be devastating. The mouth of the river is at the global megacity of Shanghai. Shanghai is one of China's manufacturing and shipping hubs, as well as its wealthiest city. Floods could potentially threaten the city, so the dam was built quickly. These benefits illuminate the political incentive to build the dam.

Because the dam was built in haste, many environmental problems have surfaced. Although the Chinese government was dismissive about the potential of these problems before the dam was built, it reluctantly accepts them now. These environmental problems include:

1. *Landslides:* The natural river valley where the Three Gorges meet was greatly disrupted by the filling of the dam. Water flooded in to fill an area 410 miles long and up to 575 feet, which is much deeper than the natural river and twice as wide (see Figure 10.3g). The slopes around the river, then, would soak up water at and around the new surface and destabilize the thousands of tons of earth above it, thereby inducing landslides. There have been hundreds of landslides, several of which took lives.

2. *Seismic Activity:* The dam was built over the Jiuwangxi and Zigui-Badon faults. Geologists warned of the pressure water weight can have on faults, as seen previously in Oroville, California. These warnings went ignored, and there have been hundreds of earthquakes, some of which were over six on the Richter scale.

3. *Ecosystems:* The flooding of the river valley has impacted the biodiversity of the region and has induced microclimate shifts. This region of China is very biodiverse and has reduced tens of thousands of acres of habitat, disrupted fish ecosystems, and induced changes in precipitation patterns (flood, drought).

4. *Fresh/Salt Barrier:* Because the flow of the Yangtze was reduced by the dam, salt water has crept up the river further than ever before. The presence of jellyfish in the Yangtze was previously unknown, and they have affected indigenous fish populations. Salt is also getting into the groundwater, salinizing agricultural areas. Shanghai has also had water shortages. Disease has also increased the incidence of schistosomiasis, or "snail fever," because a reduction in water means more contamination of the existing water, and people who come in contact with it risk being infected.

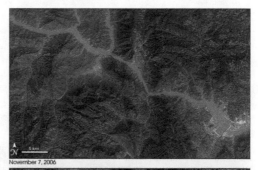

These environmental problems were the direct result of the political will to build the dam quickly. Today, the Chinese government is working with scientists and engineers to create better balance through flow dynamics.

FIGURE 10.4d. Before and after the Three Gorges Dam, from satellite.
Copyright in the Public Domain.

SOUTH KOREA: THE SIGNATURE OF SUCCESS

South Korea's loud march to success is often dampened by the economic rise of China and the powerhouse economy of Japan. South Korea lies wedged between the two and has a history of being conquered or occupied by one or the other. In many ways, South Korea is a greater story than either China or Japan. Because much of South Korea's growth has happened since 2000, their transformation has happened right under our noses. As economists, authors, and media endlessly discussed and debated China's unprecedented rise to the top and Japan's struggle to remain there, South Korea has slipped in and outcompeted them both in many ways. Today, companies like Samsung, LG, Hyundai, Kia, and Daewoo have flooded global markets with high-quality electronics and automobiles, built in some of the world's most technologically advanced factories. Like Japanese companies, South Korean conglomerates like Samsung and LG have many appendages, ranging from televisions to biopharmaceuticals. In twenty years, they have elevated their economy from one that compared to African nations to a trillion-dollar economy. South Korea's *per capita* GDP has reached about $35,000 and is rising. Both Japanese and Chinese firms view South Korea's competitiveness as fierce and, particularly for the Japanese, very annoying.

FIGURE 10.4e. Samsung is a highly desired company to work for in Korea, but typically only recruits from the top universities. Copyright © hyolee2 (CC BY-SA 3.0) at https://commons.wikimedia.org/wiki/File%3AExpo_2012_Samsung_pavilion.JPG .

South Korea has its challenges, though. Without many natural resources and raw materials, Koreans have had to focus on cultivating their *human capital*. There has, over the past decade, been a high premium put on a good education. In South Korea, grade-school education is intense, and students often spend the whole day at school and then immediately go to "tutor centers" until late in the evening. Upon completion of grade school, a single, comprehensive exam must be taken, and a student's performance on that test determines what university he or she attends. The big Korean companies often recruit from the top three or four universities only. This has led to a spike in student suicides in Korea.

BOX 10.B YOUNG WOMEN AND PLASTIC SURGERY IN SEOUL

South Korea has gained notoriety because of an unusual trend occurring within its younger generation: many girls between the ages of nineteen and twenty-six are seeking plastic surgery to change their faces. The South Korean economy has grown fast, and a larger middle class consumer market has emerged as a result. Foreign popular culture has inspired the rise of Korean popular music, known as K-Pop and K-Wave, and the girls in these groups are beautiful, colorful, and viewed as archetypes. The K-Pop stars were the first to mainstream surgery,

FIGURE 10.4f. South Korean K-Pop group, Girls' Generation are amongst those who popularized plastic surgery. Copyright © LG전자 (CC BY 2.0) at https://commons.wikimedia.org/wiki/File%3ALG_%EC%8B%9C%EB%84%A4%EB%A7%88_3D_TV_%EC%83%88_%EB%AA%A8%EB%8D%B8_%E2%80%98%EC%86%8C%EB%85%80%EC%8B%9C%EB%8C%80%E2%80%99_%EC%98%81%EC%9E%85.jpg .

and now young fans seek various facial alterations like nose jobs, narrowing of the chin and cheeks, and what is referred to in Korea as the "double eyelid" to give them a more "Western look" (see Figure 10.3i). In South Korea, so popular are these surgeries that it has become more accepted in Korean society. It is not uncommon for young women to walk around in bandages from surgery. Surgeons in Korea have specialized in facial plastic surgery, and now both middle-class Chinese and Japanese travel to Seoul to have work done.

MONGOLIA: MINING THE FUTURE

As large mining operations in Mongolia became operational, the remote nation, for the first time, saw a revenue stream that would allow its economy to grow by double digits. In 2012, the Mongolian economy grew by 12.4%, which is higher than China. The Gobi Desert and *steppe* region of Mongolia appear to have vast coal, copper, and gold reserves, amongst other metals. However, their communist regime committed to sharing the wealth, which would in turn raise *per capita* GDP, but this has not yet happened. Although mining represents about a third of the national GDP and about 90% of exports, the nation's people have yet to see the benefits. The Oyu Tolgoi copper mine, one of the largest and most advanced on Earth, is about 34% owned by the state. Many criticisms have been aired over how well Mongolia handles FDI and the potential corruption that has followed rapid economic growth.

FIGURE 10.4g. The Oyu Tolgoi mine of Mongolia is one of the largest and most advanced on Earth. Copyright in the Public Domain.

10.5 East Asia in the Twenty-First Century

As discussed in the introduction, many signs are indicating a shift of power from the West to the East. This shift is not the result of the rise of military power, particular security threats, or some deliberate strategy to dismantle Western economic controls over the global economy. In fact, the South Koreans, Japanese, Taiwanese, and Chinese are all reluctant neighbors with deep histories of conflict, confrontation, and competition. It is, instead, a combination of factors that include political and economic reforms within China and South Korea designed to catch up to—and in China's case, surpass—Japan. Taiwan, the first of these nations to attract foreign manufacturing, is still economically powerful and has, with China, created the largest belt of manufacturing in the world. East Asia, then, has become a big tent for very successful economies that are redefining many aspects of the global economic landscape.

CHINESE HEGEMONY

China has become the largest economy and superpower in the Eastern Hemisphere. Because they are such an important part of the global economy and have trillions invested in infrastructure and growing cities, they are seeking more regional control over security issues in East and Southeast Asia. Since World War II, the United States, and to a lesser degree the British, have taken it upon themselves to police the regions over the past seventy years. The Americans still have many important military bases in the region, including the ones in Okinawa, Japan. This ubiquitous presence of American military power is increasingly unwelcomed. China, as the regional hegemon, is seeking to change this.

Geopolitics

China's growing desire to reestablish domestic security forces has created tensions in regional and global political arenas. The Chinese have had conflicts with the Japanese over the *Senkaku Islands* (known as the Diaoyu Islands by China and Taiwan). Additionally, the Chinese have acquired an aircraft carrier and have

FIGURE 10.5a(1). Major Naval bases in China. Copyright in the Public Domain.

FIGURE 10.5a(2). Chinese equivalent of US Navy Seals doing training exercise. Copyright © 玄史生 (CC BY-SA 3.0) at https://commons.wikimedia.org/wiki/File%3AROCMC_ Forgmen_Balance_a_Inflatable_Boat_Over_Their_Heads_ While_Heading_toward_the_Pier_20141123.jpg .

been spotted developing artificial islands in the South China Sea near the Philippines. These moves have alarmed nations and may indicate a more assertive position in regional security.

The Environment

China's Three Gorges Dam, as discussed in *Thematic Intersection 10b*, is exclusive to one subregion within China. China's overall growth and general disinterest in anything other than economic growth has led to profound environmental problems. These problems are both regional and global. Four (4) issues of industrial growth in China include:

FIGURE 10.5b. One of thousands of factories in China.
Copyright © High Contrast (CC BY 2.0) at https://commons.wikimedia.org/wiki/File%3AFactory_in_China.jpg .

- *Industrial Pollution*: Chinese cities regularly rank high in poor-air-quality studies. Some cities, like Linfen, are known to have some of the dirtiest air on Earth.
- *Water Pollution:* Chinese rivers and estuaries are highly polluted and have affected water quality. In some cases, floating pigs and birds can be seen by the hundreds.
- *Desertification:* land-use change and changes in precipitation patterns have led to increasing desertification northeast of Beijing. This has contributed to yellow dust storms during winter.
- *Urban Air Quality:* Cars and factories have made Chinese cities so polluted that respiratory disease and cancer rates have soared.

China has identified that they have induced this on themselves and is taking steps, in some ways, to reduce their footprint. However, it is also argued that China, above all, wants to grow its economy and often accuses the United States of polluting the world as well.

NORTH KOREA: SECURITY IN EAST ASIA

North Korea is the "black sheep" of the East Asia community. Unlike its neighbor and trade partner, China, North Korea remained closed and communist, and has unwillingly remained under a totalitarian regime. The North Korean economy is abysmal, and what money they earn largely goes into military expenditures. Travel to North Korea is restricted, and those who get out illegally often find themselves in shock at the modernity and wealth of South Korea.

North Korea has remained confrontational with almost every nation except China. They conduct military drills regularly and openly declare hatred of South Korea, the United States, and Japan. A coalition of forces remains on guard at the DMZ, an armistice line that continues to be the most protected border on Earth. Under Supreme Leader Kim Jong-un, North Korea continues to decay. With no revenue to maintain infrastructure, social programs, and almost every other aspect of society, North Korea falls

FIGURE 10.5c. North Korea is one of the most closed states in the world with a struggling economy, high unemployment, and a suspiciously enthusiastic love for their leader. Copyright © Roman Harak (CC BY-SA 2.0) at https://commons.wikimedia.org/wiki/File%3ANorth_Korea_-_Kumsusan_(5015230319).jpg .

deeper into crisis. They have become less adaptable to climate change and the effects of changing precipitation patterns. In 2015, a drought reduced their agricultural output, and starvation ensued. They are not inclined to solicit help from international nonprofit agencies or the South Koreans, making the community of nations wonder if, out of desperation, they may someday use their significant military force and have the support of China.

CONCLUSION

East Asia is an extraordinary region with endless features. It has a diverse physical geography which includes the giant glacial region of the Tibetan Plateau, the expansive Gobi Desert, the temperate and picturesque east coast of China, and the islands and peninsulas of the Jakota Triangle. The cultural influences of the region are known around the world. The Chinese, for example, have not only shaped the region for millennia; they have also spread out and settled other regions around the world, making it easy to find good Chinese food almost anywhere.

The Europeans also made their mark on the region. Colonies like Hong Kong, a capitalist bastion, inadvertently became a template by which China would transform. But the region has also been the site of some of the greatest tragedies in Earth's history. The Japanese cruelty of the twentieth century, China's failed Great Leap Forward, and the American attack on Japan with nuclear weapons will never be forgotten in our collective history. However, the East Asian nations of China-Taiwan, Japan, and South Korea have become some of the largest in the world and collectively compete and cooperate within a globalized economy. It could be argued that East Asia will emerge as an epicenter of economic power and political influence in this century, as well as ground zero for climate issues.

KEY TERMS

Tibetan Plateau	Mao Zedong	Energy
Rivers	American influences	Environmental Problems
"Ways of Being"	Least Cost Theory	Mining
Imperial Japanese	Chinese manufacturing	South Korea
Hong Kong	Special Economic Zone	North Korea
World War II	(SEZ)	

CLASS DISCUSSIONS

1. Describe early Chinese social philosophies and how they differed from "Western" paradigms.
2. Discuss Japanese culture, their transition to modernity, and why they imperialized and attacked the rest of the region.
3. Discuss the rise of China as an economic power. What mistakes did they make? What are some of their successes?
4. Discuss South Korea and how they grew their economy in such a short time.
5. What are some of the environmental concerns associated with Chinese economic growth?

ADDITIONAL RESOURCES:

Chinese Environment

http://www.livescience.com/27862-china-environmental-problems.html

Energy:

http://www.eia.gov/beta/international/

http://www.korea.net/index.jsp

Oyu Tolgoi Mine:

http://ot.mn/

Special Economic Zones (SEZ):

http://blogs.worldbank.org/developmenttalk/china-s-special-economic-zones-and-industrial-clusters-success-and-challenges

Surgery in South Korea:

http://www.newyorker.com/magazine/2015/03/23/about-face

BIBLIOGRAPHY:

"Ancient Chinese Philosophies." Ancient History Encyclopedia. N.p., n.d. Web. http://www.ancient.eu/Chinese_Philosophy/. 06 June 2015.

Bergstein F.C., et al. (2006). The Balance Sheet China: What the World Needs to Know about the Emerging Superpower. Public Affairs. New York.

Booming Mongolia: Mine all mine. Economist. Jan. 21, 2012.

"China's Major Rivers." International Rivers. N.p., n.d. Web. http://www.internationalrivers.org/campaigns/china-s-major-rivers. June–July 2015.

"China's Special Economic Zones (New Areas & SEZs)." Understand China. Chinas Special Economic Zones (New Areas and SEZs). Comments. N.p., 08 Sept. 2010. Web. http://understand-china.com/special-economic-zone-sez/. May–June 2015.

Clyde, P.H and B.F. Beers (1975). The Far East. Prentice Hall. New Jersey.

Fishman, T.C. (2005). China Inc.: How the Rise of the Next Superpower Challenges America and the World. Scribner. New York.

Harvey, D. (2006). Spaces of Global Capitalism: Towards a Theory of Uneven Geographical Development. Verso. New York.

"Hong Kong." Central Intelligence Agency. Central Intelligence Agency, n.d. Web. https://www.cia.gov/library/publications/the-world-factbook/geos/hk.html May–June 2015.

Hvistendahl, M. (2008). "China's Three Gorges Dam: An Environmental Catastrophe?" Scientific American Global RSS. N.p., n.d. Web. http://www.scientificamerican.com/article/chinas-three-gorges-dam-disaster/. May–June 2015.

"Japan: The System That Soured." Bloomberg Business Week. Bloomberg, n.d. Web. http://www.businessweek.com/chapter/katz.htm. May–June 2015.

"The Opening to China Part I: The First Opium War, the United States, and the Treaty of Wangxia, 1839–1844. 1830–1860—Milestones— Office of the Historian." N.p., n.d. Web. https://history.state.gov/milestones/1830-1860/china-1. 04 June 2015.

"The Rape of Nanking, 1937." The Rape of Nanking, 1937. N.p., n.d. Web. http://www.eyewitnesstohistory.com/nanking.htm. 04 June 2015.

US Department of Energy. EIA.gov. http://www.eia.gov/beta/international/. 10 June 2015.

"The World Capital of Plastic Surgery." The New Yorker. N.p., n.d. Web. http://www.newyorker.com/magazine/2015/03/23/about-face. May–June 2015.

CHAPTER 11

Pacifica

Key Themes:

Cultural, environmental

Countries/Territories of focus:
- Australia–New Zealand
- New Guinea
- Micronesia
- Polynesian Islands
- Guam, Hawaii, other US states/territories
- North–South Poles

11.1 Three Regions, One Realm

This final chapter will combine three regions that are individually distinct but linked together by the giant Pacific Ocean. This chapter will first divide and discuss each region and then bring them under one roof, for final discussions, to highlight what they share. Generally, the region does not have the long, sophisticated histories of Europe, South or East Asia. It also lacks cohesion. Even Australia, the largest island nation on Earth, is relatively sparsely populated, with more than 90% of its people living in cities. Instead, a key theme will be the ocean realm they share and the changes many will face this century.

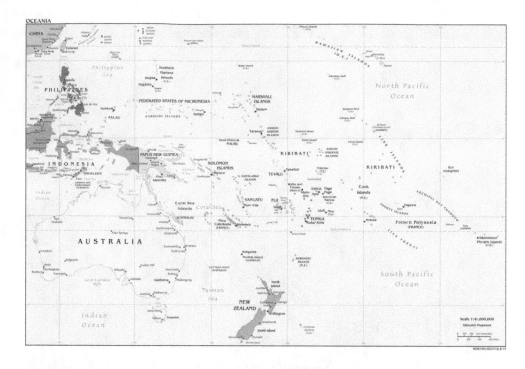

FIGURE 11.1(1). Australia, New Zealand, and Pacific Realm.
Copyright in the Public Domain.

FIGURE 11.1(2). Arctic Region.
Copyright in the Public Domain.

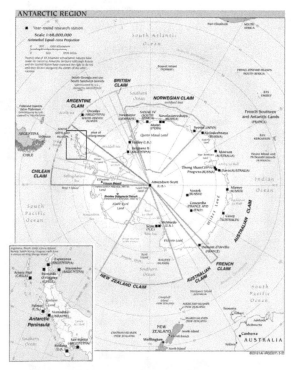

FIGURE 11.1(3). Antarctic Region.
Copyright in the Public Domain.

11.2 Australia–New Zealand

Australia and New Zealand are linked by a shared geography, a common British colonial past, and a strong political alliance. The two also belong to a community of nations that have industrialized and enjoy a high standard of living, a high level of economic security, and have low levels of corruption. They are both members of the Commonwealth of Nations, a voluntary group of former British colonies that gained independence diplomatically but still seek strong political unity with the United Kingdom. At the same time, they are actually quite different and exploit every opportunity to reinforce that distinction. If someone accidentally calls an Australian a "Kiwi" (a nickname for New Zealanders), or the other way around, they would likely be quick with a sneer and even quicker with a correction. This is because, despite these similarities, their paths have been different. This subchapter will explore both the similarities and distinctions while maintaining the important theme of the Pacific Ocean.

PHYSICAL FEATURES

Geographically, Australia and New Zealand are both exclusively in the Southern Hemisphere. That means they experience winter between June and September and summer between December and March. Whereas most of humanity in the Northern Hemisphere associates "north" with "cold," Australians and *Kiwis* associate "north" with "hot," because north is where the equator is (*see Figure 11.2a*). Physically, Australia has several flags of distinction. It is not only an island; it is the largest island on Earth, by land area. It is a sovereign state, but also is one of the seven continents. New Zealand is also an island, but is much smaller. However, its north–south axis and narrowness means it changes rapidly from north to south. Auckland in the north is tropical and humid, whereas Invercargill, on the southern tip of the South Island, has a cool and wet climate that would make an Englishman feel at home.

Physical Australia

Many physical geographers find Australia fascinating for many reasons. Geologically, Australia is one of the safest regions on Earth. It has some of the oldest rocks on Earth, which are

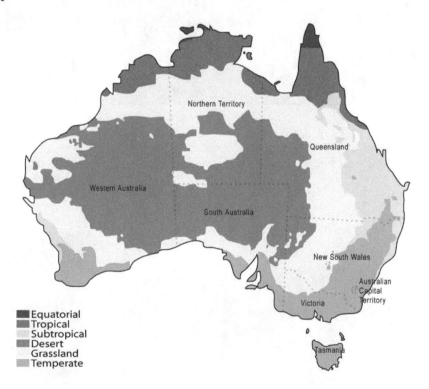

FIGURE 11.2a. Australia's Climate Distribution Map. Remember, unlike the Northern Hemisphere, the south is colder and the north is tropical and warm. Copyright © Martyman (CC BY-SA 3.0) at https://commons.wikimedia.org/wiki/File%3AAustralia-climate-map_MJC01.png .

over a billion years in age. Although it has proximity to the *Ring of Fire*, it is centrally located on its own tectonic plate. Earthquakes, then, are quite rare, as is volcanism. Australia has *three (3) climate profiles:*

- Tropical-Subtropical
- Midland desert-steppe
- Temperate-Mediterranean

The *tropical-subtropical* north falls within the *easterly trade winds*, bringing warm and moist air to the northern third of Queensland, the Northern Territories, and Western Australia. This climate area is rainy and tropical in the northernmost areas and monsoonal and subtropical as you move south. The *midland-steppe* interior is in the transition zone between the easterlies and the *westerly winds* south of the high-pressure zone. Australia's interior region is generally hot. Large deserts meet empty grassland *steppes*, which means it generates a dry climate.

FIGURE 11.2b(1). Ayers Rock, in Uluru, Australia is deep within the nation's desert interior.
Copyright in the Public Domain.

FIGURE 11.2b(2). Australia's "Outback" includes the endless grassland steppes of the country's western midlands. Copyright © Gnangarra (CC BY-SA 3.0) at https://commons.wikimedia.org/wiki/File%3AYalgoo_Shire.jpg .

FIGURE 11.2b(3). New South Wales, in eastern Australia, is a Csa climate with seasons in the interior. This region is very much like California, in the United States.
Copyright © Wyncliffe (CC BY-SA 2.0) at https://commons.wikimedia.org/wiki/File%3AHunter_Valley_Gardens.jpg .

FIGURE 11.2b(4). Mossman River in Queensland is tropical and green. Copyright © tanetahi (CC BY 2.0) at https://commons.wikimedia.org/wiki/File%3AMossman_River_during_the_wet_season.jpg .

FIGURE 11.2c(1). The Great Barrier Reef stretches 1,400 miles off the coast of Queensland, Australia in the Coral Sea. Copyright © Sarah_Ackerman (CC BY 2.0) at https://commons.wikimedia.org/wiki/File%3AAmazing_Great_Barrier_Reef_1.jpg .

FIGURE 11.2c(2). The reef is full of life, but these ecosystems are threatened by climate change. Copyright © Richard Ling (CC BY-SA 3.0) at https://commons.wikimedia.org/wiki/File%3ABlue_Linckia_Starfish.JPG .

In the south, spanning from the west coast all the way to Perth in the east, are the *temperate-Mediterranean* zones. The cooler oceans combine with the subtropical high-pressure zone to make the rare and coveted *Csa* climate type, also known as a "Mediterranean climate." This is where you will find Australia's largest cities and most of its agriculture. Geologic stability and climate diversity define Australia.

Australia is also characterized and influenced by its oceans. The Great Barrier Reef is the largest reef system in the world, stretching 1,400 hundred miles off the coast of Queensland in the Coral Sea. This biome of coral reefs took millions of years to form and have roughly been as they are for about six hundred thousand years. There are over eight hundred islands, and the coral creates a rich biome of fish, sea turtles, crustaceans, and other aquatic species. Climate change, unfortunately, threatens these reefs. Increased levels of carbon in the atmosphere mean higher absorption of carbon by the ocean. This changes the ocean's pH balance, and the higher acidity harms coral reefs. Additionally, sea surface temperature has gone up, also affecting the health of the coral biome.

FIGURE 11.2d. Box Jellyfish are the most poisonous on Earth and show up seasonally in northern Australian waters. They can cause death to humans. Copyright © TydeNet (CC BY-SA 3.0) at https://commons.wikimedia.org/wiki/File%3AMarinesting1.jpg .

FIGURE 11.2e. Australia's Inland Taipan is listed as the deadliest snake on Earth. It shares the top ten list with many other Australian snakes, making the island nation one of the most dangerous places to be bitten. Copyright © Xlerate (CC BY-SA 3.0) at https://commons.wikimedia.org/wiki/File%3AFierce_Snake-Oxyuranus_microlepidotus.jpg .

Finally, Australia is a land rich in biodiversity. Well-known animals like the kangaroo, wallaby, koala bear, and dingo can be found on land, whereas sharks, saltwater crocodiles, and the dangerous and tiny box jellyfish also occupy Australian coasts and estuaries. Perhaps most feared are Australia's many poisonous snakes. The inland taipan, common brown, king brown, death adder, and tiger snakes (amongst others) slither freely around Australia. Apart from Australia having such a wide range of dangerous creatures, it is a beautiful and fascinating physical landscape.

CASE STUDY 11A

Bunnies in Abundance from Abroad

As the English settlers arrived to Australia, they brought along about twenty-four species of rabbits from Britain for food and hunting. Although they were familiar in the landscape of Britain, they became a nightmare in Australia. Because many of these settlers would become ranchers and farmers, they brought these rabbits into the continent's coastal interior and even the "Outback." They got loose and reproduced at an alarming rate. Rabbits, a foreign species, became an invasive species. They outcompeted smaller species in the region and ate their way across Australia. Rabbits would devastate the landscape, inducing land erosion and disrupting the equilibrium of Australia's ecosystems. Foxes, dingos, and other predators had a robust food source, and themselves overpopulated. Some estimates suggest that Australia had around ten billion rabbits by 1920.

The government openly declared war on the rabbits and asked residents to kill them. Fences over a thousand miles long were constructed and are still there today. They would eventually use biological warfare against the rabbits. In 1950, they released thousands of mosquitos and fleas carrying the myxoma virus, which only infected rabbits. This was fairly successful, except for the fact that mosquitos loath dry climates, so the interior rabbits were safe. They then released thousands of flies infected with RDH (rabbit

FIGURE 11.2f(1). By 1920, rabbits were estimated to number around 10 billion in Australia. Copyright in the Public Domain.

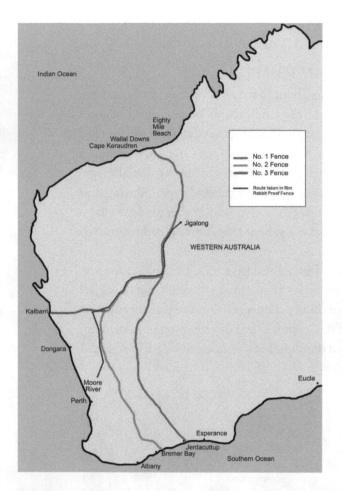

haemorrhagic disease), but flies loathed the humid areas. Together, they were effective in reducing the population by about 95%. The problem was that some rabbits were showing resistance or immunity to these diseases, and those that survived reproduced. Today, Australia still struggles with its estimated two hundred million rabbits.

FIGURE 11.2f(3). A 1884 cartoon poking fun at the limited effectiveness of the thousand miles of fence.
Copyright in the Public Domain.

FIGURE 11.2f(2). Rabbit-proof fences had limited success. Copyright © Roke~commonswiki (CC BY-SA 3.0) at https://commons.wikimedia.org/wiki/File:Rabbit_proof_fence_map_showing_route.PNG.

Physical New Zealand

New Zealand is an island nation, consisting of two major islands simply called "North Island" and "South Island." The country largely resides within the temperate latitudes, between about thirty-four degrees and forty-seven degrees south latitude. When compared to the United States, that is roughly between Los Angeles, California and Vancouver, British Columbia (Canada). However, New Zealand is surrounded by

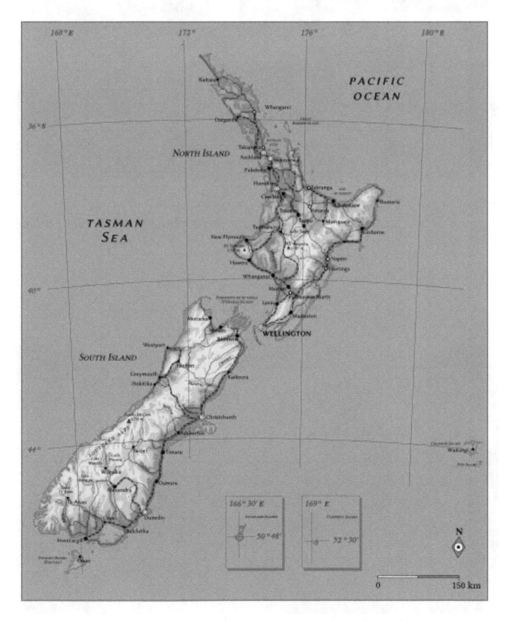

FIGURE 11.2g. Political map of New Zealand, showing the two main islands, major cities, and latitude. BohwaZ (Copyleft, Free Art License) at https://commons.wikimedia.org/wiki/File%3AMap_of_New_Zealand_(english).svg .

FIGURE 11.2h(1). Kiwis enjoying a sunny day in Wellington, North Island.
Copyright © Phillip Capper (CC BY 2.0) at https://commons.wikimedia.org/wiki/File%3AScorching_Bay.jpg .

FIGURE 11.2h(2). Southern Alps region on South Island.
Copyright © Michael Button (CC BY 2.0) at https://commons.wikimedia.org/wiki/File%3ALake_Ohau_Lodge_lupin_field%2C_NZ.jpg .

ocean, and both islands are relatively narrow. This means that seasons, though they have them, are tempered by the maritime influences.

Unlike Australia, New Zealand is tectonically active, sitting on a convergent fault between the Pacific and Australian Plates. This means they are volcanically active and experience seismic activity. The South Island is larger but more remote. It is home to the Southern Alps, which stretch hundreds of miles and have many peaks over nine thousand feet. The *Lord of the Rings* films were all shot on the South Island because of its primordial landscape that seems untouched. Also unlike Australia, New Zealand has no dangerous animals. There are no poisonous snakes, dingos, or saltwater crocodiles, and the temperate climate limits the presence of annoying pests like mosquitos.

CULTURE

Both Australia and New Zealand were occupied by native cultures before the British arrived. The British, as they had done many times, established colonies and quickly took control of lands and water resources while promoting the establishment of farms and ranches in the periphery of the colonies as supportive measures. Additionally, the Europeans brought disease, and the native populations were devastated by measles, smallpox, and other "Old World" diseases. Both Australia and New Zealand formed independent federations, and the culture of the two nations still reflect British culture.

Cultural Australia

Beginning with British Captain James Cook's exploration of the eastern coastline of Australia and the later arrival of the "First Fleet," parts of Australia became colonies of Britain around 1788. The colonies would become known as the *Seven Colonies*, which included modern-day Sydney, Adelaide, Melbourne, Perth, and Darwin. In 1901, they united and became Australia.

Several of the colonies began as penal colonies for a wide range of people from the global-scale British Empire. The most extreme criminals were imprisoned, while many others, including many women, were allowed to work off their crimes. Women, who represented about 20% of the convicts, were allowed to bring their children, and if they married free men, would be granted freedom. This "criminal past" has stigmatized Australians within the Commonwealth, and may fuel some of the disdain that exists between them and New Zealand.

FIGURE 11.2i. Several of Australia's original colonies, like Tasmania, were established as penal colonies. Copyright © Martybugs (CC BY-SA 3.0) at https://commons.wikimedia.org/wiki/File%3APortArthurPenitentiary.jpg .

FIGURE 11.2j. Sydney, Australia is the nation's largest and most international city. It is also rated one of the best cities to live in.
Copyright © Pavel (CC BY 2.0) at https://commons.wikimedia.org/wiki/File%3ASydney_Opera_house_3.jpg .

Australia has about twenty-two million people, most of whom live in cities. Urban areas are epicenters of culture, politics, and economic activities. Politically, Australia is a parliamentary democracy with a constitution. This makes it a mix between the constitutional democracy of the United States and the Westminster system of the UK. Like both the US and UK, the Australian political system separates power between legislative, judicial, and executive branches. As part of the Commonwealth of Nations, Australia maintains the symbolic position of "governor-general" to act as a representative of Her Majesty Queen Elizabeth II (currently).

Australia's cities and culture are well known. Sydney, Australia's largest city, is celebrated for its beauty, livability, and international appeal. Australians are also well weaved into "Western" popular culture and have musicians and movie stars who are recognized the world over (see *Figure 11.2k (1) and (2)*). Likewise, Australian scientists have been and continue to be amongst the most respected in the world.

FIGURE 11.2k(1). Famous Australians, Keith Urban and Nicole Kidman.
Copyright © jdeeringdavis (CC BY 2.0) at https://commons.wikimedia.org/wiki/File%3A2013_Golden_Globe_Awards_(8378775681).jpg .

FIGURE 11.2k(2). Australian super rock group AD/DC is one of the top-selling bands of all time, with over 200 million units sold.
Copyright © jameshughes (CC BY 2.0) at https://commons.wikimedia.org/wiki/File%3AACDC-Hughes-long_ago.jpg .

Australia continues to struggle with its native *Aboriginals*, in that they are often minimized, underserved, and politically ignored. The British sought to control the native population during colonial expansion, and the independent Australians, though they have made some concessions, have yet to address some fundamental concerns over tribal lands and social injustices. The Australian Constitution, until the 1960s, only mentioned the *Aborigine* twice; both times, it inferred that they were not to be considered a part of Australia's population. These references were removed, but the Australian Constitution, to this day, makes no mention of them. This has left them in a political grey area, and this group has, like Native Americans in the US and Canada, higher rates of poverty and alcoholism and lower levels of education.

Cultural New Zealand

Unlike Australia's divided colonial landscape and history of being associated as a destination for the British Empire's criminals, New Zealand has been and remains proudly British in character. They seemed to reluctantly embrace independence in 1947 after the British entered the nuclear arms race and the Cold War.

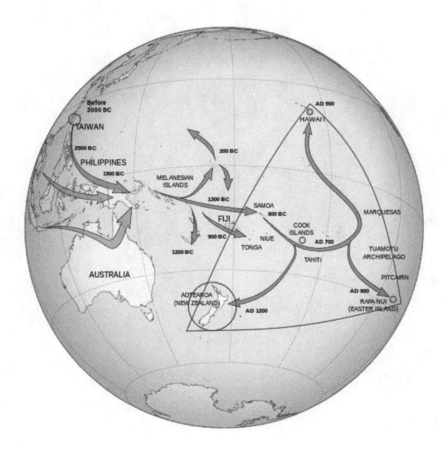

FIGURE 11.2I. The diffusion of Polynesian culture, thousands of years ago, both explains New Zealand's native Maori culture, as well as Pacific Polynesian cultures in Samoa, Tahiti, and Hawaii, for example.
Copyright © David Eccles (CC BY-SA 3.0) at https://commons.wikimedia.org/wiki/File%3APolynesian_Migration.svg .

Before then, New Zealand proudly contributed to British efforts in both World Wars, but they drew the line with nuclear weapons and amiably adopted independence with a strong commitment to remain in the Commonwealth of Nations. Like Australia, they have a parliamentary democracy with a prime minister and governor-general to represent the Queen.

The British settlers embraced a policy of equal rights for the local Maori, which made the relationship different than that between the Australians and Aboriginal tribes. However, after independence, the New Zealanders transferred land to white landowners, which impoverished the local Maori. Although

FIGURE 11.2m. Maori New Zealand soldiers, in 1941, serving with British forces in North Africa during World War II. Copyright in the Public Domain.

statistically the Maori are still poorer and less educated than the white New Zealanders, there is greater cultural camaraderie between the two.

The culture of New Zealand, though less because of lower population and greater remoteness, is known in popular culture. The *Lord of the Rings* movies, directed by native New Zealander Peter Jackson, awoke the world to the beauty of the land. These movies helped tourism significantly (see *Figure 11.2n*). Musicians like Lorde have also helped to illuminate New Zealand's contribution to popular culture.

FIGURE 11.2n. Air New Zealand jumps off the excitement generated by the Lord of the Rings movies, directed by their native son, Peter Jackson. Copyright © Ian Creek at https://commons.wikimedia.org/wiki/File%3AAir_New_Zealand_Airbus_A320_Lord_of_the_Rings_livery_Creek.jpg . Reprinted with Permission.

ECONOMIC PROFILE

Economically, both Australia and New Zealand are "core" nations with large middle classes, dominant service economies, and high *per capita* GDPs. Their tertiary sector activities are the largest in both nations, each representing nearly 70% of their economies. Australia is in the "trillion-dollar club," economically. This is driven both by its robust service economy and its raw materials. Mining in Australia is huge, and many of those raw materials are exported to China, making them Australia's number one trade partner. New Zealand, though they have a *per capita* GDP $11,000 lower than Australia's, generated about $158 billion in 2014.

Quality of life indices typically place Australia and New Zealand high on the list because of low corruption, excellent education and health care, and relatively stable unemployment (each about 6%). Although both are postured to continue doing well, both will face the growing concerns of climate change. Droughts in Australia are proving to be costly, and New Zealand may face serious issues of climate-change refugees generated by rising sea levels in the Pacific. New Zealand is the closest wealthy nation, and their shared Polynesian cultural past and ability to help may induce a flood of refugees.

11.3 Pacific Realm

The Pacific Realm is the largest region on Earth. It occupies about 68.3 million square miles and represents one-third of the earth's surface area. Although mostly remote, some island cultures have thrived in this realm. These island cultures were eventually identified and colonized by Europeans during the eighteenth and nineteenth centuries. Perhaps the most important regional narratives are the health of Earth's oceans, particularly the Pacific, and how climate change will affect the people who call this massive region home.

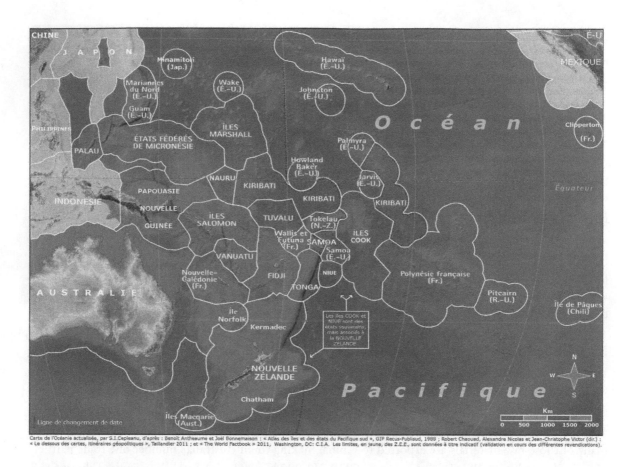

Carte de l'Océanie actualisée, par S.I.Cepleanu, d'après : Benoît Antheaume et Joël Bonnemaison : « Atlas des îles et des états du Pacifique sud », GIP Recus-Publisud, 1988 ; Robert Chaouad, Alexandre Nicolas et Jean-Christophe Victor (dir.) : « Le dessous des cartes, Itinéraires géopolitiques », Taillandier 2011 ; et « The World Factbook » 2011, Washington, DC: C.I.A. Les limites, en jaune, des Z.E.E., sont données à titre indicatif (validation en cours des différentes revendications).

FIGURE 11.3a. The Pacific Realm is all ocean, but home to many island nations and occupied archipelagos. Copyright © Spiridon Ion Cepleanu (CC BY-SA 3.0) at https://commons.wikimedia.org/wiki/File%3AOceanie.jpg .

PHYSICAL FEATURES

The Pacific Ocean holds 51% of Earth's oceanic water. It is very geologically active, especially around its rim (the before-mentioned *Ring of Fire*) and in the middle of the Northern Pacific around the Hawaiian archipelago. Like all of Earth's oceans, the Pacific Ocean is dynamic in that currents dictate the movement of water within the giant region. Ocean currents are driven by wind and help Earth share its energy more evenly.

The Pacific ocean currents, or the Pacific gyres, form dynamic looping paths for water that move clockwise in the Northern Hemisphere and counterclockwise in the Southern Hemisphere. Although these can vary during El Niño and La Niña events, they are generally reliable and help determine how precipitation is allocated, not only within the region, but also in land areas in the trajectory of the winds. Tropical cyclonic storms (hurricanes, typhoons, cyclones) are generated in this region by areas of low pressure, warm sea surface temperatures, and persistent winds. Some of the largest ever documented were in the western Pacific. Also, zones of high pressure are in the Pacific that are so large, they help determine

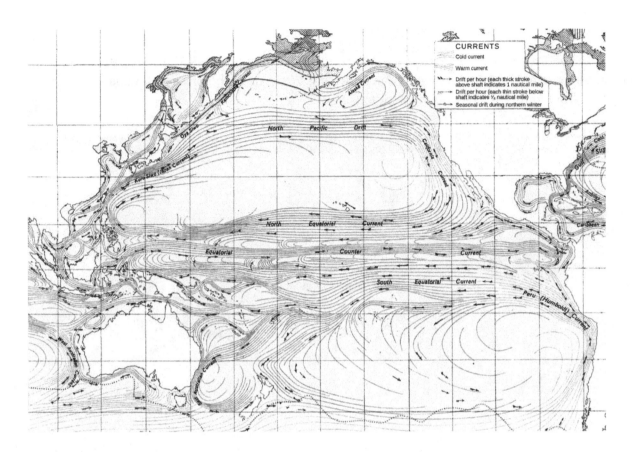

FIGURE 11.3b. Map of Pacific Ocean currents, cold and warm.
Copyright in the Public Domain.

where storms travel and the trajectory of precipitation patterns, influence the jet stream, and are engines of general wind patterns of Earth. The ocean is the world's deepest, as well. The Marianas Trench, for example, is the deepest part of the ocean on Earth, stretching about 1,700 miles in an arc around Guam. Relatively narrow, this trench reaches depths of almost seven miles. The big island of Hawaii is, measured from the sea floor, the tallest mountain in the world, easily surpassing Mt. Everest in Nepal.

BOX 11.A THE INTERNATIONAL DATE LINE (IDL)

The International Date Line is an imaginary line generally at 180 degrees longitude. It does bend and swerve to accommodate nations with islands on both sides of 180 degrees so that they may remain in the same day. The Prime Meridian is at zero longitude, in Greenwich, England. With the Prime Meridian established, a "Universal Time" could be used to calculate all other times, roughly based on longitude but politically manipulated into "Time Zones." East of the Prime Meridian advances (UTC +14) and to the west of the Prime Meridian subtracts

(UTC-12). When travelling east across the IDL (from Tokyo to San Francisco, for example), one must subtract twenty-four hours when one reaches it. When traveling west (from Los Angeles to Sydney, for example), one adds twenty-four hours.

FIGURE 11.3c. The International Date Line, as seen in the far right, is supposed to be at 180 degrees longitude, but bends to accommodate political space and keep people in the same nation in the same day. Additionally, it has been politically manipulated by nations to better coordinate commercial activities and accommodate or abolish Day Light Savings.
Copyright in the Public Domain.

FIGURE 11.3d. Three primary cultural areas of the Pacific.
Copyright in the Public Domain.

CULTURAL DIMENSIONS

The indigenous cultures of the region are predominantly Polynesian. As seen in *Figure 11.2l*, the expansion of Polynesian culture from Taiwan and the Philippines area took more than a millennium. Imagine rowing on "outriggers" across the Pacific Ocean, following sea birds and ocean currents until they, if lucky, reached a remote island. These early explorers rowed their way across the Pacific Ocean and settled islands as far away as Hawaii and Pitcairn. After settling, however, they formed cultures unique to their island homes while maintaining some basic customs in common.

FIGURE 11.3e. Hula dancing is a Polynesian tradition and still seen in Hawaii and Tahiti.
Copyright © Frank Kovalchek (CC BY 2.0) at https://commons.wikimedia.org/wiki/File%3AThree_lovely_hula_dancers_from_behind_(4829089541).jpg .

European Colonials

Even the far reaches of the Pacific Ocean were not too far for the Europeans. Beginning with Spanish explorers like Balboa and Magellan and continuing on with British Captains Drake and later Cook, many islands of the Pacific realm would eventually be colonized. The *three (3) major colonizers of the Pacific* were:

FIGURE 11.3f. Flag of Hawaii, a US state, bears the British Union Jack as a way of honoring their British past. Ironically, the native Hawaiians killed Britain's most famous explorer, Captain Cook, in 1779.
Copyright in the Public Domain.

- *British*: Including the Cook and Pitcairn Islands.
- *French*: French Polynesia, to include Tahiti.
- *Americans*: Hawaiian Islands, Midway, Guam, Marianas, and American Samoa.

The European influence in the region, though perhaps less established than other regions, can still be seen. Tahiti, for example, still speaks French and continues to be a destination for French retirees and tourists from around the world. The British have an unusually light footprint in the region, with the Cook Islands as members of the Commonwealth. However, perhaps an unusual place British presence can still be seen is on Hawaii's state flag (see *Figure 11.3f*). Really, it would be the Americans who would establish themselves as a neocolonial power in the region.

US Territories

Industrialization, increasing political power, and strengthening military force combined to shape American foreign policy during the nineteenth and twentieth centuries. The *Monroe Doctrine* and then Roosevelt's *Great White Fleet* (an armada of sixteen modern battleships ordered to circumnavigate the globe) were only two signals that the United States would soon expand or protect its interests in a larger geographical arena.

The Pacific realm was unofficially viewed as an extension of America's backyard and therefore had to be secured and controlled. The acquisition of Hawaii and the naval base at Pearl Harbor were key steps. During World War II, the Pacific theatre erupted into war. Naval engagements stretched from Alaska to Australia, and some of the bloodiest fights were over territories the United States took or protected from the Japanese. After the Japanese were defeated, the United States maintained territories in the area. Guam and the Marianas were acquired as American territories after the war, whereas American Samoa was acquired decades earlier. Hawaii, formerly a territory, was able to achieve statehood on August 21, 1959.

FIGURE 11.3g. Although the United States successfully defeated Japan and gained control over the Pacific, the loss of lives was high. Naval battles between the US and Japan were the fiercest naval engagements in modern naval history.
Copyright in the Public Domain.

THEMATIC INTERSECTION 11A

Guam, American Samoa, and the US Territories: America's Stepchildren

Themes: Political/Cultural

Unusual aspect of the territories of the United States include: their residents may enlist and serve in the military; they are US citizens (in Guam) and US nationals (in American Samoa); and they have representation in Congress, but they cannot vote. In Guam and American Samoa, enlistment in the armed services is, per capita, many times higher than that of the continental United States. In Guam, studies suggest that between one in six and one in eight join between the ages of 18 and 24. Guamanians and Samoans have fought in Vietnam, Iraq, Afghanistan, and every other military conflict, but they cannot participate in the election of representatives. Guamanians, though they cannot vote on Guam, may vote if they move to a US state. The benefits of citizenship only fully materialize if they move. Samoans, on the other hand, as American nationals, cannot vote anywhere. The allocation of funding to these territories is very low, and they are often underserved by Washington, DC in terms of education, social welfare benefits, and infrastructure. Bad roads in these territories take years to be fixed and infrastructure is aging, but they lack the budget to address the shortfalls. The US military bases, on the other hand, are highly funded and often stand in stark contrast to the territory which they occupy.

FIGURE 11.3h. Highest ranking Guamanian naval officer. Guamanians not only serve in the military at a much higher average than US mainlanders, a quarter of the island of Guam is a US military base. They just can't vote.
Copyright in the Public Domain.

CLIMATE CHANGE

This discussion will directly address the effects of climate change in the Pacific realm and how it will make the people who reside there increasingly vulnerable in this century. Although there have been some debates over how climate change might affect the ocean region, changes in sea level have already been measured. Sea level rise results from melting ice in the polar regions. It is well known that Earth has cycles that have radically changed sea level, and by extension land areas, during glacial and interglacial periods. Right now, Earth is in an "interglacial" period, as our last *Ice Age* only ended about twelve thousand years ago. During peak glacial episodes, Earth's fresh water is sequestered in ice. This lowers sea levels. Then, as the glacial episode ends, water changes into liquid form and sheds back into the ocean, raising sea level. The sea level rise measured today is the result of surplus carbon, put there by human industrial activities, energy consumption, land-use change, and so on. This added carbon, then, traps longwave radiation in Earth's atmosphere and creates an energy surplus. The polar ice is simply responding to this energy surplus in the atmosphere. Remember, as discussed in Chapter 1, Earth is a closed system.

FIGURE 11.3i. Sea level rise may intensify high tide cycles, affecting low islands in the Pacific.
Copyright in the Public Domain.

Over the course of two thousand years, Earth has seen little change in sea level. During the twentieth century, really between 1880 and 2012, the rate of SLR increased (average) 0.06 inches a year. Beginning in 1993, this rate began increasing at an accelerated rate of .11 inches per year. This rise is *absolute* SLR, which averages global variations. The variations, or regional rates of SLR, are known as *relative* SLR. Some areas, like Alaska, are experiencing lower sea levels, and others, like Tuvalu and the Solomons in the South Pacific, are seeing much higher rates of SLR. This can be confusing, but factors into whether changes in the land around the coast outpace SLR. Either way, the ocean is generally on the rise, and the Pacific island nations, along with others in the Indian Ocean (the Maldives, for example) are most vulnerable.

As oceans rise, they induce changes that are not so obvious. Clearly, water flooding the streets of Venice, Italy is measurable. However, there is often more happening. Below are the *four (4) effects of SLR:*

- *Groundwater salinization*: As salt water rises, it increasingly encroaches on land. If natural barriers are breached, even a little at a time, more salt can leech into groundwater systems; agricultural productivity decreases, vegetation dies, and drinking water has higher levels of salt.
- *Coastal erosion:* Even modest SLR can have a significant effect on coastlines. High seas move more sand, deposit more sediment (sometimes in different places), and alters coastal morphology. Human settlements and coastal industries, then, become more vulnerable because the infrastructure was built on the assumption that coasts would remain relatively stable.
- *Intensified tides:* Tides are determined by factors largely external to Earth, so they will not change. However, if sea levels change, the effect of tides changes. This can exacerbate problems associated with groundwater salinization and coastal erosion.
- *Storm frequency and intensity:* Warmer ocean surface water, low pressure, and prevailing winds are the building blocks of tropical cyclonic storms. Warming oceans give nature more opportunity to build storms, and many of these nations are already vulnerable to them. If oceans are higher, the storm surges will be more intense.

Some argue that reef islands, like many in the Pacific, are perhaps not as vulnerable as feared because they, by nature, shift and morph with change. This is true. However, human settlements, expensive infrastructure, and agriculture don't naturally shift with the islands on which they reside. This argument, then, may explain how an island will remain but fails to point out that the cultures in this region lack the resources to reengineer their island nation (sometimes with three hundred occupied islands) on time.

MARITIME POLITICS

This brief and final discussion helps explain legal and territorial dimensions in the world's oceans. The oceans of the world are essentially "commons," in that they are not, themselves, "politically owned," but shared by humanity. However, because some nations have use of waters close to foreign nations' coasts, rules had to be drawn up and agreed upon. UNCLOS, or the United Nations Convention on the Law of the Sea, facilitates the international agreements. *Legal and political features of ocean use* are below:

- **Territorial Seas:** Each sovereign nation is entitled to a barrier around its coast. UNCLOS supports a twelve-mile territorial boundary, beyond which lie *high seas.*

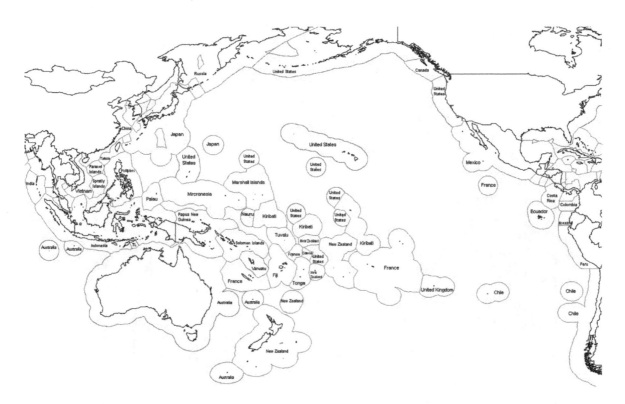

FIGURE 11.3j. EEZ (Exclusive Economic Zone) is a prescription of UNCLOS that a 200 mile distance from a sovereign nation's coast is theirs to use. Copyright © Alinor (CC BY-SA 3.0) at https://commons.wikimedia.org/wiki/File%3AOceania_Political_Map_(EEZ_based).png .

- **High Seas:** Are open and free and lie beyond territorial seas.
- **EEZ (Exclusive Economic Zones):** Because territorial seas fail to keep foreign fishing fleets from anchoring thirteen miles off a nation's coast, UNCLOS prescribed a two-hundred-mile Exclusive Economic Zone. This includes both the twelve miles of territorial seas and the remaining 188 miles of high seas. This space is used for fishing, mineral and hydrocarbon exploration and extraction, and other uses.

11.4 Polar Realms

This final region, of the three discussed in this chapter, will explore the polar regions and some key issues that are important today. First, it is important to define this region. The *Arctic Realm* includes the North Pole (at ninety degrees north latitude) and extends down to the subpolar latitudes below the *Arctic Circle*. The Arctic Circle, or the line of latitude at 66d 33" 45'.8 N, marks the beginning of the Arctic latitudes. However, the subpolar realm extends down to about sixty degrees, because during winter those latitudes are quite polar in character.

FIGURE 11.4a. Arctic Region showing the Arctic Circle.
Copyright in the Public Domain.

The same occurs in the Southern Hemisphere, where the *Antarctic Circle* demarcates the temperate southern middle latitudes from the frozen continent of Antarctica. The character of the Antarctic Circle differs slightly because it is primarily in the ocean, in the south. An important feature to remember is that the North Pole is frozen water, whereas the Antarctic is *terra firma*, or "firm land," beneath the ice. Submarines have regularly sailed beneath the Arctic ice, whereas the South Pole can only be reached by walking or flying.

FIGURE 11.4b. Penguins in Antarctica.
Copyright © Jason Auch (CC BY 2.0) at https://commons.wikimedia.org/wiki/File%3AAdelie_Penguins_on_iceberg.jpg .

CLIMATE IN THE POLES

Because both poles represent the furthest point from the direct energy Earth receives at the equator, it is cold. Although the poles receive oblique radiation (fractional energy) seasonally, temperatures typically remain cold enough to sustain giant ice sheets. These ice sheets in Antarctica cover about 98% of the continent and are about one mile thick, holding 70% of the world's fresh water.

The Arctic region is composed of sea ice or frozen sea. This sea ice is dynamic, in that in addition to it collectively moving from currents, it melts in the periphery during summer and refreezes during winter. The top ice is fresh water and when it melts adds to the sea. Greenland has the second largest ice sheet on Earth and is therefore a giant reservoir of fresh water, like the Antarctic.

Climate change, however, affects the polar regions more intensely. When the Earth receives energy in the tropics, it shares that energy around the world. Ocean currents and winds carry that energy into

FIGURE 11.4c. Antarctic is the largest reservoir of fresh water on Earth.
Copyright in the Public Domain.

the polar regions. However, added greenhouse gases in the atmosphere have induced an energy imbalance. When more energy is coming into the atmosphere than leaving, an energy surplus is achieved. And that is not a good thing. An energy surplus means a net increase in temperature, which is especially bad for the Arctic and Antarctic regions. What happens is something called a positive feedback cycle (or feedback loop), a disturbance to a cycle or system that increases the magnitude of the disturbance on the system. In the case of the Arctic, it is related to *albedo* and works like this:

1. Longwave radiation hits Arctic ice and reflects back to space (high albedo), which then maintains ice (**normal**).
2. Arctic region warms from greenhouse effect, because ocean currents and winds carry that trapped energy north (**disturbance**).
3. Ice begins to melt at a faster rate because of increased energy (**effect**).
4. Reduced ice means there is less surface ice to reflect longwave radiation, thereby reducing albedo, which then exacerbates the problem within the cycle (**feedback loop**).

The problem with positive feedback loops is that they can lead to a "tipping point," or a point where a trend cannot be reversed. Some scientists speculate we may have reached, or will soon reach, a "tipping point," at which time the Arctic ice will inevitably melt, if true. This would include not only the Arctic sea ice, but also potentially Greenland's ice sheet and Antarctic ice shelves. Or, is this already happening?

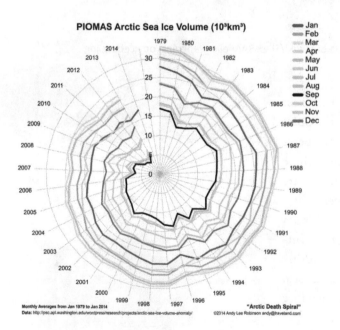

FIGURE 11.4d(1). Data suggests a steady decline in Arctic sea ice, suggesting a rapid change is occurring. Copyright © Andy Lee Robinson (CC BY-SA 3.0) at https://commons.wikimedia.org/wiki/File%3AArctic-death-spiral.png.

FIGURE 11.4d(2). Global map reflecting data that the Arctic region and parts of Antarctica have, on average, warmed. Copyright in the Public Domain.

BOX 11.B ANTARCTICA: A CONTINENT WITHOUT COUNTRIES

Antarctica is one of the seven continents on Earth, but it is the only one without any political states or permanent residents. Because it is so remote and inhospitable, it was never settled by any permanent residents. However, as technology and science improved, Antarctica has proven to be a useful natural laboratory and, as such, has been used by many nations to conduct experiments, make observations, and study climate. Nations involved have made loose territorial claims, which are observed really as lines on a map and nothing more. In a move to promote cooperation in Antarctica, the **Antarctic Treaty** (1961) was put forth and included the following international agreements:

1. Scientific collaboration
2. Military activity is forbidden
3. Environmental protection
4. Holds national claims in abeyance (state of suspension)

This treaty has been extended, but the spirit of it has resulted in international cooperation for more than fifty years.

GEOPOLITICAL IMPLICATIONS

It is important to point out that despite all the "white noise" about climate change, nations and industries have already postured themselves to exploit the riches of the north. The freeing of ice allows the exploration of hydrocarbons, extraction operations, and the potential for new shipping lanes that would save billions over the long run. Nations (like Russia, Norway, Greenland, Canada, and the United States) who have political stakes in the region are joined by nations seeking more of a voice in the region, like China, Japan, and the UK. In some ways, the economic narrative to profit from these changes dulls the grim reality that a major climate change in this area will radically change the rest of the world, particularly in the Pacific Island realm. Greenland, a nation of just sixty thousand, is already positioning themselves to capitalize from the changes occurring by issuing exploration and drilling permits within its EEZ and creating a national oil company (Nunaoil) to own 25% of all natural resources extracted. This would potentially make the relatively few Greenlanders some of the richest people on the planet, if it comes to fruition. But at what cost?

CONCLUSION

The *Pacifica* region is difficult to discuss under one roof because it really includes three distinctive regions. If a virtual classroom were to travel this region, students could visit the barren and remote *Great Victoria Desert* in Australia and roast away in 120-degree temperatures; visit the locations where they filmed the *Lord of the Rings* movies in the cool, green, temperate interior of New Zealand; snorkel in the *Atolls* of the South Pacific; and potentially freeze to death on the ice shelves of Antarctica, all in one class session. And these distinctions should be embraced. Australia and New Zealand, though they share a similar colonial past and are both industrialized nations with very high standards of living and stable political systems, are really quite different in other ways. The Pacific Realm is so big, you could literally fit all seven continents into it, with room to spare. However, there are cultures, and they have occupied their island homes long before Europeans and Americans came to claim them. They are in the "bullseye" of climate change, and their vulnerabilities will be realized in this century. The polar regions are pristine and remote but changing. They hold most of the world's fresh water, and Earth's energy surplus and reducing *albedo* will likely continue to melt the ice, thus affecting the rest of the world.

KEY TERMS

Mediterranean Climate	Pacific Ocean	Exclusive Economic
Great Barrier Reef	Gyres	Zones (EEZ)
"Kiwis"	Polynesian	Arctic Circle
Commonwealth of	Colonial landscapes	Antarctic Treaty
Nations	US territories	Positive Feedback Cycle
Aboriginals	Sea Level Rise (SLR)	Climate Change
Urbanism	United Nations	Polar geopolitics
Core economies	Convention on the Laws	
Quality of Life	of the Sea (UNCLOS)	

CLASS DISCUSSIONS

1. Compare and contrast Australia and New Zealand. Why are they similar? How are they different?
2. Discuss some physical features of the Pacific Realm. Now, discuss cultural landscapes.
3. Describe the United States territories in the Pacific. How are their residents treated differently than US citizens in the states?
4. Discuss climate change in the Pacific and polar regions. Describe how positive feedback cycles might contribute to sea level rise.

ADDITIONAL RESOURCES:

Australian Nature:

http://australian-animals.net/

http://www.australiangeographic.com.au/topics/science-environment/2012/07/australias-10-most-dangerous-snakes/

Rabbits in Australia:

http://geography.about.com/od/australiamaps/a/Feral-Rabbits-In-Australia.htm

Marianas Trench:

http://www.deepseachallenge.com/the-expedition/mariana-trench/

Sea Level Rise:

http://coast.noaa.gov/slr/

UNCLOS: http://www.admiraltylawguide.com/conven/unclostable.html

Climate change:

http://climate.nasa.gov/

http://www.npr.org/2015/03/26/395379216/big-shelves-of-antarctic-ice-melting-faster-than-scientists-thought

BIBLIOGRAPHY

"About the Mariana Trench—DEEPSEA CHALLENGE Expedition." DEEPSEA CHALLENGE. N.p., 16 Feb. 2012. Web. http://www.deepseachallenge.com/the-expedition/mariana-trench/. May–June 2015.

"Australia." Central Intelligence Agency. n.d. Web. https://www.cia.gov/library/publications/the-world-factbook/geos/as.html. May–June 2015.

"Great Barrier Reef." Great Barrier Reef. N.p., n.d. Web. http://www.greatbarrierreef.org/. June–July 2015.

"Hafa Adai, and Welcome to Guam!" U.S. Pacific Island Territory of Guam. N.p., n.d. Web. http://www.guam-online.com/. June–July 2015.

Heim, Dan. "The International Date Line, Explained." LiveScience. TechMedia Network, 21 Mar. 2014. Web. http://www.livescience.com/44292-international-date-line-explained.html. June–July 2015.

Lynas, M. (2008). Six Degrees: Our Future on a Hotter Planet. National Geographic. Washington, DC.

Mimura, N. (1999). Vulnerability of island countries in the South Pacific to Sea Level Rise and Climate Change. V. 12 pp. 137–143.

"New Zealand." Central Intelligence Agency. n.d. Web. https://www.cia.gov/library/publications/the-world-factbook/geos/nz.html. 04 July 2015.

Rosenberg, Matt. "History of Feral Rabbits in Australia." N.p., n.d. Web. http://geography.about.com/od/australiamaps/a/Feral-Rabbits-In-Australia.htm. Apr.–May 2015.

"United Nations Convention on the Law of the Sea." www.un.org (n.d.): n. pag. Web. http://www.un.org/depts/los/convention_agreements/texts/unclos/unclos_e.pdf. 15 June 2015.

Glossary

Abrahamic religions: *Judaism*, *Christianity*, and *Islam*. The reason Abraham is viewed as a common thread amongst these faiths depends on which faith is asked. Although they all view Abraham as a beginning point, the context changes between religions.

Absolute location: a precise place on Earth, like an address or Earth coordinates (latitude and longitude).

Agriculture: the practice of growing crops or raising animals for human consumption or other uses.

Altitudinal Zonation: a term used to describe what agricultural activities and crops are associated with a range of elevation in subtropical and tropical mountainous areas.

Anthropogenic: a term used to define human-caused environmental problems.

Apartheid: the South African policy or system of segregation and discrimination, based on race, between about 1948–1994.

Arab Spring: a "youth revolt" of a younger, tech-savvy generation who used social media to view both the stability and opportunities of the outside world while also documenting and sharing the atrocities from within their own countries in North Africa and Southwest Asia.

Arctic Circle: the line of latitude at 66d 33" 45'.8 N marks the beginning of the Arctic latitudes. There is also an Antarctic Circle on the same coordinates in the Southern Hemisphere.

Arithmetic population density: divides the total population into the land area of a particular state.

ASEAN: the Association of Southeast Asian Nations.

Atlantic Slave Trade: represented the largest, perhaps most organized, horrific slave operation in Africa. Beginning with the Portuguese, and later the Spanish, French, and English, the slaves from West Africa were collected and sent to the New World to be used as labor in colonial economic activities.

Axis: refers to a continent or region's east–west or north–south orientation.

Berlin Conference of 1884–1885: a meeting between Europeans to divide Africa into political space in a way that serves European economic activities and colonial operations in the region.

Birth rate: number of live births per one thousand in any given year.

Bretton-Woods Conference (1947): sought to construct global cooperation by redefining economic systems in the postwar world. This included supporting development (IMF, World Bank), controlling exchange rates, monitoring aggregate demand and methods to balance it, etc.

BRICS: 1) Brazil, Russia, India, China, and South Africa; 2) a term used for a group of industrializing nations that have high levels of FDI, GDP growth, and a growing middle class but maintain low *per capita* GDP. This includes the nations listed, but may also include nations that exhibit similar characteristics.

California Current: an ocean current in the North Pacific that flows down from the north, carrying cold water by Southern California.

Cartography: the art and science of map making.

Caste system: the inflexible system of social stratification based on birth.

City: a politically designated space often characterized by a large number of people, culture, politics, and economic activities.

Climate: an aggregate of environmental conditions (weather patterns, precipitation levels) involving heat, moisture, and motion.

Collectivization: bringing of all productive appendages of society, like manufacturing and agriculture, under government control.

Colonialism: the settlement of a foreign nation by a more powerful nation for the purpose of using their human and natural resources for the benefit of the colonizer.

Commonwealth of Nations: a voluntary group of former British colonies that gained independence diplomatically but still seek strong political unity with the United Kingdom.

Conflict: a point or episode in time when cooperation ends and transformative changes ensue.

Contagious diffusion: the spreading of an idea from person to person, in close proximity, and/or from one community or region to an adjacent community or region.

Conurbation: the growing together of two or more cities in proximity to each other, over time, for mutual benefit.

Cooperation: an abstract concept that characterizes a point or episode in time when people or nations work together.

Core-periphery model: a model primarily used by human geographers that leads to a better understanding of the diffusion of culture, ideas, technology, conflict, and so on.

Corruption: the fraudulent misconduct of those in a position of power over others, for personal gain.

Croplands: corn, rice, wheat, and other plants managed in soils.

Cultural backlash: the resentment or rejection of one culture against another, often resulting from the perception that one is impeding or overpowering the other.

Cultural complex: a particular culture's structure that houses the various elements of culture.

Cultural hearth: the heartland of a particular culture; a place of origin.

Cultural landscape: imprint of human activity over space. A broad range of human activities, over a natural landscape, that are influenced by the culture that resides within that space.

Cultural trait: a single element of culture.

Culture: an umbrella under which various traits, values, rituals, norms, and practices are held together by communication and interaction.

Cyclic movement: one's daily *activity space.* This type of movement examines the patterns of movement locally. Where people live, work, and shop can reveal something about their culture, economy, or a number of other things.

Death rate: number of deaths per one thousand in any given year.

Decolonization: the process associated with the transition from colony to independence.

Deforestation: the conversion of forested lands into nonforested land use is a potentially devastating anthropogenic activity.

Desert: a dry and often barren region that has become so from either the influence of high pressure, rain shadow, lack of proximity to a large body of water, or a combination of the three.

Devolution: the decentralization of political power into independent nations.

Diaspora: a settlement of people from one country to another, forming a community.

Diffusion: the movement of a cultural element or phenomena from a source area outward over time. This can include agricultural practices, language, religion, urban expansion, disease, and technology.

Economic geography: explores various economic activities and the trends and spatial patterns that emerge from those activities.

Emerging economies: countries that have made necessary economic and political reforms to participate in the global trade.

Emigrant: someone who leaves their home country.

ENSO: El Niño Southern Oscillation.

Environmental Determinism: the belief that the environment determines a society's successes or failures.

Ethnicity: a cultural group affiliated with a certain geographical region.

Eurasian landmass: the largest continuous landmass on Earth; includes all continental regions of Europe and Asia.

Euro: currency used by most, but not all, member nations of the EU. Also see *Eurozone.*

European exploration: the move by Europeans to establish more direct routes of trade with the Far East.

European Union (EU): a political-economic agreement between twenty-eight member nations to cooperate by way of a supranational organization.

Eurozone: the nickname given to all the countries in Europe that adopted the *Euro* as their single currency.

Exclusive Economic Zones (EEZ): a two-hundred-mile zone prescribed by UNCLOS for extended, but exclusive, economic activity for a coastal nation.

Favela: a Brazilian slum.

Federal system: a government in which the state is organized into territories that generally govern their own affairs as long as they comply with federal laws.

First Agricultural Revolution: also referred to as Neolithic Revolution; marks humanity's shift from hunter-gatherer society into cultivation of food resources (i.e., farming and animal domestication). Between eight thousand and twelve thousand years ago, this led to population rise, use of advanced tools, and specialization.

Fjord: a narrow and deep inlet between steep mountains and the sea, caused by retreating glaciers.

Forced migration: the involuntary movement of people from their homes (as a result of war, natural catastrophe, slavery, or climate change) to another region or country.

Foreign direct investment (FDI): the investment of capital, by foreign sources of revenue, into a country (manufacturing/production, services, etc.).

Formal economy: any legal economic activities that are taxed and monitored by government and counted in all measures of the economy (gross domestic product, for example).

GDP (Gross Domestic Product): measures the total value of a state's services and goods each year.

Gender preference: a culture placing a greater value on a boy at birth.

Geographic Information Systems (GIS): the computerized data management system used to capture, store, manage, retrieve, analyze, and display spatial information. This technology enables us to visualize patterns over space and even time. Maps have never been as informative as they are today because of these technologies.

Geography: the study of Earth's surface and the influences that shape both physical and human landscapes over time.

Global geography: also known as *world regional geography*; the study of both the human and physical landscapes of key world regions and the patterns that can be observed within them. Because geography often encompasses the study of large areas, it has become cooperatively divided yet eagerly interdisciplinary.

Globalization: the expansion of economic activities, to the global scale, in a way that facilitates supply chains, expands retail operations, spreads popular culture, and leverages advanced technology to orchestrate efficient communication and the movement of goods and capital.

GNP (Gross National Product): GDP plus profits and incomes earned by citizens and companies abroad.

Great Barrier Reef: the largest reef system in the world, stretching 1,400 hundred miles off the coast of Queensland in the Coral Sea.

Great Partition: (India) a final British colonial policy to divide India, religiously, by drawing a new border around a state called Pakistan for about thirty million Muslims and East Pakistan (later Bangladesh) for thirty million Muslims in the east.

Growth rate: also called *compound annual growth rate (CAGR)*; measures the increase in value of goods and services over the last year.

Gulf Stream: an ocean current that flows warm, tropical water north past the United States and then back across the Atlantic to Europe.

Gyres: dynamic looping paths for ocean water (currents) that move clockwise in the Northern Hemisphere and counterclockwise in the Southern Hemisphere.

Hacienda: a system put in place by Spanish colonial powers centuries ago. It reflects Europe's old feudal dynamic, in which a landlord (ruling class, nobility, highborn) is master of a large house and expansive lands (typically granted by a monarch or governor with royal authority).

Hadley Cell: an Earth circulation system that begins with the rising air around the equator, continues north and south as it descends and sheds its moisture in the subtropical latitudes, then spins down to the Earth's surface in subtropical high-pressure cells. This system directly influences trade winds, the jet stream, westerly winds, and deserts.

Hearth: a place or region of origin.

High Seas: are open and free and lie beyond territorial seas.

Hispanic: a term used to define individuals, cultures, or nations that have Spanish ancestry.

HIV: Human Immunodeficiency Virus, also referred to as AIDS. It is passed from one human to another through sexual intercourse, sharing needles with infected individuals, or, in rare cases, blood transfusions.

Human geography: a subdivision of the field of geography that examines human activities and phenomena, over time, and the patterns that can be observed at various scales. Human geographers embrace an interdisciplinary approach, which includes factoring in the related fields of physical geography, history, sociology, political science, and economics.

Human landscapes: any combination of human activities that shape the character of a particular place or region.

Identity: how someone sees themselves in comparison to others.

IMF: International Monetary Fund, a bank that lends money for development (associated with the World Bank).

Immigrant: someone arriving into a new country.

Indian Monsoon: a seasonal rainy season that is dictated by changes in airflow from high to low pressure.

Industrial Revolution: an era (around 1800–1825 CE) of technological innovation and mechanization resulting from a deeper understanding of science.

Informal economy: any activity not counted or measured by government or measured as a part of the economy.

International Date Line (IDL): a line of longitude that runs north to south on or about 180 degrees (opposite of the Prime Meridian) and signals the change from one calendar day to the next. The line does not always follow 180 degrees for political reasons.

Intertropical Convergence Zone (ITCZ): the point on Earth, near the equator, where the trade winds from the Northern and Southern Hemispheres converge and rise. It forms a continuous band of warm, moist air that rises, condenses, and triggers copious rainfall as it moves north and south in concert with seasonal energy.

Islamic extremism: a broad term that encompasses fundamentalism, jihadist terrorism, and the new war to create an Islamic State, or *caliphate*.

Kiwi: a nickname given to people from New Zealand.

Latin America: a nickname for the vast territories within the "Americas" that were settled by nations who spoke "Latin-based languages" like Spanish, Portuguese, and French.

License Raj: the hyper-bureaucracy in India that resulted from the democratic socialism that arose after India's independence.

Life expectancy: the average number of years a person is expected to live until death in a particular society (men/women).

Malaria: a tropical disease caused by blood parasites transmitted from person to person through the bites of infected mosquitos.

Maquiladora District: the band of manufacturing, in major cities like Ciudad Juarez and Tijuana, that stretches along the border of the United States.

Megalopolis: the continuation of urbanization from Washington, DC to Boston, Massachusetts. Locals call it "BOSNYWASH," or Boston, New York, and Washington, DC combined into one acronym.

Megaslum: smaller urban slums growing together to make a giant slum occupied by, in some cases, more than a million people.

Mental maps: the visualization of an area you know very well; allows us to think about our homes, neighborhoods, and even our towns or cities in a way that reflects our experiences and observations.

Migration: when someone leaves their country of residence or arrives to a new country, with the intention of making it permanent.

Monotheism: the worship of a single god.

Monroe Doctrine (1823): an American foreign policy declaring that any attempt by a European nation to colonize or recolonize a nation or island in North or South America would be viewed as an act of aggression, thus requiring prompt intervention

Nation-state: a group of people who share culture, a common history, and a region (nation) are given political legitimization with defined borders, sovereignty, and the right to secure their political space (state).

Neocolonialism: a new form of colonialism derived from the postwar system of economic dependency on powerful nations that lend money as their own currency for development, thus fostering or forcing political alliances.

Neolithic Revolution: *see First Agricultural Revolution.*

Occupational structure: the dominant sector that a particular nation, region, or locale engages in. Also see *Primary sector, Secondary sector, and Tertiary sector.*

OPEC: Organization of Petroleum Exporting Countries.

Pastures: livestock like dairy cows, pigs, and chickens.

Per capita GDP: the total GDP divided into total population.

Periodic movement: moving away for longer periods with the intention of returning. College students, soldiers deployed abroad, or farm hands arriving for harvest are examples of this.

Physical geography: the topical subfield of geography that examines the natural world. Physical geographers rely on a broad spectrum of scientific fields in order to spatially understand Earth's dynamic physical landscapes. These fields include climatology, hydrology, geology, geomorphology, biology, and marine studies.

Physiography: literally means to describe the physical landscape.

Physiological population density: this measurement divides total population into arable land (land used for agriculture).

Plantations: large agricultural lands, mostly in the Caribbean and American South, that included the often palatial home of the owner and used slave labor to grow, cultivate, and harvest crops to sell regionally and/or internationally.

Plate tectonics: the movement of Earth's lithosphere, in large plates, over time.

Population growth rate: $P = (b-d) + (i-e)$, or Population equals births - deaths added to immigrants - emigrants.

Positive feedback cycle: also known as a feedback loop; a disturbance to a cycle or system that increases the magnitude of the disturbance on the system.

Possibilism: the idea that the successes or failures of society are more determined by the choices they make within their environment.

Poverty: a human condition defined by low personal income and the lifestyle that is associated with it.

Primary Sector: anything directly extracted from nature, like fishing, silviculture (logging), farming, mining, etc.

Prime Meridian: a line of longitude at zero degrees in an Earth coordinate system. It runs through Greenwich, England.

Pull factor: a positive reason or perception about another location, influencing a move there.

Push factor: a negative reason or perception, influencing a move out of a particular area.

Race: distinctive physical characteristics passed from parents to children.

Rangelands: large areas used for the movement of animals used for milk, hide, or human consumption.

Rate of natural increase: birth rates minus death rates.

Refugee: a person forced to leave their country or region.

Reincarnation: a Hindu belief that the soul moves between lives and one's conduct in one's life determines his/her life form in the next.

Relocation diffusion: the transplanting of ideas, innovations, or culture from one location to another, often through migration.

River complex: a system of rivers often associated with a single major river.

Russification: a policy of assimilation stressing (even requiring) Russian culture and language as dominant, while regional culture and languages are less important.

SALT: Strategic Arms Limitations Talks between the US and China.

Scale: the ratio of map distance to ground distance, represented on a bar graph. In more practical terms, it is a mathematical way for us to distinguish close from far.

Scientific Revolution (1500–1750): the dawn of modern science, resulting from several centuries of scientific and mathematical discovery by scholars in Europe, began to change everything.

"Scramble for Africa": the rush of European powers to obtain, secure, and profit from the rich natural resources of the region.

Sea level rise (SLR): the rising of the ocean from melting ice in the polar regions.

Seasonal climate: middle-latitude climate that experiences defined seasons.

Secondary Sector: industries that transform a natural resource into a commodity, like manufacturing steel out of coal and iron ore.

Seismic activity: the processes related to the movement of Earth's crust (tectonics) that results in earthquakes.

Site: a physical feature or attribute you can still find within the city that may indicate why it was originally settled. Also see *Situation*.

Situation: a city's location determined by proximity to a natural resource, raw material, or other attribute.

Social welfare: a state's commitment and investment in the well-being of its residents.

Sovereignty: the authority of a state to self-govern within defined and recognized political space.

SEZ: Special Economic Zone.

Sprawl: the outward expansion of a city, typically for residential communities and the services and infrastructure that follow.

Steppes: an ecoregion within the drier continental midsection of central Asia.

Suburbs: smaller cities or townships on the periphery of major metropolitan areas; primarily composed of residential communities and retail services.

Subsistence agriculture: individuals farming small plots of land, tending to small numbers of livestock, or fishing for personal consumption.

Subsystem: an independent yet important component of a system.

Subtropical High Pressure: zones of descending air from the Hadley Cell at around thirty degrees north and south latitude. Although they form a band of high pressure around the world, large landmasses weaken the high pressure, whereas strong subtropical high pressure forms over oceans.

Suez Canal: a 102-mile-long human-constructed waterway connecting the Mediterranean Sea to the Red Sea.

Supranational organization: three or more nations voluntarily aligning their economic, political, and cultural interests in a way that requires them to yield some aspects of sovereignty for the benefit of all involved.

System: various elements in coordination with each other in an organized way.

Taiga: what other nations outside Russia call the *Boreal Forest*; the largest tree community on Earth.

Territoriality: a protective stance over the space which people, communities, or nations occupy.

Territorial Seas: each sovereign nation is entitled to a barrier around its coast. UNCLOS supports a twelve-mile territorial boundary, beyond which lie *high seas*.

Tertiary Sector: any person or industry providing a service. This would include retail, teaching, health care, public services, hospitality, etc.

Time-distance decay: describes how the further away a trait is from its core, and the longer it has been away, decays or dilutes the trait.

Topography: the physical features that define a landscape.

Total Fertility Rate (TFR): the number of children born to childbearing-age women.

Triangle Trade: the use of African slaves in plantation colonies to grow sugar, which then was used to distill rum, which then was shipped back to Africa to trade for more slaves, helped to keep this industry robust.

Tribal society: traditional societies held together by ethnic and cultural bonds using a simple structure of leadership (a chief), living off the land and its resources, and practicing *animistic* customs and beliefs.

Tundra: the biome situated north of the *taiga* beyond seventy degrees north latitude.

UNCLOS: United Nations Convention on the Law of the Sea.

Unitary system: where power is concentrated in a large central government in a capital city.

Urban area (or *metropolitan area*): multiple cities clustered together.

USSR: Union of Soviet Socialist Republics.

Volcanism: the processes related to the ejection of molten lava, rock fragments, hot vapor, and gas from Earth's lithosphere onto the surface and into the atmosphere.

Watershed: an area or region that drains precipitation, snow melt, and runoff through a hierarchy of streams and rivers until it reaches the sea.

Western culture: the sum of various cultures that trace origin to Europe and, later, its colonies in the Western Hemisphere.

World Systems Theory: Immanuel Wallerstein's theory that the world's nations are divided into three economic classifications: "Core" (wealthiest and industrialized); Semi-periphery (industrializing while exhibiting elements of "Core" and "Periphery"); and "Periphery" (nonindustrialized and generally poor).